THE ASSASSINATION OF LEON TROTSKY

Espionage, Scandal, and the Crime of the Century

H. KEITH MELTON & NIGEL WEST

HANOVER
SQUARE
PRESS

HANOVER SQUARE PRESS™

Recycling programs for this product may not exist in your area.

ISBN-13: 978-1-335-00066-8

The Assassination of Leon Trotsky: Espionage, Scandal, and the Crime of the Century

Hanover Square Press
22 Adelaide St. West, 41st Floor
Toronto, Ontario M5H 4E3, Canada
HanoverSqPress.com

HarperCollins Publishers
Macken House, 39/40 Mayor Street Upper,
Dublin 1, D01 C9W8, Ireland
www.HarperCollins.com

Printed in U.S.A.
26 27 28 29 30 LBC 5 4 3 2 1

CONTENTS

This book is dedicated to
Professor Hayden B. Peake (1932–2026),
a friend, a colleague, and an enduring inspiration
to all who write on the history of intelligence.

WHY THIS BOOK, WHY NOW, WHY THESE AUTHORS

This book is the result of more than five decades of investigation into one of the twentieth century's most consequential political assassinations: the murder of Leon Trotsky. The authors' interest began in the early 1970s, when H. Keith Melton encountered a little-known volume—*Murder in Mexico*—written by the Mexican colonel who led the original investigation into Trotsky's death. That discovery ignited a pursuit that would span decades, carrying the authors across continents, deep into archives, and into the homes of those who inherited the secrets of Stalin's most carefully concealed war.

At the center of their inquiry lay two persistent questions: How was the assassination planned, and what became of the weapon that ended Trotsky's life?

The answers required years to assemble. The authors traveled to Moscow, examined declassified intelligence files, interviewed retired Soviet intelligence officers, and gained access to unpublished family archives that reshaped the historical understanding of the assassination. They conducted extensive fieldwork at the Museo Trotsky in Coyoacán, photographing, measuring, and diagramming every corner of the fortified compound. These efforts exposed errors embedded in the official record and led to discoveries presented here for the first time.

What emerges is not simply a retelling of a famous murder, but a forensic reconstruction of a state-directed campaign of vengeance ordered by Joseph Stalin and executed with calculated precision. Drawing on architectural analysis, forensic review, intelligence records, and medical reassessment, the authors identify structural changes to Trotsky's "fortress" that shaped the assassin's choice of weapon; critical forensic failures that sealed Trotsky's fate; and newly uncovered medical evidence suggesting that he might have survived under different care.

This story has too often been filtered through memoir, myth, and ideological distortion. What follows is a narrative grounded in original evidence, firsthand testimony, and sustained inquiry—an effort to restore the historical record. Its relevance endures not as polemic, but as history: a reminder that state-directed political murder, refined in the twentieth century, continues to echo in the present.

—H. Keith Melton and Nigel West

NOTES ON TERMINOLOGY AND USAGE

During Trotsky's lifetime, the Bolshevik—and later Soviet—intelligence and security services underwent several name changes following the Russian Revolution: All-Russian Extraordinary Commission for Combatting Counterrevolution, Speculation, and Sabotage (Cheka) (1917–1922), State Political Directorate (GPU) (1922–1923), Unified State Political Administration (OGPU) (1923–1934), and People's Commissariat for Internal Affairs (NKVD) (1934–1943). To avoid confusing readers with shifting terminology, this book consistently uses the term **GPU**, as Trotsky himself did during his years in exile.

In the clandestine culture of the 1930s, distinctions between **cover names**, **pseudonyms**, **aliases**, and **party names** were important, even if the terminology sometimes overlapped in practice.

Within the GPU, a **cover name** was an internal operational code name used in cables, memoranda, and reports between field officers and Moscow. Its purpose was bureaucratic security: to mask real identities within the intelligence system and limit damage if communications were intercepted or archives later exposed. Not only agents but also key figures in an operation—including surveillance subjects or assassination targets—were frequently assigned cover names for internal reference, usually without their knowledge. These designations existed solely inside GPU documentation and were never intended for public use. An operative might accumulate multiple cover names over time, depending on assignment and reporting channels.

A **pseudonym**, by contrast, generally functioned in political or semi-public settings rather than in deep clandestine operations. Revolutionary movements had long traditions of adopting party pseudonyms—Lenin, Stalin, and Trotsky himself being the most famous examples. GPU officers and agents sometimes used pseudonyms when operating in émigré political circles, publishing articles, or interacting within leftist organizations. A pseudonym concealed personal identity but did not necessarily involve forged documents, fabricated citizenship, or an elaborate biographical "legend." It was a working political name rather than a fully constructed alternate life. Our principal reference for identifying such names is John Earl Haynes's *Cover Name, Cryptonym, Pseudonym, and Real Name Index*.

An **alias** was an assumed name used in real-world interactions, but it did not always require a fully developed legend. At its most elaborate, an alias could be supported by forged passports, manufactured background, and corroborating documentation designed to withstand scrutiny from police, border officials, landlords, and suspicious associates. Ramón Mercader's identities as "Jacques Mornard*" and later "Frank Jacson*" exemplify this deeper form of alias: sustained, document-backed false lives created for long-term operational penetration. Yet aliases also operated at a simpler level. A GPU officer meeting a prospective recruit in the United States might introduce himself under a basic assumed name used solely to shield his true identity during that contact. Such an alias might lack detailed backstopping or forged documentation; its purpose was compartmentation rather than long-term impersonation. Thus, an alias could range from a minimal protective layer to a fully fabricated identity. In every case, however, it functioned outwardly—shielding the operative's real name in direct dealings with others—while internal cover names continued to protect him within the intelligence bureaucracy.

The Fourth International and the Socialist Workers Party (SWP) routinely used **party names**, but for reasons distinct from GPU tradecraft. Party names functioned as protective and cultural devices within revolutionary organizations. They helped shield members from employer retaliation, social hostility, or political repression, yet they were not typically supported by forged documents or elaborate legends. A party name might be widely known within the movement and even appear in print. In that sense, it resembled a political pseudonym more than a clandestine alias. The difference lay in structure and intent: GPU aliases were instruments of espionage designed to deceive targets or authorities, whereas party names within Trotskyist circles were protective conventions rooted in revolutionary tradition rather than covert state intelligence practice.

In summary, the distinctions are structural and functional. A **cover name** protected identities inside the intelligence bureaucracy. A **pseudonym** masked identity in political or social contexts without creating a fully fabricated life. An **alias** was an outward-facing assumed name—sometimes a simple protective layer, sometimes a fully constructed false identity—used for operational purposes in the real world. And a **party name** within the Fourth International or SWP served as a movement-based protective convention—part security measure, part revolutionary tradition—rather than a tool of clandestine state espionage.

Readers may also find the multiple aliases used by Trotsky's assassin confusing. For clarity, each of Ramón Mercader's known aliases is marked with an asterisk throughout the book: Jacques Mornard*, Jacques Mornard Vandendreschd*, Frank Jacson*, Jacques*, Frank*, Jac*, and Ramón Ivanovich López*.

Sheldon Robert Harte, the GPU's mole inside Trotsky's fortress, was mistakenly known to Trotsky as "Robert Sheldon Harte." Even the memorial plaque at the villa's garden gate reverses his first and middle names. In this work, the two forms are used interchangeably.

Throughout the book, Trotsky's final residence on Avenida Viena in Coyoácan, Mexico, is referred to interchangeably as his villa, compound, or fortress. The exterior enclosed area is described as the courtyard or garden. A smaller area within the courtyard where Leon Trotsky and Natalia Sedova [Trotsky] often sat and drank tea is referred to as the patio.

ACKNOWLEDGMENTS

This book would not exist without the guidance and support of many extraordinary individuals.

We extend our heartfelt thanks to our editor, April Osborn, for her discerning judgment and invaluable guidance on the book's content, structure, and presentation. Her vision and steady hand were instrumental in shaping the final manuscript. We are equally grateful to Eden Railsback, whose mastery of Microsoft Word made it possible to integrate a lengthy text and more than a thousand endnotes into a cohesive whole. We also thank our line editor, Evan Yeong, whose meticulous attention to detail and sharp eye for clarity significantly strengthened the manuscript, and our copy editor, Jennifer Stimson, for her discerning eye and work on the final manuscript.

Our late friend Vladimir Alexeenko, a Committee for State Security (KGB) lieutenant colonel, provided invaluable assistance over more than twenty-five years. From Moscow, he translated key works in Russian and Spanish, facilitated contacts with the families of Operation UTKA officers, and helped secure materials unavailable elsewhere—including the gold wristwatch presented to Ramón Mercader by the Soviet Politburo in 1965. Through Vlad's efforts, we also met with the children of Pavel Sudoplatov and Nahum Eitingon, who shared photographs, papers, and personal recollections essential to this book.

We are deeply grateful to Anton Mironov, whose talents as a researcher, artist, and graphic designer enriched this project immeasurably. Many of the images in this book exist because of his skill and dedication.

The late Oleg Tsarev, KGB colonel, Foreign Intelligence Service (SVR) spokesperson, and historian, graciously hosted us during repeated visits to Moscow in the 1990s. His insights into Operation UTKA as one of the few people to have read the classified GPU files and his permission to reproduce rare GPU photographs were invaluable.

We are also indebted to colleagues and friends who supported this project over many years, including Dan Mulvenna, retired Royal Canadian Mounted Police counterintelligence officer; Bob Wallace, former senior Central Intelligence Agency (CIA) officer and coauthor of seven books; and Bill Kline, former director of the National Security Agency (NSA) Interagency Training Center, where Melton served as technical tradecraft historian and adjunct professor from 2003 to 2016.

We want to thank historian Terry Priest, who befriended Henry Schnautz, the last surviving member of Trotsky's personal guards. Terry shared a trove of previously unseen materials—photographs of the villa, personal letters, and daily duty logs—that shed new light on the Trotskys' villa's security protocols, the guards' routines, and the weaknesses of several entry points. Terry deserves great credit for rescuing and preserving these invaluable documents and images.

Henry R. Schlesinger, writer, photographer, and blogger, generously contributed key photographs, including images of Sylvia Ageloff's Brooklyn residence. Our thanks also extend to the late authors José Ramón Garmabella and Harry Mahoney, as well as Eric London for his hard-hitting analysis of Sylvia Ageloff, E. B. Held and Tom Sharpe for their analysis on Iosif Grigulevich's time at the GPU safe house in Santa Fe, Stefan Romic for his explanations on the use of a piolet, and many others whose research, expertise, and generosity deepened this study.

We are especially grateful to Dr. Robert Lacin, MD, whose review of the original autopsy findings provided a new medical perspective on Trotsky's fatal injury, and to Dr. Sahand Eftekari, MD, who advised us on the anatomical and surgical realities surrounding the assassin's quest to achieve a "silent death."

Our literary agent, Dan Mandel, guided this project with patience and skill. The new International Spy Museum in Washington, DC, is the home of the Trotsky assassination axe. We thank Tamara Christian, Chris Costa, Laura Hicken, and Dan Treado for their stewardship, access, and expert photography of the ice axe and other key Trotsky artifacts.

Finally, our deepest thanks go to Melton's wife, Karen, whose patience, love, and quiet endurance sustained this long journey. This book would not exist without her.

—H. Keith Melton and Nigel West

CAST OF CHARACTERS

Hilda Ageloff: Sylvia Ageloff's sister and confidant. Mexican police suspected her of failing to report private misgivings about the assassin, but she was never formally charged.

Ruth Ageloff: Sylvia Ageloff's sister, who served as a secretary and translator for Leon Trotsky and Natalia Sedova in Coyoacán during the 1937 Dewey Commission hearings. Sylvia later leveraged Ruth's established connection to the Trotsky household to obtain her own invitation to the villa in 1940.

Sylvia Ageloff [Maslow]: Brooklyn social worker, common-law wife of assassin Ramón Mercader. She was charged by Mexican investigators as a conspirator in the Trotsky assassination but never prosecuted after political intervention from the US.

Lavrentiy Beria (GPU cover name PAVEL): Soviet politician and senior security official. Head of the GPU from 1938 to 1946 and one of Joseph Stalin's most powerful enforcers.

Louis Budenz (GPU cover names BUBEN and TAMBOURINE): Managing editor of *The Daily Worker* and senior Communist Party USA (CPUSA) official. One of the GPU's principal American enablers; recruited Ruby Weil, who introduced Sylvia Ageloff to the future assassin. Rejected communism and became an FBI source in the late 1940s.

Roquelia Mendoza Buenabad: Common-law wife (1946) to Jacques Mornard*. Lived part-time with him inside Lecumberi prison.

Sylvia Callen [Franklin] (GPU cover name SATYR, party name CALDWELL): GPU agent recruited by Louis Budenz. Served as personal secretary to Socialist Workers Party (SWP) president James P. Cannon for nine years; the GPU's most significant penetration of the SWP. Later exposed by Budenz after his 1947 defection from the Communist Party. Subsequently known as Sylvia Lorraine Doxsee.

Dr. Alfonso Quiroz Cuarón: Chief criminologist of the Mexican police. Correctly identified the assassin as Ramón Mercader in September 1950.

Nahum (Leonid) Aleksandrovich Eitingon (GPU cover name TOM): Alias "General Kotov" and "Comrade Pablo" in Spain, Pavel Sudoplatov's deputy; field commander in Mexico for Operation UTKA; probable lover of Caridad Mercader.

Lilia Ginzberg Estrin [Dallin] (GPU cover name LYDIA, pseudonym PAULSEN): Wife of David J. Dallin. Possible GPU agent; secretary to Mark Zborowski in Paris after Lev Sedov's death; copublisher of the *Bulletin of the Opposition*.

Lev Lazarevich Feldbin: Senior GPU officer overseeing Soviet intelligence operations in Spain. Defected to Canada and later the United States. Defected in the summer of 1938 rather than return to Moscow during the Stalinist purges.

> **Alias: Alexander Orlov:** Used operationally by Lev Feldbin in Spain and then in the United States for the remainder of his life. In late 1938, he warned Trotsky about a GPU spy in his Paris office.

Iosif Grigulevich (GPU cover names MAKS, FELIPE, PADRE, and JOSÉ): GPU illegal. Led Operation KON (HORSE), the armed attack on Trotsky on May 24, 1940, together with David Alfaro Siqueiros.

Alias: The French Jew: Descriptive alias used by Colonel Salazar for the foreigner he believed directed the May 24 attack. Identified in Pavel Sudoplatov's 1994 memoir for the first time as Iosif Grigulevich.

Alias: Manuel Francis Rodrigez: Alias of a US-born Spaniard used by Iosif Grigulevich in Santa Fe and for travel in and out of Mexico. "Rodrigez" was misspelled by the GPU forger.

Robert Sheldon Harte (GPU cover name AMUR, pseudonym BOB SHIELDS): American guard recruited by the GPU. On duty during the raid on May 24, 1940; opened the gate for Iosif Grigulevich and the raiders. Later murdered by the GPU.

Joseph Hansen (pseudonym HENDERSON): Served as a guard and member of the Trotsky secretariat in Mexico (1937–1940). Provided information to the GPU in 1938 and to the Federal Bureau of Investigation (FBI) in 1940.

África de las Heras (GPU cover name PATRIA): GPU illegal who infiltrated Trotsky's inner circle in Europe and followed him to Mexico in 1937. Recalled to Moscow after the 1938 defection of Alexander Orlov, depriving the GPU of direct insight into Trotsky's household until 1940.

Alias: Maria de la Sierra: Alias used by África de las Heras during the Spanish Civil War and later in Europe and Mexico.

Frida Kahlo: Mexican artist; wife of Diego Rivera; former lover of Leon Trotsky.

Rita T. Kronenbitter (CIA pseudonym): An unnamed male CIA counterintelligence analyst.

Caridad Mercader (GPU cover name MOTHER): Mother of Ramón Mercader. Led Operation MAT, the second and successful assassination plot against Trotsky; probable lover of Nahum Eitingon.

Jamie Ramón Mercader [del Río Hernández] (GPU cover name GNOME, RAYMOND): The assassin.

Alias: Jac*: Shorthand alias created by Sylvia Ageloff to refer collectively to Mercader's two primary aliases, Jacques Mornard* and Frank Jacson*. Derived from the shared opening letters to avoid misspeaking.

Alias: Frank Jacson*: Alias used by Ramón Mercader in New York and Mexico City.

Alias: Jacques Mornard*: Alias used by Ramón Mercader in Paris and again following his arrest in Mexico City.

Alias: Jacques Mornard Vandendreschd*: Alias name appearing on Mercader's forged Belgian passport.

Alias: Salvador Torkof*: Previously unknown alias used by Mercader discovered during his interrogation by Colonel Salazar.

Alias: Ramón Ivanovich Lopez*: Alias used by Mercader after he returned to Moscow in 1961, and for the remainder of his life.

General José Manuel Núñez: Mexico City police chief; nominal superior to Colonel Salazar.

Diego Rivera: Mexican muralist; husband of Frida Kahlo; early political supporter of Trotsky.

Colonel Leandro Sánchez Salazar: Chief of the Mexican Secret Service; responsible for Trotsky's safety; chief investigator of both assassination attempts; author of *Murder in Mexico.*

Lev Sedov (GPU cover name SONNY or SON, pseudonym SCHWARTZ): Leon Trotsky's son. Directed Fourth International operations from Paris; widely believed to have been assassinated by the GPU in 1938.

Natalia (or Natasha) Sedova [Trotsky] (pseudonym OLD WOMAN): Trotsky's wife, mother of Lev Sedov.

David Alfaro Siqueiros (cover names KON, SONYA): Famous Mexican muralist, GPU officer, Spanish Civil War veteran, coleader of the raid on May 24, 1940 (Operation KON) against Leon Trotsky.

Pavel Sudoplatov: Senior GPU intelligence officer; overall commander of Operation UTKA, the final assassination plan.

Leon Trotsky (GPU-SWP cover name STARIK, OLD MAN); also L.D. (Lev Davidovich): Born Lev Davidovich Bronstein, Trotsky was a Russian Marxist revolutionary and cofounder of the Soviet state. He adopted the name Trotsky in 1902 while escaping Tsarist exile in Siberia using false papers bearing that name. After his escape, he joined Vladimir Lenin and the émigré editorial board of *Iskra* in Western Europe, adopting the Westernized name Leon during exile. Founder of the Fourth International and principal ideological rival of Joseph Stalin.

Ruby Weil: American Communist who befriended Sylvia Ageloff and arranged her introduction to Jacques Mornard*—an alias of Ramón Mercader—in Paris in July 1938.

Mark Zborowski (GPU cover names B-187, TULIP, MAX, MACK, and KANT, pseudonym ETIENNE, street alias E. TIENOV): The GPU's most important penetration into the Fourth International; secretary to Lev Sedov in Paris.

INTRODUCTION

"As long as Trotsky lives, no one is safe."
—Joseph Stalin

"Stalin could not sleep while his enemy still breathed."
—Isaac Deutscher, *The Prophet Outcast*

"The bullet that will kill me has already been molded."
—Leon Trotsky, 1937

How Stalin Seized the Revolution

Leon Trotsky's fall from revolutionary hero to hunted exile ranks among the most dramatic reversals in modern political history.

As Vladimir Lenin's most brilliant lieutenant and the architect of the Red Army, Trotsky was indispensable to the Bolshevik triumph of 1917. His leadership during the Russian Civil War (1918–1921) and his theory of permanent revolution established him as one of the Revolution's most formidable figures. Yet the same independence, intellect, and internationalist vision that elevated him also ensured his destruction.

By 1922, Lenin's health was failing. A series of strokes left him incapacitated and increasingly alarmed by the growing power of Joseph Stalin, the newly appointed General Secretary of the Communist Party. From his sickbed, Lenin dictated his political "Testament," warning the Central Committee that Stalin had amassed excessive authority and urging his removal. In that same document, Lenin described Trotsky as "the most capable man in the present Central Committee," a clear indication of the succession Lenin feared was slipping away.

1. Trotsky surrounded by his bodyguards in 1918.

Lenin's death in January 1924 foreclosed that outcome. Stalin and his allies suppressed the Testament and ensured it was never read aloud at the Party Congress. Control of the party bureaucracy allowed Stalin to isolate his rivals one by one. Trotsky, confident in the power of argument and revolutionary principle, found himself steadily marginalized. Their conflict was not merely personal but ideological: Trotsky's insistence on international revolution clashed irreconcilably with Stalin's doctrine of "socialism in one country."

In January 1925, Stalin orchestrated Trotsky's dismissal as People's Commissar for Military and Naval Affairs, stripping him of control over the Red Army. By 1927, the struggle was effectively over. Trotsky's alliance with Grigory Zinoviev and Lev Kamenev collapsed under staged denunciations and intimidation. That December, he was expelled from the Communist Party for "anti-Bolshevik activity." Within months, he was banished to internal exile; by early 1929, he was forced out of the Soviet Union altogether. The man who had helped create the Soviet state was now its declared enemy. Stalin's supremacy was complete.

2. Trotsky in his Moscow office in 1922.

Stalin's War on Trotsky

Exile did not end the struggle. It transformed it.

By the late 1920s, Trotsky remained the last living embodiment of Lenin's Revolution and the most visible alternative to Stalin's rule. Stalin soon concluded that banishment was insufficient and he was exiled. From abroad, he continued to write, organize, and inspire revolutionaries worldwide. By the early 1930s, this policy hardened into a formal structure with the creation of the State Political Directorate (GPU) Department of Special Tasks (DST), assigned to operations against political enemies abroad.[1]

From that moment forward, exile became provisional. GPU agents were assigned not merely to monitor Trotsky but to destroy his family, his followers, and the movement that sustained him. Surveillance deepened, networks were penetrated, and trusted associates vanished. Stalin's war against one man had become a war against an idea—a final effort to erase the last living alternative to the Revolution he claimed to defend.

A Family Targeted

The campaign against Trotsky did not stop with him. It extended deliberately and relentlessly to his family.

Trotsky was married twice and outlived all four of his children—an outcome that was neither accidental nor incidental. His family members were not collateral victims of Stalin's terror; they were targets.

Trotsky's first wife, Aleksandra Sokolovskaya, whom he married while imprisoned in the summer of 1900, bore him two daughters, Zinaida (Zina) and Nina. Although the marriage ended in divorce in 1902, Trotsky remained close to both children, particularly Zina, who resembled him closely in temperament as well as appearance.

Nina died of tuberculosis in 1928 at the age of twenty-six after being denied adequate medical treatment by Soviet authorities. Trotsky took her death badly; it was the first loss of a child he endured, and Natalia grieved deeply as well, though Nina was not her biological daughter.[2]

Zina, also suffering from tuberculosis, fled the Soviet Union in 1931 after prolonged GPU harassment. Denied permission to return home to see her ailing daughter, she fell into despair. On January 5, 1933, isolated and increasingly ill, Zina took her own life by gas asphyxiation in Berlin.[3] Her mother, Aleksandra Sokolovskaya, was later swept up in the Great Purge. Arrested in 1935, she was executed three years later.[4]

Trotsky's second wife, Natalia Sedova—his companion from 1902 onward—had two sons, Lev and Sergei. Lev Sedov, Trotsky's closest collaborator and political heir, became a central target of GPU operations in Paris. Sergei, by contrast, avoided politics entirely. A respected engineer at the Moscow Aviation Institute, he attempted to protect himself by adopting his mother's surname. It offered no safety.

On March 3, 1935, Sergei was arrested on fabricated charges. Despite brutal interrogation, he refused to denounce his father. Initially he was sentenced to five years in a labor camp, but his term was later commuted to internal exile in Krasnoyarsk. Sergei's death in 1937 was later obscured by conflicting official accounts. In 1988, Soviet authorities acknowledged that he had been returned to Moscow and executed after being accused of conspiring to assassinate Stalin.[5]

By the time Trotsky reached Mexico in 1937, three of his four children were already dead.

The following year brought the most devastating blow. In February 1938, Lev Sedov died in a Paris clinic under circumstances officially attributed to complications from appendicitis. Trotsky rejected the explanation outright. French authorities, pressured diplomatically and eager to avoid scandal, declined to investigate objectively. Trotsky never accepted the official account and remained convinced that Sedov's death was not a medical tragedy but an assassination cloaked as misfortune.[6] From that point forward, Trotsky should have understood that the Kremlin's campaign was no longer political. It was mortal.

Fleeing Across Europe

From 1929 to 1937, Trotsky lived as a fugitive—moving from country to country as each temporary refuge collapsed under Soviet pressure.

In Turkey (1929–1933), he lived under constant surveillance on the island of Prinkipo. He was guarded by Turkish police but stalked by GPU operatives posing as émigrés, sailors, and journalists. His mail was intercepted, his visitors screened, and his home watched from offshore boats. While isolation allowed him to write *The History of the Russian Revolution*, his extended family in the Soviet Union endured poverty and fear.[7]

In France (1933–1935), Trotsky found no relief. The GPU's European networks, aided by local Communist Party sympathizers, infiltrated Trotskyist circles and tracked his movements. French authorities, anxious to preserve relations with Moscow, restricted his political activity and confined him first to Barbizon and later to Royan before expelling him altogether. By 1935, few nations were willing to risk sheltering him.[8]

Norway (1935–1936) initially offered asylum, but it too succumbed to Soviet pressure. After threats of diplomatic retaliation, the Norwegian justice minister placed Trotsky under house arrest. His writings were censored, his home surrounded by armed guards, and his political activity curtailed. Failure to find a country willing to defy

Moscow would have meant extradition to the Soviet Union—and almost certain death.[9]

Mexico: The Final Trap

By late 1936, Stalin's vendetta had entered its final phase.

In October, GPU mole Sylvia Callen, embedded as the secretary to the Socialist Workers Party (SWP) president in New York, alerted Moscow that discussions over Trotsky's asylum in Mexico were supported by Mexican muralist Diego Rivera.[10] The GPU, fearful that left-leaning Mexican President Lázaro Cárdenas might be persuaded to grant asylum, began preparing to conduct clandestine operations in Mexico City.[11]

On November 11, 1936, GPU agent Caridad Mercader arrived in Veracruz with her daughter and two companions, traveling under clumsily forged passports that identified them as aid workers for Spanish orphans. Detained on arrival because of irregularities in their papers, they were released after political intervention.[12] Publicly, Mercader raised funds for the Republican cause. Privately, her mission was to identify and cultivate a cadre of operatives who would later follow her orders without question.[13]

Caridad was well-known in Spain and readily recognized by many Spanish émigrés in Mexico who had fled the Civil War. She proved adept at cultivating support among Mexico's large pro-Communist Teachers' Union as she toured Mexico. Her speeches resonated so strongly that in Yucatán, teachers replaced the Mexican flag above schoolhouses with the Soviet hammer and sickle and substituted portraits of President Cárdenas with those of Stalin.[14]

On December 6, 1936, President Cárdenas formally offered Trotsky asylum. On January 9, 1937, Trotsky and Natalia arrived in Tampico—coincidentally the same day Caridad learned that her son Pablo had been killed in Spain after defying GPU orders. His brother Ramón later remarked coldly that Pablo "got what he deserved."[15]

Caridad continued touring Mexico for two months before being ex-

3. Caridad (center) marches with Marxist labor leader Vincent Toledno (to the left of Caridad) at the Mexican Independence Day parade on November 21, 1936.

pelled in February 1937 when her Stalinist connections in the Mexican government could no longer shield her from the irregularities of her GPU-forged Spanish passport. But the trap had been laid. Her efforts in Mexico—recruiting sympathizers and building legends—formed the foundation of the plot that would unfold over the next three years. By the time Caridad returned to Spain, Ramón was already moving into position in Paris.

Final Reckoning

Trotsky's war with Stalin did not end in debate or ideology—it ended in blood.[16] From the mountains of Switzerland to the cafés of Paris, and finally to the sunlit courtyards of Coyoacán, the GPU's killers moved like shadows, eliminating one dissident after another as they stalked Stalin's number one target.

Trotsky may have outlasted exile in Europe, survived betrayal, and resisted disillusionment—but he never fully grasped the cold calculus of Stalin's methods. Stalin sought not merely to silence a man but to extinguish a movement, a lineage, and a legacy. Though Trotsky was now in Mexico, where his followers hoped he might finally find refuge and safety, Stalin had already activated the machinery that would turn this final sanctuary into his grave.

PROLOGUE

The two men stepped quietly into the dimly lit study. Overflowing bookcases crowded the walls, their contents separated into neatly stacked piles. The first man, older and distinguished, with a thick mane of gray hair, exuded a fierce intellect and restless energy. In one hand he held several folded pages—the manuscript he had been asked to examine.

He sat behind the massive worktable that dominated the room, its surface crowded but exact, every paper precisely where it belonged to reflect his well-ordered mind. Within reach lay his writing tools—pens, notes, and to the right, a loaded .25-caliber automatic pistol—no ornament, but a necessity. Three months earlier, he had survived a machine-gun assault. Six spent cartridges from that night lay nearby—tokens of survival. To his left, a newly installed alarm button could summon armed guards in seconds. Yet his attention was fixed entirely on the work before him.

The second man moved quietly—young, tense, his movements rehearsed and purposeful. He closed the door with deliberate care, sealing the room, then draped his raincoat over a low table behind the desk. No one had questioned why he carried a coat on such a sunny day. Good fortune had disguised his true intent. Hidden in a tailored inner pocket was a weapon—cold, precise, and meant for one purpose.

The older man—one of the most recognizable figures in the world—remained absorbed in the manuscript, unaware of the quiet choreography taking place behind him. From the folds of the coat, the younger man's hand emerged, gripping the handle of a shortened ice climbing axe. Its mountaineer's purpose had been transformed. The would-be assassin moved closer, steadying himself.

He stepped behind the old man's chair, breath shallow, pulse hammering. The world contracted to a single act. Then, summoning all his strength, the would-be assassin prepared to strike a single, decisive blow intended to the back of the old revolutionary's skull—expecting silence, collapse, and death. But then—just as the axe was falling—he shut his eyes.

The sound that followed was not silence, but a scream—raw, piercing, anguished, and endless. It tore through the room, freezing the air. The assassin had imagined collapse, instant death. Instead came the cry of a man who refused to die. That sound would follow him forever. More than three decades later, on his deathbed, he confessed to his wife that he no longer feared dying—but he feared what awaited him beyond. "Trotsky is waiting for me on the other side," he said. "And he is still screaming."

With a sense of foreboding, in the split second before the axe struck, the Old Man had turned in his chair. And now, as blood spattered across the table, he did not fall. Instead of dying, he rose from the chair with the energy of a wounded bull, staggering forward, blood streaming down his face, defiance burning through the pain.

The attacker froze—paralyzed by the sound, suspended between flight and murder. Trotsky, wounded but unbroken, lunged. He seized the assassin's wrist and bit down on the attacker's hand, forcing the weapon loose. The axe fell to the floor, slick with blood.

Footsteps thundered down the corridor. The guards were coming.

The assassin still carried a pistol and a dagger. He could have fought—he could have run. But the scream changed everything. Instead, when the door burst open, he stood motionless with his hands at his side as the guard's fists and gun butt crashed against him. His carefully timed escape had dissolved in the space of one scream.

Trotsky stumbled from the study, blood running down his temple. In the dining room, his wife appeared. "What's happened? What's happened?" she cried.

He looked at her—eyes steady despite the agony. "Jacson*," he said.

She eased him to the floor, cradling his head, wiping the blood from his face. "Natalia," he whispered, "I love you."

A guard knelt beside him. Trotsky's voice was faint but resolute. "He must not be killed," he said. "He must be made to talk."

Even as his strength failed, his mind remained clear—strategic, defiant to the end.

Back in the study, the beating continued. "The GPU sent you, didn't they?" a guard shouted. "Admit it!"

The assassin gasped between blows. "No—it was them!" he cried, then faltered. "They have something on me. They're holding my mother in prison." After that, he said nothing more.

The study was awash in blood. Papers, walls, and floor—all marked by the violence of that hour. The wound in Trotsky's skull was small, almost neat, but deceptive. For a moment, his doctor believed he might live.

He did not. Leon Trotsky died the following day—August 21, 1940—at the hands of Ramón Mercader, alias Frank Jacson*. The act was simple, brutal, and irrevocable. Yet the echoes of that moment carried far beyond the walls of Coyoacán. The Old Man's body fell, but his ideas did not. The scream that haunted his assassin became history's own echo—rising from the bloodstained floor of a quiet study to mark the end of a revolution, and the beginning of a legend.

CHAPTER I

THE BLUE HOUSE

Sanctuary, Subversion, and Seduction

"There are no safe houses when the state decides you must die."
—Victor Kravchenko, *I Chose Freedom*

"He [Stalin] hunted not only men, but memory. To outlive him was not enough—you had to outdistance his reach."
—Robert Conquest, *The Great Terror*

"There have been two great accidents in my life. One was the train; the other was Diego. Diego was by far the worst."
—Frida Kahlo

Life in the Blue House

At first glance, the Blue House in Coyoacán seemed an oasis of calm. Its sun-drenched courtyard, cobalt-blue walls, and sheltering gardens offered Trotsky and Natalia a rare reprieve from years of harsh exile. Inside, daily life settled into a cautious rhythm—writing, reading, mealtimes, and receiving visitors. But beneath the surface, danger lingered. Armed guards—mostly young American volunteers—patrolled the entrance and rooftop, their vigilance a thin shield against the immense power of Stalin's intelligence apparatus and its trained killers. Trotsky was no longer in control. At the Blue House, telephone calls were logged, mail was screened, and unfamiliar faces were noted with quiet suspicion. The Old Man was safe—but only just. Though half

4. Leon and Natalia disembarked, accompanied by Frida Kahlo, Max Shachtman, and George Novack.

a world away from Moscow, he remained the chief target of Stalin's wrath, protected not by an army or a state, but by a small rotating team of idealists with rifles and a conviction that the revolution he represented was still worth defending.[1]

The Old Man and Natalia arrived in the early hours of January 9, 1937, as the steamer *Ruth* approached the port of Tampico, Mexico.[2] The three-week trip from Norway had been arduous, and the ship's captain was constantly on alert for GPU plots that might interrupt their journey. The Trotskys were reportedly the ship's only passengers, but a senior Norwegian police official accompanied them as an escort. They were all instructed to remain in their cabin for greater security, enduring the ship's interior as it grew warmer each day while entering the Gulf of Mexico. As they finally passed the offshore oil derricks at the entrance to Tampico harbor, they reminded Natalia of Baku, Azerbaijan, and she likely felt relief mixed with anxiety.[3]

Years of living under the ever-present threat of Stalin's agents had left Natalia deeply cautious. She feared they had walked into a trap and refused to disembark until Leon insisted to the harbor master that they would only come ashore upon seeing familiar faces. A tense standoff followed. Just before officials were to forcibly remove them, a cutter arrived bearing Max Shachtman, founder of the American Trotskyist movement; George Novack, representing the American Committee for the Defense of Leon Trotsky; Frida Kahlo; local officials; and a throng of Mexican and foreign journalists. Reassured they were among allies, the Old Man and Natalia descended the gangplank—stepping onto Mexican soil, and into freedom.[4]

Trotsky, dressed in a cap and tweed knickerbockers, carried a briefcase and cane, walking with the bearing of a soldier. Behind him, the vibrant Frida Kahlo—draped in a long skirt and rebozo—stood out against the stern backdrop of uniforms, gunboats, and polished boots. Trotsky recalled the moment warmly, writing: "After four months of [self] imprisonment and isolation, this meeting with friends was especially cordial."[5]

To safeguard Trotsky from possible GPU attack, Mexican President Cárdenas quietly arranged for his armored presidential train, El Hidalgo ("The Nobleman"), to carry the party to Mexico City. The train had previously belonged to former President Pascual Ortiz Rubio, who survived an assassination attempt on the day of his inauguration in 1930. In the aftermath, Ortiz Rubio reinforced the railcar with steel armor plating and bullet-resistant windows—precautions that now served its unexpected passenger.[6] President Cárdenas named his presidential train in homage to Miguel Hidalgo y Costilla, the priest who launched Mexico's War of Independence in 1810. While hidalgo originally meant a minor nobleman—"Son of something"—in Mexico the name is inseparable from Miguel Hidalgo, revered as the Father of Independence. By adopting the name for his train, Cárdenas aligned his presidency with the moral authority of national liberation and revolutionary continuity.

Departing Tampico at 4:00 a.m. on the next morning, in the late morning hours of January 11, 1937, the train made an unannounced stop at Lechería, a small station on the outskirts of Mexico City, rather than the central terminal. Natalia, again fearing a trap, hesitated to disembark—until the dawn light revealed the smiling face of the rotund

Diego Rivera, flanked by Mexican Trotskyists and government officials. Surrounded by police, they exited the train for a welcoming breakfast at a nearby restaurant.[7]

Unaware of the ruse, the press, suspected GPU agents, and hired well-wishers crowded the main Mexico City rail station, eagerly awaiting Trotsky's train—which never arrived.[8]

At the station in Lechería, Trotsky embraced Diego Rivera in an emotional reunion. From there, the party departed discreetly in ordinary automobiles, winding through secondary streets to avoid attention as they headed toward Coyoacán, then a tranquil, semi-rural district south of Mexico City known for its artists and intellectuals. Their destination was Frida Kahlo's family home at 127 Avenida Londres—the now-famous Blue House.

Rivera and Kahlo had placed the residence at Trotsky's disposal, and he, Natalia Sedova, their secretaries, and security detail would occupy it without charge for more than two years. By the time the Trotskys arrived shortly before midday, Mexican authorities had already stationed seven police officers at the premises to ensure their protection. The home's prior resident—Frida's sister, Cristina—had relocated to nearby Calle Aguayo, into a house Diego, her brother-in-law and former lover, had purchased for her.[9]

Settling In

Within an hour of their arrival at the Blue House, Jean van Heijenoort ("Van")—Trotsky's trusted secretary since 1932—arrived from New York and immediately assumed responsibility for organizing the Old Man's small team of guards and staff.[10] Surveying the new residence, Van observed:

> It had a nice patio, two courtyards, and outbuildings that formed a perfect rectangle. Two opposite sides of this rectangle were situated on two parallel streets, Avenida Londres and Avenida Berlin. The third side abutted a street perpendicular to these two, Calle Allende. All windows facing these three streets had been blocked

5. La Casa Azul (the Blue House) became the Trotskys' new home in 1937.

> in with adobe bricks. The fourth side of the property formed the boundary with another property. All along this side ran a high wall, which was a drawback rather than an advantage because we could not observe what was happening on the other side. Besides, the wall was close to Trotsky and Natalia's bedroom. This layout was a constant source of worry for Diego Rivera and me.[11]

The household quickly settled in, and within two weeks, Trotsky had resumed work on his biography of Lenin, while Natalia remained bedridden with a recurring bout of malaria. In her absence, Frida Kahlo and her younger sister, Cristina, acted as hostesses and occasionally drove the Old Man. Trotsky was especially taken with Frida's appearance. Historian Bertrand Patenaude described her as "a striking and exotic beauty with black hair, audacious, almond-shaped eyes beneath batwing eyebrows, and sensuous lips."[12]

The Dewey Commission

Soon after arriving in Mexico, Trotsky called for an international tribunal to review the charges against him from the Moscow show trials

6. Leon Trotsky in exile during the 1930s.

(1936–1938) and to present his defense. The hearings, chaired by American philosopher John Dewey, were held in the largest room of the Blue House. The first of thirteen sessions began on April 10, 1937.[13] Rumors swirled in Mexico City of assassins arriving and attacks being planned. For added security, Diego Rivera had a six-foot barricade of sandbags and bricks built to protect the hearing room.[14] The sessions proceeded as scheduled and, in the final meeting, Trotsky delivered a forceful and dramatic closing statement. The tribunal later concluded that he had "demonstrated his innocence beyond the least suspicion of a doubt" and declared Stalin's Moscow trials a "judicial fraud."[15]

After the tribunal concluded, the Riveras and Trotskys often dined together and took picnics and excursions around Mexico City. Trotsky, an avid cactus enthusiast, gathered massive specimens during their outings. A wealthy American supporter even arranged a retreat in Taxco, a mountain mining town, where Trotsky rode horses over steep trails at a pace that alarmed his bodyguards.[16]

A Secret Affair

In 1937, the Old Man was regaining his health after nine grueling years in exile across Europe. Nearly six feet tall and broad-shouldered, he carried himself with the bearing of a soldier. Though he showed flashes of humor, his piercing blue eyes and set jaw conveyed intense intellect and authority.

As Trotsky's health improved, so did his confidence. Long accustomed to asserting his will, he regarded attractive women around him as fair game. According to Kahlo's biographer Hayden Herrera, Trotsky became especially animated and witty in their company, and while his opportunities were limited, his success was notable. His approach was never romantic—it was blunt.[17]

Frida Kahlo's emotional intensity, so evident in her art, was equally present in her love affairs. Though she was sometimes labeled promiscuous, that characterization misrepresents her nature. Frida was selective, expressing affection freely and deeply when truly inspired. Her lovers included both men and women, often from artistic and entertainment circles. Diego Rivera, despite his own many affairs, was fiercely jealous of her relationships with men.[18]

At fifty-seven, Trotsky was captivated by twenty-nine-year-old Frida, the daughter of a German-Jewish father and Mexican mother. Her striking beauty—jet-black hair, almond eyes, and bold eyebrows—left a powerful impression even more vivid in person than in photographs.[19]

Frida had also been quietly drawn to Trotsky since his arrival in January 1937. According to Herrera, her fascination stemmed from Trotsky's revolutionary stature, intellect, and commanding presence. She affectionately called him *piochitas* ("little goatee") or *el viejo* ("old man").[20] Resentment over Diego's past affair with her sister Cristina might also have fueled Frida's desire for revenge. Trotsky, receptive to her attention, flirted with her in English during dinners—often unnoticed by Natalia, who did not speak the language. Their bond deepened as they exchanged secret notes and began using the word *love* openly at the table.[21]

Their first intimate encounter came shortly after the Dewey Commission hearings. With Natalia out shopping and Diego away painting, the two met at Cristina Kahlo's nearby home on Calle Aguayo.[22] The location, convenient and discreet, was ironically the same house connected to Cristina's own past affair with Diego.

The Old Man's guards and household staff gradually became aware of the affair, and soon Natalia sensed it as well. Though she did not speak English, she quickly recognized the growing intimacy. By June

7. Frida Kahlo was celebrated both for her striking beauty and her remarkable talent as an artist.

1937, Natalia's distress was evident. Herrera described her as "jealous and deeply depressed . . . her wonderfully warm, intelligent face creased by deep lines."[23] Visiting Socialist Workers Party member James Farrell later remarked that Natalia had "one of the saddest faces I have ever seen."

Rivera remained unaware, but Van and the guards grew alarmed. Rivera's jealousy was legendary; he once threatened sculptor Isamu Noguchi at gunpoint after discovering him with Frida.[24] Discovery of the affair could have cost Trotsky his refuge—and endangered his asylum itself.

By July, the atmosphere inside the house was electric with strain, and the distance between Leon and Natalia had become almost unbearable.

The GPU Threat and the Cristina Ruse

By the summer of 1937, Stalin's agents were closing in. Though the Old Man's escape from Norway to Mexico had thwarted Moscow's efforts in late 1936 to extradite him back to the Union of Soviet Socialist Republics (USSR), the GPU's clandestine operations in Mexico were already underway.[25] Their goals were not only to surveil and harass the exiled revolutionary but also to infiltrate his household, gather intelligence, and prepare for his assassination. The Blue House might have seemed like a haven, but Trotsky's team was unprepared for the scale of Soviet penetration. Though barbed wire and sandbags protected against physical intrusion, the real threat came from within.[26] Soviet operatives embedded in the local Communist Party and Spanish exile community carefully cultivated relationships with those around Trotsky.

Trotsky understood the importance of codes, aliases, and compartmentalization, but within the Fourth International, their application was haphazard—more habit than protection. They might have offered comfort, but not security. Fully aware that his revolutionary movement stood as the primary target of Stalin's services, Trotsky nevertheless "was incapable of organizing even a rudimentary form of counterintelligence," leaving his household exposed to spies and informers.[27] As historian Pierre Broué argued in his major works on Trotsky and the Left Opposition, the Trotskyist movement was often organizationally loose and insufficiently prepared to guard against deep GPU penetration, reflecting broader weaknesses in internal security and trust among comrades.[28] Trotsky refused to believe that those nearest him—his comrades, his friends—could be turned into weapons. That blindness would later prove fatal.

Yet the more immediate danger came from within. The affair between Trotsky and Frida Kahlo had come to a boil. According to later testimony and accounts from close friends, Natalia Sedova [Trotsky] demanded the affair end. Whether to protect her marriage or to maintain their standing with Diego Rivera, she gave Trotsky a stark choice. Trotsky relented. Herrera, however, cites Frida's close friend Ella Wolfe, who claimed to have seen a beautifully written nine-page letter from Trotsky begging Frida not to break off relations with him, and telling her how much she meant to him during the week they had been together. Wolfe recalled that Frida instructed her to tear it up after reading and said, "I am very tired of the old man."[29] The affair ended abruptly.

Frida would later say of Trotsky, "He thought I was a pretty little thing and a good cook . . . but I thought he was too full of himself, too sure of himself." Her affection cooled, and though their affair had ended, she remained politically loyal to his cause. In later years, she would joke, "He was a great man, but a terrible lover."[30]

Herrera wrote that while Frida was flattered to have been loved by the great Russian and fascinated with his mind, she did not love him, and in the end they both retreated before there could be a disaster.[31]

Jean van Heijenoort wrote, "It was impossible to go on without committing themselves completely; the stakes were too high."[32]

Departure from the Blue House

The end came quietly. In early January 1939, Diego Rivera formally severed ties with Trotsky. His letter to the press, and his resignation from the Fourth International, were more than political—they were personal. Trotsky responded on February 14 with equal finality: "It is morally and politically impossible for me to accept the hospitality of a person who conducts himself not as a friend, but as a venomous adversary."[33]

The move was officially explained as necessary for "security reasons," but the real motivation included long-simmering tensions within the household. Rivera, long wary of Trotsky's political views and uncomfortable with his intellectual superiority, gradually withdrew his support.[34]

The rift marked the dissolution of an alliance that had shielded Trotsky for nearly two years. Rivera's political capital had ensured asylum, his resources had provided housing, and his presence had deterred many threats. Without him, the Blue House became increasingly untenable.

Van Heijenoort and the guards located a new house just a few blocks away on Avenida Viena—less picturesque, but far more secure. The walls were higher, the street quieter, and the layout better suited to defense. It lacked Rivera's artistic flair but offered something far more meaningful: distance. Though physically close, it marked a final break between former friends who had become political enemies.[35]

On May 5, 1939, the Trotskys departed the Blue House for the final time.[36] They left behind paintings, memories, and a legacy of resistance. The house would return to Frida Kahlo, whose own life would spiral further into tragedy and pain. But for Trotsky, the move was no retreat. From the soon-to-be fortified villa on Avenida Viena, he would wage the last battles of his life—against Stalin, against betrayal, and against the inescapable reach of a regime determined to silence him forever. That reach had already claimed his son, Lev Sedov, whose sudden death in Paris bore all the marks of a Soviet murder. It would not be the last.

CHAPTER II

THE ASSASSINATION OF LEV SEDOV

"I am therefore in no way inclined to commit suicide or to disappear. If something should happen to me, the cause must be sought on Stalin's side—or nowhere."
—Lev Sedov

"Even poison has fingerprints if you know where to look."
—Former GPU defector

"You kill a man like Sedov not with bullets—but with silence, delay, and a doctor on your side."
—GPU agent

Introduction: Stalin's Second Target

Lev Sedov was more than the political nerve center of the Fourth International, the strategist who matched his father's discipline and clarity, and the movement's most relentless public defender. His exposés of the Moscow Trials and his leadership of the *Bulletin of the Opposition* made him Stalin's most dangerous enemy after Trotsky.[1]

By 1936 Stalin no longer saw Sedov as a mere irritant but as a threat requiring elimination. The GPU's foreign assassination apparatus—the DST Mobile Groups—moved to silence him with a gun, a bomb, or possibly something colder and harder to trace: a compromised clinic, a manipulated operation, and betrayal from the people he trusted most.

8. Trotsky's oldest son, Lev Sedov, circa 1926.

Forged in Fire: Sedov's Early Life

Lev "Lyova" Sedov was born in 1906 while Trotsky was imprisoned for his role in the 1905 Revolution. At eleven, he witnessed the upheavals of 1917 and idolized his father's revolutionary dedication. One of his earliest memories was traveling with Trotsky on the armored train to frontline positions during the Civil War.[2]

Determined not to benefit from privilege in the new Soviet regime, Lev lied about his age to join the Komsomol and chose to live in a proletarian youth hostel rather than the Kremlin. He worked as an engineer, traveled by public transport, and cultivated a sense of independence that later made him Trotsky's most reliable collaborator in exile.

His younger brother Sergei, who remained in the Soviet Union after Trotsky was exiled in 1929 and took no part in politics, was swept up in the Great Terror and executed—an intimate family loss that only deepened Lev's resolve to fight Stalinism.[3]

Rise of a Leader in Exile

After the family's expulsion to Alma-Ata and later Turkey, Sedov began assuming core political responsibilities within the Trotskyist movement. By 1931 he had relocated to Berlin, taking charge of the *Bulletin of the Opposition* and coordinating clandestine networks.[4]

When Trotsky settled in France in 1933, Sedov became his chief lieutenant in Europe. In Paris, he directed communications, maintained secure channels between exiled groups, and managed émigré operations while under constant GPU surveillance. As historian Pierre Broué observed, Sedov evolved "from assistant to leader," the recognized center of Trotskyist resistance on the Continent.[5]

Sedov also adopted and raised his orphaned nephew, Vsevolod "Esteban" Volkov, known in the family as "Sieva," deepening his dual role as political deputy and family anchor. His rising prominence, combined with Trotsky's increasing reliance on him, placed Sedov firmly in Stalin's sights.

The GPU Closes In

Sedov's publication of *The Red Book on the Moscow Trial* in 1936 was a turning point. It systematically dismantled the regime's fabricated charges and exposed the show trials as judicial theater. "The Moscow Trial is not justice," he wrote, "but a frame-up prepared in advance and carried out under orders." The book humiliated Stalin on the world stage and sealed Sedov's fate.[6]

The essential purpose of the Moscow frame-ups was to prepare public opinion for the assassination of Trotsky. Both father and son were condemned to death in absentia by the courts in Moscow, creating the legal pretext for their elimination. In 1936, GPU chief Genrikh Yagoda appointed Sergey Mikhailovich Shpigelglas with an unlimited budget to lead the Department of Special Tasks (DST), responsible for assassinations, sabotage, and kidnappings abroad. Under Shpigelglas, Sedov was formally assigned an elimination order and placed second only to Trotsky on the GPU's international hit list.[7]

Operating from Paris, DST Mobile Groups used the GPU-controlled Union for the Repatriation of Russians Abroad (Vozvrashchenie) as a front. Staffed by GPU personnel, the "Union of Returnees" enticed homesick White Russian émigrés through a friendly-sounding front—the "Friends of the Soviet Fatherland." Many homesick White Russians naively thought it operated like a welfare organization to assist them in returning to the USSR. The reality was far different. Applicants were first coerced into proving loyalty by betraying fellow émigrés, a successful tactic that efficiently exposed Trotskyists and suspected defectors.[8] Elsa Poretsky later described the Union of Returnees as an easy hunting ground for GPU recruiters.[9] The returnees that eventually made it to Moscow were either liquidated immediately, imprisoned, or recruited as agents for operations against White Russians and Trotskyists still abroad.[10]

The Union quietly served another, more sinister purpose as a staging ground for the DST's mobile assassination teams in France and elsewhere.[11] By 1935, operating under the GPU cover name TULIP, Mark Zborowski—though nominally only an administrative employee—effectively managed the Union's Paris operation.[12]

Tasked with conducting surveillance on Lev Sedov, TULIP, supported by his possibly unwitting assistant Lilia Estrin, reported Sedov's movements and vulnerabilities directly to Moscow in daily dispatches, emerging as Stalin's most valuable asset inside the Fourth International.[13]

The Surveillance Network

GPU officer Sergei Efron—who led the DST's Paris Mobile Group—was tasked with organizing the assassination of Lev Sedov.[14] Because Sedov could not be attacked openly without political risk, the operation required luring him into a controlled environment where the killing could be executed discreetly. Efron's first priority, therefore, was a detailed "pattern-of-life" study, tracking Sedov's movements, contacts, and daily routines. When Mark Zborowski could not maintain constant surveillance, Efron's GPU teams filled the gaps.[15]

Operating undercover as refugees associated with the Union, Efron's team even secured an apartment at 28 Rue Lacretelle—variously described as located either immediately beside or directly across from Sedov's residence at number 26—providing an almost ideal observation post.[16] Yet despite repeated efforts by Zborowski to draw Sedov into isolated encounters suitable for abduction or murder, Sedov—through instinct or chance—evaded every trap.[17]

The effectiveness of this surveillance network was later confirmed during the 1937 investigation into the assassination of Ignace Reiss.

9. Renata Steiner's disarming appearance was useful in surveillance operations against Lev Sedov.

Swiss police uncovered the role of François Rossi (alias Roland Abbiat), one of the Union's key figures, in GPU operations. In his possession were maps not only of Sedov's Paris residence but also of Trotsky's first home in Coyoacán—the Blue House—revealing the breadth and coordination of the GPU's transnational campaign.[18]

Among Efron's most effective surveillance assets was Renata Steiner, whose elegance and disarming manner allowed her to infiltrate Sedov's personal life with ease.[19] Intelligence services have long understood that an attractive woman can often cross thresholds that remain closed to others. A warm smile, a sympathetic expression, or the simple disarming presence of a woman can deflect suspicion, soften vigilance, and open doors an assassin or male operative could never breach. Men often underestimate women in such contexts, dismissing them as harmless or peripheral, a cultural bias that skilled services have exploited for decades. The very stereotypes that marginalize women in ordinary life become weapons in the hands of a trained operative: they can blend into a room, coax information without appearing to seek it, and move through social spaces that would bristle at the presence of an obvious watcher. In the world of surveillance, invisibility is power—and no one is more invisible than the person a target refuses to see.

In 1936, the GPU learned of Sedov's last-minute plans for a holiday in the south of France. Efron moved quickly. Renata was sent on a "training mission" to Juan-les-Pins on the Côte d'Azur, where she registered at the Villa Marie–Maison d'Hôtes. Her assignment was simple:

befriend a young couple staying there. The targets soon became clear—Sedov and his mistress, Jeanne Martin. Acting on daily instructions from Efron, Steiner skillfully cultivated a friendship with the couple, spending much of the holiday in their company. Sedov later described her in a letter as "pleasant, young, timid, insignificant"—precisely the impression the GPU intended to project. The strike plan was nearly in place, awaiting only the arrival of the kill team. It unraveled abruptly when Sedov cut the holiday short and returned to Paris before the assassins could be deployed, unaware of how narrowly he had escaped.[20]

Wiretaps and a False Sense of Security

Between 1936 and 1937, the GPU wiretapped both Sedov's apartment as well as the home of his trusted associate Lilia Estrin to obtain advance information about Sedov's plans and meetings.[21] Sedov occasionally noticed he was being followed, but mistakenly assumed the watchers were White Guards—Russian émigrés who fled Russia after the Civil War—and far less dangerous than GPU professionals.[22]

By mid-1937, he believed the surveillance had ended. In reality, GPU attention had briefly shifted toward eliminating Reiss; once that operation concluded in September 1937, Sedov returned to the top of their hit list.

Sedov's heavy workload—editing the *Bulletin of the Opposition*, directing the Fourth International's European operations, and managing a small staff—made him increasingly dependent on Zborowski, the very person betraying him. Zborowski's masquerade was so effective that in August 1937, Sedov wrote to Trotsky, "Etienne [Zborowski] can be trusted absolutely in every respect."[23] In truth, Zborowski passed Sedov's and the Fourth International's most prized secrets to Moscow daily.

Public Warning

By late 1937, Sedov sensed danger again and issued a public warning to Stalin in a Paris newspaper: "I have in no way lost my moral balance, nor in my confidence in life. I am therefore in no way inclined to commit suicide or to disappear. If something should happen to me, the cause must be sought on Stalin's side—or nowhere."[24]

He also wrote to his father, reaffirming his mental stability in case the GPU staged an assassination to resemble suicide.

After the assassination of Ignace Reiss in September 1937, French police identified Sergei Efron as a GPU operative but failed to find incriminating evidence during searches of his office and apartment. Efron fled to the Soviet Union—where he was arrested during the purges and executed in 1941.[25]

An Unexplained Illness

On January 15, 1938, Sedov—believing himself in good health—suddenly suffered intestinal cramps. Others suggest, however, that Sedov's health in 1937 was not good and deteriorated toward the end of that year. Estrin sought help from her sister-in-law, unlicensed Russian doctor Fanny Trachtenberg, who diagnosed mild appendicitis and prescribed a simple diet. Sedov recovered by January 20 and resumed work.[26]

But in early February, the pain returned. Sedov, knowing of the GPU's fondness for poisons, feared the worst. Dr. Trachtenberg and her husband, who also claimed to be a doctor, recommended that he be moved immediately to a private clinic, the Clinique Mirabeau on Rue Narcisse-Diaz in Paris. On February 9, Jeanne Martin arranged an ambulance to take him, and Lilia Estrin came up with the money to pay for both the ambulance and his hospitalization.[27] The clinic was said to be a small private hospital run by Russian émigrés and unknown to the GPU.[28]

The Fourth International was perpetually short on funds, and Estrin's ability to quickly come up with the money for the ambulance and care was inexplicable. Sedov was admitted under the alias name of "Martin"—his mistress's maiden name—his citizenship listed as French, and his profession as a civil engineer. The choice of clinic—and the speed with which Sedov was moved there—would become one of the case's enduring fault lines. Estrin later suggested that the Clinique Mirabeau was the closest hospital. However, scholar Susan Weissman, whose research on Mark Zborowski remains foundational, points out that "the distance from Sedov's apartment on rue Lacretelle to the Mirabeau Clinic on rue Narcisse-Diaz is only 3.7 km, but there was a one hundred sixty–bed public hospital just a block away from Sedov."[29]

The Final Trap

Sedov underwent an appendectomy the day after his arrival. The French surgeon Dr. Marcel Thalheimer performed the operation and noted that the appendix appeared normal. In the immediate days after surgery, Sedov seemed to recover. Then, on the night of February 13, Zborowski abruptly dismissed the night nurse, allegedly to reduce costs. He did so without notifying Jeanne or any of Sedov's colleagues—effectively ensuring that Sedov would be alone and unprotected overnight.[30]

The next morning, February 14, Sedov was found delirious, undressed, and collapsed in a nearby office. The clinic claimed he had wandered the halls in a fevered state. No staff witnessed this supposed episode; only fellow patients reported seeing him in distress, but none called for help.[31]

Jeanne later recalled finding Sedov's bed and room "soiled with excrement," and more chillingly, Sedov whispering to her: "You know what they did to me last night?"[32]

Historian Bertrand Patenaude summarized the suspicious night in stark terms:

> Sedov had been left unattended, was seen wandering the unattended corridor, half naked and raving in Russian. He was discovered in the morning lying on a cot in a nearby office, critically ill.[33]

He was placed in a secondary room—where he spiraled into catastrophic decline. On February 15, doctors performed an emergency operation, but Sedov slipped into a coma. He died in agony just eight days short of his thirty-second birthday at 11:00 a.m. on February 16,

1938.[34] The official cause of death was peritonitis following the removal of his appendix.[35]

Aftermath and Denial

The clinic conducted an autopsy that was widely criticized as superficial and inconclusive. With the simplest explanation for his death ruled out, the likelihood was that Sedov's symptoms were caused by poisoning rather than appendicitis. Despite this, no toxicology tests were performed. Key witnesses were not interviewed; discrepancies were ignored. Multiple sources asserted that Sedov had been given a poisoned orange by Zborowski, and it was known that Sedov ate lots of oranges.[36] Jeanne Martin stated that "during that terrible Sunday night of February 13, Sedov got up 'half-naked, wearing only a pajama top' and went into another room and ate one of the oranges placed in the room, laid down in an empty bed, then got up and walked through the hallways."[37] More troubling, two men staying in rooms near Sedov's reportedly disappeared the morning after his collapse. The clinic refused to identify them, claiming patient confidentiality. Jeanne suspected that Sedov had either been beaten or poisoned, and believed his whispered remark confirmed foul play.[38]

Alexander Orlov's 1965 CIA debriefing revealed that Lilia Estrin [Dallin] was the person that brought the orange to Sedov on the night of February 13 and raised the possibility that she had been the assassin.[39] However, retired KGB Lieutenant Colonel Oleg Tsarev, who had read the entire KGB file on Zborowski, denied the poisoned orange theory and insisted that Sedov died of natural causes.[40]

Meanwhile, Zborowski—Stalin's most important mole in the Fourth International—launched a preemptive narrative campaign, dismissing Jeanne's concerns and portraying Sedov as chronically ill during 1937. Jeanne Martin, who had lived with him, however, insisted he had been in robust health and had suffered no serious illnesses that year.[41]

Trotsky fought tirelessly from Mexico to reveal the truth, but the French government was in a period of friendly diplomatic relations with Stalin and had no interest in conducting a serious probe of Sedov's death.[42]

The Shadow of TULIP

Weissman wrote that "The fact that someone so young could die, following a routine appendectomy, especially given that the young man was the leader of the opposition to Stalin in France, and the son of Leon Trotsky, invites speculation that Stalin's security forces were involved."[43]

In the weeks after Sedov's death, Zborowski provided shifting explanations for how the clinic had been chosen. He claimed that the recommendation had come from Estrin's sister-in-law, Dr. Trachtenberg, who said Sedov would feel comfortable among Russian speakers. In truth, it was Zborowski and Estrin who persuaded Sedov to "avoid a French hospital, where the GPU would surely find him, in favor of the small, little-known clinic where his whereabouts were kept secret."[44]

On the contrary, however, "the Clinique Mirabeau was run by White Russians; the Director, Dr. Boris Girmunsky, was a former Chekist [Lenin's first secret police] and GPU operative."[45] Sedov's hastily contrived alias was unlikely to withstand even a cursory examination. As Weissman observed, "Sedov's identity would have been discovered the first time he opened his mouth, and with his high fever and delirium, lapsing into his native Russian was all but certain."[46] The choice of clinic was even more troubling because the Mirabeau was regularly used by the Union for the Repatriation to Russia to treat sick émigrés prior to their return to the Soviet Union and had a reputation for being saturated with Stalinist agents and provocateurs. On the very day Sedov was admitted, TULIP notified his GPU case officer of his destination at the clinic.[47]

Weissman makes the point that it was both Zborowski and Lilia Estrin who suggested that Sedov go to the Mirabeau clinic, as her sister-in-law, Dr. Fanny Trachtenberg, worked there.[48] Weissman cited Broué's explanation that Dr. Trachtenberg recommended the small Russian clinic because the Russian staff could accept patients from a Russian doctor, even though they were illegally practicing medicine in France without a license. Weissman later commented that despite Zborowski's call to his handler after Sedov was admitted to the clinic, the GPU likely already knew of his admission before TULIP's call arrived.[49]

In 1955, Zborowski admitted that he continued funneling information to the GPU and that he had notified his handler the moment Sedov arrived at the clinic.[50]

The Mysterious Death of Lev Sedov

The supervising physician, Dr. Adolf Simkov, originally from Kyiv, quickly realized Sedov was not the "Monsieur Martin" under which he had been registered. Despite the alias, the Russian nursing staff uncovered his real identity within hours. Sedov's surgeon, Dr. Thalheimer, also had a record of several previous fatalities following relatively routine operations.[51] Weissman further noted in a footnote that in 1983, "French surgeon Jean-Michel Krivine reviewed the autopsy report and discovered symptoms of postoperative peritonitis—fifth day syndrome—which requires immediate surgery to save the patient. Krivine wrote, 'But Thalheimer, whose incompetence was legendary in the medical community, only operated two days later.'"[52]

When Jeanne Martin learned of the role played by Estrin and Zborowski in selecting the clinic, and of their later refusal to cooperate with French authorities, she accused them of complicity in Sedov's death. In response, Zborowski and Estrin—functioning as gatekeepers for the Paris office—worked aggressively to discredit her and suppress any suggestion of GPU involvement. Jeanne persisted, filing a second inquest and submitting thirteen detailed questions regarding inconsistencies in the autopsy. The clinic's replies avoided the central issues and merely reiterated its original claims.[53]

Unanswered Questions

Trotsky, devastated by his son's death, corresponded directly with the investigating judge on July 18, 1938, urging the court to abandon the theory of natural causes. He reminded the judge of Sedov's public warning the previous year: "If something should happen to me, the cause must be sought on Stalin's side—or nowhere."[54]

Trotsky's suspicion reflected the GPU's well-earned reputation for assassination techniques—particularly the use of poisons and barbiturates—whose forensic signatures could be rendered undetectable.[55]

Sedov's surgeon, Dr. Thalheimer, took refuge behind professional secrecy during the investigation, refusing to answer questions or comment further on Sedov's death.[56] Although the French court briefly reopened the case, no substantive progress followed. Several clinic staff members—potential witnesses—were never summoned, and evidentiary gaps widened rather than narrowed. Jeanne Martin's continued appeals only underscored the institution's evasiveness.

The Struggle for Truth

In the months following the inquest, Stalin's assassins continued eliminating Trotskyists across Europe. From his isolation in Mexico, Trotsky depended more heavily than ever on Zborowski and Estrin to sustain the Paris office. Their control of the Fourth International's communications network across Europe and beyond made them seem indispensable—even as mounting evidence suggested that Zborowski himself had played a direct role in Sedov's death.

Competing Interpretations

Historians remain divided over the precise mechanics of Sedov's death:

- Former Federal Bureau of Investigation (FBI) agent Ed Gazur, who protected GPU defector Alexander Orlov in the United States, argued that the GPU had previously entrusted the Clinique Mirabeau with Orlov's care after a car crash in Spain the year before—suggesting it was a known and reliable asset for sensitive operations.[57]

- Orlov later testified that once Zborowski alerted the GPU, the organization seized the opportunity, eliminated Sedov, and ensured the autopsy concealed the true cause of death.[58]
- In that same testimony, Orlov confirmed that Zborowski (TULIP) was responsible for both Reiss's and Sedov's murder.[59]
- Fellow defector Walter Krivitsky told US intelligence that Zborowski worked under Sergey Shpigelglas and participated in Mobile Group assassination operations targeting Trotskyists outside the USSR.[60]
- Years later, Soviet agent Jack Soble reiterated, "Yes, it was a GPU job."[61]
- Susan Weissman, however, cites her 1999 interview in Moscow with Lieutenant Colonel Oleg Tsarev, who claimed the GPU had pursued a different, though improbable, plan: kidnapping Sedov and transporting him to the Soviet Union for trial and execution. According to Tsarev, Zborowski's role was to lure Sedov to the abduction site, with transport envisioned either by sea or by air to Minsk and then Moscow. The GPU spread a calculated rumor that a pilot near Paris was training for a nonstop seven-hour flight to the USSR. Before Sedov could be lured into this trap—an outcome that would likely have exposed Zborowski earlier—he fell ill.[62]
- Zborowski also reported to the GPU at the time, "we want an autopsy—it should be ordered because it will be better for us—because they will find nothing."[63] The remark may be read either as the confidence of an innocent man expecting exoneration or as the assurance of someone complicit in a plot dependent on a poison advanced enough to leave no forensic trace.

Sudoplatov's Contradictions

Pavel Sudoplatov offered conflicting explanations regarding responsibility for Sedov's death:

- Sudoplatov wrote that Soviet army General Dmitri Volkogonov's biography stated that Zborowski helped kill Sedov in a French hospital after his appendix was removed, adding that Sedov's death under mysterious circumstances left little doubt it was the work of GPU chief Nikolai Yezhov's agents.[64]
- Yet Sudoplatov also claimed he found no documentation in GPU files detailing the assassination—possibly because the operation was overseen by the secretive Yashi Group, which reported directly to top leadership.[65]
- In an alternate interpretation, Sudoplatov suggested Sedov may have been more useful alive, since Zborowski's control of the Paris office—and his unparalleled access to Fourth International intelligence—only expanded after Sedov's death.[66]

These contradictions reflect both internal rivalries within Soviet services and the opacity of Stalin-era assassination operations.

The Case Against Coincidence

Despite variations in surviving accounts, the core irregularities surrounding Lev Sedov's death remain difficult to dismiss. He was treated at a compromised clinic recommended by a GPU agent, his appendix was later found to be normal, a night nurse was quietly dismissed, Sedov experienced unexplained delirium, and two nearby patients disappeared under unclear circumstances. Witness statements conflicted, the autopsy proved inconclusive, and the possibility of a fatal surgical error was never adequately addressed. These anomalies unfolded against a documented pattern of GPU assassinations carried out through medical manipulation and staged misfortune.

Taken together, they form a sequence too precise to be accidental.[67] When Trotsky's assassin, Jacques Mornard*, later appeared before the Mexican courts, he was questioned about Sedov's death and the GPU's possible role. His answer was unequivocal: "Yes, the GPU killed Lev Sedov."[68]

Conclusion: Stalin's Hand in Paris

Lev Sedov's final days in Paris unfolded amid surveillance, infiltration, and irregular medical decisions that closely resembled the GPU's established methods for eliminating high-value enemies abroad. His movements were monitored, his circle penetrated, and the circumstances of his hospitalization—the choice of clinic, the dismissal of the night nurse, the unexplained collapse, the shifting staff accounts, and the evasive autopsy—fit the architecture of prior Soviet operations.

Yet the full record does not yield an unassailable verdict. Many suspicious elements can be interpreted in more than one way. French medical incompetence in 1938 was widespread; record-keeping was poor; emergency surgery carried high risk; and even the most troubling details could plausibly be attributed to negligence, fear, or bureaucratic disorder rather than conspiracy. Occam's razor, the philosophical principle favoring the explanation that makes the fewest assumptions, can—depending on how the evidence is interpreted—support either conclusion.

What remains incontrovertible is motive and opportunity. Stalin regarded Sedov as a strategic threat: the operational brain of the Fourth International, Trotsky's closest collaborator, and a figure whose writings resonated across the European left. Eliminating him would have destabilized Trotsky's network at a critical moment, and the GPU—through Zborowski and its Paris rezidentura—was deeply embedded in Sedov's life.

But plausibility is not proof. The surviving files do not conclusively demonstrate that Sedov was murdered by GPU mobile units, nor do they establish direct operational coordination through Zborowski inside Clinique Mirabeau. The gaps in the record invite suspicion but also prevent certainty. Sedov may have fallen victim to assassination, or he might have died from a cascade of medical errors compounded by fear and haste.

What can be said with confidence is this: Sedov's death—whether the result of design or disaster—served Stalin's interests. It fractured Trotsky's inner circle, removed its most capable organizer, and cleared the ground for the next phase of the GPU's campaign. As historian Robert Service observed, "his [Sedov's] chances of growing old had always been slim."[69]

Whether Sedov died by plot or by misfortune, his absence created a vacuum the GPU quickly exploited. While Trotsky mourned in Coyoacán, Stalin's agents were already at work thousands of miles away—burrowing into unions, émigré circles, and political front groups across the United States. New York became the hub, couriers the lifeblood, and clandestine networks the architecture of a new offensive. Sedov's tragedy was not the end of the story. It marked the threshold of a new battleground—Stalin's American front—where the plot to kill Trotsky would soon take shape.

CHAPTER III

THE US PLOT TO KILL TROTSKY

Stalin's American Network

"There was no border the GPU could not cross, no friend it could not corrupt, no sanctuary it would not violate."
—Robert Conquest, *The Great Terror: A Reassessment*

"In America, the Kremlin found not only sympathizers—but volunteers."
—CIA internal review, 1972

"The hand that struck Trotsky was raised long before it crossed the border."
—Pavel Sudoplatov, *Special Tasks*

GPU Strategy from Moscow to New York

Although Leon Trotsky was ultimately assassinated in Mexico, the operation that led to his death was global in scope—conceived in Moscow, refined in Europe, and quietly set into motion from the United States. In New York, far from the revolutionary battlegrounds of Europe, GPU intelligence officers recruited and managed the individuals whose roles would prove indispensable. Operating beneath the attention of the FBI and an unsuspecting American public, they subverted loyalties, constructed false identities, and assembled the clandestine human infrastructure that made the assassination possible.

Many of the conspirators who enabled the operation were American citizens, dual nationals, or Soviet operatives active in the United States. Although the FBI would later monitor several of these figures, it took decades—along with defector testimony and international intelligence cooperation—before US counterintelligence began to untangle the web of cover names and aliases leading back to the GPU's overarching campaign to eliminate Trotsky: Operation UTKA (DUCK).[1]

GENNADY: The Spider at the Center

At the center of the American operation stood Gaik Badalovich Ovakimian, GPU cover name GENNADY. A senior officer in Soviet scientific-technical intelligence, Ovakimian arrived in the United States in 1933 under official cover as an engineer with Amtorg, the Soviet trade organization. Despite early FBI surveillance, he became one of the Soviet Union's most effective recruiters in the Western Hemisphere.[2]

The FBI described him as "rather small and stocky . . . with a medium-dark complexion, dark-brown hair, and blue eyes." Multilingual and highly educated, Ovakimian left a strong impression on those he handled. A later FBI assessment observed:

> Ovakimian's recruits were scattered as far afield as Mexico and Canada . . . Americans whom he controlled described him as charming, serious, sympathetic, well read in English literature, knowledgeable in science, and a man who inspired loyalty in his agents. He must also have been agile and politically aware, for he survived the great purges of the late 1930s which decimated the upper ranks of the Russian espionage services.[3]

That survival was not incidental. Stalin's Great Purges devastated the Soviet intelligence services, eliminating many experienced foreign operatives and shattering chains of command. Abroad, agents were recalled, denounced, or abruptly cut off from handlers. In this climate, continuity became a strategic asset. Ovakimian's ability to retain his position—and his network—gave the GPU rare operational stability in the United States at precisely the moment Stalin was escalating his campaign against Trotsky.[4]

Earl Browder and the CPUSA

One of Ovakimian's earliest and most consequential American relationships was with Earl Browder, leader of the Communist Party USA (CPUSA), known in GPU communications by the cover name HELMSMAN. Whether formally recruited or operating as a highly trusted collaborator, Browder became a critical facilitator of Soviet intelligence activity in the United States. Under his leadership, the CPUSA functioned as a recruitment pool, logistical support structure, and protective buffer for Soviet operatives.

Through Browder's influence, Ovakimian brought at least eighteen CPUSA members into GPU and Main Intelligence Directorate (GRU) networks, placing them in politically and industrially sensitive positions.[5]

Jacob Golos and the Budenz Network

Ovakimian also supervised the extensive spy apparatus run by Jacob Golos, cover name SVUK (SOUND), an illegal resident operating under the guise of a travel agent. Golos managed covert communications and recruited agents across the United States. Ovakimian later was credited with overseeing the network through which Julius and Ethel Rosenberg were eventually recruited into Soviet espionage activities, though the precise timing and mechanics of that recruitment would only be reconstructed years later.[6]

Within this ecosystem, Louis Budenz—operating under the cover names BUBEN and TAMBOURINE—emerged as one of the GPU's most valuable American assets. As managing editor of *The Daily Worker* and a senior CPUSA official, Budenz coordinated political cover, recruitment, and operational support.[7] By 1938, he had been arrested more than twenty times during labor strikes and demonstrations.

Reflecting on his activities during Stalin's purges, Budenz later recalled:

> This was the period of the Great Purges . . . I collected and took them [the GPU] all the available information . . . of secret Trotskyites . . . and their relations to left-wing socialists. At the time I had a number of agents . . . planted in the Trotsky groups.[8]

Infiltrating the Trotskyists

Another critical figure was Dr. Gregory Rabinowitz, GPU cover name HARRY, who also operated under the aliases "Robert" and "John Rich." Posing as head of the Russian Red Cross in the United States, Rabinowitz directed the systematic penetration of Trotskyist organizations.[9]

Known as an intellectual and self-styled Trotsky expert, Rabinowitz was described as "dressing conservatively to enhance his appearance of stability and solidity."[10] The Russian Red Cross provided ideal cover—humanitarian, respectable, and well positioned to access émigré communities with minimal scrutiny.

Rabinowitz identified Ruby Weil as an effective intermediary and instructed Budenz to recruit her. He also oversaw the placement of Sylvia Callen inside the Socialist Workers Party (SWP) in New York.[11]

Sylvia Callen and Ruby Weil

Budenz's recruitment of Sylvia Callen (cover name SATYR) in 1937 and Ruby Weil in 1938 proved decisive. Callen was positioned as personal secretary to James P. Cannon, leader of the SWP, giving the GPU direct access to internal correspondence, strategy, and personnel. Weil, a New York literary figure, was dispatched to Paris, where she worked with Mark Zborowski (TULIP) and facilitated the introduction between her close friend Sylvia Ageloff—one of two women named Sylvia active in Trotskyist circles—and Jacques Mornard*, the alias of Ramón Mercader.[12]

Ovakimian also explored sending Thomas L. Black (cover name BLACK and PETER) to Mexico City to monitor Trotsky's compound and intercept communications.[13] Black later claimed he declined the assignment and reported to the FBI that Rabinowitz told him GPU agents were already inside Trotsky's household.[14]

The American Web

Working in tandem, Ovakimian, Rabinowitz, Budenz, and their associates constructed the core human infrastructure that allowed Soviet intelligence to breach Trotsky's defenses. Ruby Weil's introduction of Mercader to Sylvia Ageloff initiated the deceptive relationship that enabled the assassin to penetrate Trotsky's inner circle two years later. Without that American-based facilitation, the plan might well have collapsed before reaching Mexico.

Conceived in Moscow and executed in Coyoacán, the assassination ultimately depended on an invisible network spun in New York. That network—political, personal, and clandestine—proved more valuable to Stalin than any weapon. Its decisive breakthrough was not merely the man who wielded the axe, but the quiet operative who opened the gates: Sylvia Callen. Her infiltration of the SWP's national headquarters provided Soviet intelligence with what it needed to ensure that, when the moment came, the killer would not miss.[15]

CHAPTER IV

SATYR

Stalin's Mole in the SWP

"The most dangerous enemy is the one
who already knows your secrets."
—Victor Serge, *Memoirs of a Revolutionary*

"She typed his letters by day and delivered his death by night."
—Louis Budenz

"You don't need to break a door when
someone on the inside leaves it open."
—Postwar CIA counterintelligence manual

A Secretary in the Shadows

For nearly a decade, a quiet office worker at 116 University Place—the national headquarters of the Socialist Workers Party—carried out one of Stalin's most damaging espionage operations in the United States. Known to her comrades as Sylvia Caldwell, she was in fact Sylvia Callen, a committed Communist recruited by the GPU.[1]

To the SWP, she appeared as an unpaid volunteer and loyal assistant to party leader James P. Cannon. In reality, she was a GPU mole—deeply embedded, trusted, and granted unrestricted access. For nearly nine years, Callen occupied a position that allowed her to view, copy, and transmit the most sensitive information of Trotsky's American support network—the very organization responsible for safeguarding his life.[2]

10. The pro-Trotsky SWP's national headquarters was located on the floors above the deli at 116 University Place in New York City. The site has since been redeveloped.

Each week, as others went home, Callen remained behind. Under the pretext of completing "homework," she systematically gathered internal correspondence, financial records, and confidential letters arriving from Trotsky's compound in Coyoacán. Once copied, these materials were passed to the GPU through a covert relay that included an apartment rented under the name Lucy Booker.[3]

From there, the documents were delivered to senior GPU officers—initially Dr. Gregory Rabinowitz (cover name HARRY, alias Robert), and in later years to Jack Soble (cover name ABRAM, alias Sam).[4]

Callen's access was comprehensive. She sorted and read incoming mail, typed Cannon's correspondence, and handled messages to and from Mexico. She intercepted and duplicated security updates intended for Trotsky's inner circle. As Louis Budenz—her recruiter and later a defector—testified, she "had the full run of the Trotskyite offices" and "made available to the Soviet secret police all the correspondence with Trotsky in Mexico City, and with Trotskyites throughout the world."[5]

Letters were steamed open, copied, and resealed without arousing suspicion. Her work was methodical, her demeanor unremarkable. For nine years she went undetected. In the anonymity of clerical routine, she delivered the secrets that helped destroy a movement.

Stalin's Mole: SATYR

Sylvia Callen had been groomed for this role. She was first identified within the Chicago Young Communist League and recruited by Louis Budenz under the direction of GPU officer Dr. Gregory Rabinowitz.[6]

Her husband, Zalmond Franklin—a veteran of the Abraham Lincoln Brigade in Spain—was also brought into the Soviet apparatus under the cover name CHEN.[7] The couple was instructed to relocate to New York. Sylvia would infiltrate the SWP; Zalmond would remain in the background.[8]

GPU instructions were explicit. Sylvia was to adopt a plausible cover, presenting herself as an assistant to a physician affiliated with Communist Party circles. Zalmond was to live separately, and the two were never to appear together in public. His prominence as a Spanish Civil War veteran posed an unacceptable risk to her cover.[9]

Settling into a modest midtown Manhattan apartment, Sylvia secured her unpaid "volunteer" position at SWP headquarters. Though the role came without salary, it granted unparalleled access. Working directly under Cannon, she gained routine exposure to the party's most sensitive communications. Twice each month, she delivered packets of copied materials to Rabinowitz through the Booker apartment.

Her espionage was not ideological theater. It was operationally consequential. The information she supplied fed into GPU planning for what would become Stalin's most audacious overseas murder operation: the assassination of Leon Trotsky.

Tradecraft and Compartmentation

Callen's long-term penetration of the SWP followed established rules of Soviet tradecraft. She concealed her political affiliations, posed as an apolitical office assistant, and tightly managed her personal schedule. GPU discipline extended beyond her work life. Her apartment was to remain free of known Communists—especially her husband.[10]

Her deliveries continued without interruption from 1937 for nearly a decade. The materials she smuggled included internal memoranda, financial statements, and personal information on Trotsky's guards and family members, including Natalia Sedova [Trotsky]. She also conveyed logistical details concerning Trotsky's compound, including names and duty schedules of American guards—information that later proved relevant to GPU operational planning.

Callen's importance to Soviet intelligence was later confirmed by VENONA, the top-secret US counterintelligence project that decrypted Soviet wartime cable traffic. In messages declassified in 1995, Callen was identified under the cover name SATYR.[11] These decrypts revealed the breadth of her reporting: financial intelligence, personal data, and confidential political strategy all flowed through her hands.

The Mole Revealed

In 1947, Louis Budenz publicly disclosed the existence of a GPU mole inside the SWP in his memoir *This Is My Story*, identifying her only by the alias of "Helen." US counterintelligence soon identified the individual as Sylvia Callen. Budenz later confirmed her identification in *Men Without Faces*.[12]

Even then, disbelief persisted within the SWP. Callen's quiet demeanor and long record of apparent loyalty made the betrayal difficult for many to accept. The party had no internal security protocols, no vetting of sensitive posts, and no functioning counterintelligence apparatus. That the GPU could embed an agent so deeply—and for so long—was a devastating indictment of the movement's institutional naiveté.[13]

The Key That Opened the Gate

Sylvia Callen's betrayal was not incidental. It was structurally significant. She did not merely observe the SWP; she served as a conduit through which its internal life flowed directly to Soviet intelligence.

Among the most damaging consequences of this penetration was the intelligence environment it helped create—one that facilitated the rapid vetting and assignment of Robert Sheldon Harte (cover name AMUR) to Trotsky's security detail in Mexico in early April 1940. Harte's arrival marked the first successful infiltration of Trotsky's inner circle since the departure of África de las Heras (alias Maria de la Sierra, cover name PATRIA) in late 1938. Harte would later open the gates for the armed assault on Trotsky's home on May 24, 1940.

The intelligence Callen supplied partially offset the loss of PATRIA and helped sustain GPU situational awareness. Without her reports, Soviet operatives in Mexico would have operated with diminished visibility into the Old Man's villa. With them, a steady stream of information reached Leonid Eitingon (cover name TOM), the field commander in Mexico City for Operation UTKA, who directed both assassination attempts.[14]

In Stalin's war against Trotsky, Sylvia Callen was no footnote. If Sheldon Harte physically opened the door to Trotsky's compound during the May raid, it was Callen who—figuratively—placed the key in his hand and helped swing the gate wide. Soon, others would follow—trusted operatives trained to carry out the blood work of assassination.

CHAPTER V

THE HANDS BEHIND THE AXE

Stalin's Killers

"In every revolution, there are those who kill for power—and those who kill for orders."
—Pavel Sudoplatov, *Special Tasks*

"He moved through history without leaving fingerprints—only bodies."
—Anonymous CIA profile on Nahum Eitingon

"Caridad was a crack shot with a gun or knife and bragged about executing more than twenty Trotskyites."
—Isaac Don Levine, *The Mind of an Assassin*

They came from different countries, spoke different languages, and followed divergent paths into Stalin's secret world. Yet by the spring of 1940, six individuals—artists, spies, party loyalists, and professional killers—stood at the heart of one of the boldest assassination plots of the twentieth century. They were the hands behind the axe, the architects of Operation UTKA and its two subplots, the primary plan, Operation KON (the direct assault), and the secondary plan, Operation MAT (a lone assassin). Bound by secrecy, ideological fervor, and a shared fear of Stalin's wrath, they formed a lethal web stretching from the Kremlin to the barrios of Mexico City. This was not merely the story of a mission, but of the conspirators themselves—the trusted insiders, the compromised revolutionaries, and the killers who carried Stalin's will to the doorstep of his greatest enemy.

Caridad Mercader: The Fanatic Mother

Eustacia María Caridad del Río Hernández—better known as Caridad Mercader—was one of Stalin's most fanatical operatives and among the most effective agents in the GPU's clandestine network. Though remembered primarily as the mother of Trotsky's assassin, Ramón Mercader, her own legacy runs deeper. Caridad was in Mexico City for the first eight months of 1940, but her involvement with Operation KON was limited to supervising her son, Ramón, in collecting intelligence on the Trotsky compound. Following the failure of Operation KON on May 24, however, she directed Operation MAT, the second and ultimately fatal attack on Trotsky. Far from a passive figure, she was operating under the cover name of MOTHER as the lead architect of the murder that made her son infamous and secured her place in the darkest pages of Soviet espionage.[1]

Born on March 31, 1892, in Santiago, Cuba, Caridad was raised in a wealthy Spanish family that relocated to Barcelona before Cuban independence.[2] The family belonged to the affluent Indiano class—Spaniards who returned from the Americas with wealth and social standing. She was educated at elite Catholic schools in Barcelona, Paris, and London, became fluent in both French and English, and even spent several months in a convent before rejecting a religious vocation—ultimately deciding that her wild spirit was incompatible with life in a holy order.[3]

Caridad's rebellious streak unsettled her parents, who viewed marriage as a way to temper her behavior and impose a more acceptable, ladylike decorum. In 1911, they arranged her marriage to Pablo Mercader, a member of Barcelona's industrial elite. Though it is unusual for women in Spain to take their husbands' surnames, she chose to take the name Mercader for reasons unknown. They had five children,[4] including the future assassin, Jaime Ramón Mercader del Río, their second child, who was born on February 7, 1913.[5]

Once described as strikingly beautiful[6] with piercing green eyes, Caridad became estranged from her politically conservative husband soon after the birth of their youngest child. She later claimed he had tried to "cure her sexual apathy" by making her watch prostitutes through peepholes and had her institutionalized, where she was subjected to electroshock therapy.[7] In 1925, she fled to Paris with her children, never formally divorcing him.

In Paris, Caridad gravitated toward anarchists before joining the Communist movement.[8] She caught the attention of Soviet intelligence and Leonid Eitingon by the late 1920s and worked as a courier shuttling messages between France, Belgium, and Spain[9] for the Comintern—Communist International—an organization that exported Joseph Stalin's version of communism around the world.[10] Though not formally recruited as an agent for another decade, she continued operating, uninterrupted, as part of the GPU's international espionage apparatus in the 1930s.

Caridad was arrested in Bordeaux in 1935 for her subversive activities for the Comintern, beaten by police, and expelled from France. Returning to Spain, she joined the Communist Party and became an icon of anti-Franco resistance. During the 1936 uprising, she led staged propaganda actions—peasants storming mock fascist positions—with Caridad cast as the heroic revolutionary woman. She was later wounded in a German air raid when her truck convoy was strafed. She suffered eleven shrapnel wounds and was evacuated to Lérida, where she underwent surgery and was hospitalized for eight weeks.[11]

Back in Barcelona, Caridad developed a reputation for ruthlessness. Years later—speaking from the safety of Moscow—she boasted that she had executed twenty Trotskyists and other "counterrevolutionaries" in Spain, describing herself as a seasoned killer "who could hit a target with both gun and knife at a distance of over 30 feet" and who had put down "more than twenty Trotskyite and counterrevolutionary elements."[12] But no archival record has ever substantiated those claims, which still sound, years later, like bravado. Only top GPU officers, "the elite," knew of her close relationship with "General Kotov"—Leonid Eitingon—and that during her time in Moscow she was protected under the Department of Special Tasks.[13]

11. Caridad gained notoriety for her actions during the Spanish Civil War.

In September 1936, Caridad traveled to Mexico on what appeared to be a propaganda tour to raise money for Spanish Civil War orphans. But beneath the public mission lay the real purpose of her trip: a covert assignment to evaluate whether Mexico could serve as the staging ground for a future operation against Leon Trotsky—nearly four months before the Old Man ever set foot in the country. She returned to Spain from Mexico in February 1937, and was formally recruited into the GPU by Leonid Eitingon.[14]

After Trotsky's assassination and being recognized in Moscow for her role in the operation, Caridad spent many years in exile in Moscow under GPU protection, where she remained a notorious and disruptive figure. During this period, she was remembered as a violent enforcer of Soviet doctrine by her fellow émigrés. Her relationship with Eitingon became the subject of persistent rumor, as Leonid was a known ladies' man. Decades later, however, Pavel Sudoplatov and Eitingon's children firmly denied that Caridad and Eitingon had been lovers.[15]

Ramón Mercader: The Constructed Killer

Of all the conspirators tasked with eliminating Leon Trotsky, none carried the burden—or the blade—more directly than Ramón Mercader. Handsome, disciplined, and emotionally armored by years of ideological indoctrination and maternal manipulation, Mercader

12. Ramón Mercader's 1935 passport photo.

was the ideal assassin. Shaped by his mother's fanaticism and sharpened by the GPU, he became the perfect instrument for a perfect crime. Where others plotted from the shadows, Ramón was chosen to walk into the lion's den, gain the Old Man's trust, and strike from within. He worked his lethal mission through charm, patience, and the slow erosion of suspicion.

After his mother's marriage collapsed in 1925, Ramón and his siblings followed her into exile in France. There, Ramón was raised amid his mother's circle of pro-Stalinist comrades. Some accounts suggest that as early as 1928 Caridad had come into contact with Soviet espionage and may have met Leonid Eitingon, who would recruit her into the GPU nearly a decade later.[16] Drawn to the structure and ideological certainty of Stalinism, Caridad became a fervent believer and eventually an agent of the GPU. She indoctrinated her son, Ramón, with uncompromising Communist convictions and instilled in him a deep animosity toward the enemies of the party.

When the Second Spanish Republic was proclaimed in 1931, Ramón returned to Barcelona and took a job at the Ritz Hotel.[17] During his training, he became inordinately proud of his skills with a carving knife. Historian Harry Mahoney wrote that "he delighted to display this surgical deftness at dinner parties when there was a roast or a foul to be properly cut up and served."[18]

In July 1932, at age eighteen, he volunteered for the Spanish Army, joining the Jaén Infantry Regiment. He thrived in the systematized environment, and his aptitude earned him rapid promotions—first to corporal, then to sergeant, and by 1934 to brevet lieutenant.[19]

During this time, Ramón became involved with the Círculo Artístico Recreativo Cervantes (Cervantes Artistic and Recreational Circle), a Communist front group in Barcelona dedicated to subverting the Spanish government. He participated in several sabotage missions, which gave him a taste for covert operations and false identities. Mahoney notes that Ramón relished the intrigue of undercover work.[20]

Spanish antiterrorist police, adept at dismantling clandestine networks, eventually targeted the Cervantes group. The organization held regular meetings at a bar on Calle Wilfredo 11, where the group's secretary worked as a bartender. On June 12, 1935, the police raided the establishment and arrested Ramón along with seventeen others. His police record identified him simply as a single man and writer. Due to his leadership role on the group's executive committee, he was jailed in Barcelona and later transferred to Miguel de los Reyes prison in Valencia.[21]

He remained incarcerated until February 1936, when a newly elected Popular Front government granted amnesty to imprisoned leftists. Following his release, the GPU encouraged Ramón to deepen his experience in labor agitation and strike coordination.[22]

With the outbreak of the Spanish Civil War in July 1936, Ramón and his mother responded to the Republican government's call for militia volunteers to resist Franco's uprising. He became a member of an elite commando unit and received advanced guerrilla warfare training in Barcelona. He learned how to infiltrate enemy lines, conduct ambushes, destroy infrastructure, and undertake sabotage missions. He served as a lieutenant and political commissar of the 27th Division on the Aragón Front.[23] He sustained a wound above the elbow and spent time recovering in a makeshift frontline hospital in Montejuïc before returning to Barcelona in December 1936.

In spring 1937, after returning from Mexico, Caridad held an extended private meeting with Ramón, during which she persuaded him to join the GPU. Eitingon followed up and personally made the recruitment. However, Alexander Orlov also states that as the GPU station chief, he was responsible for Ramón Mercader's recruitment in Barcelona.[24]

13. Ramón Mercader on the Aragón Front, 1936, with the 27th Division.

In his initial secret work, Ramón devoted himself to surveillance and tentative planning, probing for ways to infiltrate Trotsky's inner circle. One of his other assignments was to train David Crook, a young British Communist, in basic surveillance skills to assist in spying on Eric Blair [pen name George Orwell] in Barcelona.[25]

After their formal recruitment, Ramón's and Caridad's movements became obscured as they began advanced GPU training. Historians Julián Gorkin, Isaac Don Levine, and Mary-Kay Wilmers report that Ramón and Caridad were summoned to Moscow in July 1937,[26] where Ramón underwent training in advanced spycraft and assassination, receiving the cover name GNOME. According to Levine, while in Moscow, Ramón was granted access to the GPU's surveillance records on Trotsky's residence at the Blue House in Coyoacán.[27]

Before leaving Moscow for Paris, Ramón received a new cover identity: Jacques Mornard*, the free-spending son of a Belgian diplomat—cultured, persuasive, and fluent in French and English.[28] He reached Paris in late June 1938, where Caridad had already taken up position. Her assignment was to oversee what would become one of the GPU's most effective seduction operations.

Mercader's mission was to seduce and manipulate Sylvia Ageloff, a Brooklyn Trotskyist in Paris for the founding conference of the Fourth International and identify potential points of infiltration into Trotsky's inner circle. The dashing young Mornard* won her confidence almost immediately. Ramón followed instructions and seduced Sylvia ten days after they met in early July 1938, and for the next two years posed as her quasi-boyfriend—and later, her common-law husband. What appeared to be a romance was carefully conducted according to Moscow's script and sustained even after Sylvia returned to New York in February 1939. Ramón maintained the facade of a long-distance love affair with Sylvia through affectionate correspondence, even as he pursued his covert activities in Europe. In September 1939, Ramón journeyed to New York, a trip designed to confirm that Sylvia remained firmly under his control. As part of the ruse, he began calling her his wife, a calculated step in the larger plan, before proceeding on to Mexico City. In January 1940, Sylvia joined him.

For the first five months of 1940, Ramón's assignment was to spy on Trotsky and collect intelligence about the Old Man's guards and details of his villa's inner workings and security. However, his mission took a dramatic turn following the failure of Operation KON, the armed assault on Trotsky's residence on May 24, 1940. In its aftermath, Ramón was designated as the lone assassin for the secondary plan, Operation MAT.

Nahum (Leonid) Eitingon: Stalin's Avenging Sword

Nahum (Leonid) Aleksandrovich Eitingon was not the kind of man who shouted orders or sought recognition. He didn't need to. In the language of Soviet terror, he spoke fluently and acted decisively. Brilliant, discreet, and fanatically loyal, Eitingon served as the operational mind behind Stalin's most sensitive assassinations—none more consequential than the killing of Leon Trotsky. A master of compartmentalization, he coordinated agents, rewrote identities, and built elaborate cover stories with the precision of a chess master. While others carried out the operation, it was Eitingon who crafted the cover story, built the network, and ensured the mission eliminated its target without leaving a trace.

Born on December 6, 1899,[29] in Chernigov (now in Ukraine), Eitingon grew up in a Jewish family amid the upheaval of impe-

14. Eitingon became the field commander for Operation UTKA in Mexico in 1939.

rial collapse and revolution. He was in Moscow during 1917, joined the Red Army in 1918, and entered the Cheka, the original Bolshevik secret police, in 1920.[30] By his early twenties, he had already earned modest acclaim for suppressing a White Army uprising in Gomel. The Soviet secret police—later renamed the GPU—provided him with the counterintelligence skills that he relied upon for the rest of his career.

In the early 1930s, Eitingon was posted to Paris under diplomatic cover. There, using the cover names SAKHOV, VALERY, TOM, and PIERRE, he orchestrated a number of brazen operations that shocked Europe and galvanized opposition to the GPU's heavy-handed tactics. Although the incident ultimately damaged Soviet prestige by exposing the previously hidden activities—high-profile kidnappings, sabotage, and targeted killings of the GPU's elite Department of Special Tasks. During the Spanish Civil War, Eitingon operated the DST teams officially using the alias "General Kotov," but at other times within Communist Party circles, he was also disguised using the alias of "Comrade Pablo."[31] Eitingon also ran six schools to train saboteurs and assassins recruited from among pro-Communist volunteers.

Eitingon's record of skillfully eliminating Trotskyites was formidable, and with each success his reputation in Moscow grew. The following year, Eitingon set a trap for one of Trotsky's closest aides and former secretary, Erwin Wolf, in Spain. Forced out of Norway shortly before Trotsky departed for Mexico in December 1936, Wolf too tried to slip beyond Stalin's reach. However, he was lured into a meeting near Barcelona, where he was kidnapped, interrogated, and executed in secret. With every successful assassination, Eitingon's stature grew among his Spanish comrades, who regarded him as a ruthless killer whose lethal efficiency was hidden behind a composed and authoritative demeanor.[32]

This web of assassinations, sabotage, and political deception defined Eitingon's career. With each mission, he proved himself indispensable to Stalin's terror network. By 1940, his expertise in covert action had brought him to Mexico. There, as the on-site commander of Operation UTKA, Eitingon prepared the final act in one of the most infamous political murders of the twentieth century.[33]

Pavel Sudoplatov: Bureaucrat of Murder

Pavel Sudoplatov did not fire the shot, forge the passport, or carry the ice axe—but without him, none of it would have happened. At just thirty-three, he was the youngest and most trusted executioner in Stalin's inner circle. Coldly efficient and fiercely loyal, Sudoplatov transformed Stalin's directive—"Eliminate Trotsky within a year"[34]—into a global clandestine operation, deploying layered networks, deep-cover agents, and compartmentalized strike teams. He worked at the intersection of espionage and murder, where success was measured in silence. As chief planner of Operation UTKA, Sudoplatov coordinated every moving part and ensured the Kremlin could deny having a hand in the events even as it guided the blade.[35]

Born in the Russian Empire in what is now Zaporizhzhia Oblast, Ukraine, in 1907,[36] Sudoplatov was the son of a Russian mother and a Ukrainian father. He was raised in the traditions of the Russian Orthodox Church but left home in 1919 at just age twelve to join a Red Army unit during the Russian Civil War. The Russian Civil War was at its most intense in 1919, as the Bolsheviks fought to hold on to power and defend the revolution. They faced strong resistance from the White Russian armies, which were supported by several

European countries, including Britain and France. The fighting was brutal and widespread, with control of key cities shifting back and forth. The Red Army, short on resources and manpower, called on anyone willing to fight.

It was not unusual for children as young as twelve—and sometimes even younger—to be drawn into the ranks, particularly during the war's most chaotic and desperate periods. In the Russian Civil War (1917–1921), the Bolsheviks confronted not only White forces of monarchists and conservatives, but also Ukrainian nationalist armies seeking independence from both Moscow and the Whites. To the Soviets, both groups were mortal threats. For Sudoplatov, joining the fight against them aligned with his Bolshevik commitment, even as he proudly embraced his Ukrainian identity throughout his life.

By age fourteen, Sudoplatov had joined the Cheka (All-Russian Extraordinary Commission for Combating Counterrevolution, Speculation, and Sabotage)—the forerunner of the Soviet secret police and the GPU—and rose swiftly through the ranks.[37] By 1927, he had become a leading figure in the Secret Political Department of the Ukrainian State Political Directorate. In 1933, he was transferred to the central GPU in Moscow and began working abroad as an "illegal," or deep-cover operative.[38]

A major turning point in his career came on May 23, 1938, when Sudoplatov assassinated Yevhen Konovalets, head of the Organization of Ukrainian Nationalists (OUN), by detonating a bomb concealed in a box of chocolates. The successful mission, allegedly ordered by Stalin himself, aimed to destabilize Ukrainian nationalist resistance on the eve of war.[39] After confirming the detonation, Sudoplatov calmly departed Rotterdam and boarded a train to Paris. Dutch authorities and the OUN suspected his involvement, circulating his photograph among their ranks and closely watching for his movements, but were unable to identify the killer. Sudoplatov's success with the assassination firmly established his value to the GPU's Department of Special Tasks and led to him being appointed the next year to head Operation UTKA.[40]

He later took part in operations during the Spanish Civil War, supporting the fight against Franco's forces. In late 1938, amid the Great

15. Pavel Sudoplatov in 1935.

Purges, Sudoplatov narrowly avoided arrest and was appointed acting head of the Foreign Department of the GPU.

In March 1939, Stalin formally elevated him to deputy director of the Foreign Department and charged him with overseeing the assassination of Trotsky. His task was to mobilize all available GPU resources to eliminate Trotsky, "the worst enemy of the people."[41] The successful execution of Operation UTKA in August 1940 cemented Sudoplatov's reputation as one of Soviet intelligence's most effective and lethal strategists.

Iosif Grigulevich: The Spy in the Vatican

Iosif Romualdovich Grigulevich was a master of masks—an assassin, diplomat, intellectual, and spy. Born in the Russian Empire and raised in Argentina, he was at once urbane and ruthless, equally comfortable at a café in Paris or with a pistol in Mexico City. Recruited by Soviet intelligence in the mid-1930s, Grigulevich rose quickly through the ranks of the GPU's elite assassination squads in Spain, carving out a reputation as a loyal ideologue with an instinct for infiltration and a propensity for violence. Among the architects of Operation KON—the failed assault on Trotsky's compound—he would later attempt to

16. Iosif (Joseph) Grigulevich (cover name FELIPE) failed to assassinate Trotsky on May 24, 1940.

reinvent himself entirely, posing as a Costa Rican diplomat while secretly plotting to assassinate Yugoslavia's Marshal Tito. Few operatives blended education and violence as seamlessly—or left behind such a trail of elegant lies and bloody corpses.

Born in 1913 in Vilnius to a Polish-Jewish family, Grigulevich emigrated to Argentina in the early 1920s.[42] There he became active in Communist circles and caught the attention of Soviet recruiters. By the mid-1930s, he became a leading operative in Spain, where, using the cover names MAKS and FELIPE, he organized "mobile groups" that assassinated Trotskyists, including Workers' Party of Marxist Unification (POUM) leader Andreu Nin.[43] He collaborated in Spain with assassin Vittorio Vidali, known there as Comandante Carlos Contreras, who would later join him in Mexico.[44] Grigulevich's fluency in multiple languages and cosmopolitan demeanor made him a prized asset.

Historian Bertrand Patenaude notes that Joseph Grigulevich—fresh from the battlefields of Spain—was sent to Mexico City in the spring of 1938 intent on penetrating Trotsky's inner circle. He set up an observation post a few blocks from the Blue House and began planning operations with Siqueiros, his wife Angélica, and her brother Leopoldo Arenal.[45]

Recalled to Moscow in 1939, he was then dispatched to Mexico in early 1940 as part of Operation KON using the cover names FELIPE and JOSÉ. He served as the principal liaison between the Mexican Stalinist underground and Soviet handlers in New York and Moscow.

In 1939 he recruited the American Robert Sheldon Harte (AMUR) in New York City, grooming him as a future bodyguard for Trotsky—and as the man who would open the door to the raiders of Operation KON on May 24, 1940.[46] Grigulevich posed as a Spanish exile and worked closely with muralist and GPU operative David Alfaro Siqueiros to coordinate the failed May 24, 1940, assault on Trotsky's villa. The assault injured Trotsky's grandson and resulted in the later murder of bodyguard Sheldon Harte. Grigulevich fled Mexico City to Santa Fe, New Mexico, using the alias of Manuel Francis Rodrigez before returning to Moscow a year later.

José David Alfaro Siqueiros: The Assassin with a Brush and a Gun

David Alfaro Siqueiros was not just Mexico's second most famous muralist—he was also a fervent Communist and revolutionary who turned art into a weapon and lived by the gun. A towering figure in Mexican muralism, he was equally known for his political militancy and his unwavering loyalty to Stalin. To his admirers, he was a visionary artist with a rifle in one hand and a paintbrush in the other. To his detractors, as Mahoney noted, "he was born and raised in Mexico but spent his adult life wrapped in the cocoon of self-deluding fantasy, and the warm spit of communist ideology."[47] To Trotsky, he would become something far more dangerous: an avowed Stalinist and the field commander of the assault on his life on May 24, 1940. Siqueiros's dual life—as both cultural icon and clandestine enforcer—made him the perfect instrument for the GPU's operations in Mexico.

Siqueiros was born in 1896, and at age eighteen enlisted in Venustiano Carranza's Constitutional Army, along with fellow students from the School of Fine Arts, to fight against President Victoriano Huerta's oppressive regime.[48] Following Huerta's fall in 1914, Siqueiros became embroiled in the subsequent power struggles between Carranza's forces and the rival factions led by Pancho Villa and Emiliano Zapata. Serving in the Battalion Mama made up of teenagers, he was a battle-hardened veteran by 1915, eventually receiving a lieutenant's commission.[49] This military journey across Mexico not only deepened his appreciation for the country's rich cultural diversity but also exposed him to the harsh realities faced by the working class and rural poor.[50]

Later appointed military attaché to the Mexican Embassy in Paris, Siqueiros explored European painting techniques while embracing bohemian life. In 1920, he traveled to Moscow, where he reportedly received training in sabotage, guerrilla warfare, and assassination.[51] Soviet planners even briefly considered using guerrilla operations in Mexico as a precursor to anti-US campaigns before abandoning the idea and shifting focus to eliminating Trotsky.[52]

By 1928, Siqueiros had become a staff officer in the GPU,[53] pledging full loyalty to Stalin. Despite his covert ties, he never set aside his art.

In late January 1937, Siqueiros joined the Spanish Civil War alongside 533 volunteers from Mexico as part of the International Brigades.[54] When he arrived in Spain, he was impressively carrying an engraved pistol gifted by Mexican President Lázaro Cárdenas that he brandished to establish his political connections. His volunteers were distributed among the Republican army units while Siqueiros served as a political commissar in the Fifth Regiment led by "Carlos Contreras," the alias of Stalinist operative Vittorio Vidali, whom Mahoney noted was "a Comintern agent, tough organizer, and disciplinarian who had many cowards and deserters shot."[55] Historian Herbert L. Matthews called the highly disciplined regiment "one of the great revolutionary military units of all time."[56] And for a brief period of time, Siqueiros was placed in charge of a tank unit in the famed Fifth Regiment.[57] Reunited with Caridad Mercader—whom he had met in Mexico and was rumored to have had an affair with—he was introduced to her son Ramón for the first time.[58]

He returned to Mexico in November 1937 with his wife, journalist Angélica Arenal, and only fifty-two of the original 533 volunteers he had left with, one of the highest casualty rates of the Spanish Civil War.[59]

When Ramón Mercader—posing as Frank Jacson*—arrived in Mexico in the fall of 1939, Siqueiros welcomed him secretly while he was organizing the armed assault team for Operation KON. GPU tradecraft rules, however, required strict separation between operational units (KON and MAT), and Siqueiros's continued association with Ramón

17. David Siqueiros (cover name KON) was recruited by the GPU in 1928.

was a potential security risk.[60]

On May 24, 1940, Siqueiros led the assault team that raked Trotsky's bedroom with gunfire. Yet inexplicably, the self-described "colonel"[61] withdrew from the villa before verifying the deaths of Trotsky and Natalia—both of whom had survived. Siqueiros fled to Guadalajara, where his friend José Guadalupe Zuno hid him. He then escaped to the mountain town of Hostotipaquillo, disguised as a peasant under the alias Macario Huízar. When he was eventually captured by authorities, he was jailed in Mexico City's Lecumberri Prison.

Despite the seriousness of the charges and his central role in the attack, Siqueiros never received the judicial punishment warranted by his actions. With the intervention of diplomatic allies—including the Chilean poet Pablo Neruda[62]—he was granted permission to leave the country under the pretext of a cultural assignment. In Chile, he organized a team of artists to complete a mural in a school library in the town of Chillán. The mural, titled *Death to the Invader,* depicted heroic figures from both Mexican and Chilean history united in the struggle against foreign oppression.

Hoping to reenter the United States to contribute to the fight against fascism, Siqueiros was denied a visa. Instead, he traveled to Cuba where he completed three murals: *Allegory of Racial Equality, New Day of the Democracies*, and *Two Mountains of America: Martí and Lincoln.*

The Final Thread

These conspirators had woven a plot so intricate that even Trotsky, seasoned in betrayal and exile, failed to see its final thread until it was too late. Through false identities, compromised loyalties, and the manipulation of human affection, Stalin's assassins had breached Trotsky's last defenses. As the plot neared its climax, each player moved with disciplined precision, guided not only by ideology but by fear, obedience, and the iron will of a dictator who believed that history could—and must—be erased. The stage was set, the killer in place, and the Old Man, surrounded by steel and suspicion, stood unknowingly at the edge of what would become his undoing.

But there was still one element of the plot that even the GPU could not fully control: the heart. In the final days, it was not a bullet or a bomb that opened the gates—it was a woman. And she would open them not with treachery, but with love.

CHAPTER VI

THE SEDUCTION AND BETRAYAL OF SYLVIA AGELOFF

"Love, when wielded by the cunning, becomes
a weapon more deadly than any blade."
—Dmitri Volkogonov, retired Soviet
military general and historian

"The sharpest weapon of all is the one
that enters through the heart."
—Victor Serge, Russian revolutionary
and chronicler of Stalin's purges

"She loved a man who served a machine that
destroyed everything she believed in."
—Later reflection of Natalia Sedova [Trotsky].
(attributed in SWP correspondence)

A Weapon Named Sylvia

The affair between Sylvia Ageloff and Ramón Mercader—operating under the false identities Jacques Mornard* and later Frank Jacson*—stands as one of the most chilling case studies in psychological manipulation. The GPU's plot to assassinate Leon Trotsky demanded a weapon that could bypass bodyguards, gates, and alarm systems. It required intimacy. Seduction became the vehicle and Sylvia Ageloff the unsuspecting target.

What began as a seemingly chance encounter in Paris in 1938 was, in fact, the culmination of years of Soviet planning that reached from New York to Europe. Stalin's operatives, working through the Communist Party USA and GPU networks in Mexico and France, sought not only intelligence about Trotsky's private world but a path inside. In Sylvia—a shy, idealistic, and emotionally vulnerable social worker from Brooklyn—they found the perfect access point. Beneath her reserve lay a need for approval and belonging that often overrode reason. Educated, intelligent, and naive, she believed sincerity could be read in others as easily as she felt it in herself. That faith, coupled with her sheltered upbringing and inexperience in romantic life, left her unguarded before practiced deceit. The GPU correctly identified Sylvia's emotional needs as a vulnerability and weakness: a woman perceptive enough to sense the incongruities, yet too trusting—and too starved for affection—to confront them, knowing it might cost her the only love she had ever known.

By exploiting her trust and affection, the GPU transformed Sylvia into an unsuspecting link to Trotsky's guarded world. Her seduction was deliberate—a slow, calculated manipulation that turned companionship into access. There were clues that Jacques Mornard* was not who he claimed to be, but Sylvia, trapped between intellect and longing, refused to see them.

The American Web

Between 1936 and 1940, the GPU maintained a growing clandestine network in the United States, operating primarily through the CPUSA. Using the Russian Red Cross, trade unions, and émigré organizations as cover, Soviet intelligence embedded agents into politically active circles. One of their key objectives was to infiltrate the Socialist Workers Party, which they viewed as ideologically dangerous due to its Trotskyist affiliation. Seasoned GPU officers inside the US coordinated efforts with American Communists to gather intelligence on Trotsky's supporters and couriers.

In late 1936, American Communist Louis Budenz was summoned

to a clandestine meeting in a noisy East 14th Street restaurant in New York. There, his GPU handlers—posing as officials from the Soviet consulate—framed their appeal as a patriotic duty: to identify Trotskyites, leftist dissenters, and "fascist collaborators."[1] Budenz agreed and began reporting regularly to the GPU on Americans linked to Trotsky—small betrayals that gradually closed the net around him.[2]

Working closely with CPUSA leaders Earl Browder and Jack Stachel, Budenz helped the GPU collect intelligence on the SWP—identifying its members, uncovering its administrative practices, and laying the groundwork for infiltration. He was soon partnered with GPU operative Dr. Gregory Rabinowitz, who was the head of the Russian Red Cross in the US.[3] Rabinowitz asked Budenz a seemingly innocuous question: "Can you tell me where the Trotskyites here get their mail from Trotsky in Mexico City?" Budenz provided details, unknowingly helping the GPU inch closer to intercepting Trotsky's most sensitive correspondence.[4]

Over the next several months, Rabinowitz and Budenz continued to meet regularly. Rabinowitz brought photographs of suspected Trotskyists and sought to identify couriers or anyone with contacts to the Old Man and his entourage. One family quickly stood out: the Ageloff sisters of Brooklyn—Ruth, Hilda, and Sylvia.[5] Ruth had worked as a translator during the Dewey Commission hearings in Coyoacán, spoke Russian fluently, and had earned the trust of Leon Trotsky and Natalia Sedova.[6]

Although Ruth Ageloff had an existing relationship with the Trotskys—having worked with them in Mexico in 1937 and corresponded with them afterwards—she was not chosen as the GPU's target. Ruth was older, more politically experienced, and better known to the Trotsky household, which would have made any abrupt changes in behavior more noticeable and potentially suspicious. In contrast, Sylvia was younger, emotionally vulnerable, and less ideologically grounded—traits the GPU found ideal for exploitation. The strategy that the GPU was developing relied on emotional manipulation and seduction rather than political recruitment—tactics that would have been far less effective on Ruth. Sylvia wasn't selected because she was the most connected; she was selected because she was the weakest link.

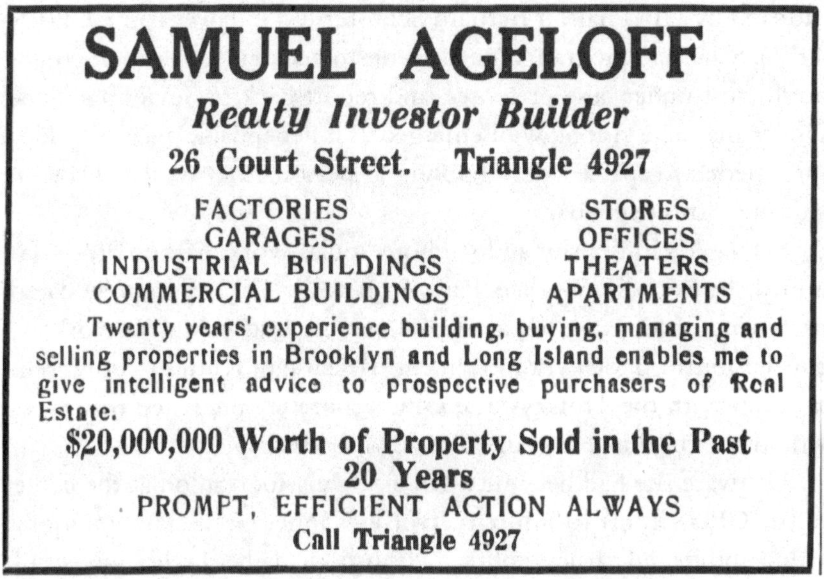

18. Samuel Ageloff was a successful investor and builder whose financial support enabled Sylvia to spend her summers volunteering as an unpaid courier for the Socialist Workers Party.

Recruiting Sylvia directly, however, was not feasible. Instead, a trusted intermediary was needed—someone who already knew Sylvia, could win her confidence, and guide her into a relationship the GPU would control from beginning to end. Rabinowitz identified that person as Ruby Weil and asked Budenz to arrange a dinner meeting.[7]

Ruby Weil and the Bridge

Ruby Weil was a longtime acquaintance of the Ageloff sisters. Weil, however, once sympathetic to Trotsky, had quietly shifted her loyalty and secretly joined the GPU-controlled Communist Party USA.[8]

Budenz had first encountered Ruby Weil during their time at the Trotskyist-leaning Conference for Progressive Labor Action (CLA) before his eventual defection to the pro-Stalinist CPUSA. After his break with the Trotskyist movement, Weil followed a similar path, secretly joining the CPUSA and enrolling in a covert infiltration program directed by GPU liaison Bernard Schuster (GPU cover name CHESTER). Schuster's program trained agents to penetrate opposition groups, build trust under false pretenses, and report back to Soviet handlers.[9] Under his supervision, Weil emerged as a dependable asset—an ideal intermediary capable of leveraging old personal ties while advancing a deadly Soviet agenda.

Sylvia Ageloff, a shy and studious social worker from Brooklyn, joined the Socialist Workers Party in January 1938. She rarely dated, preferring to focus on her academic pursuits and volunteer work as a courier for the Trotskyist movement. Because of Ruth's existing relationship with the Trotskys, the GPU accurately predicted that Sylvia would be welcomed into their circle without suspicion.

Unaware she had become a target, Sylvia soon stood at the center of the GPU's effort to infiltrate Trotsky's inner circle. Her emotional vulnerability and earnest political idealism made her highly susceptible to manipulation. As historian Isaac Don Levine noted, the GPU might have overestimated Sylvia's influence with Trotsky[10]—but even so, her seduction and recruitment became the essential first step in the chain of events that would lead to the fatal blow in Coyoacán.

Weil first met Sylvia Ageloff in the early 1930s through the Trotskyist-aligned American Workers Party.[11] Though their contact faded over time, Sylvia later heard rumors that Ruby had drifted toward Stalinist politics. This shift, however, proved ideal for GPU purposes.

To support the operation, Rabinowitz (alias "Robert") gave Budenz a large sum of cash to fund Weil's clothing, lodging, travel, and social activities. Though initially hesitant, Weil recognized the mission's strategic value and agreed to proceed, drawing on her GPU training in concealing allegiances to maintain appearances while cultivating Sylvia's trust.[12]

Once funded, Weil carefully resumed contact with Sylvia. Her infiltration was quiet but methodical—typical of GPU tradecraft. Decades later, Sylvia testified before the House Committee on Un-American Activities (HUAC), "We didn't see her [Ruby] much at all, except that we had been personally friendly in the sense that we met her sometimes to go to the movies"—a subtle but revealing trace of Ruby's covert role.[13]

19. Sylvia Ageloff had never found true love.

The Paris Setup

In spring 1938, as their friendship warmed, Weil told Budenz that Sylvia was vacationing in France during the summer. Rabinowitz quickly proposed that Ruby accompany her, and that they attend the founding conference of the Fourth International in Paris.[14] Sylvia later recalled the moment: "She [Ruby] called and said she was going to Europe too and that she would go along with me . . . her sister . . . had sent her money for passage . . . wasn't it wonderful . . . I said that was all right with me. That was in June 1938."[15]

Looking back, Sylvia's decision to travel with a known Stalinist during the peak of the Great Terror—when GPU assassins were actively hunting Trotskyists across Europe and many people were fleeing the Continent as war seemed imminent—was both tragically naive and exceptionally dangerous. However, it was Eitingon's idea to use agents who had never before been involved in operations against Trotsky or his followers.[16] Sylvia proved to be an ideal choice.

Although Ruby initially agreed to accompany Sylvia, she soon grew uneasy. Other Communists had spotted her with the Ageloff sisters—known Trotskyites—and reported her to CPUSA leadership. The Party's internal watchdogs closely monitored members for ideological deviation. Fortunately for the GPU, Budenz intervened quickly, notifying Ruby's section leader that she was on a sensitive assignment and must not be questioned. While the warning shielded her from punishment, it left a trace of suspicion, and some comrades distanced themselves.[17]

When Rabinowitz learned of Ruby's hesitation, he dispatched Budenz from Chicago to reassure her. The visit worked.[18] Ruby agreed to move forward—and the operation resumed. However, a key challenge lay ahead. How might they engineer a credible, ideologically acceptable way for Sylvia to meet her future seducer?

The Matchmaker

The GPU compiled a psychological profile of Sylvia—her romantic history, temperament, and preferences—so the GPU's chosen Romeo could tailor his approach.

Weeks before departure, Rabinowitz arranged a key meeting in Greenwich Village between Ruby Weil and Gertrude Allison, a former employee of the Jimmy Higgins Bookshop and wife of Eduardo Machado, cofounder of the Venezuelan Communist Party. Now based in Europe, Allison worked covertly as a courier for the Comintern.[19]

Stationed in Paris, Allison's visit to the US was pivotal, and for two purposes: she first coached Ruby on how to prepare Sylvia psychologically for her forthcoming romance during their Atlantic crossing, and she played a key role in the plot to introduce Sylvia to the GPU's chosen seducer in Paris. The GPU's goal was to foster anticipation in Sylvia for an exciting romantic European adventure—and soften her defenses. The trap would be ready by the time that Ruby and Sylvia arrived in Paris.[20]

Ruby and Sylvia sailed aboard the SS *Normandie* on June 15, 1938.[21] When they docked in Southampton, they met Ruby's sister, Corrine. Ruby and Corrine traveled to London by car, while Sylvia continued to her hotel by the boat train. Several days later, the sisters called her at the hotel and surprised her with new plans—for both sisters to accompany Sylvia to Paris. Though the idea made her mildly uneasy, Sylvia welcomed the company.[22]

On July 1, the trio arrived in Paris and checked into the St. Germain Hotel.[23] Ruby casually mentioned that a local acquaintance, Gertrude, had a friend who could show them the city. In her 1950 congressional testimony, Ruby recalled:

> Gertrude knew somebody in Paris . . . a young student who used to visit her at her apartment. She would get in touch with him and have him come over. So, she called him, and he came around to the hotel.[24]

The trap was now set.

Seducing Sylvia

In a reversal of the classic honeytrap, the GPU wanted to seduce the young American woman in the hope that the liaison would lead to an opportunity for them to penetrate Trotsky's inner circle. To Sylvia Ageloff, the suave, impeccably tailored stranger she met was Jacques Mornard Vandendreschd*—purportedly the cultivated son of a wealthy Belgian family and a retired senior diplomat who, he said, had served in postings around the world. As historian Harry Mahoney described him,

> He had money to take Sylvia to the best restaurants, plays and could buy her expensive gifts. He studiously avoided discussing politics with an indifference that aroused no suspicions.[25]

Jacques* claimed to have been born in Tehran, where his father was stationed as the Belgian minister to Persia. His introduction was riddled with lies and distortions—though Jacques* appeared and presented himself as being more worldly and a decade older. In 1938 he was actually only twenty-five years old and was four years younger than Sylvia. He told Sylvia that he had graduated from a Jesuit college in Brussels in 1920, then spent four reluctant years in Belgian military schools. He further explained that he moved to Paris in 1924, where he studied journalism at the Sorbonne before becoming an assistant to a French sportswriter named Paul de Lacourt who wrote for *Le Soir.* Jacques* explained that his earnings were supplemented by a family income following the death of his father in 1926, who left an estate of four million Belgian francs.[26] In truth, he was Jaime Ramón Mercader del Río Hernández—the man destined to bury an ice axe in Trotsky's skull.

At twenty-nine, Sylvia Ageloff was intelligent and well-educated, holding a master's degree in psychology from Columbia University. But her personal life was unfulfilled. Descriptions of her varied: historian Francis Wyndham described her as "moderately good looking, with a trim, attractive figure, but . . . her appearance was spoiled by her small, nearsighted eyes behind thick spectacles."[27] Others were less charitable. Isaac Deutscher characterized her as "a lonely spinster of a very unattractive appearance."[28] Wyndham also observed that "She had few, if any, love affairs, but was intelligent with a pleasing personality."[29]

In contrast, Jacques* played the part to perfection, radiating confidence and charm as he assumed the elegance, refinement, and distinguished air expected of a diplomat's son.[30] Some considered him to be only "tolerably handsome," while others described him as having "movie star looks."[31] He was worldly, attentive, and perfectly cast to charm a lonely American abroad. From their first meeting, he courted Sylvia with calculated grace—initiating a relationship that would serve the GPU's lethal mission.

Money was never an issue in their courtship.[32] Jacques Mornard* whisked Sylvia into a world of fine dining, theaters, and expensive gifts. His disinterest in politics only deepened his mystique—"He never even read ordinary news articles," she later said.[33] What Sylvia mistook as apolitical charm was calculated camouflage.

Mercader's cover was crafted to perfection: the son of a diplomat, a Sorbonne journalism student, and a part-time sportswriter.[34] Yet his behavior raised red flags that went unnoticed—or were simply ignored. He lived lavishly—too lavishly, Sylvia briefly thought, for someone with no apparent income. Oddly, for a supposed sportswriter, he never attended games, interviewed athletes, or even mentioned sports. Sylvia never saw him research or write. Instead, Jacques* devoted nearly all his time to her, showering her with affection.

Having spent years watching friends fall in love and start families, Sylvia had always felt a quiet envy. But now, she too was finding romance—and just as Ruby had predicted on their voyage across the Atlantic, Paris was indeed a city of love. Alongside Ruby Weil, she also grew close to Marie Craipeau, the warm and engaging wife of French Trotskyist Yvan Craipeau, who often joined the couple on outings and soon became Sylvia's dearest companion in Paris.[35]

Ten days after their first meeting, Jacques* seduced her.[36] His timing was hardly the stuff of romance. Their union did not spring from passion or chance but from a plan—meticulously staged by the GPU, who managed the affair like a field operation. Too soon would have seemed desperate; too late, the spark might have died. So the timing was perfect. Mercader waited just long enough for trust to blossom, then moved before doubt could take hold. For Sylvia, it felt like the natural rhythm of love. For him, it was a professional maneuver, executed with the precision of an agent who was no stranger to intimacy and knew that seduction, properly timed, was simply another form of control.

For the first time in her life, Sylvia fell head over heels in love, and her emotions quickly overrode any of her previous doubts about Jacques*. The contradictions that might have alarmed any reasonable young woman vanished in the glow of their romance. Mercader's deception was working. Love, not ideology, would open the gates to Trotsky's final redoubt.

Even then, the inconsistencies in Jacques's* life—the unexplained wealth, the absence of work, the evasive stories—should have raised alarm. Mahoney wrote that "Sylvia, ordinarily a thinking, politically oriented person, was too blinded by adoration of her suave new lover to notice his camouflage of political naïveté. He [Mornard*] also had an apparent passion, ostensibly at least, to fulfill Sylvia's every dream of what a Prince Charming should be."[37] Sylvia's mind, trained in psychology, rationalized each contradiction away. Her intelligence made her skilled at explaining behavior, but it did not protect her from misreading intent.

But then, shortly after their carefully timed union, Jacques* suddenly declared that his mother had suffered a terrible accident in Brussels and that he must rush to her side—at once. And just like that, he was gone.[38] Sylvia, of course, felt a sense of unease. While she had no reason to suspect that her lover's sudden exit was anything more than devotion, his words seemed to lack his usual warmth and genuineness and somehow seemed almost contrived. In truth, Sylvia was correct, but it would be two years before she'd understand the reasons for her suspicion. The GPU had simply yanked their very important agent from the stage as the operation now faced a far greater emergency—the imminent exposure of their entire agent network.

A Death in Paris

In July 1938, as preparations for the founding conference of the Fourth International in Paris neared completion and the seduction of Sylvia was just getting underway, a chilling drama unfolded behind the scenes. Rudolf Klement—a German-Jewish refugee, Trotsky's former secretary in Büyükada, Turkey, and now the organizational secretary overseeing the Fourth International's founding congress—vanished without a trace.[39] Days earlier, his suitcase containing sensitive conference documents and an important internal report on the Fourth International's security flaws had also been stolen from the Paris Métro.[40]

Klement's disappearance sent shockwaves through Trotskyist circles. Everyone feared the worst: that the GPU had struck again. Their fears were confirmed weeks later. On August 25, a headless and legless male body sealed in a sack was pulled from the Seine; two days later, another sack was recovered containing the legs. The limbs had been severed with surgical precision. It was Klement.[41]

As the conference organizer, Klement's mid-July disappearance had forced the postponement of the Fourth International's founding meeting—originally timed to coincide with Sylvia Ageloff's July visit. His killers, later revealed to be working for the GPU, were never identified publicly.[42] The elimination of Klement deprived Trotsky of one of his most capable organizers and silenced an important report he had been preparing on the Fourth International's internal security flaws and their possible link to the murders of Trotskyists across Europe.

Jacques's* Disappearance

On July 26, 1938, Sylvia received a letter from Mornard* postmarked from Brussels. Her absent lover wrote:

> Sylvia Darling, as I told you, my brother had given me a very bad version of my mother's accident. The thing happened like this: my father and mother were coming from Ostend to spend a day in Brussels. They were in a car driven by a chauffeur and just before getting to Brussels, my father had the car stopped for a necessary reason, and it was then that the car was hit by a ten-ton truck, killing the chauffeur and very seriously injuring my mother. My father, not having been in the car, was unhurt. My mother was operated on again yesterday (the second operation in three days) and the doctors say the greatest danger is past, but they cannot be sure for a few days.[43]

The letter from Brussels, written in his familiar affectionate tone, described a supposed family tragedy. The story, polished and precise, was crafted to appeal to Sylvia's sympathy and deflect suspicion. For the GPU, the letter served its purpose perfectly: for a while longer, it kept Sylvia compliant, disarmed, and emotionally bound to a man who had already become a weapon in Stalin's war against Trotsky.

Jacques's* disappearance was the first in a string of small, troubling moments that Sylvia would recall two years later with anguish and regret. At the time, she hadn't noticed that Jacques's* letter contained a major contradiction—only days earlier he had explained his source of income was from his deceased father's estate that was left to his mother and was worth four million francs. Now, however, his father was miraculously alive and well! The contradiction was so egregious it might have unraveled Jacques's* entire cover story. The reason for the contradiction was never revealed, but KGB historian Oleg Tsarev suggested in 1997 that the exigency of drafting the letter required that it be done by an officer in Paris rather than the Moscow specialists who had carefully built his original legend.[44] Lacking full knowledge of Jacques's* fabricated history, the letter's local author introduced inconsistencies that might have compromised the entire operation. However, luck was on the GPU's side. Sylvia, blinded by love, was apparently so relieved to hear from her lover that she either never recognized the inconsistencies or chose to simply overlook them.

Even from Mexico, however, Trotsky was no fool. He intuitively knew what had happened to his young colleague and declared to Natalia, "The GPU mowed down Klement." He was convinced the young German had either uncovered a Soviet mole inside the Fourth International or stumbled upon evidence linking the GPU to Sedov's mysterious death.[45]

Klement's disappearance and fear that another copy of his damaging report would surface might have been what forced Mercader into hiding—or perhaps to serve as an accessory to the disposal of the body.[46] As Levine later observed, Jacques's* disappearance seemed plausible to Sylvia at the time, but the truth became clear only in hindsight: "Ramón either had to go into hiding until the Klement scandal blew over, or the GPU had other and more pressing business for him than wooing Sylvia."[47]

The Return to Paris

In August, restless and heartsick, she wrote to her lover and planned a journey—first to Prague, then on to Brussels—hoping to see Jacques* again and bring him back to Paris. However, at the address he had given her, she found only a cold, businesslike woman who informed her that Mornard* had "suddenly been called to England."[48] The words hit like a door closing. Disappointed and confused, Sylvia returned to Paris alone and dejected and questioning everything about their relationship.

Then, at her lowest point, the Jacques* letters began to arrive—professionally written by the GPU. They were tender, apologetic, filled with longing. Each one pulled Sylvia back into the dream. The despair that had begun to harden inside her softened again into hope.

At the beginning of September, Jacques* unexpectedly reappeared. He claimed he had been in Brussels the entire time but had been detained under military arrest for refusing Belgian service. Even his new excuse didn't explain how he could have been under arrest but find pen, paper, and postage while in prison to write her love letters. Regardless, Sylvia didn't question it. Still wrapped in the spell of affection, she forgave him instantly. However, when she later asked, almost without thinking, to meet his family, he hesitated—then improvised a new fiction. He refused and explained that neither his mother nor father would approve of her as a daughter-in-law, as he came from a "noble Belgian family" and his father was an important diplomat.[49]

The lie was clumsy, the timing desperate. It might have ended a more perceptive romance. But Sylvia, disarmed by love and blind to absurdity, chose to believe him once more. The contradictions—so brazen they might have insulted another—seemed to her merely the eccentric charm of a complicated man.

Years later Sylvia would understand what she could not see then: Jacques's* return had nothing to do with love. The GPU had recalled him to Paris to attend the reconvened Fourth International congress—and her devotion was the passport he needed to make it possible.

The Founding Conference of the Fourth International

The delayed conference finally convened on September 3, 1938, at the Paris suburb home of Alfred and Marguerite Rosmer.[50] Sylvia Ageloff worked as a Russian translator alongside Mark Zborowski (TULIP), who—following the tragic murder of Rudolf Klement—assumed the overall responsibility for organizing the conference and represented the Russian Opposition, the anti-Stalinist White Russians. The gathering took place amid the looming Munich crisis and escalating Stalinist terror—overshadowed by the grim irony that a GPU agent controlled every detail of the event.

The Munich Crisis—then unfolding in real time—cast a grim shadow over the gathering. Britain and France's decision to appease Hitler by allowing the annexation of Czechoslovakia's Sudetenland was widely seen as a betrayal of democratic principle in exchange for temporary peace. To the delegates, it confirmed that the great powers had traded principle for delay. With Stalinist repression intensifying and Western democracies unwilling to confront fascism, the realization settled in—world war was no longer a question of *if*, but *when*.

Fearing both French police and GPU assassins, the organizers enforced tight security. The conference was compressed into a single day at a secret location. Twenty-eight Trotskyist delegates from eleven countries were led there by Zborowski, who, unbeknownst to them, was a GPU mole operating under the cover name TULIP. Because of him, the entire congress was compromised, and as delegates returned home, GPU informants and assassins were in position and awaiting their arrival.[51]

Sylvia had previously worked with Zborowski in the secretariat and, as historian Dmitri Volkogonov confirmed, knew him personally. In *Les Amants de Sylvia*, Gani Jakupi—drawing on interviews with Marie Craipeau—suggests that Zborowski was also present at the hotel when Ruby Weil first introduced Sylvia to Jacques*, though this account is not independently corroborated.[52]

Though Jacques Mornard* claimed to be apolitical, he surprisingly asked to attend the secret conference with Sylvia as a sign of support. She was not a delegate but served as a translator—fluent in French, Russian, Spanish, and English—making her indispensable. It seems implausible that the mere boyfriend of a translator to the event would be allowed at such a confidential gathering in a secret location. However, Jacques's* presence reflected both Sylvia's naiveté and the GPU's calculated and aggressive strategy orchestrating Ramón's movements behind the scenes.

Jacques's* presence allowed him to linger outside the sessions, smoking, observing, and blending in with delegates while quietly making contact with high-level figures, including James P. Cannon and others.[53] The decision proved effective and paid off two years later in Coyoacán, Mexico. Mercader exploited Sylvia's past connection to reestablish her contact with the Rosmers and, through them, gain Natalia Sedova's trust.

After the assassination, questions arose as to how the Rosmers could have granted him access to the secret conference without verifying his identity. Fortunately for the GPU, Mark Zborowski (TULIP) was now in overall charge of the conference and in a position to quietly approve Ramón's attendance and deflect any objections.

Sylvia's ability to bring her boyfriend—Mornard*—to the 1938 founding congress was also a serious breach of security. But the Socialist Workers Party—like much of the American Left—also lacked the counterintelligence awareness to recognize the threat. That failure had already cost the movement the life of Lev Sedov and many other leaders and would prove fatal once again in Mexico two years later.

The Fourth International, so pleased with their success in conducting their secret founding conference, put out a publicity release that it had been held "somewhere in Switzerland."[54]

Homesick for New York

After the congress, Sylvia told Jacques* she planned to return to New York and her job. But the GPU had other ideas. They believed Jacques* would be more accepted in Mexico in the future as Sylvia's common-law husband rather than a casual boyfriend, and more time was needed to strengthen their relationship.[55] To delay Sylvia's departure, Mornard* claimed to have secured her a lucrative freelance contract with the notional Argus Publishing Company.[56]

He told Sylvia that the company would pay three thousand francs per month—about $1,500 US in 2025—to write psychology articles with no deadlines, no editorial oversight, and no published credits, allegedly to preserve the anonymity of Argus's global syndication.[57] To bolster the ruse, letters from Argus began arriving at the apartment they shared.

When her new employment began paying Sylvia generously for her work, Marie Craipeau grew suspicious. Gani Jakupi's 2010 book *Les Amants de Sylvia (Sylvia's Lovers)* was largely based on interviews with Marie Craipeau. Marie recalled:

> Surprisingly, he [Mornard*] proposed that she translate psychology articles from English to French for an agency, and I helped Sylvia type them. We received a good salary. One day, while working, I

> stopped and said, "Listen, Sylvia, this doesn't make sense. There are no jobs this well paid." So, we sat on the bed, lit a cigarette, and talked. He wasn't interested in politics or our discussions . . . We assumed he was just madly in love and didn't want her to leave.[58]

Why Sylvia accepted such a patently implausible job remains a mystery. Perhaps, already emotionally entangled, she chose to rationalize the irrational. Ironically, her 1934 master's thesis had concluded that individuals often surrender logic under the influence of those they are enamored of—an observation she would come to embody.[59]

By late 1938, according to historian Isaac Don Levine, the Foreign Department (INO), the GPU's external spy service, was disoriented and weakened. Stalin's purges and the execution of GPU chief Nikolai Yezhov had gutted the Soviet intelligence and security services—perhaps explaining why Trotsky remained alive for another two and a half years.[60]

After a brief lull, Mornard* told Sylvia he had accepted work as an American correspondent for a Belgian newspaper and suggested she return to New York ahead of him. She sailed in February 1939 with a promise from Jacques* to follow her soon afterwards. However, a telegram from "Jacques*" reached her in Brooklyn and explained he'd been denied a US visa—but was still trying. Sylvia believed him, never questioning why the son of a Belgian diplomat would be barred entry.[61]

The truth was more nefarious. Levine pointed out that if Sylvia had been more perceptive, there was no valid reason for the United States to refuse to grant a visa to the son of a distinguished Belgian diplomatic family . . . unless he was either a Communist or criminal. Instead, Mornard* had repeatedly claimed to her that his family was of a noble bloodline, and his father had been the Belgian ambassador to Tehran during the World War.[62]

The Great Terror Strikes the GPU

There were two overriding reasons that prevented Jacques* from accompanying his "wife" back to the United States in early 1939—and neither had anything to do with travel difficulties. The first was the Great Terror, the peak of Stalin's purges in the late 1930s, during which the GPU executed or imprisoned hundreds of thousands of perceived enemies. Party officials, military commanders, intellectuals, and ordinary workers were swept up in mass arrests, forced confessions, show trials, and executions. It was a campaign of state-engineered paranoia designed to eliminate all real or imagined opposition to Stalin's rule.

No Soviet institution suffered more profound internal damage than the intelligence services. By early 1939 the GPU was still reeling, an organization at war with itself. Foreign-based officers were suspected of harboring anti-Stalinist sympathies; many were abruptly recalled to Moscow on the basis of cryptic telegrams that often concealed a death sentence. Inside rezidenturas from Paris to Shanghai, officers no longer knew to whom they reported. Superiors vanished overnight, departments were dissolved, and new directives arrived bearing signatures no one recognized. Planning became nearly impossible. Fear and rumor had become operational realities, and a single denunciation could end not just a career but a life. False reports multiplied as officers sought to eliminate rivals before being eliminated themselves.

Historian Robert Conquest describes morale in the GPU's foreign branches as "shattered by terror emanating from the center," a climate in which loyalty to Moscow became indistinguishable from suicidal trust.[63] In this atmosphere of institutional schizophrenia, men like General Alexander Orlov—who oversaw GPU operations in Spain—watched colleagues recalled and executed one after another and concluded that defection was the only path to survival. Orlov fled first to Canada and then to the United States in the summer of 1938. Across Europe, the GPU's overseas apparatus—designed to project Stalin's power—had become a mirror of his paranoia: an intelligence service consumed by internal bloodletting, scarcely capable of sustained foreign operations. Officers focused almost exclusively on personal survival, and long-range efforts to penetrate Trotsky's inner circle, including those involving Jacques Mornard*, ground to a halt.

Mercader's biographer Eduard Puigventós identifies the second reason for Ramón's delayed travel. When he was recruited in 1937 and

1938 for the operation involving Sylvia Ageloff, it was only as a Romeo; at that early stage, there was no defined long-term plan for him beyond the vague possibility that he might someday use his relationship with Sylvia to approach Trotsky's entourage. When Sylvia returned to the United States in February 1939, there was still no mission for Mercader beyond maintaining the romance.

This changed abruptly after Sudoplatov's meeting with Beria and Stalin in March 1939, when he received the order to devise a plan to eliminate Trotsky within one year.[64] The following day, he selected Nahum Eitingon as his deputy and proposed the name Operation UTKA.[65] Crucially, in UTKA, Mercader was not yet the designated assassin; his assignment was only to gather intelligence in support of the primary plan, Operation KON—the direct assault on Trotsky's villa.

Only after his mission was clarified, Ramón finally departed for Mexico from the port of Le Havre, France.

The Birth of Frank Jacson*

On September 9, 1939, Ramón Mercader—now using the alias Frank Jacson*—arrived in New York aboard the *Ile de France*, traveling on a forged Canadian passport stolen from a deceased International Brigades volunteer.[66] The GPU forger had even misspelled the name as Jacson*, a minor misspelling of Jackson that would arouse suspicion for the next twelve months.[67]

Despite stricter immigration controls following Hitler's invasion of Poland, Jacson* was granted entry under an unexplained executive order approved in Washington. No public records ever clarified how he was admitted using the passport of a dead man.

Mr. and Mrs. Jacson*

Jacson* arrived unannounced at Sylvia Ageloff's Brooklyn apartment at 50 Livingston Street, claiming to have purchased the passport for $3,500

20. Sylvia's residence at 50 Livingston Street, Brooklyn.

on the Paris black market. The money, he explained, came from a $10,000 gift from his mother to help him dodge Belgian conscription.[68]

Sylvia, now introducing Frank* as her husband, resumed their common-law relationship and moved into a Greenwich Village apartment loaned by one of Sylvia's Trotskyist friends. Her Jewish father and stepmother, Samuel and Fannie, disapproved, but Sylvia and Frank* settled into "married life." Each day, Jacson* left under the pretense of job hunting while secretly meeting with Leonid Eitingon, who quietly arrived in New York in October to set up a secret communications center to support their forthcoming operation in Mexico City.[69]

To reinforce the illusion of a stable domestic partnership with his new wife, GPU handlers instructed Jacson* to remain in the city for several weeks. Sylvia proudly introduced him as her husband at the Socialist Workers Party office, cementing his false identity. However, when a job with the New York World's Fair failed to materialize and confident that his relationship with Sylvia was still strong, the GPU moved quickly to accelerate his deployment to Mexico.

In early October, Jacson* told Sylvia that he had secured a lucrative post in Mexico City with a man named Peter Lubeck, sourcing war materials for Britain and France at $50 per week plus expenses. Before departing, he gave Sylvia $3,000 to bring when she joined him.[70]

The Bait Is Set

Confident that his control over Sylvia, and her loyalty, had been reestablished, Jacson* made his preparations to depart New York. He expected Sylvia to follow but didn't provide her with a travel date. On October 6, 1939, the Mexican consulate in New York issued Frank Jacson* a tourist card. Ramón set out for Mexico City by train and on October 12 crossed the border at Nuevo Laredo under the name F. Jacson*. On his forged Canadian passport, he listed his occupation as mechanical engineer and gave a false Montreal address.[71]

In the end, affection proved the most effective weapon of all. Seduced and deceived with precision, Sylvia Ageloff became the conduit through which Stalin's assassin was about to enter Trotsky's final refuge. Her trust, not violence, opened the gate that force alone could not breach. When the assassin's blow finally fell, it struck not only Trotsky, but also the love and faith that Sylvia had surrendered to a lie.

Behind her seduction, however, moved another betrayal, quieter but just as deadly: the double life of Mark Zborowski. For years, he had stood at Lev Sedov's side—secretly watching, reporting, and betraying him to the GPU. Together their deceptions formed the pincer that would close around Trotsky's final sanctuary and deliver Stalin the vengeance he had pursued for more than a decade.

CHAPTER VII

THE SIAMESE TWINS

Stalin's Spies Inside the Fourth International

"Mark Zborowski is a perfect informer and finger-man: he commits no thefts but points out where documents can be stolen; he commits no murder but informs on the whereabouts of people condemned by [GPU] kangaroo courts. Zborowski understands what his reports to the Soviets imply; he knows what is in store for those he shadows."

—David Dallin

"Everywhere that Mark Zborowski went, he left behind a trail of duplicity and blood worthy of a Shakespearean villain."

—Isaac Don Levine

"She didn't carry the weapon—but her actions made the killing possible."

—Oleg Tsarev

The Smile of a Killer

He arrived softly, with a smile. Nothing in Mark Zborowski's manner suggested the devastation he would unleash or the trust he would poison. Educated, courteous, and unfailingly polite, he drifted through the fractured world of Trotsky's followers like a loyal comrade. Behind the wire-rimmed glasses and scholarly gaze stood one of Stalin's most effective agents—calm, patient, and lethal.

He committed no murder with his own hands. He planted no explosives and never swung an ice axe. Yet the damage he wrought was immediate: death, division, and the slow strangulation of the Fourth International from within.[1]

Origins and Radicalization (1908–1931)

Born in Poland in 1908, Zborowski embraced communism during the upheavals of the Bolshevik Revolution. While still in high school, he joined the Communist Party in Łódź.[2]

Arrested several times, he was interrogated and beaten in the Łódź prison until a court released him in November 1930. He fled first to Berlin, then to Grenoble, France, in 1931, where he enrolled at the University of Grenoble.[3]

Recruitment and the Returnee Trap (1931–1933)

In Grenoble he encountered Russians who encouraged him to pursue his studies in the Soviet Union free of charge—if he could first prove his loyalty through the Union for the Repatriation to Russia, also called the Union of Returnees, a GPU front serving to entice White Russians to return to the USSR.

Zborowski and his wife submitted applications in 1932 to return to Russia but were refused.[4] Soon afterward, however, he was recruited by Alexander Adler of Leningrad and coded as agent B-187. Adler had orders to recruit Trotsky sympathizers among students and intellectuals in Grenoble but failed—except for Zborowski. Once he judged Zborowski prepared, Adler directed him to leave his wife behind and move to Paris to penetrate the Russian émigré Trotskyist movement. His mission: report on their activities, contacts, and especially Lev Sedov's supposed "relationship with the Hitler movement."[5]

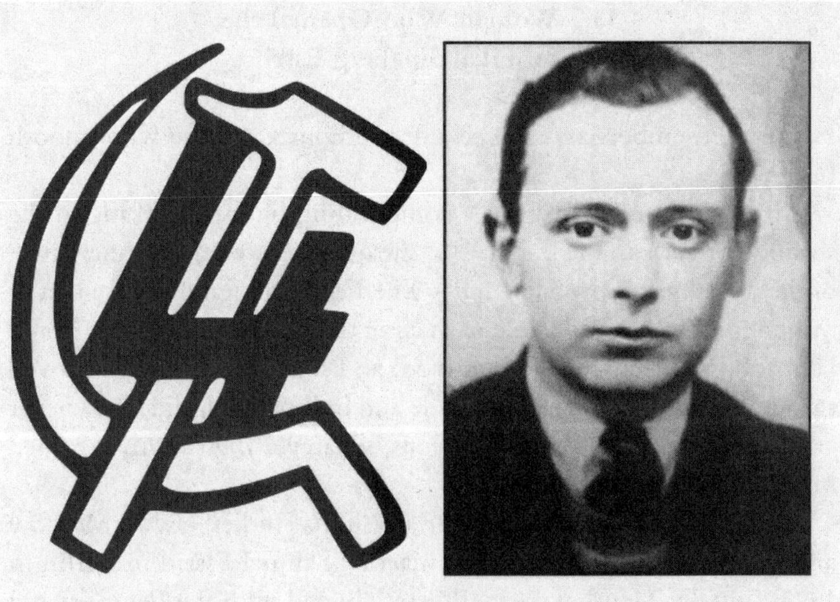

21. Mark Zborowski (cover name TULIP), who ran Trotsky's Paris office, was Stalin's most important agent embedded within the newly formed Fourth International in 1938.

Assignment to Paris (1933–1935)

Zborowski arrived in Paris in 1933 and began his employment at the Soviet-run Union of Returnees, headquartered at 12 Rue de Hoci in central Paris.[6]

During this period, he began contacting Trotskyist activists and soon met Raymond Molinier and his wife Jeanne. Different accounts describe Mark's first meeting with Lev Sedov: in one, they met "accidentally" as Russian-speaking students at university in Paris; in another, Jeanne Martin, Sedov's future partner and common-law wife, divorced from her first husband, facilitated the introduction. Both versions agree that Jeanne Martin played a central role in the Paris center—and quickly recognized Zborowski as a congenial and useful presence. Through Sedov, Zborowski met Lilia Estrin.[7]

The Woman Who Opened the Gate: Lilia Ginzberg Estrin

History remembers assassins. More insidious are those who smooth their path.

Lilia Ginzberg Estrin was a confounding figure. Working in the shadows of Paris in the mid-1930s, she quietly entered the inner circle of the Trotskyist movement and—whether by design or by a chain of misjudgments—played a role in shaping the path Stalin's killers would later follow. Intelligent, disciplined, and socially adroit, she moved through Sedov's world as a comrade and indispensable aide. She never carried the weapon—but her actions, whatever their motive, helped make the killing possible.

Born in 1898 in Liepāja, Courland, Lilia studied law in Moscow and joined the Mensheviks. She married Samuel Estrin in Berlin in 1923. Initially Mensheviks, both later aligned with the Leninists and the Left Opposition. Most accounts of Estrin's life show that after the Nazi rise to power in 1933, Lilia and her husband fled to Paris. When or even whether Lilia was formally recruited into the GPU remains uncertain, though CIA analyst Rita T. Kronenbitter's (pseudonym for a male counterintelligence analyst) 1972 Central Intelligence Agency (CIA) report offers a suggestive clue in noting that her dossier shows that she came to Paris in 1933 directly from Moscow, and not Berlin as otherwise claimed.[8] If Lilia was recruited, or received GPU training, it would most plausibly have occurred during this interlude—though definitive evidence has never surfaced.

In Paris, Estrin worked as the private secretary for Boris Nicolaevsky at the International Institute of Social History. Intelligent, poised, and socially gifted, she befriended Sedov in 1934 and a year later became an unpaid volunteer at Sedov's *Bulletin of the Opposition*. She drew a monthly salary of 1,500 francs from the institute that she used to, somehow, support herself, her husband, her brother, and her sister-in-law. Both her brother, Dr. Ralph Ginzberg, and sister-in-law, Dr. Fanny Trachtenberg, claimed to be medical doctors in Russia but were not licensed to practice in France.[9] Lilia also retained Soviet citizenship and renewed her passport annually—without consequence, despite being a known Trotskyist, an improbability unless she was already a GPU agent.[10]

Lilia was a self-described "human dynamo, capable of working on two full-time jobs, seven days a week, without respite or vacation."[11] These same qualities made her indispensable to Sedov and Trotsky. She began as Sedov's secretary before being replaced by Zborowski and handled correspondence with Trotsky and the leaders of various groups of followers in Europe and America.[12]

Entry into the Inner Circle (1935–1936)

Lilia's and Zborowski's voluntary and unpaid work for Sedov began in 1935, with Lilia arriving first and Mark later. Zborowski began by volunteering for small tasks in the International Secretariat of the Trotskyists alongside Jeanne Martin. Thanks to Martin's trust, he was soon transferred to the Russian Section and began running small errands for Sedov's assistant, Lilia Estrin. According to historian Robert Service, many of the French were already suspicious of Zborowski (Etienne):

> His story was that he was a committed Trotskyist from Ukraine who had travelled to France in 1933 to offer his services. He retained Lev's complete confidence despite the reservations expressed by French comrades. Etienne aimed to become indispensable to Lev, and he succeeded. Cool-headed and assiduous, he relieved Lev of many tasks in a heavy workload. Not everyone took to him. It was far from clear where he got his money from or even how he managed to subsist. Lev's secretary Lilia Estrin sympathetically invented jobs for him to do and paid him each time he did one of them.[13]

Zborowski's role soon surpassed Lilia's, and he became indispensable as courier, translator, and aide.[14] Working under the party pseudonym Etienne, he soon became the personal secretary to SON or SONNY—the GPU's cover name for Lev Sedov.[15] Efficient, fluent, and unpaid, Zborowski appeared the perfect revolutionary. For the GPU, he was perfect camouflage.

Sedov somehow overlooked the glaring contradiction of Etienne's ongoing employment at the Soviet-run Union of Returnees. Trotsky's Paris office, chronically short of money and personnel, gladly accepted the unpaid labor of both Zborowski and Estrin. Warnings of GPU provocateurs and spies circulated constantly in Paris, but proof was scarce, and suspicion risked tearing Trotsky's fragile movement apart. Exhausted by Stalin's assault on his family and desperate to preserve unity, Sedov repeatedly erred on the side of trust, and depended on Zborowski and Estrin to keep his office functioning.

The Siamese Twins Inside the Fourth International (1936–1939)

Zborowski and Estrin—self-described as "inseparable"[16] and the "Siamese twins"—worked in seamless coordination.[17] Robert Service wrote that a work routine was established. Etienne worked alongside Lev in the mornings, and Lilia took his place in the afternoons.[18] Equipped by his handlers with a document camera, "Etienne photographed items in the organization's files."[19] Zborowski's detailed reports, hidden inside rolled newspapers and delivered daily to his GPU handler near the Gare d'Austerlitz, were so detailed that Stalin reviewed them personally.[20]

Sedov's trust reached its zenith when he entrusted Etienne with the keys to his locked mailbox and control of his confidential correspondence—an astonishing breach of security.[21]

From 1935 to 1940, Zborowski stood at the center of the Paris office. Even after hints of his Soviet ties emerged, they were dismissed. He retained his paid position at the GPU-controlled Union for Returnees while working full-time for the Trotskyists. With no counterintelligence apparatus in their movement, Sedov and Trotsky relied on instinct and ideological affinity. They needed and depended on Estrin and Zborowski. In such an atmosphere, a trained deceiver could flourish—and Zborowski did.

Paris swirled with rumors of infiltration. Yet Zborowski and Estrin preserved Trotsky's trust by "forever whitewashing each other."[22] As CIA analyst Rita Kronenbitter (pseudonym) later noted, they "never defended themselves directly . . . instead they casually put in a good word for each other," producing what appeared to be convincing evidence of loyalty.[23]

The War Council and the Theft of the Archives (1936–1937)

In 1936, Trotskyists from around the world convened a secret War Council in Paris. With Trotsky marooned in Norway, Sedov placed Zborowski in charge of managing the event. As a result, GPU intelligence from Zborowski on the council's agenda reached Moscow even before Trotsky received his report.

That November, fifteen crates of Trotsky's manuscripts and correspondence were transferred to a new location at Boris Nicolaevsky's International Institute of Social History located at 7 Rue Michelet—supposedly for greater security.[24] Only four individuals knew the location: Nicolaevsky, Sedov, Estrin, and Zborowski.

In the early morning hours of November 7, 1936, GPU agents broke in using acetylene torches. The date—the anniversary of the Bolshevik Revolution—was symbolic. French police identified the heist as highly professional: while the burglars attempted to simulate a commonplace break-in, they left money and valuables behind, while only Trotsky's archives were removed.[25]

The police wanted to question Zborowski and Estrin about their knowledge of the papers being moved to the institute—but Sedov intervened and said that they had his full trust. Outrage erupted among the Paris Trotskyists. Accusations focused on Zborowski and Estrin. Anticipating suspicion, they were already prepared and produced a handful of documents that they had "held back" as supposed proof of loyalty. Zborowski refused to testify to French investigators but confessed his role in the robbery twenty years later during Senate hearings.[26] Zborowski told his FBI interrogators two decades later that he was furious with his GPU handler because of the break-in. He asserted that it gained very little of value but placed him under increasing scrutiny and nearly blew his cover.[27]

The theft destabilized the Paris center and granted Moscow unprecedented insight into Trotsky's thinking.

Murder by Proxy (1937)

GPU agents were everywhere, and even they were no longer safe. The theft of the archives was only the beginning. The intelligence Zborowski passed to Moscow soon had fatal consequences. Etienne's and Lilia's mutual alibis reassured Sedov and Trotsky time and again—while "Stalin's Department of Special Tasks drew up the lists of those to be killed, and international revolutionaries sympathetic to Trotsky began to 'disappear,' at least until their bodies surfaced, sometimes in pieces."[28] Trotsky's continued reliance on the twins' alibis proved fatal to him and to those around him.

In July 1937, Etienne betrayed Erwin Wolf, a rising young Trotskyist whom Sedov had dispatched to Spain. Zborowski relayed Wolf's travel plans to the GPU. Wolf vanished near the Spanish border—intercepted, murdered, and erased.[29]

Just weeks later, in September 1937, he provided information that facilitated the assassination of Ignace Reiss, a senior GPU officer who had defected and denounced Stalin in a public letter addressed to Sedov.[30] Reiss's murder sent shockwaves through the Trotskyist movement. The Paris center had become a magnet for doom: correspondence sent there made individuals targets; proximity to Sedov made them vulnerable.

The Warning Sedov Couldn't Hear

Walter Krivitsky, once a seasoned GPU officer, chose to defect after the assassination of Reiss and upon learning that Moscow had recalled and executed trusted GPU colleagues such as Theodore Maly and Vladimir Antonov-Ovseenko. Alarmed by the tightening noose of Stalin's terror, Krivitsky arranged a discreet meeting with Lev Sedov and warned him that a GPU informer operated within his inner circle. Krivitsky even ventured a name: Mark Zborowski. As historian Gary Kern observed, "Krivitsky had no desire to join the Trotskyists, but was impressed by Sedov, admiring his revolutionary fervor, hard work and austere lifestyle."[31]

Yet the warning fell short of persuasion.

Sedov—embattled, exhausted, and surrounded by competing rumors—hesitated to accept the accusation against a man who had become indispensable to his daily work. Zborowski, acutely attuned to the shifting political winds, recognized the threat posed by Krivitsky and moved swiftly to secure his position. He ingratiated himself once more, dispensing minor favors, supplying useful intelligence, and offering a steady flow of explanations that, amid the confusion of Paris, appeared entirely plausible.

Meanwhile, Krivitsky's intelligence—hard-won and precise—was lost in the swirl of disinformation carefully seeded by the GPU. What might have been a decisive moment of exposure dissolved into another unverified rumor, allowing Zborowski to retain his place at the heart of Sedov's operation and continue feeding Moscow the lifeblood of the Trotskyist network.

Lilia's role during this period, though less explicitly documented, was intertwined with Zborowski's. Her access to Sedov, her influence within his office, and her synchronized activities with Zborowski helped shape the atmosphere the GPU needed—one of trust, confusion, and deliberate misdirection. Every reassurance she offered, every deflection she made, reinforced Zborowski's position and gave Moscow both time and actionable intelligence.

The Death of Sedov (February 1938)

The most intimate betrayal unfolded in February 1938. When Sedov suddenly fell ill with acute abdominal pain, he relied almost entirely on Lilia and Mark. In his weakened state, they urged him to seek treatment at the private Clinique Mirabeau, a facility known to Soviet intelligence and linked to the Union for Returnees.[32]

How Lilia produced the money for the ambulance and hospitalization remains a glaring point of suspicion. Mahoney observed that Lilia "always seemed to be able to come up with large sums of money whenever they were needed."[33]

Admitted under an alias of a French engineer, Mr. Martin, Sedov was reported immediately to Moscow by Zborowski. Sedov survived the first operation but deteriorated rapidly and died on February 16, 1938, after a second emergency surgery.[34]

Whether the GPU directly murdered him or merely exploited his vulnerability is still debated. Jeanne Martin, Sedov's partner, believed he was killed. Her inquiries uncovered troubling evidence, including the clinic's ties to the Union of Returnees—controlled by none other than Zborowski.[35]

Years later, Zborowski confessed to Elsa Poretsky, Ignace Reiss's widow, that Sedov's death was "the happiest day of my life" because he would no longer have to spy on him or denounce him.[36]

Jeanne Martin's Accusation

Trotsky immediately blamed the GPU and demanded a full police investigation.[37] His suspicions deepened when both Mark and Lilia refused to cooperate with French authorities, privately claiming that as Communists, they feared their travel documents used to enter France in the early 1930s were forged and if discovered would be used against them.[38]

Jeanne Martin begged them to assist the investigation, to no avail. Their refusal, combined with the details of Sedov's hospitalization and the role Zborowski played, confirmed her fears. She wrote to Trotsky and Natalia accusing both Mark and Lilia of being Soviet agents.

Lilia struck back viciously. Anticipating the attack, she dismissed Jeanne as "neurasthenic with a lunatic imagination of foul play . . . [who] sees the GPU everywhere."[39]

Jeanne and Lilia exchanged bitter letters. Jeanne accused; Lilia deflected. Amid this turmoil, Zborowski offered to conduct an "internal inquiry"—a gesture as absurd as it was effective, for Trotsky found it reassuring.[40]

Further complicating matters was Trotsky's agonizing struggle over custody of his grandson Sieva Volkov, who had been adopted by Lev and Jeanne.[41] Trotsky wanted the boy in Mexico. Jeanne refused. Trotsky engaged a Paris lawyer; the matter dragged on until October 1939, when Marguerite Rosmer had to "tear Sieva from Jeanne's clutches" and deliver him to Coyoacán.[42]

The GPU, meanwhile, opened a second front to protect "the twins." Anonymous denunciations circulated through the movement, accusing loyal Trotskyists of treason and flooding Paris with suspicion. The atmosphere thickened into a fog of paranoia that nearly shattered the office. Piece by piece, Trotsky's confidence in his Paris network eroded. The whispers, accusations, countercharges, and endless turmoil blinded him to the conspirators in his midst.

This blindness would continue into 1939—and prove fatal.

After Sedov's Death: A Vacuum of Leadership

As the office began functioning, "Etienne and Lilia handled most of Trotsky's correspondence for Europe. They were a transmission channel for communications with the Fourth International in Paris, the leaders of oppositionist groups and various countries, Soviet defectors, and other figures of importance to the movement, as well as the Paris courts. They knew who suspected them of disloyalty and when and how to counteract them."[43] It was an amazing result for the GPU.

The twins continued to write skillful letters to Trotsky and his wife. Etienne's letters were businesslike and reflected his image as a loyal and dependable successor to Sedov in managing the movement's affairs. Lilia's letters we primarily sent to Natalia Sedova [Trotsky] and expressed sympathy, adulation to the family, and their undying devotion to the cause. Interspersed between the lines were frequent barbs at Jeanne Martin, who was consistently labeling Lilia and Mark as traitors.[44]

From March to June 1938, Trotsky remained uncertain about Lilia and Etienne, his doubts sharpened by Sedov's sudden death and by Jeanne Martin's insistence that her husband had not died of natural causes. Jeanne grew frustrated that Lilia and Etienne refused to provide statements for the inquest. After a long silence, Trotsky demanded clarification. Lilia replied with a stream of condolences and recollections of Sedov—letters that, intentionally or not, emphasized her own steadfastness and devotion.

Rumors, Reassurances, and the Battle for Trotsky's Confidence

Seeking to counter Jeanne's accusations, Lilia and Etienne encouraged several comrades to describe Jeanne as unstable and overwhelmed by grief. Their efforts persuaded Trotsky that the pair had been wrongly maligned and that the allegations against them likely stemmed from a single hostile source, interpreted at the time as GPU-inspired slander. Their competent work on the *Bulletin* further reinforced his confidence.

Trotsky's renewed endorsement came just as rumors circulated again that both Etienne and Lilia might be connected—wittingly or unwittingly—to Soviet intelligence. Henk Sneevliet described Etienne as "a filthy Polish Jew spying for the GPU," while Victor Serge voiced quiet suspicions about the pair. Lilia and Etienne warned Trotsky of these whispers before they reached him, urging that Etienne take the initiative in forming a commission with the International Secretariat to settle the matter. Trotsky advised them simply, "Make the necessary initiative yourselves."[45]

Ironically, the rumors that Lilia and Etienne were Soviet spies ended up strengthening their prestige and winning Trotsky's full confidence. Instead of allowing an outside commission to examine the accusations, Etienne conducted his own inquiry, interviewing comrades and producing a detailed report meant to demonstrate that he was no spy and that Lilia was equally blameless. In this strange reversal, their self-directed "investigation" persuaded Trotsky that both were innocent victims of malicious rumor—rumor he believed had been stirred up by GPU agents.

Trotsky's letters soon reflected this shift. He praised the pair frequently and instructed that future mail be addressed to either of them interchangeably. Even when he was not managing correspondence, Etienne handled significant tasks for him. Convinced by their report, Trotsky took further steps: he broke with Jeanne Martin, Sedov's most persistent accuser of the couple. From the GPU's perspective—assuming they were watching—this rupture was a major victory, for it widened an already growing divide between the International Secretariat and the French Section of the Fourth International. Jeanne's former husband, Raymond Molinier, and his brother Henri were central figures in that factional struggle.

Lilia and Etienne ultimately persuaded Trotsky that Jeanne and the "French clique" were aligned with hostile forces. His decision to sever ties was final, despite the objections of many French supporters. From that point on, Trotsky wrote additional letters commending Etienne, and in response to Lilia's continued offers of assistance, he invited her to visit him in Mexico in May 1939.[46]

Lilia's Trip to Mexico

Lilia Estrin's trip to Mexico in the spring of 1939 unfolded at the edge of two worlds—Trotsky's beleaguered household and the shadow war tightening around it. Whether she understood the stakes is unclear. What is certain is that her movements, letters, and access placed her near currents that would soon converge on Coyoacán.

After Sedov's death, Etienne—already tied to Soviet intelligence—served as the replacement for the murdered Rudolf Klement, handling logistics for the upcoming Fourth International conference in Paris. Through him, Lilia moved easily among delegates, greeting figures like Sylvia Ageloff and her boyfriend Jacques Mornard*, the future assassin.[47] Amid this swirl, Lilia proposed a simple offer: she would travel to Mexico on her own dime to assist Trotsky with his book on Stalin. Trotsky declined, but she kept writing. Lilia's letters to Natalia Sedova [Trotsky] and the secretariat were warm, loyal, and edged with quiet warnings about Jeanne Martin, who accused her and Etienne of treason. The intention behind the letters was unmistakable—she wanted an invitation.[48]

In early 1939, she tried again. This time she had a new passport and a firmer plan: New York first to obtain a Mexican visa, then Mexico. Trotsky relented and extended an invitation in March 1939. Van Heijenoort made her arrangements.[49]

Lilia left Paris on April 19. She spent several weeks in New York, then rode a bus south through Texas and across the border, arriving in Mexico City on May 29. Her visit raised no alarms. She talked with Trotsky about revisions to his Stalin biography, the possible transfer of his grandson Sieva away from Jeanne Martin in Paris, and Etienne's old idea for an inner circle of Russian Trotskyists in Paris.[50]

Orlov's Warning in Early 1939

During Lilia Estrin's visit, Trotsky showed her an unsigned registered letter dated December 27, 1938, that he had received in January—an alarming warning that Etienne was an GPU agent. The writer claimed ties to General Lyushkov, the high-ranking GPU defector in Japan, and provided enough accurate detail about Soviet leadership and operations to give the message weight. The letter identified "Mark" as the GPU courier who had sent Trotsky's stolen documents to Moscow and asserted, unequivocally, that Etienne was "Mark."[51]

The writer made an urgent appeal to the Old Man: "Believe no one, male or female, coming to you from that provocateur [Etienne's circle]." He further asked Trotsky to acknowledge the warning through a coded notice in the Socialist Appeal. Trotsky complied—but no one ever came forward.[52] The anonymous writer attempted to reach Trotsky by telephone but got only as far as his secretary. Wary that the caller might be just another persistent newspaperman, Trotsky would not come to the telephone. The writer was GPU General Alexander Orlov, a recent defector who had recently been in charge of all GPU operations in Spain.[53] Despite the letter's pointed instructions, Trotsky did something difficult to explain—he ignored them and showed the letter to the very person who had just arrived from the Paris office—Lilia.

Trotsky's motives for taking such a foolish and reckless action remain unclear. For nearly a year, he had heard accusations directed at both Lilia and Etienne; sharing such a letter with her ran counter to his usual caution. Whether he sought to test her reaction or simply dismissed the danger is impossible to know. Lilia later recalled feeling deeply uncomfortable and told him that the letter could be nothing else but "a dirty job of the GPU who wanted to deprive Trotsky of his few dependable collaborators in France."[54]

Trotsky accepted her interpretation. Far from weakening their stand-

22. GPU General Alexander Orlov, pictured in his forged 1934 US passport, defected in 1938 and tried—without success—to warn Trotsky of a mole in his Paris office.

ing, the incident strengthened the pair's position. The Old Man also ignored renewed allegations from Europe and praised their work.

Lilia departed after a week—and by June was assisting Etienne more closely while continuing as Trotsky's primary correspondent on Russian Section matters and the *Bulletin*. In one instance, the Old Man was so elated with Etienne's performance that he even sent him an autographed picture . . . something that he rarely did. Etienne responded with a note of gratitude and devotion—fitting for a moment when Trotsky's confidence in both of them had never been higher.[55]

Lilia's purpose in Mexico had been fulfilled, though her true role, if any, is still uncertain. No document proves she aided GPU preparations for the attacks the next year or even had any idea of GPU long-range plans, but none rules it out. What remains is a pattern:

access, mobility, persistence, and proximity to the very people the GPU would soon rely upon. In the narrowing world around Trotsky, even routine visits carried weight. Lilia's was no exception.

VENONA and the Evidence Trail

A VENONA cable dated May 1, 1944, refers to Lilia by her maiden name ESTRINA in connection with the Victor Kravchenko defection in Washington, DC. Yet the decrypt itself offers no definitive internal evidence that Lilia was acting as a witting Soviet asset. The most pointed reference—the New York–to–Moscow message of May 1, 1944—reports Zborowski's failure to make contact with Kravchenko and includes Stepan Apresyan's warning (communicating on behalf of the rezidentura) that "one cannot insist strongly . . . as this would arouse suspicion."

The surrounding context could suggest that Zborowski or Lilia, or both, were being used—knowingly or unknowingly—in efforts to approach the defector. Since Zborowski is conclusively identified as a trained GPU operative (code name TULIP), the implication is that Lilia might not have understood the true purpose of the tasking. At the same time, the decrypt notes that she had "promised to have a detailed chat" about Kravchenko, a phrase that can be read as indicating at least some degree of voluntary involvement.

In the end, the VENONA material remains inherently ambiguous and is capable of neither proving Lilia Estrin's complicity as a GPU agent nor establishing her innocence.

Susan Weissman, however, felt the case for Estrin's innocence to be even stronger and pointed out that the VENONA messages show Lilia to be an innocent source who trusted and confided in the agent TULIP (Zborowski), believing him to be a fellow anti-Stalinist.[56] Weissman further noted that Estrin continued to work for the American Trotskyists, and after her death in 1981, it was learned that she had been paying for the upkeep of Lev Sedov's grave in Paris since 1938.[57]

The Final Thread (1938–1940)

By the late 1930s, TULIP—Mark Zborowski—had already fractured Trotsky's European network beyond repair, aided in ways that might or might not have been fully understood by Lilia Estrin. The intelligence he funneled to Moscow enabled the murders of Wolf, Reiss, Sedov, and likely Klement, leaving the Fourth International hollowed by suspicion and incapable of recovery.

Two years before the ice axe fell, the decisive thread of the operation was woven in Paris. In September 1938, Zborowski—and, to an uncertain degree, Estrin—helped introduce American Trotskyist Sylvia Ageloff and her new boyfriend, Jacques Mornard*, to delegates at the founding conference of the Fourth International.[58] The event was held at the home of Alfred and Marguerite Rosmer outside Paris. It seemed a trivial courtesy. It was not. Zborowski was later asked under oath if he introduced Sylvia Ageloff to Jacques Mornard*. Zborowski responded evasively. He initially denied knowing Ageloff, though he conceded that he might have seen her at the conference, and ultimately claimed that he could not remember.[59]

Behind the Mornard* alias, Ramón Mercader relied on the Paris office's credibility to circulate freely among Trotskyist ranks. Zborowski's reputation opened doors; Mercader stepped through them without challenge, studying the movement's personalities and vulnerabilities with the patience of a trained operative. Whether Estrin grasped the moment's larger significance remains unclear. Yet the introduction she helped facilitate would reverberate all the way to Coyoacán.

Zborowski never carried a gun. He never crept toward a bedroom door. His weapon was access—quiet words, redirected letters, and small shifts of trust that blunted Trotsky's defenses long before Mercader arrived. Estrin's role, whatever its intent, enabled and amplified that damage from within.

When the ice axe finally struck in Coyoacán, it was only the final blow. The killing had begun years earlier, in whispers and handshakes, in offices and café corridors, and in the confidence that Trotsky placed in people who stood smiling at his side.

Reinvention and Shadows in America

After Trotsky's murder, Lilia Estrin reappeared in the United States under a new name and a new life. She married the historian David Dallin—once a Menshevik, now a respected anti-Communist voice—and together they seemed to embody a familiar émigré arc: former revolutionaries who had broken with Stalin and remade themselves in America.

But questions trailed behind them.

After the fall of France, Mark Zborowski also surfaced in the United States. In a twist that unsettled many Trotskyists, it was the Dallins who helped secure his immigration papers and found him work in a Brooklyn screw factory. Soon after, Zborowski rented an apartment in the same upscale Manhattan building where the Dallins lived—its rent covered by money from an unnamed source.

In New York, Zborowski quietly resumed espionage for the GPU. The renewed proximity between him and the Dallins rekindled old suspicions. Was Lilia merely haunted by the past—or still entangled in it?

In 1955, General Alexander Orlov—the man who had once tried to warn Trotsky—told the Dallins that Zborowski had been a GPU agent from the beginning. In CIA debriefings, Orlov went further, voicing his belief that Lilia herself might also have been an agent, part of the same hidden structure. He even alleged that David Dallin had been a paid Soviet source in Berlin in the 1920s—a charge never proven but disturbing in its specificity.

Lilia testified before the US Senate Subcommittee on Internal Security in 1956. Her calm manner and careful recollections reassured some. Others thought they detected something else: the poise of someone long accustomed to navigating secrets.

After the hearings, the Dallins withdrew from the spotlight, burying themselves in scholarship and letting the Orlov controversy slip from public view. But the shadows around them never fully disappeared.

The Verdict on Lilia

Lilia Estrin's life mirrors the fate of an entire revolutionary generation—idealistic, driven, and ultimately consumed by the very forces it once believed it could command. She entered politics as a principled socialist, crossed continents in the name of justice, and ended her days as a quiet New York intellectual. Between those points lies a shadowed path history cannot fully illuminate.

What remains clear is her proximity to the men and moments that shaped Trotsky's final years. Her collaboration—whether deliberate or unwitting—with Mark Zborowski helped hollow out the Paris center, isolate Sedov, and misdirect Trotsky's trust. In America, their intertwined trajectories continued to raise questions that no archive has yet answered. The evidence, fragmentary but persistent, reveals a pattern of actions that repeatedly advantaged Soviet intelligence at decisive moments.

Was Lilia Estrin a conscious agent, a manipulated intermediary, or a loyal comrade swept along by currents she barely understood? The record declines to answer. Yet the consequences of her actions do not. Every reassurance she gave Sedov, every carefully worded message she sent to Trotsky, narrowed the circle of trust and bought the GPU precious time. Intention might be unknowable, but impact is not. Across two continents and over the span of years, her conduct—whatever its inner motive—aligned perfectly with the needs of Mark Zborowski and the interests of the GPU. That alignment shaped outcomes far larger than she might have imagined.

The verdict on Lilia is therefore not a conclusion but a tension: a life that may never surrender its secrets, yet one whose choices helped pave the road on which Mercader eventually walked. Whether she was a witting operative or an unwitting accomplice, the path she helped lay led to the same place—the study in Coyoacán, the raised arm, the falling blow.

Trotsky's murder was not foreordained; it was the terminus of a chain of misjudgments, loyalties, and deceptions stretching back through Paris, back through the fractured exile community, and ultimately back to Stalin's own fatal miscalculation.

CHAPTER VIII

STALIN'S MISTAKE

The One Who Got Away

"To send Trotsky abroad in exile [and alive] was my greatest mistake."
—Joseph Stalin

"The most dangerous enemy is the one who refuses to die."
—Vasili Mitrokhin Papers

"Exile protects the body. Truth protects the idea."
—Anonymous Trotskyist leaflet, 1939

The Decision That Set Everything in Motion

In 1928, the generation that had marched with Trotsky through the October Revolution and the Civil War still held real weight inside the Soviet Union. Their presence left Stalin's Political Bureau wary and exposed. To kill Trotsky outright was to risk offending the veterans who saw him as the architect of Red Army victory and the living embodiment of October's triumph. Stalin did not yet command the Politburo with the iron certainty he later enjoyed, and executing Trotsky at that moment threatened backlash he could not fully contain.

And so, uncharacteristically, Stalin hesitated. That pause—born of caution rather than mercy—became the most consequential miscalculation of his political life. Instead, exile seemed safer. First internal. Then external.

Remove Trotsky from the center; push him to the margins. Let distance accomplish what a bullet might provoke.

It was, as one contemporary wrote, "Stalin's greatest mistake,"[1] for exile freed Trotsky to become the regime's most dangerous external critic—loud, uncompromising, and beyond Soviet censorship.

A Martyr Avoided, a Problem Deferred

Given the risk of executing Trotsky on Soviet soil, Stalin remarked to a comrade: "Why make a martyr out of Trotsky who will be defeated anyway?"[2] Exile appeared to solve the immediate political dilemma: no spectacle, no shrine, no internal blowback.

But Trotsky did not vanish. Instead, he grew louder. And the farther he moved from Moscow, the more his defiance carried.

Stalin had misread the terrain. Exile had not eliminated Trotsky—it had merely repositioned him beyond the Kremlin's immediate reach.

Robert Service captured the shift precisely: "Once Trotsky had been deported from the Soviet Union, Stalin could pursue him abroad without the political complications of a show trial or an execution at home."[3]

Removal created opportunity. Distance created deniability. And the logic of assassination began to take shape.

A Letter, an Order, a Trajectory Toward Violence

From Prinkipo, Trotsky continued to behave like a man who believed logic might still move the Soviet leadership. He wrote to the Politburo. He annotated reports. And on April 27, 1931, he sent Stalin a personal appeal—measured, political, almost imploring.

Stalin read it with mounting fury.

Across the bottom he scrawled a line that ended all ambiguity:

> Trotsky, this criminal gang-boss and Menshevik charlatan, has to be bumped on the head.[4]

Volkogonov later noted that Stalin's elliptical phrases often masked death sentences. Here, the code required no interpreter. "Bumped on the head"[5] was not improvisation. It was authorization—private, informal, unmistakable.

With those words, the trajectory toward violence—already forming in the GPU's upper ranks—became irreversible. The machinery of assassination had not yet been assembled, but the directive existed.

And once Stalin issued a directive, the GPU's task was never if—only when and how.

Murder Becomes Policy: Exile and the First Attempts

By the late 1920s, the GPU under Vyacheslav Menzhinsky had already formed a specialized group, the Ninth Directorate, devoted to "liquidation" operations—kidnappings, disappearances, and assassinations carried out against enemies of the regime.[6] Successful missions were rewarded; failure was fatal. Assassination was becoming institutionalized within the GPU's Foreign and Political Sections.

The first attempt to act on Stalin's "bumped on the head" order was only a matter of time. But Turkey, unwilling to host an international scandal, demanded formal assurances from Moscow that no attempt would be made on its soil. Ankara imposed strict limits on Trotsky himself: he was to avoid Turkish politics and publish nothing domestically.

Even under Turkish protection in Istanbul and on Prinkipo, Trotsky remained "under threat not only from the Stalinist GPU, but also from the White Russian émigrés his Red Army had defeated in the Civil War."[7] From the outset of his exile, the GPU began penetrating his household and the circles of the Left Opposition surrounding him—laying the networks and surveillance that would later enable the assassination campaigns culminating in Mexico.[8]

Eager to proceed with Stalin's order to eliminate Trotsky, "Menzhinsky and Yagoda attempted to carry out their masters [sic] wish on Prinkipo, covering their tracks by launching rumors in the Communist-friendly press about an impending attack on Trotsky's life by White émigrés. Efforts indeed were made to provoke Whites into carrying out the murder, Trotsky left Prinkipo for France at the crucial moment. This ended the first, rather slack, attempt to fulfill Stalin's wishes."[9]

When early GPU plans in Turkey collapsed in 1931, Stalin's fury was volcanic. Several planners were recalled to Moscow and disappeared into the prisons of the Lubyanka. The message to Soviet intelligence was unmistakable: success meant survival; failure meant a bullet. In Stalin's system, even the executioners could be executed.

Nowhere to Hide: France, 1933–1935

After four years of exile on the Turkish island of Prinkipo (1929–1933), Leon Trotsky was deported to France, arriving at Marseille on July 24, 1933, where he was immediately placed under strict police supervision. The French government—under Premier Édouard Daladier—reluctantly granted him entry on humanitarian grounds on the condition that he refrain from political activity within France. Yet even this fragile refuge soon proved perilous.

Stalin's agents wasted no time in extending their reach, and Communist newspapers, acting as proxies for Moscow, demanded Trotsky's expulsion as a "counterrevolutionary criminal." The French government, increasingly wary of alienating Stalin amid the rising threat of Nazi Germany, imposed severe restrictions on Trotsky's freedom. He was prohibited from granting interviews, writing for the French press, or attending political meetings. GPU surveillance became constant, and by the mid-1930s, intelligence began streaming into Moscow from the GPU's master-operative embedded inside his son Lev Sedov's Paris circle—Mark Zborowski (cover name TULIP).

Trotsky's followers were trailed, his correspondence intercepted, and his inner circle compromised. Behind diplomatic channels, the Soviet Embassy in Paris pressed for his extradition, accusing him of conspiring with fascists. French officials, eager to maintain good relations with Moscow, hinted that his continued presence was untenable.

For the first year, he lived at Saint-Palais-sur-Mer near Royan on the Atlantic Coast. However, in 1934, when the French Minister of Internal Affairs signed a degree to deport Trotsky, no foreign government would accept him. French authorities then instructed Trotsky to move to a residence in the village of Barbizon, which was under strict surveillance. He was confined under virtual house arrest, and his contact with the world was even more limited and restricted than in Turkey.[10]

Fleeing to Norway, 1935–1936

Under unrelenting pressure from Stalin's diplomats and the French Communist Party, Trotsky searched for a new refuge. In June 1935, the Norwegian Labor government unexpectedly offered sanctuary, and Trotsky and Natalia Sedova [Trotsky] left Saint-Palais-sur-Mer aboard a small coastal vessel, arriving in Norway on June 19, 1935. For a moment, he hoped for calm.

Instead Norway became another cage. Although Justice Minister Trygve Lie approved his stay, and Trotsky lived with Konrad Knudsen at Norderhov from June 18, 1935, to September 2, 1936, the GPU quickly rebuilt its network in Oslo, while Stalin's diplomats worked to undermine his hosts.[11] By 1936, Trotsky's articles supporting the French May–June strikers had angered Paris, intensified Soviet pressure, and emboldened Vidkun Quisling's fascist Nasjonal Samling.[12]

The pressure turned violent on August 5, 1936, when Nasjonal Samling militants broke into Knudsen's home searching for Trotsky's papers. Knudsen's daughter Hjørdis stopped most of the theft, though some documents were taken.[13] The government then used fragments of the stolen material against Trotsky.[14]

Days later the Kremlin escalated: the Telegraph Agency of the Soviet Union (TASS) declared the fabricated "Trotskyist–Zinovievist" conspiracy and opened the Moscow Trials. After Zinoviev, Kamenev, and others were executed on August 25, Norwegian police arrived at Norderhov with gag conditions—no political writing, no interviews, full censorship. Trotsky refused, and interrogators soon recast him as a "witness" to the fascist raid.[15]

Under direct pressure from Moscow, the Norwegian government tightened the noose. On September 2, 1936, Lie ordered Trotsky and Natalia moved to a farm in Hurum, placing them under armed guard and, effectively, house arrest.[16] By autumn, Trotsky was locked indoors twenty-two hours a day, barred from sending letters, denied nearly all visitors except his lawyers and Labor leader Olav Scheflo, and eventually forbidden even to walk outside.[17] The GPU continued its campaign; Norwegian Communists staged violent demonstrations outside his residence, and Soviet envoys pressed for his arrest.

Cut off from the world, Trotsky smuggled out a single text—the Moscow "Confessions"—on December 18, 1936.[18] The following day, the government yielded completely. Under the supervision of Norwegian police official Jonas Lie—no relation to Justice Minister Trygve Lie—Trotsky and Natalia were escorted aboard the tanker *Ruth* and deported on December 19, 1936.

From Mexico, Trotsky wrote the final judgment on his treatment: "Never, anywhere . . . was I persecuted with as much miserable cynicism as by the Norwegian 'Socialist' government . . . They held me in a stranglehold to prevent me from protesting the greatest crime history may ever know."[19]

And so, on that winter morning aboard the *Ruth*, bound for Mexico City, Trotsky left Norway behind—exile yielding once more to defiance—as he sailed toward the uncertain refuge he hoped awaited him behind the blue walls of the Casa Azul.

The New Campaign: Liquidation by Infiltration

In 1935, Stalin ordered GPU chief Genrikh Yagoda to "speed up the liquidation of Trotsky."[20] Sergey Shpigelglas, head of the GPU's Foreign Department (INO), responded with a two-pronged approach: plant an agent inside Trotsky's household and prepare for a direct assault. África de las Heras (cover name PATRIA), posing as Maria de la Sierra, infiltrated the Old Man's Norwegian circle and later followed him to Coyoacán, supplying Moscow with detailed layouts of the Blue House—including sleeping quarters and security routines.[21]

Silence in the Record

Yet one anomaly remains difficult to ignore. PATRIA—Maria de la Sierra—does not appear in any of Trotsky's biographies, nor is she mentioned in the memoirs or later accounts of Trotsky's secretaries or guards, whose writings document the daily rhythms of the household in unusual detail. Her absence from these sources complicates claims that she was a permanent or visible member of the household.

All post-1995 references to Maria de la Sierra as Trotsky's "secretary" and "our best agent" appear to trace back to a single source: Pavel Sudoplatov.[22] In *Special Tasks*, Sudoplatov wrote that "the Siqueiros group had to rely on a floor plan of Trotsky's villa that had been smuggled out by Maria de la Sierra before she was recalled to Moscow. She made an assessment of Trotsky's bodyguards and gave me a detailed character analysis of his secretariat. This very useful information was forwarded to Eitingon."[23] A careful reading of this passage, taken in isolation, does not require that she was a visible or permanent member of the household. Sudoplatov's account is equally consistent with an operative operating at the fringes—close enough to gather sensitive information directly or serving as a handler for an unnamed source who moved inside the compound before the floor plans were removed.

The most plausible explanation is that Sudoplatov's memory faltered—an unsurprising lapse given his age and the treatment he endured—and that PATRIA did not serve as a domestic presence or secretary but instead operated at the margins: close enough to the inner circle to be useful yet sufficiently removed to avoid notice. If her function was to report rather than to belong, her value would have depended on controlled proximity: access without visibility, familiarity without recognition. In such a role, absence from memoir and recollection would not be anomalous but functional—an indication not of failure but of successful concealment.

The Purge of the Executioners

Stalin's war on his enemies tolerated no incompetence. Within the Soviet security organs, failure to complete an assassination could be fatal.

23. África de las Heras (cover name PATRIA) was either embedded inside Trotsky's inner circle in Norway and Mexico or close enough to provide valuable information.

When plots against Trotsky and other "traitors" faltered, Stalin turned his fury inward, purging the very men he had entrusted to kill.

Genrikh Yagoda, who as GPU chief had overseen early foreign "liquidations" and the expansion of the Gulag, was arrested in 1937 and executed the following year for "wrecking" and "espionage."[24] His successor, Nikolai Yezhov—whose reign of terror claimed hundreds of thousands—likewise fell victim to Stalin's paranoia; by 1940 he was shot in the same cellars where his victims died.[25]

Even mid-level operatives were not spared. GPU rezident Mikhail Trilisser, head of foreign intelligence in the 1920s, was executed in 1940 after being blamed for "failures" in penetrating émigré networks.[26]

Later, Pavel Sudoplatov confirmed that the GPU's Foreign Section took orders directly from the Party Central Committee and routinely recruited foreign exiles and refugees—so-called "COMINTERN personalities"—for espionage, sabotage, kidnappings, and assassinations.

Sergey Shpigelglas, the GPU's specialist in the "liquidation operations," engineered and oversaw the assassination of the Ukrainian nationalist Yevhen Konovalets in Rotterdam in May 1938,[27] the execution of the defector Ignace Reiss in Switzerland in September 1937,[28] and the kidnapping of the leader of the Russian All-Military Union (ROVS), General Evgenii Miller, in France in September 1937.[29] It has also been suggested that he was the mastermind of the murder and decapitation of the Trotskyist leader of the Fourth International, Rudolf Klement, in

France in July 1938[30] and of the murder of the defector Georges Agabekov killed by Soviet GPU agents in the Pyrenees in August 1937.[31]

However, Stalin's patience was exhausted. He publicly declared "the one thing we lack is the willingness to liquidate our own carelessness, our own placidity, our own shortsightedness."[32] Stalin said that the elimination of Trotsky had first been assigned to Shpigelglas in 1937, but he had failed to fulfill this important government mission.[33] Sudoplatov later stated, "He [Shpigelglas] didn't carry out the job of killing Trotsky. So, he couldn't be forgiven."[34] Failure to produce results cost him his life. Shpigelglas was recalled to Moscow, arrested on November 2, 1938, and executed on January 29, 1941. Yagoda, his superior, was tried and summarily shot in March 1938. In their place, Stalin elevated Nikolai Yezhov to head the GPU and gave Sudoplatov operational control of the operation to eliminate Trotsky.

Ironically, Trotsky's security improved briefly in late 1938 when África de las Heras (cover name PATRIA) was recalled from Mexico following Orlov's defection. Her departure blinded the GPU inside the household. That delay—unintended and uncontrollable—set back plans for an armed assault on the Blue House and bought Trotsky nearly eighteen more months to live.

Stalin Tightens the Noose

At the end of 1938, desperate to replace de las Heras as an informant within Trotsky's entourage, the GPU wanted to send Zborowski to Mexico as her successor. Trotsky's secretary, Jean van Heijenoort, however, blocked the move on the counsel of their French comrades in the Fourth International who were highly suspicious of Zborowski and Lilia following the suspicious death of Lev Sedov months earlier. As the effort to penetrate the household stalled, frustration in Moscow grew over the GPU's failure to kill the Old Man. To produce immediate results, one GPU officer even floated the idea of using the "Sofia method"—blowing up the villa with dynamite while the family was having dinner. The plan didn't proceed for a fear of collateral deaths to the Mexican staff and guards.[35] Instead, Stalin began dispatching additional thugs and assorted operatives from Spain and the Soviet Union to Mexico to stage a final strike.

The Reckoning Nears

For more than a decade, Stalin's greatest mistake, sending Trotsky into exile, had defied every effort to erase him—surviving betrayal, purges, and the full machinery of a state built on terror and silence. Trotsky had outlasted the Moscow Trials, denounced Stalin before the world, and kept the spirit of the revolution alive. But no exile lasts forever, and the final reckoning had come. It would not arrive by court or decree—but by two unseen assassins. Stalin's silence was at last within reach. Behind the high walls of a modest villa on Avenida Viena, the final phase of Trotsky's life unfolded—an ending shaped by shadows, steel, and the tightening grip of fate.

CHAPTER IX

AVENIDA VIENA

Trotsky's Final Refuge

"What precautions the old revolutionary
had had to take to protect his life!"
—Colonel Leandro Sánchez Salazar, *Murder in Mexico*

"In a fortress built of stone, it was trust that killed him."
—Anonymous memoir of an SWP guard

"We defended against shadows . . . while the real
danger stood at the door with a smile."
—Joseph Hansen, Trotsky's secretary

A New Fortress

On May 5, 1939, Leon Trotsky and his entourage moved just three blocks—but it felt like crossing into another world.[1] The revolutionary, haunted by conspiracies and exiles, relocated from Frida Kahlo's Blue House to a villa at Avenida Viena 19. Once a summer mansion for Mexico's elite, the abandoned compound would soon become one of the most closely watched fortresses in the world—and the last place Trotsky would ever call home.[2]

Built in 1903 as a summer retreat for the wealthy Turati family, the villa had later served as the Instituto Óptico Científico (Scientific Optical Institute) until 1935 and had fallen into disrepair.[3] In prepa-

24. The Mexican police built a casita at the southeast corner of the property. The eastern wing of the villa along Calle Morelos contained the Trotskys' office and library, dining room, and kitchen.

ration for Trotsky's arrival, the once-modest walls that surrounded the property, constructed from brick and stone, were elevated to an imposing height of nearly fourteen feet. The former central entrance gate on Avenida Viena, initially intended for horse-drawn carriages, was permanently sealed, leaving only the sturdy twin wooden garage doors as the sole point of entry for individuals and Trotsky's two vehicles.

Layout and Early Modifications

The property had stood abandoned when Jean van Heijenoort identified it as a potential residence earlier in the spring of 1939.[4] Its layout was distinctive: a T-shaped floor plan with the top of the T forming the eastern wall of the compound. This section held the library, dining room, kitchen, lavatory, and an adjoining bedroom, all connected. Four barred windows faced a strip of no-man's land and a distant cornfield. Extending into the courtyard was the T's stem, which included Trotsky's study, the bedroom he shared with Natalia, and the adjoining room used by their grandson, Sieva Volkov. A family dressing room and bathroom were added nearby. The rest of the villa included sparsely furnished spaces for secretaries and guards. Trotsky's study and the secretaries' office soon overflowed with books, periodicals, and correspondence.[5]

The structure was primarily one story, except for a two-story torreón—an old observation tower from the Mexican Revolution—shaded by a towering eucalyptus tree. Brick outbuildings for the guards lined the north wall, while a small casita outside the walls at the southeast corner was being constructed for the Mexican police with firing ports to control the approaches to Avenida Viena and Calle Morelos.

Domestic Routine and Security

Initially, security was minimal: only barred windows and a barbed-wire fence stood between Trotsky and the outside world. Concerns that GPU agents might attempt to purchase the property and evict him prompted an urgent appeal to the Socialist Workers Party. A sum of $2,000 was quickly raised from American sympathizers that enabled Trotsky to buy the house outright, making him a reluctant homeowner for the first time.[6]

The Courtyard and the Commanding General

Within his new fortress, Trotsky found solace and embraced routine. At dawn, he tended to a small farm of rabbits and chickens in the courtyard's northwest corner. The task, far from trivial, reflected his scientific rigor; he meticulously researched animal diets and illnesses. Guard Charles Cornell remembered Trotsky's insistence on spotless pens and health inspections. By early 1940, the rabbit population exceeded one hundred, prompting him to design multitier hutches. Even Max Eastman, visiting from the United States, found it surreal to be "introduced to a flock of rabbits by the former Commander-in-Chief of the Red Army."[7]

He also cultivated a diverse cactus garden, collecting native species from across Mexico. The grueling excursions to gather them—called "picnics"—involved hauling plants weighing up to two hundred pounds. Natalia likened the tasks to penal labor, but Trotsky's infectious enthusiasm carried the household through. These outings grew rare as threats to his life escalated.[8]

Dictation and Debate

A strict disciplinarian, Trotsky spent most of his time dictating articles, letters, and manuscripts into a Dictaphone—switching effortlessly between Russian, English, and French.[9] He focused on his biography of Stalin in early 1940 to pay the bills, though he often confided to Natalia that he would rather write about Marx or Engels. Secretaries worked frantically to keep pace with the transcriptions. After a short siesta, he resumed work until evening.

Though visitors often disrupted his schedule, Trotsky tolerated them for practical reasons—many were SWP comrades whose financial support was vital. Meetings were supposed to be monitored by guards, but in practice, Trotsky often insisted on privacy—an openness the GPU identified and later exploited.

Guard Charles Cornell recalled Trotsky's vitality during meetings with visitors: "his head held high, gestures animated, and his sentences—whether in English, French, or German—precisely constructed." Despite advancing age and heavy burdens, Trotsky's intellect remained undimmed. Though he jokingly referred to the villa as "prison," life within its walls was anything but dull.[10] Meals, supervised by Natalia at a large pine table in the dining room, became spirited forums for political debate. Trotsky presided at the head, blending daily family ritual with ideological reflection. Guards and secretaries affectionately called him "the Old Man."

25. Marguerite and Alfred Rosmer were the Trotskys' closest friends and the only houseguests who didn't overstay their welcome.

Marguerite Rosmer and the False Friend

Of all those who passed through Avenida Viena, only Marguerite and Alfred Rosmer—veterans of the revolutionary struggle and friends since the days of the First World War—truly earned Natalia's trust. After the death of Lev Sedov in Paris, it was the Rosmers who helped bring young Sieva Volkov, Trotsky's grandson, to safety in Mexico on August 8, 1939.[11] Marguerite's bond with Natalia deepened into quiet companionship—an emotional refuge amid growing isolation. The GPU, ever watchful, saw an opening. In early 1940, Ramón Mercader—operating under the alias Frank Jacson*—identified Marguerite's influence as a vulnerability to exploit. With calculated charm, he used her trusted presence as a bridge, to insinuate himself into the household and edge ever closer to the man he had been sent to kill.

Camera, Alarm, Betrayal

From late 1939 through early 1940, secretary-guard Alex Buchman documented life at Avenida Viena with a Leica camera and an 8-mm Bell & Howell film recorder. His archive of photographs—some in rare color—offers the most comprehensive visual record of Trotsky's final year.[12] Beyond his camera work, the skilled Buchman also played a key role in enhancing the villa's security by rebuilding the compound's complex alarm system and installing additional switches. His service as a guard ended in mid-April 1940 with the arrival of his replacement from New York—Robert Sheldon Harte—who was secretly a GPU agent, cover name AMUR.[13]

The Illusion of Safety

Yet for all the vigilance, Avenida Viena was a fortress only in appearance. The real danger had already crossed the threshold—disguised as a friend, concealed by routine, and embedded in the trusted patterns of daily life. The Old Man, brilliant and cautious as he was, would not fully confront how deeply the GPU had infiltrated the Fourth International—nor how close the blade now lay to his throat.

Beneath the quiet streets of Coyoacán, a slow and silent catastrophe was unfolding—scripted in Moscow, rehearsed in New York, and carried out by agents who understood the patience of murder. Trotsky's routines masked the mounting peril, the rabbit pens, the cactus garden, the guarded gates all part of a fortress that looked secure but had already been breached. By the summer of 1939, Stalin's most ambitious operation to eliminate the Old Man was in motion: a plot built on infiltration, deception, and blood. Its cover name was Operation UTKA. And the final reckoning was about to begin.

CHAPTER X

OPERATION UTKA

Stalin's Secret War on Trotsky

"The only way to destroy an idea is to
kill the man who carries it."
—Soviet proverb attributed to Stalin-
era political police (GPU)

"Stalin wanted not only to destroy Trotsky,
but to erase him from memory."
—Natalia Sedova [Trotsky]

"We have to get rid of Trotsky and his gang once and for all."
—Joseph Stalin, to Politburo colleagues, 1939

The Final Order

Stalin's war against Trotsky had entered its final, most ruthless phase in 1939. Across Europe, the Trotskyites, or Polecats,[1] as Stalin called them, the revolutionaries of the Left Opposition, were being hunted down—one by one—by Stalin's secret police. Their organizations, once vibrant, were now fractured by infiltration, betrayal, and fear. Yet the man Stalin feared most—his former comrade and ideological rival—remained defiant, alive, and still publishing from a modest villa in Mexico City. From there, Trotsky continued to rally followers, expose Stalin's crimes, and defend the vision of the October Revolution.

For Stalin, this was more than defiance. It was a provocation that had to be silenced—not with words, but with death.

As war clouds gathered over Europe, Stalin resolved that Trotsky must die—and soon. The failures of past attempts had become an embarrassment. The efforts overseen by GPU foreign operations chief Sergey Shpigelglas had collapsed in scandal. Stalin was done waiting.

In March 1939, deep within the marble corridors of the Kremlin, the final order was delivered. Stalin convened a private meeting with Lavrentiy Beria, the newly appointed chief of the GPU, and a young intelligence officer named Pavel Sudoplatov. Sudoplatov was known for his loyalty, discretion, and a cold efficiency that Stalin admired. Beria made the recommendation:

> Comrade Stalin, having exposed the GPU Foreign Department's former leadership's treachery, we suggest comrade Sudoplatov be appointed Deputy Director of the GPU Foreign Department to assist newly mobilized party activists in fulfilling government orders.[2]

Stalin, pausing only briefly, gave his reply. The threat of Trotskyism would be ended once and for all. "There are no more important political figures in the Trotskyite movement except Trotsky," Stalin declared. "If Trotsky is finished, the threat will be eliminated."[3]

By the summer of 1939, Joseph Stalin was certain that another world war was inevitable, a conclusion shaped by his assessment that a major clash between the capitalist powers was approaching and that the Soviet Union needed to position itself to benefit from it.[4] He intended to enter that conflict with every threat to his authority eliminated—a goal that had driven the purges of the late 1930s and the systematic destruction of perceived political rivals.[5] Chief among those threats was Leon Trotsky, whose survival in exile continued to represent a political and ideological danger, a point underscored by Stalin's fixation on eliminating Trotsky's influence abroad.[6] Stalin also understood that any coming conflict would reorder Europe and present the USSR with new opportunities for expansion—opportunities the Kremlin could seize only if internal and external enemies were silenced before the first shot was fired.[7]

The Munich Agreement of 1938 had convinced Stalin that the Western democracies were weak and divided. Britain's and France's appeasement of Hitler signaled that they would never form a strong alliance against Germany—or against him. To Stalin, war between the capitalist powers was not just possible but historically inevitable. He believed that if the West and Nazi Germany turned on one another, the Soviet Union could bide its time, intervene when both sides were exhausted, and emerge dominant. Yet Trotsky, from exile, threatened that vision. Through his writings and the Fourth International, Trotsky called for revolutionary opposition to both fascism and Stalinism. His voice—still respected across the socialist world—risked undermining Stalin's moral legitimacy just as the Soviet Union prepared to present itself as the defender of peace and socialism.

Intelligence from the GPU confirmed that Hitler's next target would be Poland, and Stalin saw his moment. Negotiations with Britain and France had stalled, so he turned to Hitler, signing the Molotov–Ribbentrop Pact in August 1939. The agreement secretly divided Eastern Europe and guaranteed that Germany's attack on Poland would ignite the very world war Stalin expected. Before that happened, however, Trotsky had to die. The last surviving symbol of the 1917 Revolution opposed Stalin's regime more effectively than any army. His assassination, Stalin believed, would close the final chapter of internal dissent and ensure that, when the global conflict erupted, the Soviet leader could act without ideological challenge.

Thus, as Europe drifted toward catastrophe, Stalin's gaze was fixed not only on maps of Poland and Germany but also on a single villa in Coyoacán, Mexico, where his most dangerous rival still lived—and where, before the war began, he would order the final blow.

Stalin's directive was absolute: kill Trotsky within a year, before the war began.[8] Sudoplatov was to report only to Beria. No excuses. No further delays. He would select his own team and draw from the ranks of Spanish Civil War veterans. When Sudoplatov protested that he did not speak Spanish, Stalin was unmoved. "Find suitable personnel," he said. "Responsibility is yours."[9]

Sudoplatov's assignment was both an extraordinary honor and a silent death warrant should he fail. Shpigelglas didn't liquidate Trotsky and was later executed. Sudoplatov understood that failure to produce results now would earn him the same fate.[10]

Building the UTKA Network

Trotsky was unaware that his death had been ordered in the Kremlin. But he understood well the reach of Stalin's killers. As early as the 1920s, Soviet intelligence had developed the tools for covert assassination: poisons, silent pistols, and disguised weapons. At the 1938 show trial of Genrikh Yagoda, former head of the GPU, Prosecutor Andrey Vyshinsky had declared that Yagoda had perfected "the technology of killing people in the most devious ways." The USSR had turned murder into a bureaucratized craft.

The day after receiving his directive, Sudoplatov turned to Nahum Eitingon, a seasoned operative fluent in Spanish and a veteran of clandestine campaigns in Spain and France, and placed him in charge of the Mexico task force. Together, Sudoplatov and Eitingon drafted a one-page proposal for Stalin's review titled "Plan for Agent and Operational Measures for UTKA." Stalin approved the document in August 1939.[11]

The plan was explicit in both purpose and means. Its sole objective was the elimination of UTKA, Leon Trotsky. It authorized a wide range of methods, including poisoning, car bombing, suffocation, stabbing, shooting, or an armed group assault. Responsibility for execution was assigned to organizer TOM (Eitingon), supported by MAT (Caridad Mercader) and RAYMOND (Ramón Mercader).

Eitingon gave the operation its cover name: UTKA, or *duck* in Russian. In Soviet slang, it also meant *canard*, or *disinformation*. It was a suitable label for a multipronged plot built on deception.

Two operational lines were created under the UTKA umbrella. The first, Operation KON, was a paramilitary-style raid on Trotsky's villa that was to be coordinated by the Mexican muralist and GPU operative David Alfaro Siqueiros. The famous painter had returned from Spain a hardened veteran of the war and a devout Stalinist.[12] The second line, Operation MAT, relied on seduction and deep infiltration. It centered on Ramón Mercader—already embedded under a false

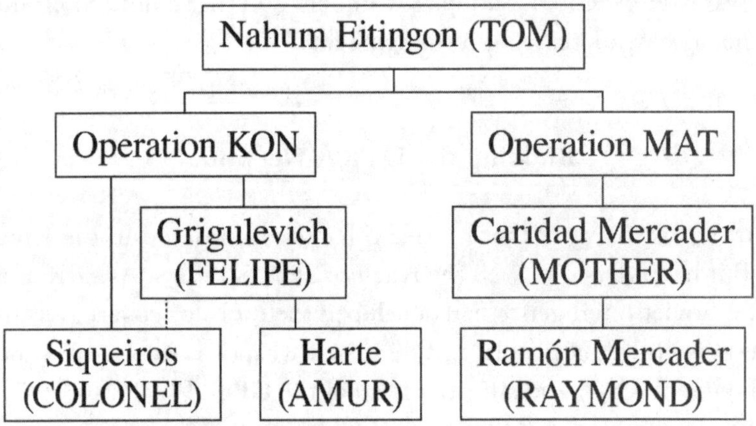

26. Operation UTKA's network in Mexico.

identity in Paris—who had begun a calculated romance with a young American Trotskyist named Sylvia Ageloff a year earlier. Because operation KON was closer to fruition, Operation MAT was in place as a reserve contingency.

Beria and Eitingon understood that Ramón, operating under the alias Frank Jacson*, had not yet secured the direct access to Trotsky's household that an assassin would require for Operation MAT. Until that infiltration could be completed, only the coordinated armed assault as envisioned in Operation KON offered a plausible path to immediate success.

Sudoplatov estimated that both operations, KON and MAT, would take six months and cost up to $300,000.[13] It was to operate independent from the regular Soviet diplomatic and intelligence channels—isolated from both the GPU rezidentura in Mexico and its counterpart in the United States. The operation would operate in the shadows, answering only to Beria and Stalin.

Preparations and Deployments

To maintain secrecy, Sudoplatov and Eitingon traveled to Paris under false identities, using forged papers provided by GPU forger Georgy

Miller. There, they met Caridad and Ramón Mercader separately from the KON group to ensure strict compartmentalization.[14] Sudoplatov found the mother and son pair reliable but insisted they undergo further training in intelligence tradecraft. That training delayed their deployment—nearly fatally.[15]

In August 1939 they prepared to depart from Le Havre for the Americas, then on September 1 Hitler invaded Poland, and Europe descended into war. Eitingon, traveling under false Polish papers, was at risk of internment or conscription.[16] He vanished into hiding, faking mental illness and checking himself into a Paris asylum under a Syrian-Jewish alias. Only after GPU illegal Maksim Steinberg secured an emergency visa through contacts in the US did Eitingon escape arrest and travel to New York in October 1939.[17]

Eitingon had established himself in Brooklyn under commercial cover, operating an import–export firm. This enterprise provided funding and logistical support for Ramón Mercader's next transformation.[18] Ramón, operating using the alias of Frank Jacson*, carried an altered passport that had been appropriated by the GPU from a deceased International Brigades veteran.[19] His assignment: go to Mexico, have Sylvia Ageloff join him, and establish proximity to Trotsky.

In New York, Ramón, as Frank Jacson*, resumed his romantic relationship with Sylvia, now referring to her in public as his wife. Ramón was handsome with good looks and a magnetic charm that helped smooth over their seven-month separation.[20] Eitingon also arranged to discreetly observe Jacson* and Ageloff over lunch before Ramón departed for Mexico City.[21]

While Sudoplatov remained in Moscow to coordinate operations from the center, Eitingon and the field teams worked steadily toward their final objective.

Operation KON: The First Strike

The initial intelligence that helped shape the attack plan did not come from GPU agent África de las Heras (PATRIA) as is mistakenly believed. Though GPU sources correctly credited PATRIA with providing a floor plan of

27. Kitty Harris (cover name AIDA) purchased Zook's Pharmacy for the GPU and later ran it as a safe house for atomic espionage during World War II.

Trotsky's residence, her 1938 layout of the Casa Azul (Blue House) had become obsolete.[22] Trotsky's relocation to a new, more defendable compound on Avenida Viena in May 1939—five months after de las Heras's recall—rendered the earlier blueprint useless.[23]

The first detailed sketches of Trotsky's new Avenida Viena address more likely came from Trotsky guard Sheldon Harte (cover name AMUR, pseudonym BOB SHIELDS),[24] who arrived at the villa on April 7, 1940, seven weeks before the raid.[25] The young American Stalinist was recruited in New York in 1939 by Grigulevich to pose as a Trotskyite and volunteer to serve as a guard in Coyoacán.[26] Harte supplied not only updated floor plans but also detailed knowledge of the Old Man's guard shifts and internal routines.

Joseph Grigulevich, an experienced illegal operative, was added to UTKA by Beria at the end of 1939.[27] Working with the cover name FELIPE, Grigulevich had earlier failed to mount a successful assault on the Blue House in 1938 while Trotsky was still in residence, likely because of PATRIA's withdrawal. But his plans impressed Beria, and his tactical discipline was viewed as a necessary counterweight to the erratic behavior of David Alfaro Siqueiros, the Mexican muralist leading the KON raiders.[28]

One of Grigulevich's earliest proposals for eliminating the Old Man—a booby-trapped cactus packed with explosives—was rejected by the GPU rezidentura in New York in 1938 for fear of civilian collateral casualties.[29] But his initiative and organizational contributions were invaluable.

Using the alias of Manuel Francis Rodrigez, Grigulevich acquired a safe house in Santa Fe, New Mexico, through GPU courier Kitty Harris (AIDA), using it beginning in late 1939 to fabricate documents for the KON raid team.[30] Then he returned to Mexico to help direct the final assault planning in early 1940.

The key to Operation KON's success was for the raiders to gain entry unopposed into the central courtyard of Trotsky's villa before the alarm was raised. And Harte's arrival to Trotsky's household became the linchpin of the raid's success. His duties on the night guard rotation and solo operation of the main garage gates provided the opening that the raiders needed during the predawn hours of May 24, 1940. When the raiders reached the gates, Harte would have them unlocked from within.

Operation MAT: The Assassin in Waiting

While Operation KON moved toward execution, Operation MAT—the GPU's more surgical contingency employing Ramón Mercader as the lone assassin—remained in reserve.

When successfully reestablishing his relationship with Sylvia in New York in September 1939, Ramón presented himself to her as a man deeply in love, offering affection, security, and plans for a shared life. She introduced him to others in the Socialist Workers Party as her husband and accompanied him in Trotskyist circles. Meanwhile he was receiving operational guidance and funding from Eitingon, who was also in New York in the fall of 1939 making preparations for Operation KON before departing for Mexico.

Mercader departed New York and arrived in Mexico in October of 1939 with a single objective: to get inside the Old Man's household. His first strategy was simple—use Sylvia. If he could leverage their relationship to convince Natalia Sedova of his legitimacy, the gate to Avenida Viena might open on its own. But he brought a second plan as well.

Alfred and Marguerite Rosmer, revered veterans of the revolutionary movement, were then living with the Trotskys. The Rosmers likely remembered Sylvia favorably from the Fourth International Conference in Paris in September 1938, and their shared history offered Mercader a second line of approach. If the Rosmers accepted Frank* as Sylvia's new husband, they could quietly vouch for him to Natalia. And Natalia, who regarded Marguerite as her closest friend, would be inclined to trust her word.

With this in mind, Mercader weighed the possibility that the Rosmers—not Sylvia alone—might be the ones to "open the door" for him into Avenida Viena.

Ramón's eventual access unfolded gradually: first through indirect social visits with Sylvia and the Rosmers, and then by befriending the Rosmers and Trotsky's guards. As the guards became more relaxed when he appeared at the gates, the GPU's potential scenario for Operation MAT slowly developed. Unlike KON, MAT was meant to leave a smaller trail—just one attacker, one weapon, and one violent act.

For now, though, Ramón was told simply to wait and gather intelligence.

Eitingon's coded instructions from Moscow in late 1939, delivered through agricultural metaphors, were precise and urged patience: "tend the field, wait for the harvest, and protect the plantation," and "Do not make experiments that are not well thought out, go for obtaining results for certain, and you will indeed make a valuable contribution to science." As Eitingon later put it: "The seeds had been planted. Now we had to watch them grow."[31]

The final blow might come from a team of raiders, or from a lone assassin with an ice axe. Only time would tell.

Convergence: Stalin's Noose Tightens

By the spring of 1940, Operation UTKA had shifted from concept to execution. The deception layers were in place. Surveillance teams were active. Intelligence streamed in from infiltrators planted across Trotsky's circle. And for the first time, the mechanisms of KON, MAT, and the networks supporting them aligned under Eitingon's coordinated command.

Yet coordination across continents remained an ordeal. With no diplomatic ties between the USSR and Mexico, secure radio contact was nearly impossible. Moscow had supplied substandard transmitters, Mexican authorities monitored the airwaves, and every message had to zigzag across half the world. Signals were first sent to a Soviet merchant ship anchored in New York harbor, then relayed to the rezidentura in Paris, and only then forwarded to Moscow. At each stop, messages were laboriously encoded and decoded by hand. A single instruction could take a week to reach Moscow or Mexico.[32]

Stalin's impatience grew by the hour. He demanded constant reports, interrogating Beria and his principal deputy, Vsevolod Nikolayevich Merkulov—who would himself assume leadership of the security apparatus the year after Trotsky's assassination—about every detail of the operation. He pressed for updates, demanded timetables, and fumed at delay. For Stalin, Trotsky's death was not a question; it was an overdue obligation. Shpigelglas had disappointed him. Orlov had betrayed him. But Eitingon and Sudoplatov could not fail. Their lives—and the lives of those beneath them—depended on success.

In April 1940, preparations for Operation KON advanced to their final stage. Grigulevich tightened the logistics for the assault. David Alfaro Siqueiros, volatile yet indispensable, gathered arms, uniforms, and assembled a cadre of trusted fighters, many of them civil war veterans hardened by years of killing in Spain. Inside Trotsky's villa, one final piece fell into place: newly arrived guard Sheldon Harte was scheduled for the overnight shift on the critical date and held the keys to the garage and courtyard gates. The assault team needed only his cooperation.

At the same time, Operation MAT advanced quietly in the background. Ramón Mercader, hidden behind the face of Frank Jacson*, played a patient, meticulous game. He behaved as a harmless admirer of Trotsky's ideas from afar, deepened his rapport with the Rosmers in an attempt to gain Natalia's trust, and wrote tender, reassuring letters to Sylvia, who had returned to her job in Brooklyn on March 26, 1940. Frank* presented himself as everyone's friend. He made no sudden moves. He waited.

Now the twin blades of UTKA—KON and MAT—were converging on the same target. Stalin's machinery of murder was fully in motion. In Coyoacán, Siqueiros and his raiders were preparing to breach the walls of Trotsky's villa. In the shadows, Ramón Mercader quietly gathered minutiae on the household's routines. And in the midst of it all, the Old Man, surrounded by comrades he believed loyal, remained unaware of how close the danger had crept.

The noose had tightened. The clock was almost out.

All that remained was the arrival of a squad of hardened killers from Spain—men for whom killing was not ideology, but habit.

CHAPTER XI

THUGS, ENFORCERS, AND ASSASSINS

"Eliminating a political enemy was not murder; it was necessary surgery."
—Pavel Sudoplatov

"Terror is the quickest path to obedience."
—Felix Dzerzhinsky, founder of the Soviet Cheka (forerunner of the GPU)

"From the blood-soaked sewers of Spain, the GPU sent its wolves to finish Trotsky in Mexico."
—Anatoli Sudoplatov

A Dress Rehearsal for Murder

The Spanish Civil War became far more than a clash between Republican democracy and Francoist rebellion. It became a laboratory for Stalinist repression, a proving ground where the GPU exported the logic of the Great Terror into a foreign war. Soviet advisers—foremost among them Alexander Orlov, the GPU's rezident in Spain—embedded themselves within Republican security structures and shaped their methods with techniques tested in Moscow's prisons.[1] They brought with them the full repertoire of Stalin's terror: fabricated accusations, forced confessions, theatrical trials, and the conviction that failing to uncover enemies was itself evidence of guilt.[2]

Historians have since shown that Soviet involvement quickly fused military assistance with political policing, factional purges, and the

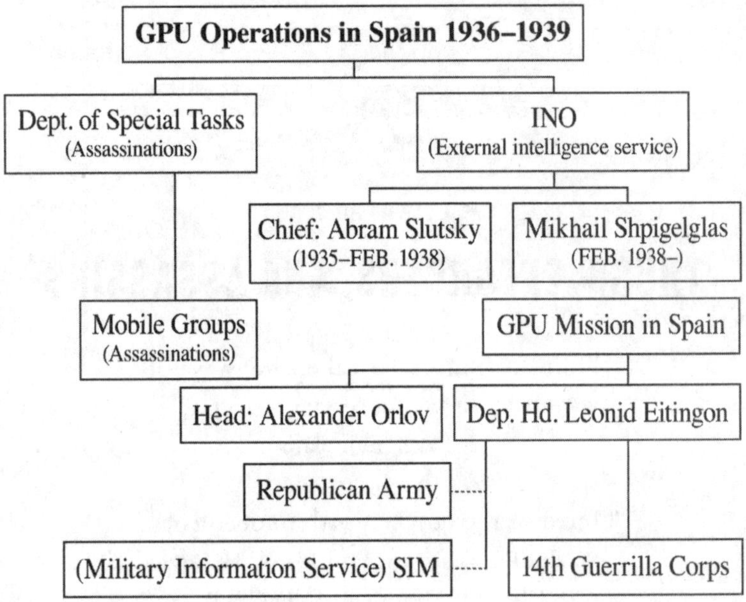

28.

elimination of ideological rivals, particularly Trotskyists, anarchists, and dissident Marxists.[3] Declassified Comintern and GPU records reveal that Moscow's operatives wielded a mandate that blended political oversight with covert security work, mirroring the purgative logic of Stalinist rule.[4] The result was a campaign of organized political violence inside Republican Spain that reflected—almost in miniature—the architecture of Stalin's terror at home.[5]

Under the sanction of the Comintern and the tight, disciplined direction of the GPU, Spain became the clearest foreign case study of Stalin's methods: intervention, infiltration, and political terror executed under the cover of revolutionary war.

The Architecture of Terror: Orlov's Network and the Men Who Did the Killing

By 1937, the GPU had effectively seized control of the Republican security services. What began as an international defense of a threatened Republic mutated into a Stalinist counterrevolution inside the revolution. The GPU redirected its fire—not toward Franco's Nationalists but toward rival left-wing groups. The POUM, fiercely critical of Stalin and sympathetic to Trotsky, was outlawed; its leaders were arrested, tortured, or disappeared in a purge documented extensively across contemporary testimony and modern scholarship.[6]

No case symbolized this internal war more starkly than that of Andreu Nin. Kidnapped by Soviet-directed operatives, Nin was taken to a clandestine GPU prison near Alcalá de Henares—its interrogation rooms modeled on the Lubyanka—and murdered when he refused to confess to fictional crimes.[7] His death was not an anomaly. It formed part of a coordinated purge of Trotskyists, anarchists, and dissident Marxists across Catalonia, orchestrated with the cold logic then devouring the USSR.

Behind the camouflage of war, Orlov's killers operated with near-total impunity. Among them were men who would later resurface in Mexico: Ilya Grigulevich, a brilliant illegal whose career would span continents; Victorio Codovilla, the Comintern's Argentine enforcer; Vittorio Vidali, the Italian assassin known as Comandante Carlos; and George Mink, a Philadelphia-born hatchet man feared for his brutality. Their activities—interrogations, sabotage, disappearances—are corroborated by Comintern archives and multiple historians.[8] Spain did not tame these men. Spain weaponized them.

As the Republic collapsed in 1938 and 1939, the Stalinist project in Spain unraveled with it. The GPU began a silent evacuation. Its most valued operatives fled under forged identities—first into France, then into Latin America—along escape routes maintained by the Soviet rezidentura.[9] From the back alleys of Barcelona, the GPU dispatched its wolves toward Mexico. Their mission was no longer political policing inside a civil war. It was the assassination of a single man.

They brought with them an operational toolkit refined amid Spain's chaos: forged passports, deep cover identities, compartmentalized cells, secret apartments, and covert funding streams—methods documented across Comintern records and confirmed by leading scholars.[10] The terror had not ended with the fall of Barcelona; it metastasized. The same operatives who had filled Catalonia's prisons and consigned Nin to an unmarked grave now advanced toward a new battlefield: the quiet bougainvillea-lined streets of Coyoacán.

What began as repression in Spain evolved into a program of targeted assassination abroad. The methods honed in Barcelona and Valencia—surveillance, infiltration, staged denunciations, false-flag operations—were repurposed for a singular objective: the elimination of Leon Trotsky.[11] In Mexico, Stalin's agents encountered a more permissive environment, more malleable allies, and a political landscape unprepared for the sophistication of Soviet clandestine work. Before the blow could be struck, the GPU reshaped Mexico's political terrain. The once-marginal Mexican Communist Party (PCM) became a weapon of denunciation, echoing Moscow's demands and amplifying the call to erase Trotsky from public life.[12]

Thus the terror born in Spain became the dress rehearsal for the political murder carried out inside a fortified villa in August 1940.

The Killers Arrive

The GPU's solution was simple, direct, and unmistakably Stalinist: send in the killers. These were not faceless agents. They were men already bloodied in Spain—veterans of purges, disappearances, and clandestine executions. As historian Paul Preston notes, Mexico became "the scene of a portentous concentration of veteran Stalinist killers and conspirators," many of them arriving between late 1938 and late 1939.[13] Their task was not subtle. They were to reshape Mexico's political climate until Trotsky could be denounced, isolated, and killed.

They infiltrated the PCM, labor unions, student groups, arts organizations, and newspapers, pushing a harsh anti-Trotsky line and intimidating editors who resisted.[14] Demonstrations were organized, threats delivered, and wavering party members disciplined. Within months, the GPU had engineered a climate of hostility that made violence against Trotsky seem not only acceptable but inevitable.

Victorio Codovilla: The Enforcer

The first major operative to reach Mexico was the Argentine-based Italian Communist Victorio Codovilla. Stocky, blunt, and politically ruthless, Codovilla had spent the 1930s as the Comintern's chief representative in Spain and had worked closely with Soviet security operatives there. His role in Spain is well documented in books by both Burnett Bolloten and Ron Radosh: he aided Soviet agents in suppressing Trotskyists and helped coordinate the elimination of the POUM and its leader, Andreu Nin.[15]

By the late 1930s, Codovilla had become one of the Comintern's most trusted field enforcers. According to historian Angel Viñas, he held "a decisive role in shaping the political repression inside the Republican zone," closely aligned with GPU general Leonid Eitingon.[16]

Once in Mexico City, Codovilla quickly aligned with painter-turned-militant David Alfaro Siqueiros. Together they assembled a paramilitary group of Spanish Civil War veterans and hardened Mexican miners—men who had already killed for Stalin in Spain and were prepared to kill again.[17]

Vittorio Vidali: Stalin's General of Terror

If Codovilla acted as the enforcer, Vittorio Vidali was its general—the most feared Comintern hitter in the Western Hemisphere. Known variously as Carlos Contreras, General Carlos, and Comandante Carlos, Vidali had arrived in Spain in 1936 and quickly became one of the most powerful figures in the International Brigades. Historian Antony Beevor describes how Vidali built the Fifth Regiment into a fearsome shock force through a mixture of military discipline and extrajudicial violence.[18]

Desertion under Vidali was often met with summary execution. His presence in Mexico in 1939 sent a clear signal: Stalin's punishment of dissent within the PCM was about to begin. Hernán Laborde and Valentín Campa—moderate party leaders who had tolerated Trotsky's asylum—were purged by Vidali's Comintern tribunal on charges of "ideological deviation" and "Trotskyite tolerance."[19]

By March 1940, Vidali had installed a new PCM leadership fully subordinate to Moscow. Their first public demand: Trotsky must be expelled from Mexico.[20]

Trotsky watched these events carefully. The PCM purge, he wrote, was "the moral preparation for assassination."[21]

George Mink: The Wolf with the Golden Tooth

The last to arrive was the most infamous: George Mink. Born in Russia and raised on the Philadelphia docks, Mink had risen in the Marine Workers Industrial Union through a combination of street brutality and criminal cunning. Federal investigative reports from the 1930s described him as "ruthless, wary, and violent," a man whose loyalty lay only with the GPU.[22]

In 1932, Mink murdered Hans Wissinger, a fellow party member suspected of disloyalty, boasting afterward: "We never strike at innocent men."[23] Arrested in Denmark in 1935 with false passports and cipher pads, he was deported to the USSR—only to resurface in Spain under the alias Alfred Hertz, enforcing discipline through night raids and terror tactics against anti-Stalinist militants.[24]

In 1938, Mink entered Mexico on a visa obtained through a sympathetic diplomat in Paris. Trotsky immediately recognized the danger and publicly identified Mink as a GPU assassin sent to kill him.[25]

Rumors soon spread that Mink was assembling a death squad of Spanish veterans and Mexican militants. By early 1940, he had vanished from public view entirely. In February 1941, the Russian-language newspaper *Novoye Russkoye Slovo* reported that Mink had been "liquidated in December 1940." Trotsky's secretary Joseph Hansen similarly told the FBI that Mink was killed "by men who took him to a crater thirty miles from Mexico City."[26]

Whatever the truth, Mink was never seen again.

29.

Setting the Stage for Assassination

The killers Stalin sent to Mexico acted not as revolutionaries, but as executioners-in-waiting. Under their pressure, the PCM transformed from a fractured party into a ferocious weapon of denunciation. Those who questioned the escalating anti-Trotsky rhetoric vanished from public life. Newspapers carried shriller accusations. Demonstrations grew larger and more violent.

The crescendo came on May 1, 1940.

Over twenty thousand marchers filled the streets of Mexico City carrying red flags and chanting "¡Trotsky debe morir!"—a mass spectacle of hatred carefully engineered by PCM leadership aligned with Vidali.[27]

Trotsky understood instantly. This was not protest. It was prelude.

The walls of his villa—reinforced, guarded, electrified—were no longer symbolic defenses. They were the last barrier between him and a political murder being scripted in Moscow.

By late spring, all the pieces of Operation UTKA were assembled:

the political agitation, the armed paramilitary cells, the killers from Spain—and one final weapon making his rehearsed entrance under the alias Frank Jacson*.

Ramón Mercader had arrived.

And Sylvia Ageloff, believing herself his wife, was already taking her place in the tragedy he would write with an ice axe.

CHAPTER XII

COMRADES AND LOVERS

Mexico (January to March 1940)

"No fortress is so strong that it cannot be breached from within."
—Soviet counterintelligence proverb

"The cruelest weapon is not forged of steel but of trust. Affection can conceal an order, and a kiss can complete a mission."
—Nahum Eitingon, 1941

"In Coyoacán, the Revolution devoured its own heart. A man died for ideas, but it was love that opened the door."
—Rita Kronenbitter, CIA intelligence analyst

Mexico: Spycraft and Sanctuary

He arrived with flowers, but he carried a weapon sharpened by betrayal. Mexico in 1940 was no mere refuge—it was a geopolitical paradox: a land that offered asylum to the exiled yet harbored the agents of their destruction. It was a country where revolution lingered in the air, and where embassies, cafés, and artists' studios became battlegrounds for ideologies at war. For Ramón Mercader, it was the final theater in Stalin's relentless campaign to annihilate his rival. Beneath the mask of affection, he bore a directive conceived in Paris, sanctioned in Moscow, and now poised for its bloody conclusion in Coyoacán. His entry into the compound would not require force—only trust, and Sylvia Ageloff.

Dispatched by Moscow, backed by Stalin, and managed by Nahum

Eitingon (TOM) and his own mother, Caridad (MOTHER), Ramón Mercader returned to Sylvia Ageloff under the guise of love. She had once fallen for him in Paris and now presented herself in Mexico as his supposed wife. What she believed was a rekindled romance was, in truth, a covert operation. Unwittingly, she was delivering a spy to the threshold of Trotsky's inner circle—there to penetrate the Old Man's final refuge through the most vulnerable entry point imaginable: love.

Mexico's political volatility and permissive stance toward political exiles made it ideal for espionage. President Lázaro Cárdenas had granted Trotsky asylum and protection, but the country teemed with Stalinist loyalists eager to win favor with Moscow. Mercader's mission was to solidify his relationship with Sylvia and use her to gain intelligence and access to the villa at Avenida Viena. Operation KON—the planned armed assault—depended on intimate knowledge of guard routines and vulnerabilities. That intelligence was one of Ramón's responsibilities, and the pressure from Eitingon and Caridad to deliver details about the villa was mounting.

Traveling under a tourist visa as Frank Jacson*, Ramón Mercader crossed into Mexico on October 12, 1939, at Nuevo Laredo, and arrived in Mexico City a few days later.[1] Caridad and Eitingon, traveling separately, arrived in October also. Ramón settled into a modest hotel and began mapping his target. He studied the villa's routines from afar, asking innocuous questions, posing as a curious tourist. The house had become a small fortress, ringed with concrete walls and guard posts. Mercader understood that the path past stone walls would be paved with trust—and Sylvia was his access.

Cover Stories and Climbing

As Mercader awaited further direction from the GPU regarding the final details of his commercial cover in Mexico City, he refined the identity first outlined during his October 1939 meeting with Eitingon in New York. The original plan had envisioned his remaining in the United States—particularly in the New York area—for several months. There, he was to reestablish himself with Sylvia Ageloff, cultivate local familiarity,

30. Frank Jacson's* forged passport photo.

and construct a more durable, convincingly backstopped professional persona. The GPU believed it had access to a sympathetic contact in the personnel office of the New York World's Fair who could secure Jacson* a position as a guide or driver, thereby providing legitimate employment and institutional cover. For reasons that remain unclear, that arrangement collapsed before it could be solidified.

Time, however, was no longer on Moscow's side. Stalin's impatience for Trotsky's elimination was intensifying. In late spring 1939, Pavel Sudoplatov had been made to understand that the "Trotsky problem" was to be resolved within a year. As that deadline approached, pressure mounted sharply. Earlier failures had already tested Stalin's tolerance; another delay could carry lethal consequences for those responsible. Rather than rebuild and properly backstop the American cover, the GPU accelerated the timetable and ordered Mercader to proceed to Mexico ahead of schedule.

Under these revised instructions, Jacson* informed Sylvia that he had been offered a promising position in Mexico City. The earlier Belgian newspaper story quietly disappeared. In its place emerged a new explanation. He told her he had obtained employment as secretary to one "Peter Lubeck"—elsewhere rendered in various records as Frank Lubec, Lubek, or Luback—a Belgian national allegedly serving as a purchasing agent for the British government in both the United States and Mexico. According to Jacson's* account, Lubeck had previously been an importer-exporter in

Belgium but had fled before the outbreak of war. He was said to maintain offices in either San Francisco or Los Angeles, as well as in Mexico City. Jacson* claimed he would earn fifty dollars per week managing Lubeck's affairs and assisting in the procurement of critically needed war materials—copra, sugar, oil, and other commodities—for shipment to Britain and France in their struggle against Nazi Germany.[2]

Sylvia later told investigators that Jacson* spoke fluently about commodity prices, described labor difficulties in Mexico, and complained of shipping delays—details that persuaded her that his employment was genuine. Precisely when Mercader first introduced the Lubeck name to Sylvia remains uncertain. What is clear is that the name surfaced most prominently in the documentary record after his arrest. In his initial statements to Mexican authorities, Mercader invoked Frank Lubeck as the man behind his employment and as part of his fabricated explanation for the crime—a version of events that Sylvia Ageloff likewise repeated during her own police interrogation.[3]

The lull in his schedule allowed Ramón a rare opportunity to pursue his passion in mountain climbing. Among those he met under his alias of Frank Jacson*, while climbing, was Senor Patino of the Pan American Airways office. Patino was an experienced climber and listened to Jacson's* boastful tales of climbing Mont Blanc and other impressive mountains in Europe.[4]

In November, Patino organized an ascent of Popocatépetl. The majestic mountain, along with its companion Iztaccihuatl, is frequently adorned with snow and can be glimpsed from Mexico City on clear days. When the designated time arrived, Jacson* arrived with an abundance of climbing gear, a typical oversight among novices. As they commenced the ascent, Patino's initial assessment was validated: Jacson*, laden with excess equipment, quickly succumbed to fatigue halfway up the slope due to poor conditioning. Instead of pressing on, they made the decision to leave him utterly exhausted at a resting point.[5]

On December 7, 1939, the GPU authorized Mercader's purchase of a prestigious four-door Buick sedan at the Hernandez Agency to provide transportation for Sylvia and others.[6] It was beige in color and stood out. Such an expensive luxury car was consistent with Jacson's* cover and later proved useful to provide an entrée into the Old Man's household.

Sylvia's Reawakening

Ramón had last seen Sylvia in October 1939, and left saying that he expected her to join him. He even gave her $3,000 for her expenses, but beyond that, he made no plans.[7] Making it even worse for Sylvia, she heard nothing more from him for more than two months.

As Sylvia waited for his summons, her patience began to wear thin. Reluctant to spend the $3,000 he had entrusted to her, she took a job with the New York Home Relief Bureau as a social worker to support herself. By December 1939, however, she was growing increasingly frustrated by his silence and decided to act. She finally obtained a doctor's note citing a sinus condition that "required" a warmer climate. Historian Bertrand Patenaude suggests the illness was fabricated: "As the Christmas break approached, Sylvia feigned illness to leave her job . . . supported by a doctor's note claiming sinus pain."[8]

Sylvia flew to Mexico City on New Year's Day of 1940 to reunite with her husband and moved into Frank's* well-situated apartment at 159 Colonia Juarez in Hamburgo.[9] Unbeknownst to Sylvia, Ramón was following Eitingon's instructions to strengthen their common-law marriage. Sylvia's presence in Mexico was the best of the options remaining to them to penetrate Trotsky's inner circle to collect the intelligence on the villa.[10]

Trotsky's Last Year: 1940

The year 1940 would be Trotsky's last, as the GPU's network of spies, infiltrators, and assassins were closing in. Sylvia Ageloff—emotionally vulnerable and unwitting—had been maneuvered into position through deception, seduction, and psychological manipulation. What she believed was a chance romance with Jacques Mornard* that began eighteen months earlier in Paris was, in fact, a carefully crafted operation to penetrate Trotsky's inner circle. With blissful ignorance, she ignored mounting signs of duplicity and became a pawn in one of the twentieth century's most notorious assassinations—an endgame that would soon unfold in the walled courtyards of Coyoacán.

Each night, Jac* convincingly played the part of a devoted lover. By day, however, while he was supposedly at his notional job, he met with his mother, Caridad, and Eitingon at their safe house at 55 Calle Dinamarka.[11] GPU handlers were satisfied—the long game was progressing exactly as intended.

Soon after she arrived, Sylvia reached out to Trotsky through her sister Ruth, who had a relationship with the Trotskys from 1937, and received an invitation to visit Avenida Viena. Frank* drove her to the meeting and called for her again in the late afternoon, a pattern that they repeated later. Over time, this allowed Frank* to become a familiar sight to the guards and the Mexican police outside the villa. Trotsky's guards quickly took notice of Frank*—the man with the sleek new car who drove recklessly through the streets, braking hard in a swirl of dust just before reaching the gates. However, Frank* never made an effort to enter the villa as he seemed to be one of the few people in Mexico without an interest in meeting the famous Old Man.

A decade later, when Sylvia testified before the House Committee on Un-American Activities, she remembered that Frank* had adopted a slightly new course: "When I was in Mexico from January to March, he showed a little more interest in politics as a concession to me, but nothing that would give a clue to his feelings."[12]

In the Company of the Rosmers

Sylvia's first meeting with the Trotskys went well, and in early February, she was invited to return. As she was leaving the villa, she unexpectedly crossed paths with Alfred Rosmer, whom she had met previously at the founding congress of the Fourth International, held at the Rosmers' home outside Paris in 1938. Now guests of the Trotsky family in Coyoacán, the Rosmers had come to Mexico the previous summer escorting Trotsky's grandson, Sieva Volkov, from Paris following the death of his uncle and adopted father, Lev Sedov. Renewing their acquaintance, Sylvia invited the Rosmers to visit her apartment, where they were introduced for the first time to Frank*, her new common-law husband.[13]

Their friendship resumed easily. They dined together frequently, and Frank* often treated the couple to drives through the Mexican countryside in his shiny new Buick. These relaxed social interactions gradually helped normalize his presence within Trotsky's circle and reinforced the impression of him as a charming, generous, and trustworthy companion—an image the GPU would later exploit to devastating effect.

As their friendship deepened, in late February, the Rosmers invited Sylvia and Frank* on a picnic to Mount Toluca. The outing went smoothly, though Patenaude later noted that Frank* was seen as a political lightweight and not taken seriously during discussions. The Rosmers were also puzzled that Frank*, a supposed Canadian, spoke such fluent Parisian French. Frank* had a ready explanation: he claimed to have been educated in Paris.[14] The GPU recognized the value of the Rosmer connection immediately and exploited it in the months ahead.

Puigventós explained that "Sylvia had a very close relationship with the Rosmers, principally with Marguerite, to whom she confided her worries and her doubts," while "Ramón fell into the Rosmers' good graces" as well.[15] They often spoke at the entry gate of Trotsky's house, and "he [Frank*] obtained their confidence quickly; they exchanged some words, and they invited Jacson* to eat or to go on walks." The bond was strongest with Marguerite, who viewed Frank* as "a smart, considerate and generous boy, a likable type and very handsome."[16] Slowly Frank* also began to ingratiate himself with members of the Trotsky household—running errands for the Rosmers and offering the use of his Buick to assist with household needs. Guard Jake Cooper later said that the household began to think of Frank* "as a friend."

The Office That Didn't Exist

In February Ageloff decided to extend her stay in Mexico City by informing her employer that she was still sick and needed additional time off work. Historian Gregorio Luri explains,

> On February 26, Sylvia wired New York officials requesting an extension of her medical leave through April 1, citing worsening

sinusitis. She enclosed a February 24 certificate from Dr. A. Zollinger in Mexico recommending she remain in a warmer climate.[17]

Mercader's initial role in Mexico City was solely for reconnaissance, and he was prepared to play his part well. At the time, the future assassin had no idea of how his role might change if the raid on Trotsky's villa (Operation KON) should fail.[18] In his autobiography, Sudoplatov insists that Mercader did not even know of KON, but that seems doubtful given his close friendship with the talkative and boastful Siqueiros.[19]

The GPU Takes Control

In 1940 Trotsky believed (correctly) that Stalin's ability to liquidate him would first necessitate his absolute dominance over the local Communist Party. In 1937, when he first arrived in Mexico, the Mexican Communist Party (PCM) was led by Hernán Laborde, an esteemed anarchist and poet known for his genteel demeanor and humanitarian principles. Laborde wielded authority within the party with a commanding presence, often donning a striking long black cape and carrying a pair of pistols to local gatherings for impact. However, his strong individualistic streak led him to bristle at Stalin's Comintern enforcers, who sought to meddle in PCM affairs.[20]

The PCM staunchly backed the leftist administration of Mexican President Lázaro Cárdenas and felt obligated to endorse his choice to offer asylum to political refugees, including Trotsky. The GPU, however, needed the PCM to support their position seeking to liquidate the Old Man, and for that reversal to take place, Laborde had to be replaced as party head.[21]

To accomplish the task, the GPU established a "purge commission" consisting of CPUSA member James Ford and the Comintern's South American troublemaker Victorio Codovilla to oust Laborde's group from power. The presiding judge for the hearing was to be Vittorio Vidali, who had gained fame as the GPU's arch assassin in the Spanish Civil War, when he operated under the alias of Carlos Contreras.[22]

The commission met secretly in March 1940 to hear the matter of "The Struggle Against Trotskyism and Other Enemies of the People." The purge was, of course, rigged, and the outcome was never in doubt. Laborde and his followers were ousted from the PCM and replaced by new leadership who were committed to Trotsky's elimination, regardless of President Cárdenas's position.[23]

Doubts and Deceptions

In early March 1940, Sylvia confided in Marguerite Rosmer her concerns that her husband was in Mexico on a forged Canadian passport under the name of Frank Jacson*. She explained the reason for the subterfuge was that Jacques Mornard* was a fugitive from military conscription in Belgium.[24]

Something else was bothering Sylvia. She asked Marguerite to investigate and confirm Frank's* office, located in room 820 of the well-known Edificio Ermita in the neighborhood of Tacubaya, a bustling business center hosting several companies engaged in global commerce. Sylvia was concerned that when her visiting sister Hilda had attempted to confirm the location earlier in March, she learned that there was no room 820.[25] When Hilda and Sylvia tried to make sense of it, they rationalized that Frank* was in reality collaborating secretly with the British government, or that "he was involved in work, which was not strictly legal, and that he consequently refused to divulge its nature."[26] Sylvia told all of this to Marguerite Rosmer, including her fears that Jac* was a British agent. Marguerite, however, calmed her.[27]

When Sylvia confronted Frank* with the inconsistency, he explained that he simply misspoke, and the correct room was 620. According to information available to Trotsky's attorney and SWP National Committee member Albert Goldman, "Marguerite Rosmer went to the building and actually found an office boy who told her that it was Jacson's* office."[28]

Shortly after the failed assassination attempt on May 24, 1940, however, it emerged that room 620 in the Edificio Ermita—previously linked to Frank Jacson*—had been leased by none other than ardent

Stalinist David Alfaro Siqueiros, the leader of the Operation KON assault squad.[29] This revelation, relayed by Ageloff to Mexican police during the post-assassination investigation, was deeply troubling. It showed that as early as March 1940, five months before the murder, Sylvia had begun to question Jacson's* credibility and even voiced suspicions that he might be a British agent. If Sylvia truly feared Jac* was involved in covert or illegal activity, why did she remain by his side? Or alert the Old Man's guards to her suspicions? Sylvia's concerns should have raised alarms about being manipulated for a hidden—and likely criminal—agenda. It also casts doubt on Marguerite Rosmer's role in "calming Sylvia" and raises the critical question: Did Marguerite relay these inconsistencies to her close friend Natalia Sedova [Trotsky]? Evidently not, as Natalia first learned of the Edificio Ermita incident and Sylvia's fear that Frank* might be a foreign agent only after the Old Man's death.

Sylvia grew increasingly anxious about the implications of Frank's* presence in Mexico under a false passport, fearing that "guilt by association" could damage both her own reputation and Trotsky's. She worried the PCM might exploit their relationship in its propaganda attacks against the Old Man. Determined that Trotsky hear it from her rather than from Marguerite, she chose to disclose only the false passport—omitting the troubling incident at the Edificio Ermita. After the assassination, Mexican Trotskyist Octavio Fernández confirmed that Ageloff never informed Trotsky or his guards about Jacson's* supposed office at the Edificio Ermita, even once it was revealed that the same address had been used by Siqueiros and linked directly to the GPU.[30] Had that connection been known, Jacson's* cover would inevitably have been blown and Sylvia's dream of a life with her new husband shattered.[31]

Surveying the Target

By late March, Sylvia's medical leave was no longer extended, and her employer warned she would lose her job if she didn't return to Brooklyn. Before departing on March 26, she visited the villa once more—bringing Frank* inside its walls for the first time to help with some luggage. Though Jac* did not meet Trotsky, the visit allowed him to observe the entry procedures and likely note the small guard shack alongside the garage where the alarm system was fitted.

Frank* had only dropped her off at work for the previous three months and then called for her at the end of the day. This visit, however, marked a turning point for Eitingon as Ramón was finally getting closer to being in a position to provide the needed intelligence about the villa.

After Trotsky's murder, Sylvia told the police investigators that, before departing for New York in late March, she had made Frank* promise that he would not visit the Trotsky household again in her absence.[32]

The defenses at Avenida Viena had been built to repel soldiers, to absorb gunfire, to survive an armed raid. But no steel gate could stop a man already inside. Sylvia, manipulated by affection, was serving her intended purpose. Under the guise of errands, Frank* circled the villa, tracked guards, noted routines. He was becoming a friend to all—as the final approach had begun. The future killer had made it past the walls the first time—and was beginning to exploit his advantage.

CHAPTER XIII

THE INVISIBLE SIEGE

Stalin's Spies Encircle Trotsky (April to May 1940)

"An assassin is only the final act. The real work is done by those who make the target vulnerable."
—GPU training manual (circa 1938)

"It is not the bullet that kills the revolution—but the whisper that aims it."
—Soviet intelligence doctrine

"First, you listen. Then you learn how to be trusted. Then you remove the locks."
—Soviet tradecraft aphorism

By May 1940, the Soviet war on Trotsky had reached its climax. No longer satisfied with poisoning sons or planting rumors, Stalin's agents moved toward decisive action. A dense lattice of wiretaps, forged friendships, faked identities, and stolen correspondence encircled the Old Man like an invisible noose. What began as espionage was about to become murder. Inside the villa, doors were unlocking. Outside, weapons were loaded. Trotsky's enemies were not approaching—they were already inside the gates.

The Noose Tightens

Ramón Mercader—armed with a polished cover story and patient malice—tightened his orbit around the Old Man. No longer constrained by Sylvia's watchful presence, he accelerated his campaign to infiltrate the villa. Under the guise of running errands, offering casual assistance, and building friendships with the Rosmers and the villa's handful of defenders, he transformed himself from an outsider into a trusted fixture. Every small favor, every routine conversation, chipped away at the vigilance that stood between Trotsky and Operation UTKA. Unseen and unsuspected, Stalin's assassin was already inside the gates.

The Intel Gap After PATRIA

Only the small group planning the raid on Trotsky's villa fully understood the urgency of Mercader's mission: to gather intelligence on the compound's layout and defenses. The situation turned critical in late 1938 when África de las Heras (PATRIA) was quietly withdrawn, leaving the GPU without access to insider intelligence. With Sylvia Ageloff back in New York, Mercader's connection to her remained their most viable path inside. Without the necessary intelligence, Operation KON was likely doomed.

The "Impregnable" Fortress

The villa underwent near-constant renovations and security upgrades during their first year of occupancy. Trotsky's guards further complicated matters for the GPU planners by deliberately spreading false rumors to the Mexican press about the villa's advanced security systems, including notional "automatic firing devices" said to kill intruders in the Old Man's living quarters. While seemingly far-fetched, the rumors were taken seriously enough that Siqueiros feared a trap.[1]

From Sylvia's Lips to the GPU

For the first three months of 1940, while Sylvia was still in Mexico City, Ramón had picked up only fragments of secondhand intelligence

31. The Bar Kit-Kat offered the overworked guards a heady mix: whiskey, jazz, and women whose affection could be bought by the hour.

from her and the villa's guards. Frank* engaged only in idle chat with the guards during Sylvia's shift changes and occasionally smoked with them at the gate. But the information proved incomplete and didn't provide the comprehensive details and sketches of the villa's interior layout that Operation KON required. For that, Ramón needed a set of eyes inside the compound.

The Harte Connection

In his effort to get inside, Ramón first turned his attention to befriending the guards, especially the newly arrived Sheldon Harte, whom he found "easygoing and gullible."[2] Ramón joined Harte and other guards at the popular Bar Kit-Kat and Salon México, where drinks and local prostitutes facilitated rapport.[3]

According to Eitingon's memoir, Harte (AMUR) and Mercader (RAYMOND) were unaware of each other's roles in the planned attack.[4] Harte might have remained in the dark, but Mercader likely learned of the new guard's recruitment and planned participation in the upcoming raid from his buddy and comrade Siqueiros. When Harte arrived at the villa in early April, he soon began supplying the room layouts, duty schedules, and a map detailing the location of Trotsky's archive to Grigulevich.[5] However, more intelligence was needed, and Eitingon believed that it could be found if they could access the Old Man's external communications.

Letters, Wiretaps, and Whispers

The GPU monitored Trotsky's primary written communications along three main channels: (1) with James Cannon, head of the SWP in New York; (2) with his Paris office managing European and global operations; and (3) with his New York publisher, Harper & Brothers.

The SWP funded the villa's operations, and Trotsky corresponded with Cannon almost daily about financial matters and ongoing security improvements. Sedov and later Zborowski coordinated the activities of the Fourth International abroad, while Trotsky's publisher remained his principal source of income. Their monitored exchanges likely included regular updates on his forthcoming exposé—the scathing biography of Soviet leader Joseph Stalin. While the three channels provided valuable strategic insight and funding for the villa's new defenses, they offered little information about security entry and exit protocols or visitor procedures—precisely the details Eitingon and Siqueiros needed most.

GPU operatives were embedded in all three channels to intercept written communications. In New York, Sylvia Callen served as James P. Cannon's secretary from 1937–1947 using the name Sylvia Caldwell, and virtually nothing passed through the Socialist Workers Party headquarters that Callen (SATYR) did not promptly relay to the GPU.[6] In Paris, the GPU was equally well positioned: Mark Zborowski (TULIP) was already embedded in Lev Sedov's office, where he routinely handled Sedov's correspondence and made copies for transmission to Moscow.

To penetrate Trotsky's communications with Harper & Brothers—the publisher of his forthcoming biography of Stalin—the GPU enlisted Louis Budenz to manipulate Harper journalist Leigh White into revealing that Trotsky's letters were being forwarded to a cutout, Sara Wolf, in New Jersey. GPU operatives, likely with the assistance of a bribed postal worker, intercepted the mail en route, opening, photographing, and resealing it before it reached Wolf.[7]

These intercepted communications provided the GPU with valuable insight into Trotsky's financial condition, publishing deadlines, and—most critically—the evolving security measures at the villa. Trotsky's near-daily letters to Cannon frequently addressed concerns about infiltration, guard rotations, and architectural modifications intended to strengthen defenses. Correspondence with Harper & Brothers, meanwhile, hinted at the timing and substance of Trotsky's planned exposé on Stalin, a publication Moscow was determined to prevent. Together, this steady stream of intelligence enabled the GPU to refine the timing of its attack and adapt its operations in response to developments inside the compound.

Intercepting written correspondence was only part of the GPU's broader surveillance strategy. Equally important were Trotsky's real-time conversations—especially those with James Cannon, who often discussed security logistics and funding by phone. To capture this valuable stream of intelligence, GPU handlers turned to wiretaps. These gave Moscow immediate access to confidential discussions that might never be recorded in writing. By monitoring Cannon's private line, the GPU hoped to uncover not only plans and vulnerabilities at the villa but also the timing and scope of financial support critical to maintaining Trotsky's protective perimeter.

James Cannon worked from a seventh-floor apartment at 126 West 11th Street, and Rabinowitz arranged a wiretap on his home phone through GPU technician Joseph Katz, who posed as a repairman. Skilled in surveillance and deception, Katz accessed the junction box atop a nearby pole and ran a line into an apartment where Floyd Cleveland Miller, cover name HELL, monitored the call logs. The wiretap lasted about a year, with calls recorded on wax cylinders. Miller later joined the SWP and contributed to its publications under the alias Michael Cort.[8]

Although they could monitor Cannon's conversations, Eitingon also needed intelligence on the villa's guards. Hoping for similar access to Trotsky's own telephone line, the GPU leveraged PCM operatives inside the Mexican Telephone and Telegraph Company to bug his phone.[9]

The PCM already had a number of supporters embedded in the large telephone company. In early 1937, PCM agents sabotaged a live phone speech Trotsky attempted to deliver to a large assembled crowd at New York's Hippodrome.[10] The connection cut out seconds after he began, and though technicians scrambled to fix it, silence followed. Shachtman read the prepared text aloud instead.

The botched address triggered the formation of the Dewey Commission two months later.[11]

Tapping the Old Man's phone line was much simpler than the Hippodrome operation. By 1940, the GPU established a safe house near the villa that served as a listening post for a tap on Trotsky's line, installed by an agent dispatched from New York.[12]

For Operation KON to succeed, the villa's five-man Mexican police contingent, located outside the villa, needed to be quietly neutralized. Somehow they needed to be bribed, sedated, or restrained during the raid—and without suffering any fatalities that could turn public opinion against the raiders. Identifying which guards were lax or inattentive became essential. Fortunately, Sheldon Harte (AMUR), the GPU's first foothold inside Trotsky's entourage since Maria de la Sierra's 1938 recall, began providing the needed information.

The Shirley Courts Hideout

Without Sylvia around, Jacson* moved from his apartment into the Shirley Courts Motor Hotel on April 11,[13] located at 151 Calzada Manuel Villalongín—and just nine blocks from Eitingon's safe house at the apartment of Spanish emigrant Marta Meller. There he set up his operating base and stored documents, money, and their operational plans.[14]

Shirley Courts was a modern motor court catering to affluent and adventurous American travelers who traveled to Mexico City by automobile. It offered sanitized American food and car services that were essential for coping with the largely unimproved Mexican roads and inevitable breakdowns. Jacson* posed as a Canadian road engineer delayed by rainstorms on the Chiapas highway. He used his room as a GPU safe house until June 12.[15]

The hotel's owner, James Shirley, later told Colonel Salazar that the Canadian guest (Frank Jacson*) received frequent calls, including from a woman with a Russian accent—likely Caridad. He noted Jacson's* guarded demeanor, always facing the door while using the public phone and hosting visitors only in the garden where he could position himself to observe the entrances.[16]

32. Shirley Courts was a popular stop for American tourists bold enough to undertake the drive to Mexico City.

Jacson* had other habits that raised Shirley's suspicions. Each time Frank* returned from a countryside trip, his Buick was caked in dust, but his odometer showed no changes—he had disconnected it for each trip. He explained this was to preserve the mileage for resale.

Upon checking in, Jacson* left a trunk and two suitcases—each heavy, especially the trunk—locked in the hotel's storage room. He claimed they contained engineering tools. But on the night of May 23, he moved them to his Buick and drove off. Shirley and Colonel Salazar later suspected the luggage held the weapons used in the attack on Trotsky's villa.[17]

All of the elements needed for the forthcoming attack were moving into place: maps, weapons, blueprints, betrayals. What the GPU could not obtain through bribery or seduction, it had extracted through wiretaps and whispers. The villa would not be stormed—it would be opened from within. Operation KON was no longer just a plan. It was a date, a team, a house with a gate about to swing open. The final act was no longer in Moscow's hands. It would begin in Coyoacán—with the guards asleep, the assassin watching, and the door unlatched from the inside.

CHAPTER XIV

ASSASSINS AT THE GATES

Operation KON Begins

"For more than three years, we have been waiting, with sure knowledge, for the assassins."
—Natalia Sedova [Trotsky], May 24, 1940

"It was not a raid—it was a message, written in gunfire, and signed by Stalin."
—Joseph Hansen

"Assassination is the final argument of the bankrupt regime."
—Leon Trotsky, 1937

The Raid Begins

The assassins came at four in the morning, beneath the black sky of Coyoacán. For Leon Trotsky and Natalia, it was the end of years of vigilance—and the moment Stalin's death sentence was to be delivered. The group of about twenty-five men—many of them veterans of the International Brigades from the Spanish Civil War—were dressed in a mixture of police and military uniforms. After disabling the drowsy, intoxicated police guards outside the compound and passing through the unlocked gates, the attackers silently infiltrated the grounds of Leon Trotsky's fortified villa on Avenida Viena in Mexico City on May 24, 1940. The assailants, now acting under the command of the GPU, displayed intimate knowledge of the compound and its defenses. They

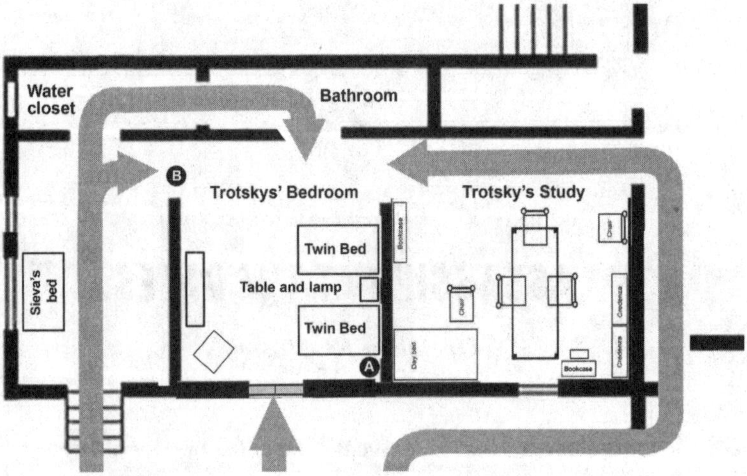

The killers fired into Trotsky's bedroom from four directions in the early hours of May 24, 1940.
Ⓐ Trotskys' hiding place Ⓑ Siquerios fired the *coup de grâce*

33.

cut the main telephone line and disabled the alarm system linking the villa to the Coyoacán police station.[1]

Once inside, they waited until the raiders were all in place and unleashed automatic gunfire into the guards' quarters and bedroom where Trotsky and his wife, Natalia, were sleeping. (See diagram for the attack plan.) Their goal was a swift assassination without resistance. During the raid, the only guard on duty, a young American named Sheldon Harte, disappeared.[2] His body was discovered weeks later in a shallow grave treated with lime, evidence of a premeditated execution.[3]

At first, Trotsky mistook the distant noise for celebratory fireworks, which are common in Coyoacán's town square.[4] But the acrid smell of gunpowder and the closeness of the explosions quickly shattered that illusion. He realized that the long-expected attack had finally arrived—an event he had anticipated during twelve years of exile. Disoriented but alert, he questioned how the attackers had breached the villa's defenses. Why had the alarm not sounded? Where was Harte? Had he been taken or killed? Where were his guards? Had the Mexican police been overpowered—or worse, were they complicit?

34.

Gunfire tore through the walls and ceilings—into Trotsky's study, Sieva's room, the courtyard, and even the bathroom.[5] He and Natalia first dove beneath their beds, then crawled to the southeast corner of the room—the only blind spot in the crossfire. It was a narrow refuge, offering their only sliver of protection. (See diagrams.)

Then, from his grandson's doorway, an attacker tossed an incendiary device and stepped briefly into view. Illuminated by the blaze, Natalia saw his silhouette as he scanned the room, then fired from the door directly into the bedding on both twin beds.[6] The gunman, likely mistaking the covered shapes for corpses, rather than entering to confirm the kill with shots at close range, withdrew—convinced the Old Man was already dead.[7]

Trotsky remained silent throughout the assault. His pistol was nearby but useless against the volume of fire pouring into their bedroom. Choosing not to return fire might have helped conceal their position and saved their lives. Outside, his guards had been trapped in their quarters, outgunned, and disoriented. Minutes passed with no sign of help.

The attacker in Sieva's doorway fired one final round into Sieva's empty bed before withdrawing. Unknown to him, the boy had already rolled beneath it, though the shot struck him in the toe.[8] Believing his

35. Raiders left three unexploded improvised incendiary devices in the courtyard outside the Trotskys' bedroom.

grandparents were dead, Sieva fled in panic through the courtyard to the library, leaving a trail of blood.

As the shooting ended, Trotsky and Natalia emerged slowly to assess the damage. Bullet holes riddled the walls, glass littered the floors, and fires smoldered in several rooms. Yet against all odds, everyone in the villa had survived—except for Sheldon Harte, who was missing. Among the courtyard debris, three unexploded incendiary bombs were later recovered.[9] Their presence confirmed the assailants' intent: not just assassination, but total destruction.[10]

An illustration shows the compound's exterior defenses along the southern wall. The attackers had entered through the southwest garage gate—the only point of access to the villa—without firing a shot.

The Investigation

Before the smoke cleared from Trotsky's villa, Colonel Leandro Sánchez Salazar was already on his way.[11] He wasn't just responding to a crime—he was walking into a war zone shaped by foreign ideolo-

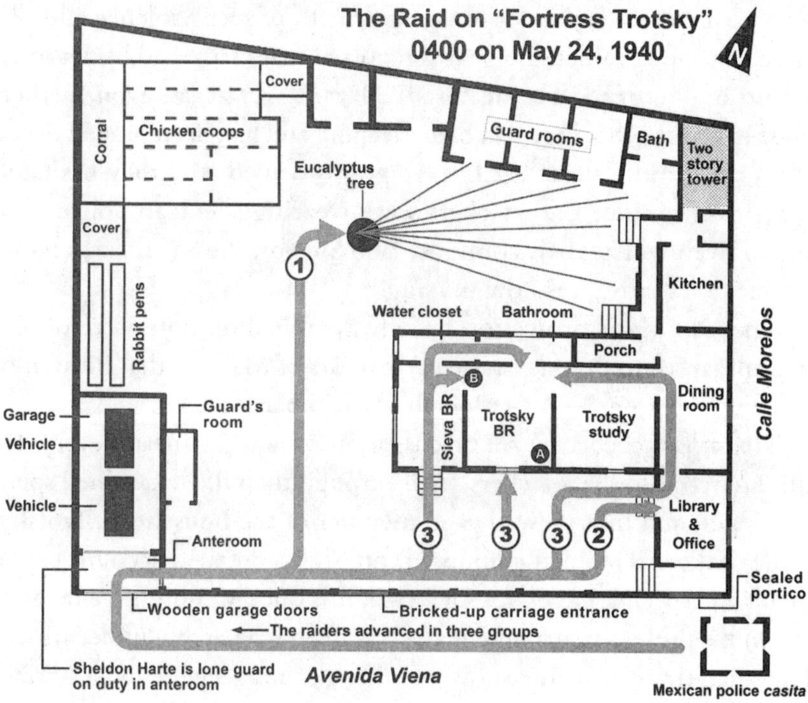

At 0400 on the morning of 24 May 1940 the 25 raiders advanced in three groups:
Group One: Blocking group with a submachine gun to pin down the guards,
Group Two: Sabotage group to destroy Trotsky's archive and the Stalin manuscript,
Group Three: Killing teams asaulted the Old Man's bedroom from four directions
Ⓐ Leon and Natalia huddled in the South East corner of the room
Ⓑ Siqueiros fires into the beds before the raiders withdraw.

36.

gies, ruthless ambition, and a campaign of shadows. Salazar, a man of reason and order, had been appointed precisely because he was neither a Communist nor a Trotskyist. But the scene that awaited him was something different altogether: seventy-three bullet holes in the bedroom, silence where there should have been resistance, and a target who had somehow survived the full force of Stalin's will. Salazar wasn't only hunting gunmen—he was chasing the truth through a maze of deception—and what he found would alter Mexico's role in the global war of shadows.

As Colonel Salazar began his inquiry, he was struck by the Old

Man's composed demeanor in the aftermath of such violence and became suspicious. When the guards reported that Harte had been armed but no one returned fire, it raised Salazar's skepticism even further. They explained that they had been sleeping and had been pinned down when the gunfire started. All were poorly armed, and they hesitated to return fire since the attackers were wearing Mexican police uniforms. Even worse, their comrade, Bob Shields, the SWP party name for Sheldon Harte, was now missing.[12]

The Old Man's protection had always relied on limited resources and uneasy assumptions. In the early hours of May 24, that illusion of safety was shattered—his vulnerability laid bare.

Salazar launched a formal investigation, skeptical of nearly every detail. He retraced the attackers' path through the villa, examined spent cartridges, and interviewed each member of the household. Trotsky, while shaken, remained composed, offering a detailed account of the assault and speculating on its Soviet origins. But the confidence he once had in his protective arrangements had been irreparably undermined. The villa, thought secure, now stood as a crime scene—and a symbol of how close the assassins had come to success.

Colonel Salazar was taken aback by Trotsky's immediate claim that Stalin and the GPU were behind the attack—a charge that only deepened the colonel's skepticism.[13] If professional Soviet assassins had truly carried out the assault, he reasoned, why had they failed to kill the unarmed couple before withdrawing? The raid's effectiveness and ease in penetrating the villa stood in contrast to its ultimate failure, a contradiction that fueled Salazar's doubts and cast a shadow over Trotsky's account.

Further confusion emerged from the testimony of the two Mexican policemen found bound in the casita at the southeast corner of the building. They claimed that Sheldon Harte had not been abducted but had left voluntarily with the attackers, using the household's own vehicles.[14] Though Harte had only been with the household for seven weeks, he had earned the trust to serve overnight guard duty—indicating his perceived loyalty and dependability. Trotsky, however, immediately rejected any suggestion of betrayal. He insisted that Harte had been kidnapped and murdered, though persuading Mexican officials of this proved difficult.

37. The raiders burned files in the office hoping to destroy the manuscript of Trotsky's upcoming biography of Joseph Stalin.

The Attack Plan

Regardless of how the attackers entered the villa without raising an alarm, their actions reflected detailed planning and disciplined execution. The raiders had divided into three teams, each assigned to a specific section of the villa—further evidence of a carefully coordinated operation. (See diagram.)

The raiders' plan of attack called for the three groups to move into place silently and await the signal to begin firing. The raiders split into three main groups:

Blocking Force (1): Positioned behind a eucalyptus tree on the north wall, this group established a machine-gun position and unleashed a fusillade of gunfire to suppress and pin down the minimally armed guards. This group effectively thwarted any attempts at resistance and isolated Trotsky from his rescuers.

38. Chief guard Harold Robins checking credentials at the wooden front gates hours after the May 24 assault.

Incendiary Team (2): Advanced towards the library, wielding incendiary bombs to destroy the Old Man's manuscript of the forthcoming biography of Stalin and his valuable archive.

Assassins (3): Divided into four teams, each moved to flank the bedroom: through Sieva's room, the bathroom, the courtyard, and the study.

The first group behind the eucalyptus tree opened fire on the left-hand side of the house, spraying machine-gun slugs into the doorways of the rooms where the guards off shift were sleeping. The gunfire lasted three to five minutes, and more than three hundred rounds were fired.[15] The poorly armed guards had been caught by surprise and were unable to come to Trotsky's defense.

Escape and Fallout

In the aftermath of the onslaught, as the raiders retreated into the night, they absconded with both of the compound's automobiles[16]—a Ford typically used for transporting supplies and a Dodge. In their wake, they left behind a disturbing array of tools: an electric saw, scaling ladders, rope ladders, drills, a defective bomb with enough dynamite to obliterate the entire house, several unused incendiary bombs, and one incendiary bomb that had shattered on a lawn, scorching the grass.[17] A third incendiary bomb ignited at the entrance to Sieva's room, prompting Natalia to quell the flames with blankets, causing burns on her arm and leg.

The Ford had stalled a short distance away, while the Dodge was later abandoned in one of the upscale districts of Mexico City.[18]

The abandoned tools, along with the telltale remnants of police uniforms used as disguises, served as damning evidence of a meticulously orchestrated plot, crafted by seasoned professionals. Scaling ladders, electric saws, and drills bore witness to the assailants' intent to breach the compound's defenses with ruthless efficiency if Harte had not allowed them to enter the villa quietly through the garage gates.[19]

The failed assassination, splashed across headlines worldwide, ignited a storm of speculation, outrage, and fear. For Trotsky, it was not just a narrow escape—it was a grim confirmation that Stalin's reach was unbroken. The household tightened its defenses, yet the Old Man grasped a harsher reality: the next blow would not arrive as midnight gunfire but as a silent betrayal—quite possibly from someone already inside the gates.

And as Trotsky braced for what lay ahead, Stalin's assassins scattered into the shadows, scrambling to escape Mexico City—and the police now hunting them.

CHAPTER XV

ON THE RUN

Stalin's Assassins Vanish

"The hardest part of an assassination is
not the kill. It's the getaway."
—Pavel Sudoplatov

"A single loose end could unravel the whole thread."
—GPU operational maxim

"In a country of shadows, even traitors disappear like smoke."
—Colonel Salazar's case file, 1940

At dawn on May 24, 1940, the acrid smoke from the failed assault on Trotsky's villa still hung in the air. Stalin's gunmen had missed their mark, and panic spread through the shadows of Mexico City. Trotsky had survived, and the GPU's hand had been shown. For Nahum Eitingon (TOM), the next hours were a desperate race against time. The chain of command stretched all the way to the Kremlin—he had to minimize the fallout while he could. That meant extracting deep-cover illegals, eliminating liabilities, and preserving the next phase of the plan.

Damage Control

By midmorning, receiving confirmation of the failure, Eitingon turned to damage control. His priorities were threefold: (1) composing a ciphered radio message to Sudoplatov and Beria in Moscow explaining the disaster, (2) ensuring Joseph Grigulevich escaped before authorities identified him, and (3) safeguarding the integrity of Operation MAT, which depended on protecting Caridad and the still-covert future assassin, Ramón Mercader.

Grigulevich's Escape

Joseph Grigulevich (PADRE or FELIPE), the chief planner of the KON assault, had taken part in the May 24 attack himself. He also suspected—correctly—that the Mexican police guards bound near the entrance gates had seen and recognized him. Investigators didn't yet know his name, but they had his description. Colonel Salazar began referring to him as "the French Jew" and launched a citywide manhunt.[1] Levine, writing in 1959, correctly identified his importance and labeled him the "shadowy chief of the operation."[2] Grigulevich's identity was so well protected that it remained secret for over fifty years—until Pavel Sudoplatov finally exposed him in his post-Soviet memoir.[3]

The Zook Safe House

To avoid compromising Operation MAT, or the separate illegal network in New Mexico, Nahum Eitingon ordered Grigulevich (PADRE) to leave Mexico City at once. He fled north to the border—more than 1,200 miles—and then to Santa Fe, New Mexico, arriving in June. Months earlier, the GPU had quietly established a safe house inside Zook's Pharmacy, managed by the possibly unsuspecting Katherine "Katie" Zook.[4]

Zook's Pharmacy at 56 San Francisco Street in Santa Fe offered ideal conditions for clandestine work: steady foot traffic, a discreet rear exit, and a courtyard opening behind what is now Café Pasqual's. Its unmarked back door blended into the adobe alleys of the old quarter—perfect camouflage for GPU operations.[5]

Intelligence sources later concluded that Zook's Pharmacy was

39. The GPU purchased Zook's Pharmacy in Santa Fe for use as a safe house.

identified in 1939 through Grigulevich's family connections in the pharmaceutical trade and purportedly acquired with the help of GPU courier Kitty Harris (AIDA).[6] By then, John Zook, a Lithuanian-American pharmacist, had retired, leaving the business in the hands of his thirty-three-year-old daughter, Katie—a poised, cosmopolitan woman well-known in Santa Fe society.

Seduction as Tradecraft

In Santa Fe, Grigulevich used the alias of Manuel Francis Rodriguez, a twenty-seven-year-old historian gathering material for a forthcoming book on Latin American history.[7] His cover was plausible: Joseph was a skilled writer who would later publish several volumes under his own name, and his family background in pharmacy gave him an air of professional familiarity.[8] How these skills enabled his quiet takeover

40. Joseph Grigulevich was reputed to be adept with women.

of Zook's as a GPU safe house—before and after the failed May 24, 1940, assault on Trotsky's villa (Operation KON)—remains unclear.[9]

Historian E. B. Held, an experienced CIA operations officer, has privately advanced a theory that Katie Zook was no accidental acquaintance but the carefully chosen target of a practiced seducer. According to Held, Grigulevich possibly recruited her on one of her overseas trips through a calculated blend of romance and manipulation. He was charming, articulate, and confident, and considered to be a ladies' man—and a skilled recruiter who understood the use of seduction as a tool of tradecraft. Held described Katie as tall, self-assured, and stylish, her long braids often coiled beneath one of her signature hats.[10] Through sustained flattery, attention, and controlled intimacy, he could blur emotional and physical boundaries until loyalty, or dependence, took hold.

Held goes further, proposing that the Santa Fe safe house was not managed by the GPU courier Kitty Harris but by Katie Zook instead.[11] Although no surviving documents confirm Katie's knowing involvement in the safe house operation, Held's hypothesis offers a plausible explanation for why the GPU continued to use the pharmacy even after Grigulevich left in 1941: Katie and her mother retained ownership of Zook's Pharmacy until at least the mid-1960s.

Aftermath

According to Sudoplatov, Zook's Pharmacy continued to serve Soviet intelligence for years afterward, allegedly under the direction of Kitty Harris, even aiding atomic espionage operations during the war. However, Sudoplatov also wrote that when Grigulevich left Santa Fe and the United States in 1941, he transferred the ownership of the pharmacy "to one of his agents" and that "it was simply good luck that a previous mission left us with a safe house in Santa Fe."[12] Since Katie Zook was the owner of the shop until 1965, Sudoplatov's autobiography appears to be confirming Held's theory that Katie Zook's role may have been much greater than is known!

Held's theory remains, for now, the only one that plausibly explains the GPU's continued use of the site operated by Katie rather than Kitty—perhaps even accounting for confusion arising from the similarity of their names. Katie Zook's involvement—whether as a witting accomplice, recruited agent, manipulated lover, or unwitting pawn—remains one of the most intriguing unresolved mysteries in the GPU's long pursuit of Leon Trotsky.

Grigulevich left Santa Fe in 1941, though the date and route of his return to Moscow remain unknown. Historian E. P. Sharapov notes that PADRE reappeared in Moscow that June and was soon awarded the Order of the Red Star for his role in the assassination of Leon Trotsky.[13]

Siqueiros's Evasion and Capture

Trotsky wasted no time naming "Stalin's gangsters"—and he put David Alfaro Siqueiros at the top of the list.[14] The press scoffed, but Colonel Leandro Sánchez Salazar soon verified Trotsky's suspicion. On June 17, police arrested two dozen conspirators and publicly declared Siqueiros the ringleader.[15] By then, the muralist had already vanished.

41. Siqueiros disguised as a farmer under the name of Macario Huízar in October 1940.

According to his biographer, Philip Stein, Siqueiros continued painting for several days after the May 24 assault before slipping underground.[16] It was a prudent move: Trotsky mentioned his name to investigators exactly one week after the attack.[17] Rumors multiplied, and Salazar launched a national manhunt for the famous muralist.

The first solid lead came from Mexico City's train station. Witnesses reported that Siqueiros's wife, Angélica Arenal, carrying two valises, had boarded a train for Guadalajara. State investigators confirmed that on June 2, 1940, Siqueiros passed through the city on his way to Hostotipaquillo, a mining region in the Sierra Madre foothills where he had organized labor fifteen years earlier and could expect fierce loyalty.[18]

There Angélica joined him. The couple adopted peasant clothing, false names, and a rhythm of constant movement—sleeping in miners' homes, at a municipal secretary's house, and in the high country above the town, often reached on horseback.[19] From time to time, Angélica slipped back into Mexico City, disguised as a campesina (female peasant), posting Siqueiros's letters to sympathetic newspapers—letters that tried to recast the assault as retaliation for Trotsky's alleged betrayal of the Spanish Republic. Salazar, however, quickly realized the Mexico City postmarks were only a ruse.[20]

Meanwhile, Moscow's political machinery worked to distance the Kremlin from the failed raid. Comintern and PCM representatives advanced the false claim that the assault was a staged "self-attack" inside Trotsky's home.[21] The PCM reinforced the line in the *El Nacional*

42. Following his capture, Siqueiros (seated right) posed for this photo with General Núñez (seated center) and Colonel Salazar (seated left).

newspaper, branding the raiders "uncontrollable elements" whose actions violated proletarian norms and had "nothing to do with us."[22]

Yet the longer Siqueiros evaded capture, the more his image changed. Segments of the public began to cast him not as a criminal but as a renegade revolutionary. Each police bulletin and narrow escape fed the legend.

Hidden in the Hostotipaquillo sierra under the names Macario and Eusebita, he and Angélica were sheltered by locals who treated them as honored fugitives—taking from their own meals so the couple could eat better.[23] In later accounts, the pair acquired a cinematic aura, their disguises and cave hideouts echoing the outlaw couples of Mexican film culture.[24] The networks that protected them were not GPU constructs but ties of loyalty—miners and officials who remembered Siqueiros from earlier battles.

Trotsky's assassination on August 20 temporarily shifted Salazar's priorities, but once the case of the attack was solved, he returned to the hunt. On September 25, acting on new intelligence, he vowed not to leave Jalisco until Siqueiros was found.[25] Disguised as peddlers and guided by a local priest, Salazar's investigators finally traced the fugitives to a remote farm near San Blasito. They arrested Siqueiros in the brush near the home—exhausted, unarmed, unresisting.

According to Siqueiros's account, federal troops honored him at the moment of his capture. Furthermore, he recounted that Salazar is said to have addressed his men, praising Siqueiros as a veteran of the revolution and a "great painter and glory of the nation" before local officials hosted a banquet in his honor at the municipal palace.[26] By then, he had become—at least in the public imagination—a revolutionary artist turned guerrilla whose flight from justice seemed an extension of the spirit he had once painted on walls.

The return to Mexico City, however, broke the spell. Siqueiros was charged with murder, weapons violations, impersonating military personnel, and related crimes. While imprisoned, he received visits from Pablo Neruda, the Chilean poet, diplomat, and political figure who attempted unsuccessfully to secure his release through diplomatic channels. Before the judge, Siqueiros admitted his role in the raid but framed it as revolutionary justice. Despite Natalia Sedova's objections, the judge dropped the most serious charges. After five months, Siqueiros posted bail and left for Chile—where he resumed painting, completing his famous mural, *Death to the Invader*, a title now sharpened by irony.

Colonel Sánchez Salazar sensed it before anyone else. From the first moments of his investigation, he became convinced that the attack on Trotsky could not have been mounted without help from within. If the GPU had reached the gates once, he reasoned, they might already be past them now.

The failed raid was over. Operation KON had ended. Operation MAT had begun.

And as Salazar turned inward—toward the villa, toward the guards, toward the possibility of a traitor—the hunt for the mole was about to start.

CHAPTER XVI

INSIDE JOB

The Mole Hunt

"They [the GPU] missed. They missed everything. And that, more than the bullets, is what terrified me."

—Leon Trotsky, reflecting on the May 24, 1940, assault

"The aim was not only to kill Trotsky, but to kill the idea of resistance."

—Colonel Leandro Sánchez Salazar (reflecting years later)

"The greatest danger is not the enemy at the wall, but the friend with the key."

—Mexican investigative proverb, attributed to Colonel Leandro Sánchez Salazar

The Crime Scene

Trotsky was still in his bathrobe when Colonel Leandro Sánchez Salazar began questioning him—less than an hour after the attack. What struck Salazar immediately was Trotsky's composure. Most victims he had interviewed after violent assaults were dazed or in shock. Trotsky, by contrast, was controlled, precise, already thinking like an analyst rather than a survivor.[1]

The guards, too, seemed strangely calm. Their answers came measured, almost rehearsed. For men who had just endured a near-fatal assault, their demeanor did not match the chaos still visible around them.[2]

To both investigators and the press, Trotsky was unequivocal: the raid had been orchestrated by Stalin and executed by elite GPU operatives.[3] May Day demonstrators in Mexico City had marched with banners reading "¡Trotsky debe morir!"—"Trotsky must die!"—and to Trotsky the assault on his villa was simply the logical next step. Any attempt to explore alternative theories, he told Salazar, was a diversion from the real culprits in Moscow and their allies in the Mexican Communist Party.[4]

Inside the bedroom, Salazar's team counted seventy-three bullet holes in the walls, furniture, and doors—including two that ripped through the very bed where Trotsky had been lying.[5] Trotsky later insisted that an analysis of the trajectories proved at least eight shots could only have been fired from inside the room.[6]

Natalia, crouched with him in the southeast corner of the bedroom, remembered a brief, surreal glimpse. In the glare of an incendiary bomb thrown onto the threshold between their room and their grandson's, she saw "the curve of a helmet, shining buttons, and an elongated face that flashed by me as in a dream."[7]

And yet improbably, this Chaplinesque gunman—major's uniform, dark glasses, false moustache, caught in the flare of his own incendiary explosion—missed both targets at point-blank range.[8]

The beds were shredded. The plaster was chipped and pocked. But how could the Old Man and Natalia have survived?

The Geometry of Survival

The original twin beds made it possible for the Trotskys to conceal themselves in the southeast corner of the bedroom. Those bullet-riddled beds were replaced soon after the attack with a single double bed that remains in place today. Viewed from the doorway to Sieva's bedroom, the twin-bed arrangement created both visual and physical concealment from the gunman's line of sight—a geometry the present-day configuration no longer conveys.

43 and 44. The Trotskys originally slept in twin beds, which were destroyed during the May 24 raid and later replaced by the double bed seen today. The twin-bed arrangement had partially shielded the couple in the corner from the assassin's view—protection the later double bed would not have provided.

Questions Without Answers

What most puzzled Salazar was not the violence of the attack, but its failure. "So many attackers, so many firearms, even bombs, and nothing happened to them [the Trotskys]!" he wrote later. "All that is very strange!"[9] Trotsky and Natalia had been utterly defenseless—no more than twenty-five paces from the garage where, Salazar believed, the "real instigator" of the attack, "the French Jew," remained in the company of guard Sheldon Harte.[10]

The guards were pinned down or immobilized. The alarm system was dead. The police posted at the nearby casita had been bound and gagged. If, as Trotsky insisted, this was a professional GPU operation, why had the raiders abandoned the villa with their primary target still breathing?

Evidence outside the walls deepened the mystery. Investigators found Trotsky's Ford stuck in the mud along the Río Churubusco near Avenida Viena, surrounded by discarded tools and gear for scaling the villa's perimeter.[11] If Harte had not opened the gate, the equipment suggested, the attackers were prepared to go over the wall.

A second car, a Dodge, was discovered abandoned in Colonia Roma. Inside were civilian clothes made to resemble police uniforms, leather belts, film cartridges, and an axe. Police impounded both vehicles, leaving the Rosmers—Trotsky's houseguests—without transportation for Alfred's hospital visits.

Frank Jacson*, always alert for openings and opportunities, quickly offered the use of his own car to the villa. The gesture allowed him to present himself as a helpful friend to the household and guards. The visits that followed allowed Jacson* to better understand the routines of the besieged household.

Theories and Misdirection

In the days after the assault, explanations multiplied faster than hard facts.

Former Mexican ambassador to France Narciso Bassols suggested that Trotsky himself had orchestrated the attack—a staged provocation meant to discredit the Communist Party.[12] The PCM, not to be outdone in creativity, claimed the raid had been arranged by the anti-Communist Dies Committee in the US Congress to embarrass Moscow.[13]

Trotsky rejected these theories outright. For him, the line ran straight from the Kremlin to Coyoacán: Stalin's police, Stalin's agents, Stalin's orders. Salazar, however, could not ignore the internal contradictions—nor the strange behavior of those who were supposed to protect the Old Man.

Origins of the Raid

The roots of the May 24 assault reached back to the Spanish Civil War. Joseph Grigulevich, a veteran of Soviet operations in Spain, arrived in Mexico City in the spring of 1938 with orders to penetrate Trotsky's defenses. After Operation UTKA was launched in the summer of 1939 and key agents were being maneuvered into position in Mexico, FELIPE was abruptly summoned to Moscow.

In the climate of the Great Terror, recall often amounted to a death sentence. Yet Grigulevich returned and survived. He impressed his superiors with "his detailed knowledge of the Mexican terrain and of Trotsky's situation on Avenida Viena" and presented a plan to storm the villa directly.[14]

GPU chief Lavrentiy Beria approved the proposal and, according to historian Bertrand Patenaude, urged that Siqueiros be named to lead the fighting group.[15] Grigulevich returned to Mexico City in February 1940 and met with Nahum Eitingon to coordinate the operational details of what would become Operation KON.[16]

By the time Salazar walked the bullet-scarred hallways of Trotsky's home, the colonel did not yet know the full story. But he could see the results. The assault might have failed to kill its target, yet it bore all the hallmarks of a Soviet operation tested in the crucible of Spain.

Under Suspicion: Guards and Staff

From the beginning, the behavior of the guards nagged at Salazar. Had the attackers been stopped in a gun battle outside the walls, local police might have arrived in time. Instead, the intruders slipped into the courtyard, confirmed that the alarms were off and the phone lines were cut, took up positions, and opened fire—catching the defenders completely by surprise.

At about four in the morning, Chief of Guards Harold Robins saw a man in a police uniform near the large eucalyptus tree, a protected and commanding position in the courtyard. A submachine gun opened up from behind it. "Keep your heads down and you won't get hurt," a voice called in accented English.[17] Some later believed the gunman was Leopoldo Arenal, Siqueiros's brother-in-law, though Salazar's notes point instead to Antonio Pujol as the man carrying the submachine gun in the lead-up to the attack.[18] American guards, for their part, claimed the voice did not belong to anyone they knew.[19]

Guard Charles Cornell, jolted awake by the gunfire, scrambled for his weapon—then remembered he had lent it to Robins. When he peered out into the courtyard, Robins shouted, "Put your head down, Charles!" Though armed, Robins never returned fire. Later he claimed to have fired once and missed.[20] New guard Jake Cooper opened his door, was greeted immediately by bullets, and wisely stayed inside.

Why had none of the guards engaged the attackers with gunfire? Some later argued that they feared killing someone who might be a Mexican policeman. Others blamed Joseph Hansen for supplying the wrong ammunition.[21] Robins himself claimed their weapons jammed and that the guards had received little training.[22]

In 1975, the International Committee of the Fourth International revealed that Hansen had been in contact with the FBI through the American consul in Mexico City and had allegedly "played along with the GPU" when they attempted to recruit him earlier. Robins and others concluded from this that Hansen had been a GPU agent, though some historians maintain that he remained loyal to Trotsky until the end.[23] Hansen's defenders argue that if he had truly been working for the GPU with the intention of eliminating Trotsky, his proximity to the Old Man would have afforded far simpler opportunities than the complex and risky assault embodied in Operation KON.

Salazar's suspicions extended beyond the guards. On May 26, he had the Mexican cook, Carmen Palma, and the maid, Belén Estrada, arrested and sent to El Pocito Prison, a grim detention facility on the outskirts of Mexico City.[24] The name—El Pocito, "the little well" or "pit"—captured its nature: a dark, airless holding site where suspects in the May 24 case were crammed into windowless, damp cells lit by a single bulb that burned day and night. Political prisoners, Communists, and petty criminals were kept side by side in conditions designed to break resistance.[25]

Under interrogation, Palma said she had seen guard Otto Schüssler with a revolver during the attack, though he never fired. Both she and Estrada remarked how nervous Schüssler and Cornell had seemed before and after the raid. They came to suspect that the attack had been staged or at least anticipated.[26]

Trotsky was furious. He insisted to Salazar that the line of investigation was misdirected: the real culprits were GPU operatives such as Siqueiros, not his loyal household staff. President Lázaro Cárdenas ultimately agreed. He ordered Palma and Estrada released and instructed Salazar to apologize.[27]

Trotsky also defended the guards' anxiety as natural under constant threat. Yet even his own recollections implicated one of them. Around 5:00 p.m. on May 23, guard Sheldon Harte had asked for the key to the alarm system. The villa's security network, wired with contact sensors, triggered both a bell and a pinpoint light on the control panel if breached.[28] Salazar later wrote mistakenly that the alarm ran to the "guard tower." However, the command tower in the southeast corner was not built until after the raid. In May 1940, the alarm was still monitored from the small guardroom alongside the garage in the southwest corner of the villa.[29]

When investigators examined the alarm system after the raid, it was switched off, and the phone lines were severed.[30] Harte had been the last person known to access the controls.[31] Either he had made a catastrophic mistake—or he had sabotaged the system deliberately.

Salazar's eye also fell on Diego Rivera's abrupt departure for San Francisco after the assault. Some believed Rivera feared GPU retaliation for sheltering Trotsky three years earlier; others argued he was chasing publicity—and commissions—for paintings and a mural project in the United States.[32] Rivera's exit added another layer of unease but did not resolve the central question.

Though he had flirted with the idea that Trotsky might have staged the raid, Salazar eventually abandoned that theory. Someone inside the orbit of the villa had clearly helped the raiders. Harte remained the prime suspect, but without hard proof—and with the guards fearing any hint of a leak to the GPU—the truth stayed just beyond his reach.

Breaking the Illusion of Safety

As arrests mounted and surveillance tightened on suspected raiders, a pattern emerged that confirmed what Trotsky had claimed from the first hour. Many of the attackers had served in the International Brigades during the Spanish Civil War. Their paths intersected with Siqueiros, and others whose loyalties were not to Mexico, but to Moscow.[33]

The raid, Salazar concluded, had been conceived, coordinated, and sanctioned by Stalin's secret police. It was more than an act of violence. It was a projection of power. The bullets fired into the adobe walls of the Coyoacán villa were intended not only to kill one man, but to silence a symbol of resistance.

For Salazar, the investigation turned into a slow dismantling of the illusion that Trotsky's sanctuary had ever truly been safe. What began as a straightforward criminal inquiry became something darker and more complex: an autopsy of a breached fortress. The evidence pointed in two directions at once—toward the GPU operatives who planned the assault and toward the possibility that the assassin's path had been cleared from within.

A Hint in a Bar

By early June, the case seemed stuck in a maze of half-truths and silences. Harte had vanished. The guards were defensive. The household was wary. The political stakes climbed with every new lead that pointed toward Soviet involvement.

And then, on June 17, in a modest bar far from the villa's high walls, Colonel Salazar overheard a fragment of conversation—just a few careless words, spoken over drinks—that changed everything.[34]

The breakthrough did not come through brilliant deduction or a dramatic confession. It arrived as a chance remark in a smoky room. The case did not slowly unravel. It snapped open.

The hunt for the mole was about to begin in earnest.

CHAPTER XVII

OPERATION CASA CHICAS

Sex, Lies, and the Road to Coyoacán

"I do not believe in mysteries. Only in unanswered questions."
—Colonel Sánchez Salazar, Chief of
Investigation, Mexico City

"The revolutionaries came with bullets, but it took a
policeman with a notebook to bring them down."
—Luis Arenal Bastar, a May 24 raider in custody

"It wasn't bullets or ideology that undid us. It was
tequila, women, and one loose tongue."
—Attributed to a PCM member
arrested after the May 24 raid

A Voice in the Crowd

For more than three weeks after the failed raid, the investigation had stalled—until a chance remark cracked it open. On June 17, 1940, Colonel Salazar was seated quietly in a bar near Luis Moya Street when he overheard a group of tramway workers discussing the attack on Trotsky's villa. One older, drunken worker in a greasy navy-blue suit declared loudly, "The police want to hush up the affair. They've got their reasons, but that's how it is." Salazar leaned closer. The man continued, claiming that a Tacubaya police magistrate, during a drunken boast, had admitted to supplying police uniforms for the raid.[1]

Salazar withdrew immediately and returned to headquarters. Acting on the overheard lead, he followed the trail to Captain Néstor Sánchez, a twenty-three-year-old law student and Spanish Civil War veteran living at 54 Avenida Guatemala.[2] Arrested two days later, Sánchez recognized Salazar from their military service in Oaxaca.

Under interrogation, Sánchez soon admitted he had been recruited by David Alfaro Siqueiros—motivated by loyalty to a comrade from the International Brigades and unaware of the full scope of the operation.[3] He identified Siqueiros as "the organizer and chief director" of the May 24 assault.[4] Sánchez also described secretive planning meetings and named painter Antonio Pujol as part of the hit team. Crucially, he revealed that Trotsky guard Sheldon Harte had been bribed by the "French Jew (Joseph Grigulevich)," suggesting a long-standing connection between Harte and the GPU.[5]

The Network Exposed

Sánchez's confession led to more than two dozen arrests among members and sympathizers of the Mexican Communist Party (PCM) and International Brigades. A clearer picture of the conspiracy emerged: Siqueiros—assisted by Luis and Leopoldo Arenal and Pujol—directed the raid,[6] while PCM Political Bureau member David Serrano managed a spy network in Coyoacán. This ring tracked the villa's layout, its recent fortifications, and the guards' rotations, providing essential timing information. With this intelligence in hand, Salazar imposed strict monitoring on all telephone lines connected to the case, beginning with Trotsky's own.[7]

Meanwhile, the PCM and Stalinist press scrambled to distance themselves from Siqueiros, branding him "mad," "undisciplined," and acting without party sanction.

The Weak Link: Trotsky's Guards

The raiders understood the operation depended on neutralizing the five Mexican policemen guarding Trotsky's residence. Among them,

45. Julie Barradas (left) and Ana López (right) with Mexican police guards they seduced for intelligence about Trotsky's villa.

Jesús Rodríguez Casas—sub-officer of the Seventeenth Company—was both competent and loyal.[8] When on duty, Casas ensured his men stayed sober, awake, and engaged. For Siqueiros and his handlers, the raid could only succeed on a night when Casas was absent—and that required intimate knowledge of the guards' schedules.

The GPU found its solution through seduction, alcohol, and engineered intimacy.

Casa Chicas (House of Chics): The Brothel with a Mission

In April 1940, one month before the raid, the conspirators rented a yellow two-story house at 85 Abasolo Street, just two blocks from Trotsky's villa.[9] There they built a covert brothel—Casa Chicas (House of Chics)—staffed not with the unreliable prostitutes of Calle de la

Soledad but with trusted party women whose political loyalty and discretion were unquestioned. Casa Chicas was designed to cultivate intimate access to Trotsky's guards, extract their schedules and weaknesses, and monitor the villa's daily routines.

Foremost among the recruits was Serrano's estranged wife, Julia Barradas—fearless, alluring, and deeply committed to Stalinism. She and Serrano were so devoted to the Soviet project that they named their daughter Sovietina.[10] She was joined by Ana López Chávez, lover of Siqueiros's associate Mariano Herrera, and another PCM loyalist. Their assignment was simple: charm, seduce, and extract whatever intelligence the party required.

Siqueiros personally supervised the brothel's progress daily, frequently arriving in his LaSalle sedan—behavior that attracted notice in the quiet neighborhood and jeopardized the entire operation, given Trotsky's compound was only a few blocks away.[11] Even so, Trotsky's American guards remained unaware of Casa Chicas until after the raid.

The women's efforts proved highly effective. Barradas, the most assertive, boasted openly of her sexual conquests.[12] One infatuated guard even gifted the women a photograph of the entire police detail—highly useful for identification. When Salazar's team raided the house after the failed attack, they discovered sketches of the villa, internal notes, and PCM documents tied directly to Julia scattered throughout the rooms.[13]

Author Isaac Don Levine later wrote that police also recovered a notebook in which Julia had recorded, "Trotsky was not to be killed, but because he stood in the way of the triumph of communism, his archives had to be stolen." This explanation may have been the same fabricated story used by Grigulevich to manipulate Harte into participating in the operation.[14]

On June 17, Barradas and López were arrested. Unlike the men, who broke quickly under interrogation, the women endured seventy-two hours without confessing. Salazar then changed tactics. He positioned Julia behind a door to listen and brought her husband, David Serrano, into the room. Salazar began questioning him about Julia's sexual skills and then listened as Serrano made a series of crude and hurtful remarks about her sexual behavior. Enraged, Julia burst out from behind the door, emotionally overwhelmed, and confessed everything. Ana López succumbed to psychological pressure and confessed also.[15]

The women revealed that in the early morning hours of May 24, they performed final reconnaissance at the villa and found the guards asleep or drunk at 2:00 a.m.—conditions ideal for the attack.[16]

Masquerade of Violence

Sánchez's full confession reconstructed the raid with striking detail. As rain fell over Coyoacán, the attackers assembled around 10:00 p.m. on Calle República de Cuba. Wearing stolen police and military uniforms and armed with submachine guns, revolvers, thermos bombs, and gloves, they joked among themselves as if preparing for a party. Around 2:00 a.m., Siqueiros returned in full army major regalia—sunglasses and a fake moustache included—and asked, "How do I look?" to laughter.[17]

The raiders loaded into vehicles, including Siqueiros's LaSalle, and moved toward Avenida Viena. At 4:00 a.m., shouting, "Viva Almazán!"[18] they quietly overpowered the Mexican guards, who were either drunk or sleeping in the casita. They then linked up with a second group positioned near the southwest corner by the wooden entrance gates.

When Sánchez expressed concern about being machine-gunned, Siqueiros smiled and replied, "There's no danger of that!"[19] Sánchez revealed that the guard at the gate, Sheldon Harte, had been compromised. "The attack occurred when he was on duty. He opened the door. The French Jew (Joseph Grigulevich) had bribed him. I remember—they were in the same car after the attack. Sheldon drove it when I exited."[20]

Once Harte opened the gates, roughly two dozen attackers rushed in. One team moved behind the eucalyptus tree to cover the guard quarters; another targeted the office and library; and a third, led by Siqueiros, forced entry into Sieva's bedroom, Trotsky's study, and the French windows leading into Trotsky's own room. The operation was underway.

Treachery Revealed

As the conspiracy unraveled, it became clear that the May 24 raid was not simply an attempted murder but a complex act of political warfare carried out on Mexican soil. Through Sánchez's confession, the arrest of Barradas and López, and the discovery of Casa Chicas, Salazar exposed an extensive Stalinist network operating through Mexico's political left. The plot stretched from a brothel in Coyoacán to the upper ranks of the PCM and ultimately to Moscow—just as Trotsky had warned Salazar on the morning of the attack.

For Trotsky, the raid was a warning. For Mexico, it was a revelation: Stalin's war against his enemies was no longer distant—it had arrived within their borders.

Salazar now turned to the deeper mystery: uncovering the mole inside Trotsky's villa. Dozens had been arrested, but one figure remained missing—the guard Sheldon Harte.

CHAPTER XVIII

PAWN OF STALIN

The Tragedy of Sheldon Harte

"I am absolutely sure that Robert Sheldon Harte remained faithful to his ideas . . . and to me in the end."
—Leon Trotsky

"One of Trotsky's guards [Harte] had been bought."
—David Alfaro Siqueiros

"In the world of espionage, loyalty is only a matter of timing."
—Soviet intelligence maxim

Arrival and Assignment

On May 31, Trotsky provided his official statement on the May 24 attack to the public prosecutor, writing that "the attempt could have been organized only by the Kremlin, by Stalin" and the "foreign section of the GPU." And, perhaps intuitively, Trotsky named David Alfaro Siqueiros as someone who knew the principal members of the GPU who had arrived from Spain and Paris.[1]

Journalists from around the globe descended on Mexico City as they competed for public attention. Amid the chaos and unanswered questions, one detail dominated the headlines: the sudden disappearance of Robert Sheldon Harte. His vanishing ignited a massive and unprecedented manhunt and thrust the young American into a storm of speculation, mythmaking, and manipulation. As hard facts proved elusive, rumor began to replace reporting.

At first, the GPU worked to shield Moscow from the May 24 attack by promoting the fiction that muralist David Siqueiros had acted alone—a rogue idealist driven by personal indignation rather than Soviet direction. The pro-Stalinist press quickly echoed the line. *El Popular*, Moscow's primary outlet in Latin America; *La Voz de México*, official organ of the Mexican Communist Party; and *Nacional*, the government newspaper heavily staffed with Communist editors and correspondents, published supportive narratives, severing any public ties with the muralist.[2]

The Manhunt for Harte and Siqueiros

When Trotsky's statement to the prosecutor was released naming Siqueiros, the muralist went on the run. As weeks passed and Siqueiros repeatedly escaped capture, his defiance began to resonate with the Mexican public, which loves to champion the underdog. Each narrow evasion burnished his reputation as a revolutionary outlaw, admired even by those who condemned his violence. Sensing this shift, the Communist Party and the pro-Soviet press reversed course—moving from denunciation to celebration. By early June, the loyalist newspapers launched a coordinated campaign to deflect blame away from Siqueiros, casting the missing Sheldon Harte and supposed "Trotskyite conspirators" as the true culprits. The new narrative protected both the PCM and Moscow, reframing a failed assassination as spontaneous revolutionary passion gone awry.

Harte had arrived in Coyoacán in early April, only seven weeks before the May 24 attack. Yet soon after the raid, leftist papers depicted him as the treacherous mastermind of the assault. He was caricatured as a "typical Russian gangster" despite being an American-born idealist with a university education. They falsely claimed he handed attackers the car keys—ignoring that the guards routinely left keys in ignitions as protocol. He was even linked to the mysterious "French Jew" rumored to have directed the operation from the shadows. Iron-

46. Sheldon Robert Harte (cover name AMUR) was recruited in New York City by Joseph Grigulevich.

ically, one element of the smear campaign later proved true: archival revelations and memoirs by Sudoplatov, Sharapov, and other Soviet insiders five decades later confirmed that Harte had indeed been recruited by the GPU, validating the very suspicions once dismissed as slander.

The Road to Trotsky's Gate

Colonel Leandro Sánchez Salazar, working with support from the FBI, launched an investigation into Harte's background. What they uncovered deepened the mystery. Harte, a recent Duke University graduate and aspiring playwright, had grown up in privilege—his father was a wealthy silk importer—but Harte's political sympathies leaned toward revolutionary socialism. He wore his hair long, cultivated a rebellious demeanor, and openly admired Marxist ideals.

Harte's road toward espionage began innocently. In February 1939, he attended an anti-Nazi rally at Madison Square Garden, where he met Albert Goldman, Trotsky's American attorney. Inspired by the event, he soon joined a left-wing newspaper staff and immersed himself in the Socialist Workers Party (SWP), where his intelligence and enthusiasm earned him a role on the Manhattan Executive Committee.[3]

Only decades later would the full story emerge. Pavel Sudoplatov's 1994 memoir[4] revealed that during his activities in New York, Harte had been secretly recruited by GPU officer Joseph Grigulevich—the same operative who designed the attack plan for Operation KON and the May 24, 1940, assault on Trotsky's villa. Under Grigulevich's direction,

Harte's role shifted from political activism to espionage, providing the GPU with critical insight into Trotsky's American support network and facilitating Harte's appointment as one of the guards in Mexico City.[5]

It was likely that Harte's rapid selection to join Trotsky's handful of guards occurred with the unseen assistance of Sylvia Callen—GPU agent SATYR—embedded within the SWP office. Before departure, Harte underwent firearms training, yet upon arrival, he found Trotsky's household more relaxed than militant and having "a summer camp-like atmosphere."[6] He concealed the true nature of his assignment from his family, telling his father he was traveling on routine business.

Despite his brief tenure of seven weeks, Harte earned a reputation as reliable and earnest. Trotsky and his secretary Joseph Hansen later defended him, maintaining that Harte had been deceived rather than corrupted. Hansen theorized that someone dressed in uniform—possibly carrying forged documents—could have persuaded Harte to open the gate on the morning of the raid with a message such as, "Bob, these officials have a message of extreme importance for Trotsky."[7]

Disappearance and Suspicion

However, the investigation of Harte's absence after the raid raised troubling questions. One of the Mexican guards testified that Harte was not bound or a prisoner but left "without showing any signs of having been violently treated by the attackers."[8]

On June 15, the investigation broke open. A captured raider, Spanish Civil War veteran Néstor Sánchez, confessed under interrogation. He identified Siqueiros and Antonio Pujol as leaders of the assault and recounted a remark Siqueiros made en route to the villa: "One of Trotsky's guards has been bought."[9] Salazar increasingly suspected that Harte had opened the gate to the attackers. Harte was the sole guard on duty that night—and he vanished with the fleeing raiders.

Circumstantial evidence mounted. In Harte's room at the villa, investigators found a Spanish-English dictionary inscribed by Siqueiros, a known Stalinist; a key to room 37 at the Hotel Europa; and a trunk marked as originating in Moscow. A local prostitute reported Harte had spent the night with her at the hotel on May 21, visibly intoxicated and in possession of a large sum of cash.[10]

The Father's Arrival and Hoover's Warning

Jesse Harte, Sheldon's father, president of the International Factors Corporation and a politically influential figure in the United States, arrived in Mexico City on May 25, deeply troubled by the accusations against his son.[11] He carried letters of introduction to Mexican officials and to the US ambassador from prominent American politicians and FBI Director J. Edgar Hoover.[12]

Harte admitted his son had concealed his work for Trotsky and confided that Sheldon was "a committed Stalinist." Rumors circulated that Sheldon had kept a portrait of Stalin in his New York room—claims Trotsky quickly refuted showing a cable from Jesse Harte: "DEFINITELY DETERMINED STALIN'S PICTURE NOT IN SHELDON'S ROOM."[13]

Another oddity further fueled suspicions—contemporary investigators later suggested that, unlike other SWP guards who arrived economically by bus, Harte might have traveled by air. That extravagance, if true, would have sat awkwardly with the SWP's finances and suggests the likelihood that it was paid from another source . . . perhaps even the GPU, who were desperate for intelligence about the layout inside Trotsky's villa to finalize plans for their May 24 attack.

After a short visit, Jesse Harte offered a $2,000 reward ($46,000 today). He returned to the United States and met with Hoover, who expressed sympathy but warned bluntly that his son had become a political fanatic with a "cause fixation."[14]

The Santa Rosa Discovery

The break came on June 17.[15] Salazar's investigation broke the case open, and after a week of surveillance, culminated in a June 25 raid[16] on a

47. Sheldon Harte was murdered in this remote cabin to keep him silent.

remote adobe house on the outskirts of Mexico City, rented under a false name by Siqueiros. A detained conspirator, Mariano Herrera, directed police to the location near the Desert of Lions on the outskirts of the city.[17] Neighbors recalled seeing a tall, red-haired American arrive there on May 24—presumably Harte.[18]

Inside, officers found a canvas, scattered art supplies, a slashed mattress, and blood in an upstairs room. As they prepared to leave, one officer noticed disturbed soil beneath the kitchen's dirt floor. Digging into the soil, they uncovered a decomposing corpse buried in quicklime. Harte was easily identifiable by his reddish hair.[19]

Salazar returned after midnight with firefighters and ordered a full exhumation. The body showed bullet wounds consistent with execution at close range. At 4:00 a.m., Trotsky was notified. Otto Schüssler identified the remains. Later that morning, Trotsky visited the San Ángel morgue to confirm the body himself.

Salazar later recorded Trotsky's reaction: "The man had directed a revolution, survived battles, and seen friends and family perish . . . now he wept in silence."[20]

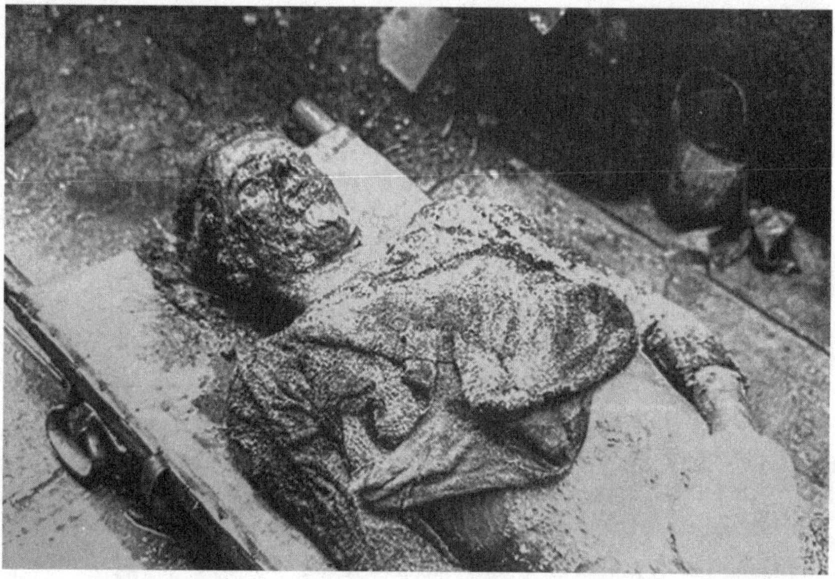

48. The remains of Sheldon Harte, following the discovery by Colonel Salazar.

The Evidence Trail

For decades, Harte's role remained contested. Trotsky never wavered from his conviction that the young American had been deceived rather than complicit: "Bob perished because he placed himself in the path of the assassins," and "his memory is spotless."[21] In early August 1940, Trotsky mounted a memorial plaque at the garden gate inscribed "MURDERED BY STALIN."[22] At the Museo Trotsky today, the weathered chain-link gate and Harte's modest plaque in the villa's southwest corner still stand—overlooked by most visitors, and almost never fully understood in the weight of what they commemorate.

Colonel Salazar reached his own conclusion: "Siqueiros had taken Harte off with him as an accomplice, and for some reason had decided to murder him. Possibly these were his orders from Moscow."[23]

Historian Harry Mahoney offered another plausible motive: Harte may have discovered that Ramón Mercader was a GPU agent. Although Mercader denied any friendship with Harte, the two were

49. Mounted by Trotsky at the garden gate in early August 1940, this plaque reflected his unwavering belief in Harte's innocence. He never learned Harte's true name—Sheldon Robert Harte.

reportedly seen drinking together at the Bar Kit-Kat and consorting with prostitutes.[24] After the failure of Operation KON, Soviet planners shifted to Operation MAT, and Harte—if interrogated—posed a direct threat to Mercader's cover. Eliminating him became an act of operational damage control.[25]

Sudoplatov, in overall command of Operation UTKA, later wrote that Harte was liquidated because he knew Grigulevich and could have exposed the network.[26] Yet Sudoplatov's explanation came half a century later in his memoir and reflected retrospective justification rather than contemporary documentation.

Fortunately, there exists a contemporaneous record originating from GPU files—preserved in E.P. Sharapov's 2003 biography of Nahum Eitingon. Granted access to some internal documents, Sharapov reproduced the exact operative explanations submitted to Moscow shortly after the attack:

> During the operation, it was discovered that Sheldon turned out to be a traitor. Although he had opened the door of the gate, in the room where he led the participants in the raid there were nei-

> ther archives nor Trotsky himself. When the participants in the raid opened fire, Sheldon stated to them that if he had known all of this, as an American, he would not have agreed to participate in this affair. Such behavior served as the grounds for making the decision on the spot about his elimination.[27]

In 1954, Eitingon confirmed that he also reported to Moscow that Harte was killed in his sleep by two bullets to the head by Siqueiros's brother-in-law Luis Arenal.[28] Grigulevich's account was similar: "Moscow ordered: shoot the traitor. And that's what we did."[29]

Final Verdict

In New York in 1939, Joseph Grigulevich saw in Harte an ideal recruit: intelligent, earnest, eager to serve a cause larger than himself. The GPU targeted not the cynical but the idealistic—individuals whose moral certainty made them susceptible to manipulation. Harte fit this pattern perfectly. Flattered by the attentions of seasoned revolutionaries, he was guided into a world where clandestine service was framed not as betrayal but as duty.

By the spring of 1940, Harte stood inside an operation he could neither direct nor escape. His position within Trotsky's household made him indispensable—and expendable. Acting under assurances from Grigulevich and those coordinating with Siqueiros, Harte most likely believed the raid's objective was limited: the destruction of Trotsky's archives. He had no idea that the mission's true goal was assassination. Only when automatic fire tore through the villa did he comprehend how deeply he had been deceived. His usefulness ended in that moment.

When the GPU no longer needed him, Harte was silenced—buried beneath quicklime in a remote adobe hut, erased by the very revolution he believed he served.

He did not die a martyr. He died as both a traitor and a victim—caught between idealism and a machinery that consumed its own.

And with Harte's elimination, the last obstacle to the security of Stalin's second strike—Operation MAT—quietly disappeared.

CHAPTER XIX

THE SPY WHO LOVED AND LIED

"He who is loved is easily trusted. He
who is trusted, easily feared."
—Graham Greene, *The Human Factor*

"The best spy is the one who never seems interested."
—GPU training manual

"A spy must wear a mask so convincingly that
even he forgets who lies beneath it."
—Attributed to Pavel Sudoplatov

After the Raid: A New Opening

The May 24, 1940, assault on Leon Trotsky's villa created a vacuum—and an opening—for Ramón Mercader. Operating under the alias Frank Jacson* and posing as Sylvia Ageloff's husband, he stepped forward with quiet usefulness. Until then, Trotsky's guards had known him only as the man who dropped Sylvia off in the mornings and collected her in the evenings: a familiar outsider, visible but never invited inside. But the raid had stolen the household's two vehicles, disrupted daily routines, and left the compound suddenly dependent on outside help.

Mercader recognized the opportunity immediately. When Trotsky's longtime comrade and houseguest Alfred Rosmer fell ill and required repeated trips to the French hospital in Mexico City, the household had no means of transport. Jacson* promptly offered his Buick and personally drove Rosmer and his wife to their hospital appointments on Niño Perdido Street—a gesture calculated to ingratiate himself to the couple and, through them, to Natalia Sedova, who trusted Marguerite Rosmer's judgment implicitly. What began as a convenience quickly became routine. Frank* carried messages, ferried visitors, and quietly relieved the daily pressures of a household still shaken by the attack.

Within days, Jacson* was no longer an observer lingering at the gate but a regular presence moving through it. Guards nodded and admitted him without hesitation. Trotsky's circle began to accept him as Sylvia's helpful spouse—quiet, obliging, and seemingly devoted. His presence felt routine; his assistance seemed natural. Behind the wheel, however, sat a trained assassin preparing for a second attempt—one that would rely not on gunmen but on trust.

What unfolded in Coyoacán mirrored a far more violent reckoning in Moscow. According to Dmitri Volkogonov, news of the failed May 24 assault sent Stalin into a rage. Lavrentiy Beria absorbed his fury, while those associated with the operation faced the prospect of arrest or worse. One senior intelligence officer, Shpigelglas, was already under detention. From that moment forward, Volkogonov wrote, "everything would now be staked on the action of an individual operator who had long been installed in Mexico, and who was preparing to carry out his mission."[1]

That operator, Mercader, did not expect to be the executioner himself when he arrived in Mexico months earlier. Volkogonov records that only days after the failed raid—on May 26 or 27—Nahum Eitingon summoned him and made the situation unmistakably clear. Mercader was told he would be "carrying out a just sentence" handed down in Moscow, an act framed as an honor that would secure his place as a revolutionary hero. Refusal was unthinkable. Mercader had already learned in Spain how dissent ended. Suspected weakness meant disappearance. "The law of the revolution," Volkogonov noted, "was that the weak and unreliable are liquidated." Mercader understood the lesson.[2]

Sylvia, then in New York, had explicitly warned Frank* not to visit the villa in her absence when she departed in late March. He ignored her. The failed raid—and the theft of the household's automobiles—

had created precisely the conditions he needed. Under the guise of helpfulness, Ramón Mercader began threading himself into the life of the besieged household, one small favor at a time.

Moscow Reacts: The Fall of KON and the Rise of MAT

In the early hours of May 24, Nahum Eitingon (TOM) received the news he had dreaded: Operation KON had failed. Despite the storm of gunfire and David Alfaro Siqueiros's confident assurances, Leon Trotsky—the Old Man—had somehow survived. Against expectation, against probability, the target was still alive.

Eitingon knew Moscow's reaction would be swift. The news reached Beria and Stalin on Sunday, May 26, via a TASS (the official Soviet news agency) report.[3] Years later Sudoplatov offered his explanation for the botched assassination:

> The assassination was thwarted due to the fact that the group was not professionally trained for the specific action. Eitingon, for reasons of secrecy, did not participate in this attack. He certainly would have corrected the actions of the attackers. There was no one in the Siqueiros group who would have had experience in searching and checking the rooms or houses. The members of this group were peasants and miners with basic training in conducting partisan warfare and sabotage.[4]

Unable to reach Moscow directly because of underpowered radio equipment, Eitingon sent a lengthy encrypted message:

> On May 23, 1940, an attack was made on Trotsky's home . . . Assuming no complications arise, we intend to rectify the mistakes in 2–3 weeks . . . and require an additional $10,000–15,000 to complete the mission. I fully accept the blame for this nightmarish failure and am prepared . . . to face the punishment it warrants.[5]

In Stalin's Russia, such candor was perilous. Many had been executed for far less. Beria summoned Sudoplatov to his dacha and erupted in fury. Sudoplatov confirmed that the attackers were politically reliable but militarily untrained. He advised that Ramón Mercader—the embedded agent already inside Trotsky's orbit—was now the most viable option.

With Stalin's approval, Beria ordered Sudoplatov to activate Operation MAT. Mercader's role shifted decisively from observer, lover, and spy to presumptive assassin. Despite the failure of Siqueiros, Moscow instructed that Eitingon be reassured of their continued confidence. Within days, Eitingon met with Caridad and Ramón. Though the final method had not yet been chosen, they agreed to regroup in New York on June 15. Stalin's directive was unambiguous: Trotsky must not escape.[6]

The KON raid had also compromised security. Too many conspirators had been involved; no escape plan had been prepared. The GPU's hand was now suspected. Moscow insisted that the next attempt be carried out by a single man, face-to-face, without witnesses and without a trail.[7]

Espionage from the Inside

Although Mercader had been collecting intelligence since arriving in Mexico, his access to the villa had previously been limited. Now, as Moscow's chosen instrument, pressure from Caridad and Eitingon intensified. He needed to master every detail of the compound—its layout, routines, guard rotations, and defensive measures.

Despite having promised Sylvia not to visit the villa in her absence,[8] Mercader had never intended to keep that pledge. His attentiveness after the raid impressed Marguerite Rosmer and gradually softened even Natalia Sedova's lingering doubts about Frank*. Determined to control the narrative, Mercader insisted on telling Sylvia himself that he had broken his promise. He framed his actions as deliberate and benevolent, fearing she might otherwise hear the truth from others in a less favorable light. When he explained his conduct, her response was supportive.

50. Ramón Mercader, alias Frank Jacson*.

With each appearance at the villa, Frank's* credibility—and his access—deepened. From late March through mid-August, the future assassin systematically absorbed details of the villa's defenses. Rumors circulated in the press and among exiles after the May 24 raid claiming that Trotsky's compound was protected by automatic firing devices.[9] Whether exaggerated or false, these claims underscored the need for confirmation. Mercader set out to distinguish myth from reality through direct observation.

Casing the Fortress: Observation by Leica

Photographic reconnaissance became central to Mercader's task. His objective was no longer casual familiarity but the precise documentation of security features—perimeter walls, gates, guard positions, alarm systems, and approaches—that would allow Moscow to plan a single-agent attack.

On May 28, Jacson* arrived at Trotsky's villa at 7:58 a.m. and drove Alfred and Marguerite Rosmer to Veracruz for their return voyage to France.[10] He returned on May 30 from 3:42 p.m. to 4:12 p.m.[11] Each visit was brief but purposeful, allowing him to observe the compound under ordinary conditions. Isaac Don Levine later remarked on Mercader's "extraordinary visual memory," noting his capacity to absorb spatial detail during seemingly mundane encounters.[12]

Police and security records show that Frank* also visited the villa on June 4 (2:31–2:55 p.m.), on June 7 (4:30–4:45 p.m.), and again briefly on June 12 (10:35–10:40 a.m.), ostensibly to offer the use of his car.[13] After returning from New York, he made six additional visits.

Each visit served an intelligence purpose. By varying the timing of his appearances, Mercader was able to observe guard changes, routines, and vulnerabilities. Reports—including photographs—were transmitted to Moscow and reviewed in 1948 by GPU defector Vladimir Petrov, who confirmed the thoroughness of Mercader's documentation:

> There was complete photographic documentation of Trotsky's life . . . including images taken inside the fortified villa, perhaps by Mornard* himself, showing guards, fences, courtyards, Trotsky with his wife, sharing tea with friends, even Trotsky's dog.[14]

Levine wrote that Jacson* "took numerous snapshots, probably with a concealed miniature camera, of the household and all its occupants."[15] Operationally, however, this is unlikely. In 1940, the Riga Minox—the only practical subminiature camera then available commercially—had only just appeared and was very expensive and difficult to obtain. Soviet intelligence would not produce a purpose-built miniature camera until 1955 with the introduction of the ARNICA for copying documents.[16]

A standard 35-mm Leica camera, however, widely used by tourists and professionals alike, was far more plausible for surveillance purposes. Compact and unremarkable, it would have allowed Mercader to photograph architectural features—alarm boxes, telephone lines, gates, and perimeter walls—openly and without attracting attention. Trotsky's many guests always documented their visits to one of the world's most famous men, and the guards were accustomed to visitors taking pictures. The Minox, by contrast, remained a novelty in 1940 and would likely have drawn unwanted scrutiny.

A trunk shipped by the assassin to New York in June 1940 may provide the missing clue to the mystery of Mercader's camera. Shortly before departing for New York in mid-June, Jacson* consigned a trunk to himself at his New York address.[17] After the assassination, a man identifying himself as H. Christie attempted to retrieve it but was refused for lack of proper identification. The trunk was subsequently seized by FBI agents. Among its contents were a Leica lens, a Lios-SCOP light meter, a yellow-green filter, a film canister, and a copy of *Manuel Leica*, a 1933 French photography manual for the Leica camera. The Leica camera body itself was never recovered. It is likely that Frank* retained the camera in Mexico City for continued use in reconnaissance operations throughout the summer.[18]

By the time of Mercader's final dry-run visit to the villa on August 17, 1940, his photographic work was complete. The camera was no longer required and was most likely left with Caridad Mercader or Nahum Eitingon for disposal.[19]

Final Visits: Charm, Trust, and the Silent Breach

By the time Jacson* boarded his plane to New York on June 14, the groundwork had been laid. His forged travel documents were convincing, but it was his practiced denunciations of Stalin that truly opened doors. In conversations with Sylvia Ageloff, the guards, and even members of Trotsky's inner circle, he learned that condemning Stalin was the surest way to gain trust. He spoke bitterly of the purges, of the corruption of the revolution, of comrades betrayed by the bureaucracy—each remark carefully calibrated to echo the language of the disillusioned left.

What appeared to be spontaneous outrage was, in reality, a rehearsed performance. Through this mimicry of sincerity, Mercader cultivated credibility, winning sympathy and access no known Stalinist could ever have achieved. By the time he departed, suspicion had been eroded not by force, but by familiarity.

Operation MAT did not begin with a pistol or a rifle. It began with a soft voice, a generous would-be husband, and a future assassin walking through an open gate. The walls around Trotsky had not yet fallen—but they had been breached, and from that moment forward, the outcome would depend less on perimeter defenses than on personal access.

CHAPTER XX

OPERATION MAT

License to Kill

"A single blow must destroy the enemy,
without regard for the consequences."
—Joseph Stalin

"Let him say he acted for love."
—Stalin, allegedly, to Beria and Merkulov

"Say nothing. Write nothing. Admit nothing—you will
become a ghost—and we will never forget you."
—Eitingon's instructions to Ramón

Inside the Walls

Operation MAT did not arise from measured deliberation. It crystallized from failure and overconfidence. In the early hours of May 24, 1940, the raiders withdrew from the villa believing their mission accomplished. David Alfaro Siqueiros, who led the assault inside the compound, assured Grigulevich (PADRE) that he had delivered the *coup de grâce* and that Trotsky was dead. On that assurance they dispersed. Only hours later did Eitingon learn the truth: Trotsky had survived.

The debacle was not simply tactical—it was an embarrassment to the GPU professionals who had designed it. A heavily armed assault force, encountering almost no resistance and firing at close range into an undefended bedroom, had failed to kill its target. The humiliation was as damaging as the failure itself.

From that moment, the logic changed. If a coordinated squad could not guarantee success, the method itself had to change. The next strike would not depend on volume of fire or numbers, but on proximity and precision. Operation MAT—already sketched in outline—now moved from contingency to commitment.

Yet at that moment Ramón Mercader remained outside the inner circle. He had been inside the compound only once before—on March 26—for a few brief moments while handling luggage. He had never stood face-to-face with Trotsky. He possessed limited access through Sylvia Ageloff, but not entry into the inner sanctum.

From the wreckage of the raid emerged an opportunity no one had anticipated. As the attackers fled in the early hours of May 24, they took with them the compound's two automobiles. The theft produced immediate logistical paralysis. The villa was effectively immobilized. Routine errands became ordeals. Even the smallest necessity required outside assistance and careful coordination.

That inconvenience created an opening. Mercader had long sought a practical reason to be helpful—something that would justify his presence inside the gates rather than lingering at their edge. Four days later, the pretext appeared. On May 28, 1940, he was invited inside.

It seemed a minor crossing, almost incidental. Yet for the planners in Moscow, it marked a decisive breach. The future assassin entered Trotsky's household as a guest and, for the first time, met the man he had been prepared to kill—a quiet encounter that signified everything.[1]

The household was still raw from the raid: bullet holes scarred the walls, and the guards moved with rigid vigilance.[2] Inside the compound, the air was tight. The Rosmers were preparing to return to France from the port of Veracruz, and without transportation, daily life had become a logistical burden—one that presented Ramón with an opening.[3]

Mercader exploited the disruption with calculated ease. Presenting himself as the helpful acquaintance who had offered to drive the Rosmers to the port himself—correctly calculating that "chauffeuring the Rosmers would cement his relationship with them, and through them, he might gain a better entrée to Trotsky."[4] The offer appeared generous, precisely the sort of courtesy Sylvia Ageloff's husband might extend. Natalia Sedova [Trotsky] welcomed the assistance and joined them for the drive.[5]

The guards, still shaken by the raid, raised no objections. Nor did they seize the opportunity to conduct even a cursory background check on Jacson*, their new and increasingly familiar visitor. What none of them knew was that this seemingly improvised gesture had been envisioned two years earlier—part of the GPU's final and most elaborate design, Operation MAT, to eliminate Leon Trotsky.

At 8:17 a.m. Jacson* finally crossed the threshold to meet the Old Man. Leon Trotsky was there, feeding his rabbits, a basket of grain tucked under one arm. Jacson* approached, hat in hand, his manner easy, deferential. Trotsky looked up, met the stranger's gaze, and extended his hand.[6] They spoke only a few words—civil, unmemorable—but that instant marked years of clandestine labor. A once distant order from Moscow was now embodied as Stalin's assassin stood within arm's reach of his target.

Placing Jacson* in direct contact with Trotsky had been the GPU's objective for years. What began with Sylvia Ageloff in New York in 1938, refined in Paris, and carried back across the Atlantic culminated in a single handshake beneath the Mexican sun.

By day's end, Stalin's assassin had not only met his prey; he had begun the slow work of normalizing his presence—one visit at a time—toward the blow that would fall eleven weeks later.

Scouting the Escape Route

Access alone was not enough. The assassin had entered the compound, but entry was only the first problem. Every successful assassination required not only proximity to the target, but a path of withdrawal. If the strike succeeded, survival would depend on seconds—on architecture, sightlines, and the movements of others inside the house.

The Old Man's study had only two doors: the east door into the dining room, and a private west door into his bedroom. Visitors normally entered and departed through the east dining room door. An assassin soaked in blood, however, could not safely take that route without risking an encounter with Natalia or a guard.

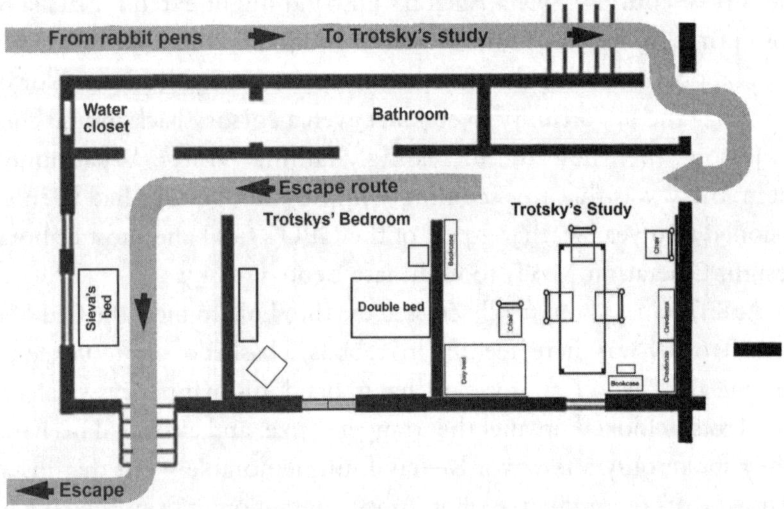

Jacson's* Planned Escape Route

51.

On May 28, his first visit, Mercader needed to confirm the alternative exit: the passage from the study through the Old Man's bedroom and then through Sieva's room into the garden and to the exit gate. Bringing a small wooden airplane,[7] he entered the boy's room under the guise of presenting the gift and confirmed the passage through the study appeared to be unobstructed by the recent security changes. Trotsky and Natalia noticed his presence and found it odd but registered no alarm. The route through Sieva's bedroom, hidden from the dining room guards, offered the assassin a likely corridor to the garden gate, garage, and a waiting Buick—enough time, perhaps, to reach his escape before anyone discovered the body.[8]

From Access to Authorization

With proximity established on May 28, the operation moved beyond infiltration and into decision. Confirmation that Mercader had entered the compound and shaken Trotsky's hand triggered the next phase.

What remained was not access, but authorization of the final plan and selecting the assassination weapon. Those would be fixed at a series of secret meetings to be held in New York.

On June 14, 1940, Ramón Mercader boarded his flight to New York City under his alias Frank Jacson*, leaving behind a villa he had spent months infiltrating. To the Old Man's guards, he was a courteous helper who even left his vehicle for the guards to use;[9] to Sylvia Ageloff, still in Brooklyn, he was a lover and supposed husband.[10] But to the GPU, he had become the chosen weapon.

The journey north was not improvised. Awaiting him were Nahum Eitingon, Caridad Mercader, and Gaik Ovakimian, the GPU's rezident in the United States.[11] Ovakimian's network had long monitored Trotskyist activity, and he now played a pivotal role in coordinating the final phase. Operation MAT was no longer only a possibility—it was now to be a scheduled assassination.

Love as Cover

Ramón's journey to the United States demanded a careful deception. At the US consulate in Mexico City, presenting himself as Canadian citizen Frank Jacson*, he requested a two-day transit stop in New York on his way to Montreal. However, the second part of the trip was a ruse as he never intended to continue past New York.[12] He later told the police that "I was only [in New York City] with Sylvia and her family and friends, all were Trotskyists except for the family. I had no other contacts; I was not on a business trip but only to see Sylvia."[13]

When Ramón arrived in New York, Gaik Ovakimian, the GPU's senior officer in America, held all the operational threads of the Trotsky plot in the United States. Jacson* checked into the Pierrepont Hotel with his wife Sylvia, paying fifteen dollars a week, and used June to solidify his domestic facade.[14] During this period, he mingled with Sylvia's sisters and the Rosmers. Their voyage to France included a scheduled stop in New York City, which they used as an opportunity to visit with Sylvia and Frank*, as well as friends within the Socialist Workers Party (SWP). Their brief reunion reinforced Jacson's* standing within Trotsky's

52. Gaik Ovakimian (cover name GENNADY) was the GPU rezident—top spy—in the United States from 1933 to 1941.

American circle and lent continued authenticity to his assumed identity. Frank* explained his frequent daytime absences to Sylvia as business with his elusive millionaire employer Peter Lubeck, a wholly fictitious figure—part of the carefully constructed GPU legend created to justify Jacson's* presence in Mexico, the trip to New York, income, documents, and periodic disappearances. In truth, these absences masked clandestine meetings with Ovakimian, Nahum Eitingon, Gregory Rabinowitz, and Caridad Mercader at the larger Hotel Lexington.[15]

To Sylvia, Frank* remained the quiet, attentive husband, with no trace of political extremism or capacity for violence. This apparent ordinariness was deliberate. The GPU understood that emotional intimacy could be the most effective disguise: her trust gave him cover, social legitimacy, and a direct path into Trotsky's guarded circle. Proudly telling friends of her husband's helpfulness to her family and SWP comrades, Sylvia never suspected that the man she loved was offering—inside a New York hotel room—to kill Leon Trotsky with his own hands.[16]

In New York hotel rooms, beneath the cover of domestic normalcy,

53. Mr. and Mrs. Jacson* stayed at the Hotel Pierrepont, while the Operation MAT planners met at the Lexington Hotel.

the mechanics of assassination were debated with clinical precision. What remained undecided was not intent—but instrument.

The Final Plan Takes Shape

Before meeting with Caridad and Ramón, Eitingon received ciphered instructions from Sudoplatov and Beria to finalize the assassination plan.[17] The method for the assassination had not yet been settled. Eitingon had proposed a hybrid assault when he met in Mexico City with Ramón and Caridad in late May.[18] Eitingon, Caridad, and five armed operatives would launch an external attack to draw Trotsky's guards to the perimeter walls. With the guards engaged in the fighting, Mercader—already inside the villa—would seize the moment to kill Trotsky while he was exposed and undefended.[19]

The GPU, however, recognized that its assassination protocols only worked when undertaken with precision. The May 24 failure proved that involving too many operatives increased complications and decreased their operational security. Beria also feared that if any assailant were caught, the newly built MAT network and its safe house in New Mexico and links to Moscow might be exposed. The risk of compromise grew with every additional participant. Moscow came to a resolution: the next attempt would rely on a single assassin. It would be personal and face-to-face and leave no room for Trotsky's escape—or survival.[20]

By late June, the outline was fixed: one man, one room, one moment. What remained was the instrument—what Mercader would carry into the study, and what Moscow would permit him to use.

Selecting the Weapon

Sudoplatov was no stranger to political murder. In Rotterdam in 1938, acting on Stalin's orders, he assassinated Ukrainian nationalist leader Yevhen Konovalets, who had contacted Hitler and was plotting an uprising. Sudoplatov was to meet him in a café and present him with a gift containing an explosive device. Sudoplatov recalled:

> The bomb in the candy box was prepared with a timing device and did not depend upon a hidden switch. The bomb was to explode thirty minutes after the position of the box was changed from vertical to horizontal. I had to keep the box in an upright position in the inner pocket of my jacket. I was to present the gift to Konovalets and leave before it exploded.[21]

Watching from a café across the street until the explosion, Sudoplatov later quietly slipped away to Brussels, then Paris, and finally back to Moscow, where he was hailed as a hero and introduced to GPU chief Nikolai Yezhov and his successor, Lavrentiy Beria.[22]

Despite Sudoplatov's success in other operations with disguised explosives, there's no solid indication that a bomb was ever a serious op-

54. The piolet, or Eispickel (ice axe), was used for cutting steps in ice while climbing.

tion for Operation MAT. The technical failure of multiple improvised incendiary devices during the May 24 raid likely discouraged the idea. Ironically, the small device little larger than a can of soda left in the courtyard just outside Trotsky's bedroom might have destroyed the entire room had it been filled with high explosives instead of incendiary compounds and placed directly against the bedroom wall with a simple, and far more dependable, lit fuse.

According to Eitingon, Ramón assured them he could kill Trotsky alone from within the heart of the fortified villa.[23] He drew confidence from his combat experience in Spain, where he'd sharpened his marksmanship, fought hand-to-hand, and once fatally stabbed a sentry guarding a bridge. He claimed he was mentally prepared for three possible methods: shooting, stabbing, or using a blunt force weapon.[24] Each had pros and cons. Despite that risk, Ramón projected confidence in his readiness for whatever means proved necessary.

Knife wounds, unlike cinematic portrayals, rarely bring instant, silent death. Even fatal stabs often result in a noisy end. That left blunt force as the most viable option. If Ramón could strike Trotsky from behind, a heavy weapon might kill without making a sound—offering the best chance to escape before anyone reacted.

To support Ramón's plan, Eitingon cited a successful, if unorthodox, assassination from two years earlier. In 1938, the GPU learned of a Soviet ambassador preparing to defect in the Middle East. Beria summoned Bokov, a Red Navy cipher officer known for his strength, and asked one question: "Are you strong enough to kill a man with a single blow of an iron bar?" Bokov replied, "Yes, comrade commissar."[25] Traveling on a fake diplomatic passport, Bokov arrived at the embassy, was handed a short iron bar, and entered the ambassador's office posing as a visitor. Once inside, he stepped behind the target and delivered a fatal blow to the ambassador's skull—inaudible, swift, and final.[26]

Though an iron bar was effective, Ramón proposed an even better option. As an experienced climber, he claimed he could split a granite boulder with a single swing of a piolet—ice axe—and Trotsky's skull, he quipped, would be softer than the granite.[27] A precise blow to the back of the head could be both soundless and fatal, allowing time for escape. The weapons discussion ended with Eitingon instructing Ramón to carry all three options—a dagger, an axe, and a firearm—in case he needed to fight his way out after the killing.[28]

Dead Men Tell Nothing

As one unspoken intelligence maxim held, the less an agent knows—and survives to tell—the better. In Operation MAT, one omission heretofore undiscussed stands out with particular force. The GPU sent a trained assassin into a fortified compound without a suppressed pistol—the single weapon that would have given him the greatest chance to kill Leon Trotsky quietly and with certainty while also providing the only realistic means of escaping before the alarm sounded.

A suppressed firearm would have been the optimal instrument for such an operation. The ice axe, by contrast, was a contact—or impact—weapon that imposed severe operational liabilities. To use it, Mercader had to stand directly behind Trotsky, strike with sufficient force to penetrate the skull, and remain physically engaged during and after the blow. This necessarily extended the duration of the attack from a fraction of a second—as with a firearm—to several seconds. Those seconds mattered. They allowed the victim to react, increased the risk that the attacker could lose balance or control, and created a window for nearby guards to intervene.

That risk was not theoretical. Because the ice axe did not immediately incapacitate Trotsky, resistance was structurally built into the weapon choice. Trotsky screamed. He fought back. The struggle itself—audible, violent, and prolonged—drew instant attention from those outside the room. A firearm discharged at close range, particularly a suppressed one, would almost certainly have caused immediate incapacitation, eliminating the possibility of resistance altogether.

The same factors ensured detection. The combination of Trotsky's scream, the noise of the struggle, and the delay between the blow and loss of consciousness meant that discovery was inevitable within seconds. Even without gunfire, the attack announced itself. In this sense, the ice axe did more than increase risk; it virtually guaranteed exposure. A suppressed pistol, by contrast, would have minimized audible signature, reduced time on target, and increased the likelihood that Mercader could have exited the room before guards fully grasped what had occurred.

Speed was central to this distinction. A suppressed firearm allowed the assassin to act and move almost simultaneously—delivering the fatal act and disengaging in one continuous motion. The ice axe required a sequence of actions, each dependent on the success of the previous one, magnifying uncertainty at every step.

Control was equally decisive. A firearm would have given Mercader control over distance, timing, and outcome. It would have avoided physical entanglement with the victim and reduced unpredictability. Once Mercader struck with the ice axe and failed to achieve instant incapacitation, control passed irretrievably out of his hands.

Most significant was the loss of tactical flexibility. A suppressed pistol would have allowed Mercader to respond if interrupted, fire multiple shots if the first failed, threaten or neutralize guards, and—however slim the odds—attempt to disengage and flee. The ice axe permitted

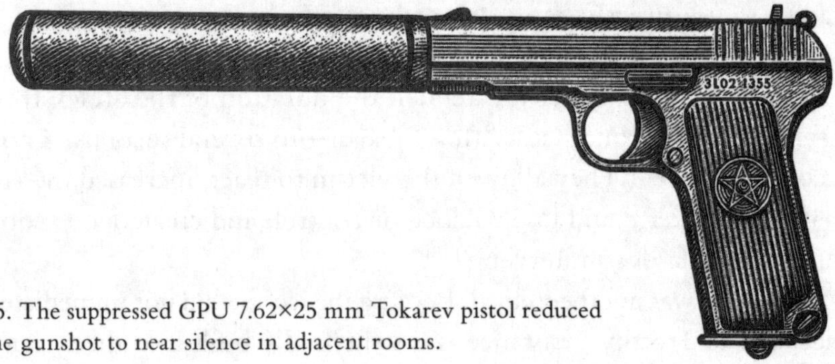

55. The suppressed GPU 7.62×25 mm Tokarev pistol reduced the gunshot to near silence in adjacent rooms.

only a single action: strike. When that strike failed to kill immediately, Mercader had no tactical options left.

Weapon Choice as Evidence

Pavel Sudoplatov later claimed that no "special laboratory" was available to prepare a suppressed firearm for the operation, implying a technical limitation rather than a deliberate choice.[29] Taken at face value, this explanation is difficult to reconcile with the broader record. Sudoplatov himself acknowledged that Stalin authorized the assassination with extraordinary latitude, granting access to any personnel or resources deemed necessary. The GPU of 1940 was not constrained by scarcity or improvisation.

By that time, Soviet security services possessed decades of experience with suppressed weapons, including a suppressed revolver developed during the Russian Civil War and improved suppressed semiautomatic pistols introduced in the 1930s—well before the Trotsky operation.[30] The decision not to employ a suppressed firearm therefore cannot be credibly attributed to technical incapacity.

Instead, the absence of a silenced weapon points to a different objective. The GPU did not require a quiet killing; it required a permanently silent assassin. The weapon choice—ensuring capture rather than escape—was not a failure of preparation but an operational signal of intent.

Operation UTKA itself demonstrated a level of technical and logistical sophistication that further undermines claims of limitation. The operation relied on forged documents, compartmented handlers, safe houses across multiple countries, covert travel, secure communications, and a carefully drafted confession letter calibrated for political effect. Against this backdrop, the absence of a suppressed pistol cannot plausibly be explained as a logistical failure. With months of preparation, such a weapon could have been smuggled into Mexico by sea through any major port or carried covertly across its land borders.

What the GPU did provide sharpens the contrast. Mercader was equipped with a concealed strike weapon, a meticulously constructed cover identity, carefully cultivated emotional access through Sylvia Ageloff, and a written confession designed to shape the political narrative after the killing. What he was not given was the means to disengage quietly or escape decisively. The operation was provisioned for assassination—not extraction.

Operational Finality and the Value of Silence

Had Jacson* been killed in a gunfight while attempting to flee the compound, the narrative would have ended at the scene. The only explanation left behind would have been the confession letter carried in his jacket pocket. From the GPU's perspective, the advantages were obvious. A dead assassin could not be interrogated, could not contradict his prepared statement, and could not expose the chain of command leading back to Moscow.

That assessment aligns with contemporaneous intelligence understanding within Trotskyist and anti-Stalinist circles. In a private discussion with members of the Fourth International's directing committee in New York shortly after the assassination, Whittaker Chambers—a former GPU courier with firsthand knowledge of Soviet operational practice—warned that "the death of Jacson* is the central concern now of the GPU."[31]

Caridad Mercader would never have accepted such an outcome.

Her emotional investment in her son made that inconceivable. But Eitingon and Sudoplatov were not guided by maternal loyalty. As professional intelligence officers, they understood that an operation truly concluded only when all liabilities were neutralized. A heroic death at the scene—framed as the desperate act of a lone fanatic—would have sealed the assassination cleanly.

By August 1940, escape was increasingly implausible in any case. Trotsky's villa had become a fortified enclosure. The addition of a sallyport and two remotely controlled electric locks meant that once the alarm sounded, flight was effectively sealed off. In that context, the absence of a suppressed pistol reads not as an oversight but as a statement of priorities. Mercader was equipped to kill with certainty—but not necessarily to survive.

His death would have solved multiple problems at once: no interrogation, no trial, no decades of secrecy to maintain. It was a fate Caridad Mercader could never have accepted—but one that Eitingon and Sudoplatov, operating under Stalin's explicit authorization, might well have regarded as acceptable, even optimal.

Some have argued that the ice axe was chosen for symbolic or psychological reasons—that it was intended to convey brutality, intimacy, or ideological hatred rather than operational efficiency. That interpretation misunderstands Soviet intelligence practice. The GPU did not privilege symbolism over success, nor did it rely on theatrical violence when quieter, more reliable means were available. When symbolism mattered, it was layered onto outcomes already secured, not substituted for them. In this case, the choice of a contact weapon added risk, reduced control, and virtually guaranteed detection. If the overriding objective had been a silent, certain killing followed by escape, a suppressed firearm would have been the logical instrument. That it was not provided suggests that operational finality—not symbolism—governed the decision.

With method and means now fixed, one remaining task carried outsized importance: the story that would explain the killing after the fact—especially if Mercader died at the scene or refused to speak. That script was drafted in New York.

The Alibi and the Exit

Julián Gorkin later contended—convincingly—in *Murder in Mexico* that the June 1940 trip to New York was primarily to construct Jacson's* alibi and confession letter.[32] GPU operatives there understood its importance and political sensitivity and approached the wording with extreme care. Multiple scenarios were considered, and crafting the document might have taken more time than planning the assassination itself.

Historian Julián Gorkin provides the best explanation for the creation of Jackson's alibi or confession letter.

> Yes, all is lies and deceit about this human robot [Jacson*]. Above all, the letter which was found on him. There is no doubt that it was written in New York, examined, discussed and re-written. To cover up this fact, the assassin had to invent a fantastic typewriter. It is proved by the signature and the date written in pencil at the last minute, and the fact that in his declaration he did not remember its contents very well. The GPU agents in New York had very carefully composed it, as though it were a document of high policy on which depended the future of Russia, a document more careful for them than all the theories of the Comintern. There was one major preoccupation in the minds of its composers: to give satisfaction to the leaders and, above all, to the supreme leader.[33]

While Jacson* carried the letter on his person—concealed like a device waiting to detonate—another copy had almost certainly already been dispatched to Moscow, sealed in a diplomatic pouch. That was standard GPU practice. The letter was designed to serve two purposes at once: to depict Trotsky as an implacable enemy of the Russian people and the supposed architect of a plot against Stalin, and to destroy Trotskyism itself by depriving it of both its leader and its moral standing. The movement would be left headless, undone by the claim that one of its own, "disillusioned," had turned against him and struck the fatal blow.

This dual purpose reflected a familiar GPU pattern. Killing the victim was never enough; the crime had to be followed by character assassination, the transfer of guilt, and the corruption of meaning. In this way, the GPU repeatedly revealed its own signature—an instinct for duplicity so consistent it amounted to a calling card. The letter was therefore not merely cynical but profoundly inept: a blunder by its very existence, and an even greater one in its content. It was as if the GPU had slipped its own visiting card into the assassin's pocket.[34]

Gorkin explains that the killing was meant to appear as a private act of revenge. Jacson* would be portrayed as a man driven to violence by Trotsky's interference in Sylvia Ageloff's decision to marry him. If captured, he could further claim that Trotsky's followers had abused his financial support, or that Trotsky himself had attempted to draw him into an international terrorist conspiracy to assassinate Stalin. Each of these narratives was calibrated not only for public plausibility but also for how Beria and Stalin might judge the operation's political utility.

Aware that their own futures depended on the outcome, the conspirators' two-week stay in New York likely provided sufficient time for a written confession to be drafted, encoded, forwarded to Moscow for approval, and then typed. The plan was for Ramón to carry the signed letter in his jacket pocket, ensuring that—whether he was arrested or killed—a ready-made account of his "motives" would exist, severing any visible link between the assassin and Moscow.[35]

There is little doubt that the plan assumed Jacson* would not survive. The GPU sought three outcomes in a single act: Trotsky's death, the silencing of its own agent, and the transformation of that agent's death into a final "testament." Trotsky's intervention—mortally wounded yet fully lucid—upended that calculation. By ordering his guards not to kill his attacker, he asserted political judgment to the very end, ensuring that the web of lies and treachery would be exposed—if not completely, then nearly so.[36]

Return to Mexico

Ramón also needed operating funds for the next two months—and possibly for his escape. The GPU gave him sealed packets of cash, secured with red wax to prevent tampering. To keep them from Sylvia's view, he stored them in the hotel's office safe. Before leaving for Mexico, he shipped his luggage ahead, then used a smuggler's trick: strapping the packets to his forearms with rubber bands beneath his shirtsleeves. When Sylvia asked about them, he claimed they held bulky Mexican currency, not US dollars, and didn't show her. The money, it later emerged, was provided by the GPU to finance both the assassination and his possible escape.[37]

Ramón Mercader departed New York on June 30 transformed. He curiously didn't fly all the way to Mexico City. Instead, he purchased tickets on Eastern Airlines for flights to New Orleans, and then a day later, to San Antonio. From there he was to travel by bus to the US–Mexico border at Laredo, where he would cross on foot.[38] From the Mexican side of the border, he was supposed to take a train to Mexico City. It is interesting that Mercader didn't arrive in Mexico City until the last week in July. His whereabouts for most of July have never been determined.

The future assassin was no longer perfecting a cover story or preparing for a mission. His role had been cast, his "confession" letter accepted, and the murder plot approved at the highest level. The weapons had been chosen, and the route mapped. Even his escape from the villa had been planned. Yet to Sylvia Ageloff, his departure from New York seemed like just another chapter in their tangled romance. She had no idea that the man she adored was now carrying cash, forged papers, and final instructions for an execution. For Mercader, the line between espionage and murder had been crossed. What lay ahead was no longer subterfuge—it was the kill.

With his mission set in New York, the assassin returned to Mexico—only to find the villa transformed. Alarmed comrades in the United States had funded sweeping security upgrades: reinforced walls, additional guards, and tightened routines. Each change would now dictate how he planned his next move.

CHAPTER XXI

FORTRESS TROTSKY

The House Under Siege

"The walls grew higher, but the danger was already inside."
—Anonymous GPU defector

"Every fortress invites its own siege."
—Leon Trotsky

"In the end, we defended against shadows—while the assassin walked through the front gate."
—Joseph Hansen

Prologue: A Chilling Warning

One afternoon in the summer of 1940, as guards hauled sandbags and laid steel mesh across the villa's walls, Trotsky turned to a visitor—Ramón Mercader, using the alias Frank Jacson*—and asked, almost playfully, what he thought of the upgrades.

"In the next attack," Mercader replied coolly, "the GPU will use other methods."[1]

Nearby, guards Charles Cornell and Joseph Hansen looked at each other. As Joseph Hansen later recalled, Trotsky answered that "a single agent of the GPU, who could pass himself off as my friend, could assassinate me in my own home."[2]

The exchange captured the contradiction that would define Trotsky's final months. Steel, concrete, and vigilance would soon harden the

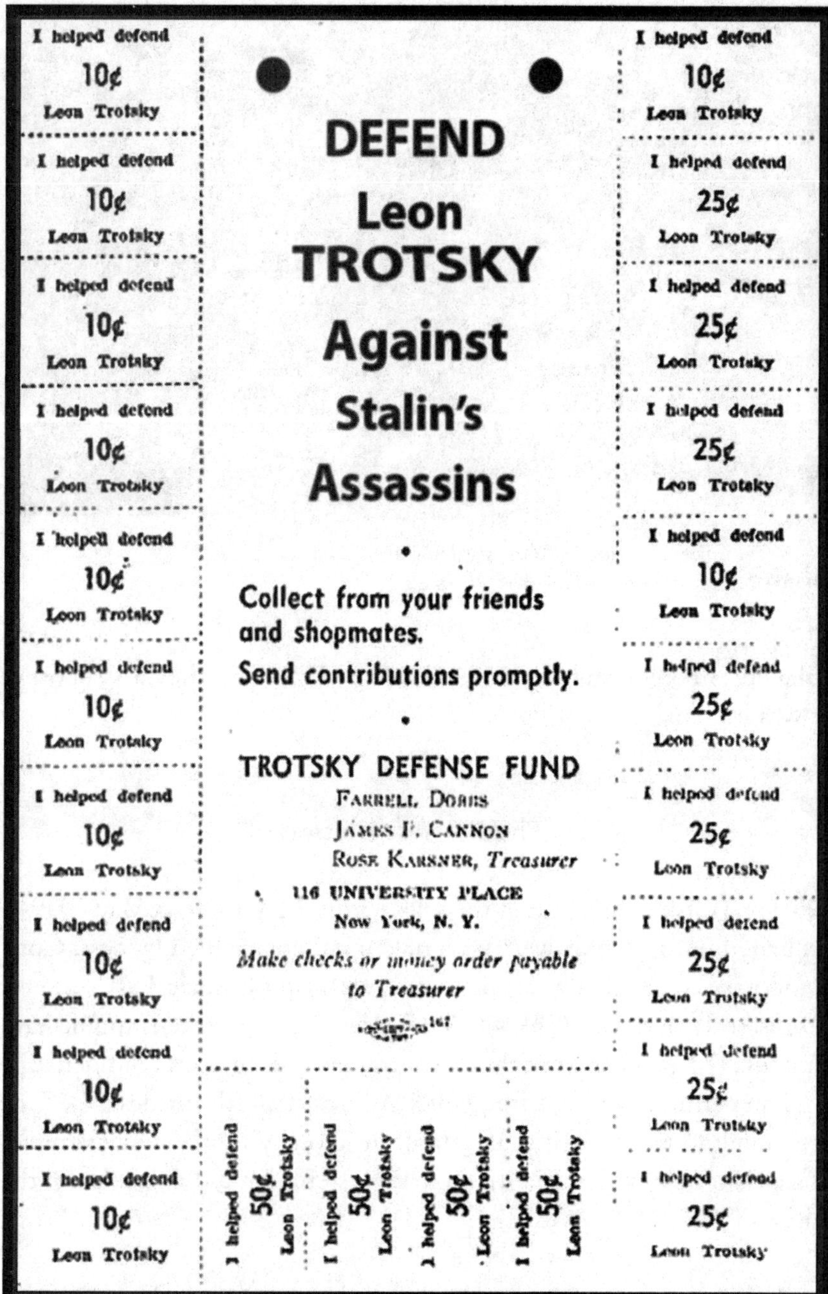

56. Fundraising leaflets distributed in union shops across the United States to support security upgrades.

57. A rare image showing both the garden gate (1) and guard's hut (2), as seen from Tower A.

villa's perimeter—but the danger he feared most was never structural. It was human.

The Fortress Illusion

During Trotsky's first year at the villa—from May 1939 to May 1940—security improvements were undertaken but constrained by cost. Contemporary newspaper accounts, along with later historical assessments, consistently overstated the villa's defenses. Such portrayals might have discouraged attackers, but they also fostered a dangerous confidence.

Later historians have frequently misunderstood, misdescribed, or exaggerated the security safeguards at Trotsky's villa. For example, Isaac Don Levine described a security system that did not exist on the night of May 24:

> The security precautions at the villa had been carefully designed to prevent the guard from being surprised and overcome by a hostile force. The guard was supposed to draw the first bolt, opening the

58. New steel garage doors with inset pedestrian door and remote lock system.

main door a few inches and flooding the face of the person seeking admittance with a strong light.[3]

In reality, the wooden garage doors on May 24 lacked external lighting and were secured only by a wooden crossbar. Even had more sophisticated mechanisms existed, they would have failed that night—when Sheldon Harte (code name AMUR), alone at the garage gate, simply opened it to the raiders.

From Failure to Fortification

Following the failed May raid, SWP President James Cannon and Ferrell Dobbs traveled from New York to Coyoacán. Their urgency was unmistakable. SWP branches swiftly raised $2,250, while Trotsky contributed an additional $6,000 from the sale of his archive to Harvard.[4]

As the funds arrived, the villa underwent a sober reassessment of its defenses. The alarm system consisted of sensors placed around the

59. The newly installed electric gate featured a remotely controlled lock (see arrow), with the small anteroom and chain-link garden gate visible in the background.

60. Seen from the patio, the plaque honoring Sheldon Harte and the electric gate lock (see arrow), both installed in early August 1940, remained visible as of 2009.

house and garden, all linked to a central control panel in the lean-to guard hut beside the garage. Along the brick and masonry wall encircling the property, electric contacts ensured that scaling the wall undetected was theoretically impossible. The slightest pressure triggered a bell at the command post and illuminated a bulb pinpointing the breach.[5] In practice, however, the system proved unreliable and heavily dependent on exhausted guards for maintenance.

Within weeks, however, guards and volunteers reinforced the compound with steel garage doors, wire mesh, barbed wire, and perimeter traps. The labor strained the small American guard force. Mealtimes grew tense, routines frayed, and Trotsky's moods fluctuated sharply. Loyalty, however, did not.

Unfortunately, beyond the villa—and beyond Mexico itself—details of the upgrades were already being secretly copied and relayed to Moscow, giving GPU planners a parallel view of the fortress taking shape.

61. Tower A and the main command post were constructed above the portico and were manned twenty-four hours a day.

The Sallyport and the Electric Lock System

Among the most consequential changes was a redesign of the compound's entry and exit system. Hank Schultz, an SWP member and skilled mechanic from Minnesota, rushed to the villa after hearing of the attack. To prevent the vulnerability of betrayal by a single guard on duty at the front gates, he proposed a double-gated sallyport—an enclosed passage with two electrically locked gates, remotely controlled from a command post atop Tower A. No single guard could admit or release a visitor alone without the concurrence of Tower A, which was to be manned twenty-four hours daily.[6]

Trotsky was impressed with the design and praised Schultz's work, calling him "indefatigable, absolutely selfless, and inventive."[7]

The sallyport incorporated steel garage doors replacing the original

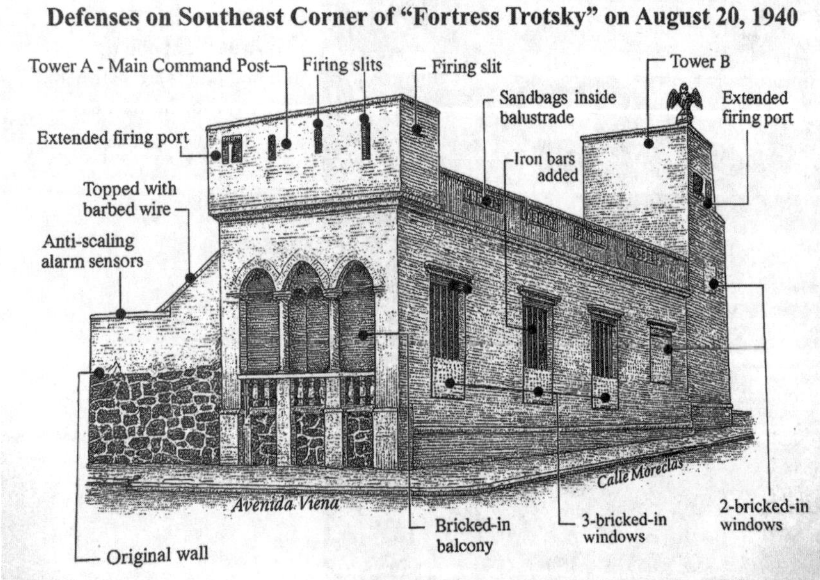

62.

wooden gates, an electrically locked pedestrian door inset into the right-hand garage door, and a small anteroom leading to an electrically locked chain-link garden gate that opened into the courtyard.

When Schultz departed in late July, he could not have known how pivotal his design would become. Within weeks, it would alter Mercader's escape plan and shape his choice of weapon. Schultz recommended Ray Rainbolt as his replacement, a proven organizer with military experience from Minnesota, but Trotsky balked at the cost and turned him down.[8]

Tower A and the Command Post

Before May 24, no centralized command existed—only a lean-to guard hut beside the garage controlling the alarm system and telephone lines. Tower A, completed in July, transformed the southeastern portico into a fortified command post. Elevated and manned around the clock, it controlled all access, locks, lights, and alarms.

63. C: Mini tower, and G: the two-story guards' quarters.

Command and Surveillance Towers

By late July 1940, three newly constructed towers—A, C, and D—supplemented the reinforced northeast tower (B), forming a four-point defensive system around the compound. Tower A, positioned at the southeast corner, served as the main command post and housed the electrical controls. Tower B, the original northeast tower, was reinforced with firing ports covering the Churubusco River and Calle Morelos. Tower C, a smaller structure set along the mid-north wall, overlooked only the patio and courtyard. Tower D, located at the northwest corner, commanded both the garden and the river.

Historian Bertrand Patenaude described the transformation:

> The tower atop the roof at the northeast corner of the property was converted into a two-story bombproof redoubt, with cement floors and ceilings. Three new brick turrets appeared above the walls, each with loopholes overlooking the patio and the neighborhood.

64. The only known photograph of the north wall of Fortress Trotsky. Tower B is at the northeast corner of the villa.

> Two of these blockhouses—one at the northwest corner [Tower D] and another at the center of the north wall directly above the guards' quarters—looked out onto the river [Tower C]. The one at the southeast corner [Tower A], built on the roof of the house and looking down on the police casita and Avenida Viena, as well as the gardens and the remotely controlled locked garden gate, served as the main guard station [Main Control Tower] and housed the electronic switches to the garage doors.[9]

Despite these advances, one vulnerability remained unchanged. Trotsky refused to allow guards to search visitors. As Albert Goldman recorded, Trotsky insisted, "Either we trust the people and admit them without a search, or we do not admit them at all."[10]

He also rejected proposals to raise the north wall against sniper fire from across the Churubusco River, arguing it would turn life

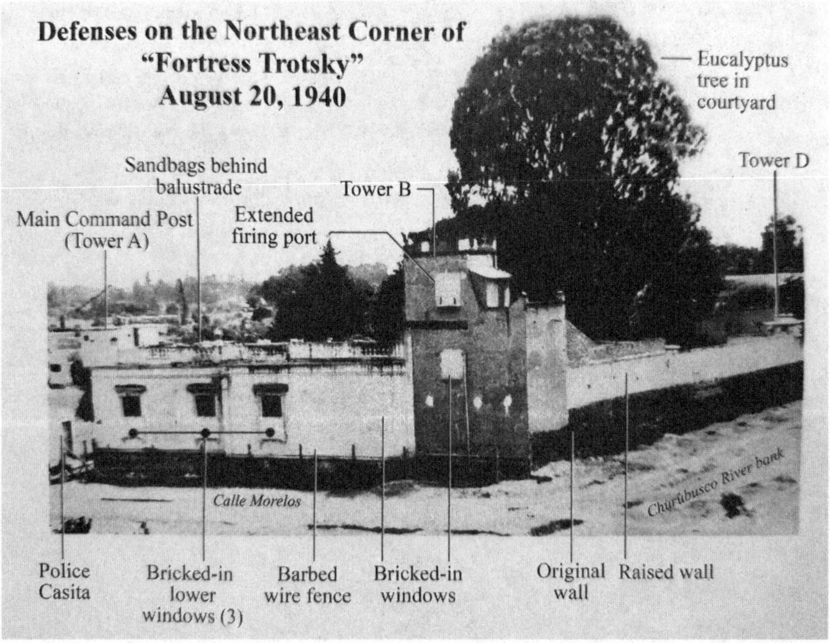

65.

inside the villa into imprisonment. Instead, a second story was added to the north guardhouse—ultimately exceeding the height originally requested.

Weapons, Rumors, and No Sleep

After the May raid, Joseph Hansen, the Old Man's former secretary, returned to the villa to serve as a guard and help coordinate security. He feared not only renewed GPU plots but the possibility of mass action by the Mexican Communist Party. On May Day 1940, some twenty thousand marchers flooded the streets of Mexico City shouting, "Death to Trotsky!" Hansen rightly wondered that if such a crowd turned toward Coyoacán, whether there was anything capable of stopping it from overrunning the compound.[11]

From June through August, exhaustion set in. Newly arrived guard

66. Jake Cooper stands in the doorway of the two-story guardhouse, August 1940. Bullet damage from the May 24 assault is visible.

Henry Schnautz wrote on August 15, 1940, that the work was grueling and he averaged less than five hours a night of sleep.

Schnautz organized firearms training with Chávez, a Mexican policeman and expert marksman. The guards' accuracy improved quickly.[12]

Rumors multiplied—tunneling saboteurs, poisoned food parcels, car bombs, even dive-bombing aircraft. A proposed photoelectric wall alarm was abandoned, and funds were redirected to barbed wire and bomb-resistant netting. Hansen warned Dobbs on July 31 that bombs posed the greatest threat.[13]

Surveillance, Delays, and Denial

Colonel Salazar's investigation delayed construction in July when a judge ordered the villa preserved for inspection. On July 16, the site was examined by the court for five hours, including interviews with Trotsky's grandson Sieva. Communist defense attorneys were granted access, alarming the guards.[14]

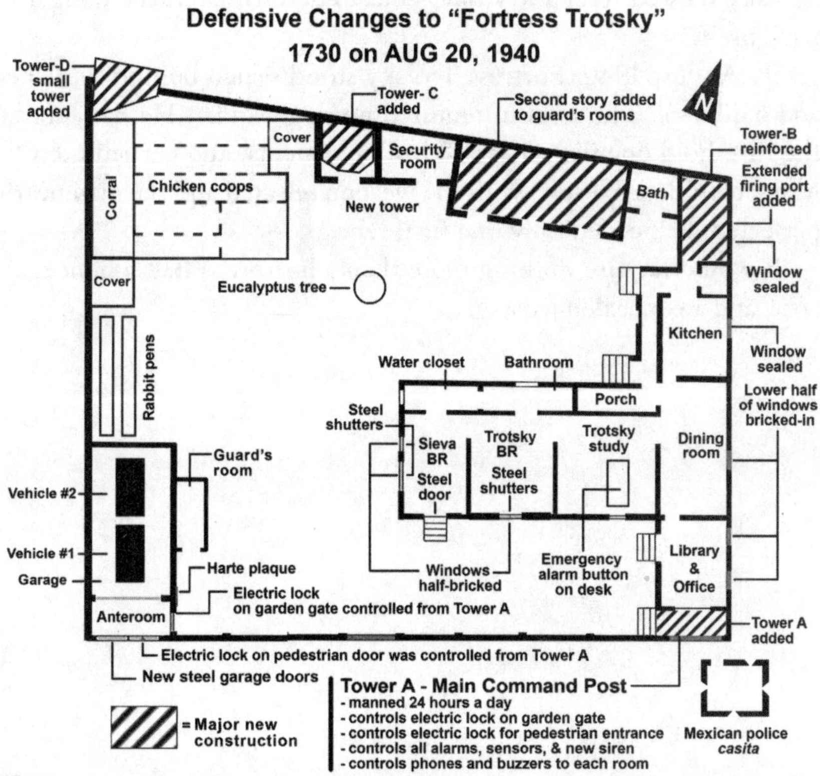

67.

The PCM exploited exaggerated newspaper accounts of the villa's defenses to pressure President Cárdenas into reducing police protection. When Trotsky first arrived in Coyoacán in 1937, the police detachment stationed outside the gate had already been cut to just ten men. Only after the failed assault of May 24, 1940, was the force restored to its original strength of twenty-five.[15]

Fatal Faith

Trotsky accepted structural safeguards but resisted personal ones, agreeing only after pressure to duck down in his car when entering or leaving the villa. Decades of survival had bred overconfidence.

Trotsky trusted steel and stone—but underestimated the danger of trust itself.

By August 1940, Fortress Trotsky stood sealed behind vigilance and hardware. The assassin required no siege ladder. He had crossed the threshold openly, rehearsed his movements, and earned the Old Man's confidence. Now, with the weapon selected and the plan nearly perfected, he needed only one final rehearsal.

It would require nothing more than a borrowed hat, a light raincoat, and a concealed ice axe.

CHAPTER XXII

FINAL REHEARSAL

Hat, Raincoat, and Axe

"I will be killed either by one of them in here or by one of my friends from the outside, by someone who has access to the house. Because Stalin cannot spare my life."
—Leon Trotsky

"Trotsky knew the hour was near—but not the hand that would strike."
—José Ramón Garmabella, interview with the author, 2009

"The most dangerous enemies wear your uniform, speak your language, and ask for your trust."
—GPU chief Genrikh Yagoda

The Quiet Before the Storm

Ramón Mercader returned to Mexico on July 5, 1940. Over the following three weeks, he stayed intermittently at the María Cristina Hotel, a period during which his daily movements remain largely undocumented.[1] The pressures of the assignment appear to have weighed heavily upon him. Eric London notes that "the success of his mission was a matter of life or death for all those involved, including himself, his mother, Caridad, and Eitingon."[2] Dmitri Volkogonov likewise described Mercader as deeply shaken by his orders, writing that the mission "sent a chill down Ramón's spine."[3]

According to a later recollection by Sylvia Ageloff, shared with her friend Marie Craipeau, Jacques*—Mercader's alias—responded to the news that Trotsky had survived the May 24 attack not with relief but with visible anger and frustration, as though the Old Man's survival represented failure rather than reprieve. Ageloff later claimed that she was so unnerved by Jac's* reaction that she destroyed what she described as her most compromising papers.[4] Even then, she maintained that she did not grasp the full significance of his behavior. In a later interview, the Mexican writer José Ramón Garmabella suggested that Ageloff believed Mercader's agitation in the weeks preceding the assassination reflected his awareness that responsibility for the act now rested solely with him.[5]

Suspicion and Naiveté

On July 29, at 2:40 p.m., Jacson* reappeared at the Coyoacán villa, ostensibly to collect his Buick, which had been parked there for six weeks for the guards' use.[6] Instead, he used the seventy-minute visit to tour the compound and listen as the guards boasted about newly installed security upgrades. When asked whether he had visited the Socialist Workers Party headquarters while in New York, he slipped—claiming he had been too busy meeting with "Wall Street brokers." Harry Mahoney observed that skipping a visit to the SWP was like visiting Rome and "a Catholic skipping the Vatican."[7] Attempting to recover, Jacson* explained that he had spent the trip persuading Sylvia's family that Trotsky's position—defending the USSR even under Stalin—was correct. The guards were unconvinced and reported his behavior to Trotsky.

Trotsky responded with characteristic generosity:

> He [Jacson*] is rather light-minded and will probably not become a strong member of the Fourth International. Nevertheless, he can be won closer. In order to build a party, we must have confidence that people can be changed.[8]

Tragically, Trotsky, forever optimistic, remained convinced that Jacson* could be molded into a comrade—never realizing that he was already a killer. Rather than ordering an investigation into Jacson's* background, he instructed his guards to "try harder to be friendly."[9] The GPU's long game had worked.

The Assassin with a Fever

By July 31, Operation MAT had entered its final phase. That day, Jacson* again visited the villa, bringing chocolate for Natalia Sedova [Trotsky], who was struck by how bad he looked and remarked on his obvious physical decline.[10] In the weeks that followed, his condition steadily worsened. Once robust and self-assured, Mercader became pale, gaunt, and increasingly agitated.

Historian Nicholas Mosley observed that he "began to be so ill that he was not able to get out of bed," lying for days in his darkened room. The man who had once been an effortless talker now "flitted from subject to subject and petered out at a loss for words." Formerly meticulous in his appearance, he spent half the day in his pajamas and, on more than one occasion, hinted at thoughts of suicide.[11]

Despite these warning signs, no renewed scrutiny followed. No inquiries were made at the Edificio Ermita office he claimed to share with Siqueiros. No effort was made to verify his supposed employer, Peter Lubeck, or to reconcile the contradictions in his shifting cover—engineer, broker, diamond dealer. Earlier warning signs also went unexamined. Though Jacson* claimed to travel regularly to Veracruz, he became lost on May 28 while driving the Rosmers and Natalia to the well-known port, requiring outside assistance—an odd lapse for a businessman supposedly familiar with the route.[12] No alarms were raised.

Nor did American contacts—airline staff, consular figures, and others—press questions about the mysterious Canadian.

At the same moment, Trotsky received a telegram from his former guard Jean van Heijenoort, offering to return and assume responsibility for security at the villa. A gifted linguist and seasoned observer of GPU tradecraft, van Heijenoort might have detected Jacson's* accent—neither Parisian, Belgian, nor convincingly Canadian. Trotsky declined. Writing on August 2, he explained, "It would really be too cruel to force you to return to this prison . . . not in the modern manner, it is true, but rather more like in medieval days."[13]

The decision quietly closed one of the last remaining avenues by which the assassin might have been exposed.

The Final Reconnaissance

Jacson* returned to the villa on August 10 for a brief visit. Mahoney mistakenly described that meeting as the rehearsal. It was not. The true dry run came a week later.

Natalia Sedova later recalled Jacson's* visit of August 17, 1940, at 4:35 p.m., with unease. She had not been at home when he arrived, but Trotsky described the encounter to her afterward and admitted that something about it had surprised him.

Jacson* brought what he called an outline of an article for Trotsky's review. In reality, it amounted to only a few muddled phrases. Trotsky offered several suggestions and withheld judgment, saying they would see how it developed. Yet what stayed with him was not the manuscript but Jacson's* manner.

Trotsky remarked that the visitor had not resembled a Frenchman at all that day. More curious still, he had seated himself on Trotsky's desk and kept his hat on throughout the meeting. Natalia found this detail striking. Jacson* never wore a hat indoors. Trotsky confirmed that on this occasion he had done so—and then pursued the matter no further.[14]

The hat was not merely eccentric; it was tactical. Jacson* may have observed that the guards' attention was drawn to the distinctive trilby and its unusual band, diverting notice from the raincoat draped over his arm—precisely the configuration he would employ three days later.

68. Trotsky's study and desk in 2021.

Tools of the Trade

Inside Trotsky's study, Jacson* took careful note of everything. Mosley described the room as sparsely furnished, roughly two hundred twenty-five square feet in size, containing a long wooden worktable positioned at a right angle to the window, several high-backed painted Mexican chairs, a daybed, two or three bookcases, and stacks of books and newspapers. On the worktable sat a push-button alarm to summon the guards and a .38-caliber Colt revolver. Along the eastern wall stood a low narrow table used to hold overflow documents.[15]

Trotsky sat with his back to the interior wall, a large map of Mexico behind him, the courtyard window to his left. As he read, Jacson* moved behind him and slightly to the left, into the narrow space between the desk and the low table beneath the map, silently observing both the Old Man and the room.[16] The future assassin likely absorbed every detail as Trotsky annotated the article.

69. The narrow space behind the chair, constrained by the rear console, was where the assassin maneuvered to deliver the fatal blow. (Photograph taken in 2010.)

This visit, however, was a rehearsal—not an attack. Jacson* carried his hat and raincoat exactly as he would on the day of the assassination, but on this occasion, the garment concealed no weapons. Its purpose was positional and procedural: to test movement, sightlines, and the guards' indifference to familiar ritual.

On his next and final visit, the raincoat would be altered into a weapon carrier. Sewn into its inner lining would be a thirteen-inch poniard. On the opposite side, concealed in a modified inner pocket, would be the shortened piolet—the weapon he had chosen for the killing.[17] Unlike a pistol or knife, the axe offered the prospect of a swift, silent blow. Left-handed, Jacson* would also carry a Spanish-made Star .45-caliber semiautomatic pistol in his left trouser pocket.[18]

Mosley later noted that the ice axe was concealed within the raincoat but misstated the width of its head as seven inches.[19] The actual head measured eleven inches—too large for any outer pocket. Instead, the shaft had been inserted through a slit cut into the lining, allowing it to slide between the lining and the outer fabric.[20]

70. The powerful Star .45-caliber pistol was a favorite during the Spanish Civil War.

When Jacson* returned for the assassination and laid the raincoat on the low table parallel to Trotsky's desk, the axe could be withdrawn quickly and without sound. By then, the guards—accustomed to his presence and reassured by repetition—took no notice as the two men remained alone in the study.

A Fateful Goodbye

Later that day, Trotsky granted an interview to journalist Eduardo Téllez Vargas. Without naming names, he issued a stark warning: "I will be killed either by one of them in here or by one of my friends from the outside, by someone who has access to the house. Because Stalin cannot spare my life."[21]

The warning was unmistakable. Its urgency went unrecognized.

Whether Jacson* intended to kill Trotsky on August 17 and recoiled cannot be established. What is clear is that no preparations consistent with an imminent attack were in place—no arrangements for document destruction, no prepared confession letter, and no escape plan for

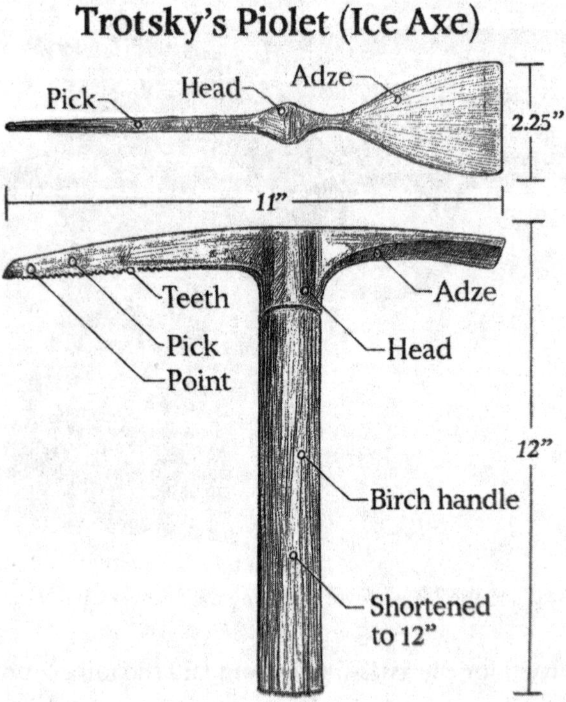

71. The shortened piolet became an efficient murder weapon.

Ramón, Caridad, or Eitingon. The rehearsal, however, confirmed the effectiveness of his deception.

As Ramón Mercader stepped out of Trotsky's study on August 17, 1940, the final countdown had begun. The charm, the chocolate, the hat, the raincoat—it had all worked. The guards were disarmed. The Old Man remained unsuspecting. The final defenses had been quietly dismantled.

What Trotsky failed to recognize—what no one around him could yet see—was that death had already entered the compound. Not with bombs or gunfire but cloaked in friendship and ideology. While the guards watched the gate, Mercader memorized the study. He had rehearsed his part, tested his disguise, and measured the room. With less than seventy-two hours remaining, he was ready. Stalin's hand was already at Trotsky's throat. The die was cast.

That day would begin like any other—quiet, routine, and fatally unremarkable.

CHAPTER XXIII

AUGUST 20, 1940

Trotsky's Final Day

"Whoever recalled it later, remembered the exceptional peace and serenity in the house up to the final hour!"
—Isaac Deutscher, *The Prophet Outcast*

"You see, they didn't kill us last night after all, and yet you are still dissatisfied."
—Leon Trotsky, recalled by Natalia Sedova [Trotsky]

"The blow must be delivered in such a way that no suspicion will fall upon us."
—Pavel Sudoplatov

Morning Routine

Harry Mahoney wrote that Tuesday, August 20, 1940, dawned "cloudless, sunny and crystal clear." It was a lovely day, Mahoney observed, as only a day can be in the clear, sparkling mountain air of Mexico City at that time of year—after the rains, when everything was green and blooming and the dust had settled.[1]

One of the precautions taken after the May 24 attack had been the installation of steel shutters that bolted over the courtyard windows and were opened and closed each morning and evening. They effectively prevented a future attacker from firing directly into the bedroom. According to Natalia, Trotsky sometimes joked as he opened or closed the shutters, "Well, now no Siqueiros can get at us." On waking, he often greeted her with dry gallows humor: "You see, they didn't kill us last night after all—and still you're dissatisfied." When she protested, he once added more quietly, "Yes, Natasha [Natalia], we received a reprieve."[2]

What began as an unremarkable summer day would, by nightfall, become the scene of one of the most consequential political assassinations of the twentieth century.

A Rare Sense of Peace

On the morning of August 20, those earlier musings seemed distant. Trotsky awoke around 7:00 a.m. feeling unusually refreshed. A double dose of sleeping powder had given him rare, uninterrupted rest—momentary relief from the strain that had shadowed him since the May attack.[3] Three months earlier, he had survived a coordinated assault by more than twenty armed men. Another attempt felt inevitable, though the timing and method remained unknown. Still, a sense of guarded calm lingered. Even under constant threat, Trotsky often remarked that exile was preferable to "dying in a bed in the Kremlin"—a sentiment Natalia Sedova [Trotsky] and other contemporaries later recalled in their memoirs.[4]

That morning, his spirits were noticeably high. Restored by sleep and renewed strength, he dressed quickly and stepped into the courtyard to tend to his rabbits—a ritual he never abandoned, even during periods of illness. He said the work gave him solace, though the labor left him tired. Mindful of his limits, he paced himself carefully, conserving energy for the intellectual work that awaited him each day. Whether cleaning a cage or composing a polemic, he approached the task with full intensity.[5]

A Day of Work

Trotsky's daily animal chores usually began around 7:15 a.m. and continued until 9:00 a.m. Occasionally he paused to jot down ideas or dictate

72. Trotsky appeared temporarily strengthened during the summer of 1940.

a phrase to Natalia. Then they took breakfast together. That morning, he read a letter from his attorney, Albert Goldman, confirming that his personal archives had arrived safely at Harvard University. The sale had brought only $6,000—far less than Trotsky had hoped. The funds were urgently needed to pay for recent security improvements to the villa.[6]

The morning passed without interruption. Afterward, Trotsky told Natalia that he felt strong enough to begin dictating a new article—this one addressing the politically sensitive issue of conscription in the United States. As he worked, he framed the American debate over conscription not merely as a policy question but as a test of revolutionary principle, and his language reflected that urgency.[7]

Following a short siesta, his good spirits remained. Though recent weeks had been marked by fatigue, today brought a noticeable improvement. Natalia occasionally peeked into the study and saw him in his familiar pose: hunched slightly over the desk, pen in hand, his brow furrowed in concentration.

To Natalia, her husband often resembled either a prisoner or a hermit, locked behind steel-reinforced doors and flanked by guards. But unlike either, he remained immersed in the ceaseless battle against Stalin and his ideological enemies. Isolation did not silence him—it sharpened his defiance.

Approaching Shadows

At five o'clock, as was their custom, Trotsky and Natalia sat down for tea. Twenty or thirty minutes later, Natalia stepped onto the kitchen balcony for fresh air. Looking down into the courtyard, she saw her husband standing beside an open rabbit hutch, gently feeding the animals. Another man stood nearby, wearing a hat, with his topcoat slung over one arm. At first she did not recognize him.

Only when the man removed his hat and stepped toward the house did his face come into focus.

It was Jacson*—Ramón Mercader.[8]

CHAPTER XXIV

THE ASSASSIN'S LAST DAY

"I did not choose the time to live, die, or kill . . ."
—Ramón Mercader, 1969

"Every assassin is convinced of his own necessity."
—GPU intelligence manual

"The hardest step is not the first. It is the one after."
—GPU training proverb

Morning in Room 113

Just before 8:00 a.m. on August 20, Ramón Mercader—alias Frank Jacson*—woke from a fitful sleep. He and Sylvia were registered as Mr. and Mrs. Frank Jacson* in room 113 of the Hotel Montejo,[1] a discreet four-story colonial-style inn along the busy Paseo de la Reforma. With "50 rooms, 50 baths, and moderate prices,"[2] the Montejo catered to businessmen and visiting Americans. Room 113, with its private bath and "modern and luxurious furniture," offered comfort—but for Jacson* and Sylvia, it would be their final refuge.

Desperate to see her husband, Sylvia had left New York by air on August 7 and arrived in Mexico City the next day by Eastern Airlines from Brownsville, Texas.[3] The couple spent two nights at the Waldorf Hotel before checking in to the Montejo on August 11. They had not seen one another since late June, and Sylvia grew increasingly anxious after weeks without word. Then, after nearly three weeks of silence,

73. Hotel Montejo was a popular and conveniently located choice for American travelers.

she sent him a telegraph on July 29 in care of the American Express office in Mexico City. It read:

> No letter for many weeks, Worried. Wire immediately present plans. (signed) SYLVIA.[4]

It must have worked as Frank* finally telephoned from Mexico at the end of July, claiming he had fallen ill in Puebla and had been too sick to write or call.[5] His health, he said, was failing, and he begged Sylvia to come at once.

Sylvia had hoped to nurse him back to health, but despite her efforts, he remained pale, gaunt, and miserable. Persistent digestive trouble and bouts of diarrhea left him weak and irritable. His light olive complexion had taken on a greenish cast. She attributed the decline to amoebic dysentery, chronic diarrhea, and exhaustion aggravated by Mexico City's altitude. Sylvia urged him to see a doctor—but not in

Mexico—insisting that he wait until their return to New York, where he could consult her own physician in Brooklyn.[6]

In a letter to her sister Hilda dated August 15, Sylvia wrote, "I'm glad I came [to Mexico City] from Jac's* point of view because he really looks terrible and needs care." He attributed his weight loss to a chronic condition requiring surgery. With their return to New York scheduled for the following day and tickets already purchased, Sylvia hoped her Brooklyn family doctor would uncover the true cause.

His illness was not of the stomach, though it might have appeared that way. The twitching, the restlessness, the bone-deep fatigue—these were outward signs of collapse. Tormented by dread and sleepless anxiety, he found no moment of peace. Every waking hour was shadowed by the knowledge of what he was preparing to do—and by the near certainty that it would destroy him.

Adding to Mercader's strain were signs that Moscow had begun to question Jacson's* effectiveness. More than a month had passed since his return to Mexico, yet no decisive action had followed. Trotsky remained alive—and active—publicly dissecting the GPU's role in the failed May 24 assault. In Moscow, patience was wearing thin.

As Eric London has pointed out, around August 7 or 8, Jacson* received a terse telegram in English, which Eduard Puigventós attributes to Nahum Eitingon. Its message was unmistakable and ominous: "PLEASE COME BACK TO NEW YORK AT ONCE."[7] For an operative trained to read implication as closely as instruction, the summons carried a clear warning. Failure was no longer a distant possibility but an imminent reckoning. If his nerves were not already frayed, the message almost certainly pushed him to the breaking point.

Jacson* struggled to steady his nerves and summon the will to carry out a single, brutal act: to drive an ice axe into the skull of an aging man who trusted him as a friend. The blow, if it succeeded, would silence Stalin's most dangerous critic. It would also mark the beginning of his own undoing.

The Escape Plan

Jacson* planned to kill Trotsky noiselessly and exit through Trotsky and Natalia's bedroom, then through Sieva's, avoiding the dining room, the guard, and Natalia herself. From there he would reach the courtyard, cross roughly twenty-five steps under the gaze of guards stationed at the new main command post atop Tower A, smile and wave, and hope they would remotely unlock the garden gate and pedestrian door. All this needed to happen before Trotsky's body was discovered and the siren sounded. He would then pass through the small pedestrian door in the steel garage gate and out past armed Mexican police. The odds were against him, but it just might work.

The exit procedure, however, had recently been altered by the installation of two remotely controlled electric locks—one on the garden gate and one on the pedestrian door. This was a significant improvement in villa security and had a decisive impact on Mercader's escape plan. Previously, he might have used any of his three weapons—ice axe, dagger, or pistol—and, even if the attack alerted the guards, still had a chance to shoot his way into the courtyard and flee through the garage gate. The electric locks completely eliminated that option.

Now his only hope of escape depended on killing Trotsky instantly and without a sound—before the alarm could be raised and the gates sealed. These constraints hardened his decision to use the ice axe, the weapon most likely to deliver a silent, incapacitating blow.

His objective was to reach his Buick parked outside the compound or, in an emergency, to rendezvous with his mother, Caridad, waiting nearby in a taxi. But he understood that the odds of surviving until nightfall were slim.

A Visit—and a Lie

Sylvia believed that she and her husband would fly to New York the next day and she spent the morning making final arrangements. Around 9:00 a.m., Jacson* left the hotel, telling her he was going to the US embassy to renew his visa.[8] It was a lie—intended to distance himself from her. Everything would soon be over, and Sylvia was not part of his escape plan.

Señorita Noriega, the hotel's manager, later recalled seeing him pass through the lobby with a raincoat draped over his arm—an odd choice on such a bright day.[9]

Sylvia waited anxiously in their room, irritated by his prolonged absence. He returned nearly three hours later, evasive and short-tempered, blaming long lines at the embassy.[10] Police later attempted, unsuccessfully, to trace his whereabouts during those hours.

According to later journalistic accounts, Mercader met with Nahum Eitingon (TOM) in Chapultepec Park, where he received final instructions and the typed confession he was to carry in his pocket.[11]

A Final Walk

In their hotel room, Jacson* was irritable and pacing. Hoping to calm him, Sylvia suggested a short walk and perhaps lunch. They left together, heading north along Avenida Reforma before turning east on Juárez toward San Juan de Letrán.[12]

Jacson* remained distant and withdrawn until the couple unexpectedly encountered one of Trotsky's younger guards, Otto Schüssler, and his fiancée outside the Palacio de Bellas Artes. During the conversation, Sylvia mentioned that they were returning to the United States the following day and hoped to say goodbye to the Trotskys that afternoon. At that point, Jacson* abruptly proposed that the two couples meet for a farewell dinner that evening at 7:30 p.m.[13] Eric London, however, disputes this version, writing that it was Sylvia—not Jacson*—who extended the dinner invitation. The distinction is significant. If London's account is correct, police later concluded that Sylvia may have been deliberately arranging to keep Schüssler away from the villa that night.[14] Then, without explanation, Frank* abruptly excused himself—claiming to have forgotten an appointment—and walked away.

Sylvia was stunned. Embarrassed, she covered for him, blaming the altitude and his sensitive stomach. Schüssler nodded and promised to see them that evening.

Returning alone to the Hotel Montejo, Sylvia tried to make sense of his behavior. She later told authorities that Jacson*, once "gentle and accessible" when they first met in Paris, had become volatile and withdrawn since her return to Mexico. When he failed to reappear that afternoon, she asked Noriega about him but received no answers. Jacson* eventually returned without explanation. Fearing his temper, Sylvia did not press him.

Operation MAT—the GPU's second assassination plan—depended entirely on Jacson* maintaining Trotsky's trust. His relationship with Sylvia had made that possible. Had she shared her doubts about him with the Trotskys at any point, the entire operation might have unraveled.

Knowing her preferences, Jacson* took Sylvia for a drink and a light lunch at the Salon Don Quixote in the nearby Regis Hotel. The outing seemed to calm her. Back at the Montejo, he told her he needed to quickly retrieve mail from the Wells Fargo office and would return in time for their visit to Coyoacán.[15]

At approximately 2:10 p.m., Frank* left the room carrying his raincoat, fully aware that he would never see Sylvia again.[16] Eric London later asserted that concealed inside the raincoat were the ice axe used in the attack, along with a dagger and a pistol.[17] That claim warrants skepticism. It is difficult to believe that a seasoned GPU operative would leave three concealed weapons unattended in a raincoat inside a hotel room shared with Sylvia before the attack. Such behavior would have been exceptionally reckless and incompatible with even rudimentary GPU tradecraft.

Preparations

Jacson* later told police that he stopped briefly at Wells Fargo, then drove to the outskirts of the city, where he burned his passport and all identification as Frank Jacson*. In his suit pocket was the confession prepared two months earlier in New York by the GPU, blaming the assassination on a rogue Trotskyist faction. Typed in French to match his alias, Jacques Mornard*, it had been left undated—until that afternoon, when he penciled in "August 20" and signed it "Jac*." He claimed he had typed it the previous day in Chapultepec Woods.[18] In another pocket, he carried the typed political article he intended Trotsky to review.

74. Mercader's three weapons and his Clifton raincoat were photographed after the assassination.

Mercader had no intention of taking Sylvia with him to Coyoacán. Her presence would complicate his plan to meet Trotsky alone. However, he was confident in his control over her and did not fear that she would visit Trotsky's villa without him. Isaac Don Levine later observed, "Sylvia was submissive, dependent on him and perhaps a little afraid of him . . . not in the habit of acting independently."[19]

By midafternoon, Jacson's* top priority was retrieving his weapons and destroying anything linking him to Stalin or the GPU. Police never located his weapons cache. Levine suggested that Mercader might have stored them at one point in a large suitcase occasionally kept at Shirley Courts, where he stayed from April to June. Most likely, however, Caridad took care of their disposal.

Three Weapons

That afternoon, Jacson* carried three concealed weapons: a .45-caliber Star Modelo P semiautomatic pistol, a poniard with a 13¾-inch blade, and a shortened ice axe (piolet).

The plan rested on a single brutal premise: for Frank* to have any chance of escape, Trotsky had to be instantly incapacitated and die without a sound. GPU training emphasized a surprise attack from behind designed to cause catastrophic cranial injury.[20]

The pretext for the visit was a farewell call and Trotsky's review of Frank's* article. On August 17, Jacson* had, for the first time, been allowed alone with Trotsky in the Old Man's study to discuss such a draft. He intended to reenact that moment—using the article as bait once again.

The Road to Coyoacán

At approximately 4:45 p.m., Mercader climbed into his Buick and drove toward Coyoacán, raincoat concealing his weapons, hands steady, mind fixed.

A block from the villa waited his mother, Caridad. Another block beyond, Leonid Eitingon sat parked with binoculars and ready to assist if escape became possible. Both were parked along Avenida Viena, had a view of the compound, and were alert for the first sign of trouble. But before any escape could be attempted, the task remained.

The city's clamor faded as Mercader neared the fortified villa. Each turn of the wheel drew him closer to the moment that would define—and damn—his life. The deception was complete. The tools were ready.

As Jacson* approached the gate, he turned the car around and parked the Buick near the entry garage door. Later, some bystanders would claim that he left the engine running.

Now, after months of preparation, deception, and rehearsal, the moment had come. The assassin stood at the gate—his weapons hidden, his exit mapped, the final act minutes away.

There would be no turning back. This time there could be no excuse.

The Old Man had to die.

CHAPTER XXV

THE AXE FALLS

Trotsky's Final Battle

"He [Stalin] seeks not to strike at ideas of his opponent, but at his skull."
—Leon Trotsky

"After the [May 24] attack, we were certain Stalin would try again. We expected a new method—perhaps a solitary individual secretly dispatched by them."
—Natalia Sedova [Trotsky]

"In the end, Trotsky was not felled by Stalin's army, but by his illusion of safety."
—Anonymous GPU defector

"We could have withstood an attack by 50 men unless armed with artillery. No defense is possible against treachery."
—Guard Henry Schnautz

5:20 p.m.

The fortified villa in Coyoacán stood ready for the wrong kind of danger.

For nearly three months, Trotsky's household had lived under the expectation of another armed assault—rifles, grenades, a second

Siqueiros-style raid, perhaps even an attack from the air. Steel shutters had been bolted into place. Gates reinforced with electric locks. Guards doubled. Every defense pointed outward, toward force.

But the threat approaching the gates that afternoon carried no rifle.

A beige Buick came to a hard stop on the dusty street outside the compound. The guards were not expecting a visitor, but the driver was familiar enough to avoid immediate alarm.

Inside the walls, Trotsky moved through the routines that steadied him—tending his animals, preparing to return to his desk. Natalia watched with the alert unease of someone who had already survived one attack and expected another.

Beyond the compound, unseen from the courtyard, two figures waited—Caridad Mercader and Nahum Eitingon—watching the gates and listening for the siren. If it sounded too soon, the escape would fail. If it remained silent long enough for Ramón to emerge, the mission might yet succeed.

The villa had been hardened against violence. It had not been hardened against trust.

The Siren Is Installed

On the rooftop near the main guard tower, Charles Cornell, Joseph Hansen, and handyman Melquiades Benitez worked in the fading light, installing a new siren recently sent by a supporter in Los Angeles. Hardwired into the villa's alarm system and triggered by a button newly installed on Trotsky's desk, it was intended to be the first warning of attack.

"It's loud enough to be heard all the way to Los Angeles," Trotsky joked—never knowing it would soon become his funeral bell.[1]

Within hours, the siren would wail for the first time—not as a drill, but as a cry of alarm. Its sound would not stop at the gates. It would carry beyond Coyoacán and into history, marking the moment the Fourth International suffered its most grievous wound—the day the axe fell.[2]

A Familiar Visitor

Hansen looked down from the rooftop and saw a beige Buick pull up and park. The driver—Frank Jacson*—was known to the guards, though his arrival was unexpected.

Unlike earlier visits, there was no theatrical flourish. This time he parked deliberately, angling the car toward the road leading back to Coyoacán. The position later suggested forethought—a planned exit and the hope of escape. "Has Sylvia arrived yet?" Jacson* called up, waving toward the rooftop.

His unexpected arrival drew attention. Following the May 24 attack, visitors were logged carefully, and no one had been told to expect Sylvia—or anyone on her behalf. Still, Trotsky was known to arrange last-minute meetings without notifying staff.[3] From Main Control Tower A, Charles Cornell flipped the switches that opened the locks on the pedestrian door and the garden gate, and Harold Robins, the chief of guards, went to meet Jacson*.

Trotsky was in the courtyard tending to his rabbits and chickens. Robins stayed close, as protocol required a guard to be present when the Old Man met visitors. Under the tightened security routines adopted after the May 24 raid, the precaution now seemed warranted.

Jacson* Appears

Natalia and Leon had sat down for tea at 5:00 p.m. before Trotsky went out to tend the animals. Between 5:20 and 5:30 p.m., Natalia recalled stepping onto the kitchen balcony and seeing a man speaking with her husband near the rabbit pens. When he removed his hat, she recognized him at once: Jacson*.

Her reaction was immediate and visceral. *He's here again*, she thought. *Why is he coming so often—and without warning?* A wave of dislike passed through her, accompanied by a sense of something unnatural. Something was wrong.[4]

Jacson* greeted her and asked for a glass of water. She offered tea instead. "No, no," he replied. "I dined too late and feel that the food is up here," he said, pointing to his throat. "It's choking me."[5] Harry Mahoney later described Mercader's thirst as "the guilty dry mouth caused by his dread and fear of what he was about to do."[6]

His appearance struck her. His complexion had taken on a sickly green-gray pallor, his demeanor strained, as if he were struggling to maintain composure while concealing panic.[7]

She asked why he was wearing his hat and carrying his topcoat—it was sunny, and he was pressing the coat awkwardly against his left side. He replied that the weather might not last; it could rain.[8] When she asked about Sylvia, Jacson* seemed confused, lost in his own thoughts. "Sylvia? . . . Sylvia?" he repeated, before adding casually, "She's always well." Still gripping his coat, he produced several pages—his supposed article.[9]

Natalia recalled that three days earlier, Jacson* had arrived with another article, dressed exactly as before. She had not been home at the time, but Trotsky later described the encounter with unease. "He didn't resemble a Frenchman at all," he remarked. "He sat down at my desk and kept his hat on the entire time." Now he was back again. Had that earlier visit been a rehearsal?[10]

After the May 24 attack, Natalia had urged Trotsky to place a guard outside his study window. He declined, citing limited manpower, though other security measures were under review.[11]

Trotsky, attempting to ease Natalia's angst over Jacson's* unexpected visit, explained that Sylvia was leaving for New York the next day and that he had invited her to stop by, forgetting to mention it. Natalia said she would have prepared packages had she known. Jacson* offered—disingenuously—to return the next day to collect them. She declined.[12]

Into the Study

"You're looking unwell again," Trotsky said reproachfully. Then, after a pause, he added, "Well then, shall we take a look at your article?"[13]

Trotsky usually met guests in his study with a guard present but sometimes made exceptions, as he had for Mercader's visit three days earlier. Though Jacson* was a frequent visitor, he remained an outsider; in hindsight, a guard should have been present.

Natalia followed but stopped in the dining room. As the study door closed, she noticed Jacson* still gripping his raincoat—and wearing his hat.[14]

She could not explain why but later recalled that it felt—without proof or cause—as if the final act had already begun.

The Axe Falls

Trotsky's desk dominated the study, its broad surface cluttered with drafts and papers. A gooseneck lamp supplemented the fading daylight from the south-facing windows. By his right hand lay a loaded .25-caliber pistol; nearby sat six spent shell casings from the May 24 attack. His .38-caliber Colt revolver[15] had recently been removed during a desk reorganization.[16] To his left was the new alarm button wired to the siren installed that day.[17]

Trotsky sat down as Jacson* placed his coat and hat on the low console table behind him, then moved quietly to the Old Man's left in the cramped space behind the desk—blocking access to the alarm button.

Trotsky began reading and had just gotten through the first page.[18] Dissatisfied with the article he had seen three days earlier, he lifted the pages and turned slightly clockwise to catch the fading light coming in through the French windows—unaware of the danger closing in behind him.

In his statement to police, Jacson* later said what happened next:

> I put my raincoat on the table so I could take out the ice axe . . . when Trotsky started to read my article, I took the piolet in my fist, and, closing my eyes, gave him a tremendous blow on the head.[19]

The attacker they feared had slipped past them not with bullets, but with trust.

Mercader's eyes were closed. Trotsky's were not. In the split second before the strike, Mercader edged farther to his left, preemptively

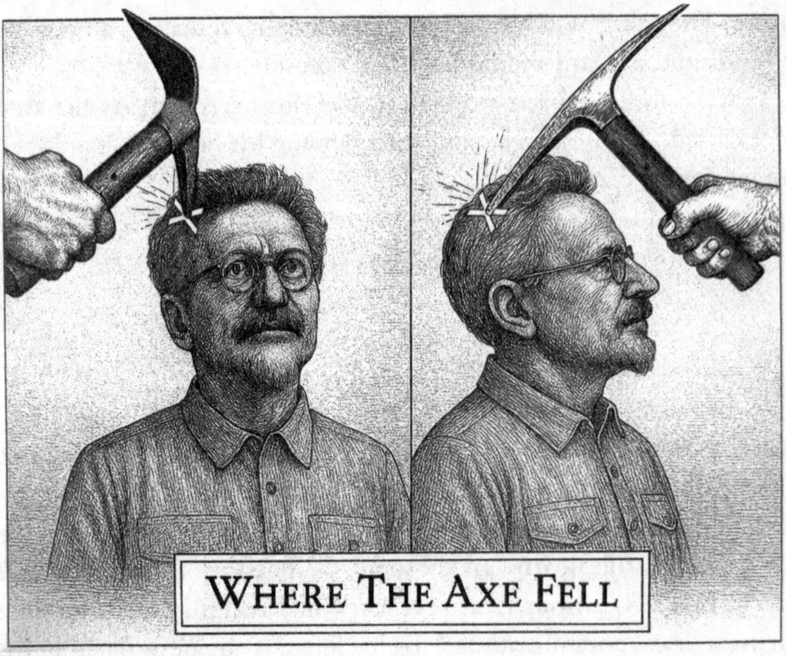

75. Trotsky had just turned and was nearly face-to-face with his assassin when the blow fell.

cutting off the Old Man's reach toward the alarm. Trotsky sensed the movement and turned—rotating roughly one hundred thirty to one hundred fifty degrees clockwise in his chair—just in time to look up before the axe struck.

Fifty years later, Pavel Sudoplatov introduced a conflicting description of the attack after meeting with Ramón Mercader in Moscow in 1969:

> Ramón did not close his eyes. Trotsky, engrossed in the article, turned his head. This changed the direction of the blow and weakened its force. That is why he wasn't killed immediately and screamed, calling for help.[20]

The axe did not strike from behind as planned. It fell with Trotsky almost facing the man who swung it. That small deviation changed everything.

The Struggle

Trotsky did not collapse and fall from the chair. Instead, a scream tore from his lungs and echoed through the villa. At sixty, grievously wounded, he surged to his feet "like a madman," blood pouring down his face, and lunged at Jacson* with ferocity born of will, not strength.[21]

The old warrior hurled books and a heavy pen holder, then wrenched the piolet from Jacson's* hands. In the melee, he bit down hard on Jacson's* finger, drawing a second scream.[22]

The Scream

At that moment, Melquiades Benitez and guards Charles Cornell and Joseph Hansen were in the new Main Control Tower A labeling switches on the unfinished alarm panel. The photoelectric system designed by Hank Schultz had never been completed after his departure; Hansen formally canceled it on July 31, 1940, instead diverting funds to wire netting to prevent bombs being thrown over the walls.[23]

What shattered the calm was not the alarm but the scream.

Mercader later described it as "AAaaa, very long, infinitely long," a sound that pierced his brain and lingered there.[24] Hansen described the scream as prolonged and agonized, half scream, half sob, chilling him to the bone.[25]

Hansen ran out onto the adjacent rooftop as sounds of violent struggle erupted below. He claimed to glimpse Trotsky locked body to body with another man and shouted to Benitez, who was armed with a rifle and preparing to fire. He yelled to stop.[26] However, this account must be treated with caution. From the rooftop and Tower A, the view into the study was obstructed by the room's southern wall. Architecturally, it would have been impossible from Hansen's position on the roof to see the area behind Trotsky's desk where the blow was struck.

What could be seen and heard was the aftermath—movement, resistance, chaos behind the study walls.[27]

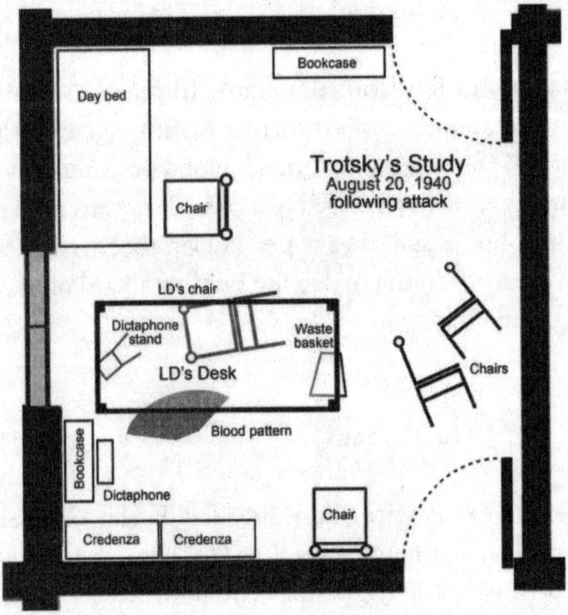

76. A schematic of Trotsky's study following the attack.

Blood Everywhere

Hansen triggered the general alarm and slid down the ladder. As he entered the dining room, Trotsky staggered out of the study, blood streaming down his face. Through sheer will, he pushed forward—determined to reach Natalia and warn those outside.[28]

Natalia and Harold Robins rushed to him, guiding him toward the kitchen balcony before he collapsed near the far end of the dining room table. For a moment, Natalia thought part of the roof had collapsed. Within seconds, however, she understood it was an attack.[29]

Behind them, Jacson* stood frozen in the study, his Star pistol hanging loosely from his hand. The floor was covered with blood.

The Beating

Robins and Hansen rushed Jacson* and began walloping him with blows. Robins drove Jacson* into a corner, striking him with the butt of his revolver. Hansen followed, landing blows so violent he fractured his own hand.[30] The beating was savage. Jacson* soon lost consciousness.

Hansen would later recall,

> My first impulse was to kill him. But I held back—I felt sure he'd talk. We kept the police out. Robins, then I, then Robins again worked him over. He wouldn't talk. I think he went unconscious twice. That's when I realized how hard this person really was. He would rather die than talk.[31]

On the floor lay the weapon: a shortened mountaineer's piolet (ice axe), its forged iron pick spattered with blood.

Years later, Ramón's brother Luis asked why he had not fought his way out. Purportedly, Ramón admitted he had never killed before—and that Trotsky's scream nearly paralyzed him. Before he could use the pistol, the guards were already upon him.[32]

Natalia's Recollection

Natalia knelt beside Trotsky, wiping blood from his face. As she cradled his head, he spoke quietly. Only then—after the blow—did Trotsky recall a fleeting thought from moments earlier as they entered his study: *This man could kill me.*[33]

He had dismissed it—out of politeness.[34]

Natalia would remember those words for the rest of her life.

The Final Hour

At 5:50 p.m., Hansen climbed back to the guard tower and shouted toward the police casita. It was unnecessary. The scream—and then the siren—had already alerted authorities. The Green Cross Hospital received the call at 6:00 p.m., and the ambulance was dispatched immediately.[35]

A few blocks away, Caridad Mercader waited in a taxi, tense and silent, while Nahum Eitingon sat another block farther along in a separate vehicle. Ramón had been expected to exit the gate calmly and drive away in the Buick. Their exfiltration plan called for a quick rendezvous and a private flight out of the country—probably to Cuba. Eitingon monitored the property from a distance with binoculars. But by 5:45 p.m., they observed an ominous uptick in activity at the police casita. Then the siren wailed—long, high-pitched, and unmistakable. That siren wasn't part of the plan—it told them that something major had happened.

Ramón was meant to step out bloodless and composed, slip into the Buick, and vanish down the escape route they had meticulously prepared. But the siren shattered that plan. He hadn't come out. The clean getaway was lost.

And yet this had always been one of the most likely outcomes—one Caridad had prepared for. Still, she clung to hope that he might emerge. But if Trotsky was dead, then the mission she had planned—and forced upon her son—would still have succeeded.

The Doctor and the Wounded Revolutionary

Hansen immediately sent Charles Cornell to fetch a doctor. Cornell first attempted to use Jacson's* Buick but could not locate the key; instead, he took one of the household cars and sped off. He returned quickly with Dr. Wenceslao Dutrem Domínguez, the Spanish exile physician who had treated the family after the failed May 24 attack and was trusted within Trotsky's circle.[36]

Dutrem arrived breathless, medical bag in hand. He cleaned the wound, applied antiseptic, and at first tried to reassure those gathered that the injury did not appear fatal. Trotsky did not respond immediately. A faint, ironic smile crossed his lips. Then he spoke quietly: "I feel it here . . . this is the end . . . this time . . . they've succeeded."[37]

Struggling to remain conscious, Trotsky turned toward Hansen. "Take care of Natalia," he said. "She has been with me many, many years." Drawing Hansen closer, he added—analytical even now—"He was a political assassin. Jacson* was GPU—or perhaps a fascist. Most likely the GPU."[38]

Natalia placed a pillow beneath her husband's head and pressed ice against the swelling wound. Hansen examined it closely. There had been no gunshot; he concluded the attacker must have used a heavy instrument—something like a prospector's pick or a mountaineer's piolet.

Trotsky drifted in and out of consciousness. Each time he stirred, he reached for Natalia's hand and kissed it gently. Once he whispered, "Natasha [Natalia], I love you." At another moment his thoughts turned outward again: "Sieva must be taken away from this."[39] She whispered in response, "No one, no one must be allowed to see you without being searched."[40] Her words carried a tragic optimism, revealing that she had not yet grasped the severity of his wound—or that there would be no future visitors at all.

He Must Talk

Holding her husband, Natalia suddenly thought of the chaos unfolding behind them. "What about that one?" she asked—meaning Jacson*. "They [Trotsky's guards] will kill him." At that moment, Cornell rushed past with his pistol drawn. In the study, Jacson* sat bloodied and dazed while Harold Robins held him pinned against the wall.

From the dining room, Trotsky's voice rose faintly but unmistakably: "No . . . impermissible to kill. He must be . . . forced to talk."[41]

Jacson* then broke down. "They made me do it! They've got my mother!" he cried. "Sylvia had nothing to do with this. The GPU had nothing to do with this." The guards did not believe him. The beating resumed. Bruised and slumped in the corner, Jacson* finally looked up and asked, "Why don't you kill me?"[42]

Though his outburst momentarily appeared to implicate the GPU, Jacson* never repeated the claim—not once during the lengthy interrogations that followed. As he drifted back to consciousness, his words came in a confused torrent: his mother was imprisoned; Sylvia Ageloff was innocent; he denied—too insistently—any connection to Soviet intelligence.[43]

Dr. Dutrem stayed close, trying to calm Natalia, but Trotsky's

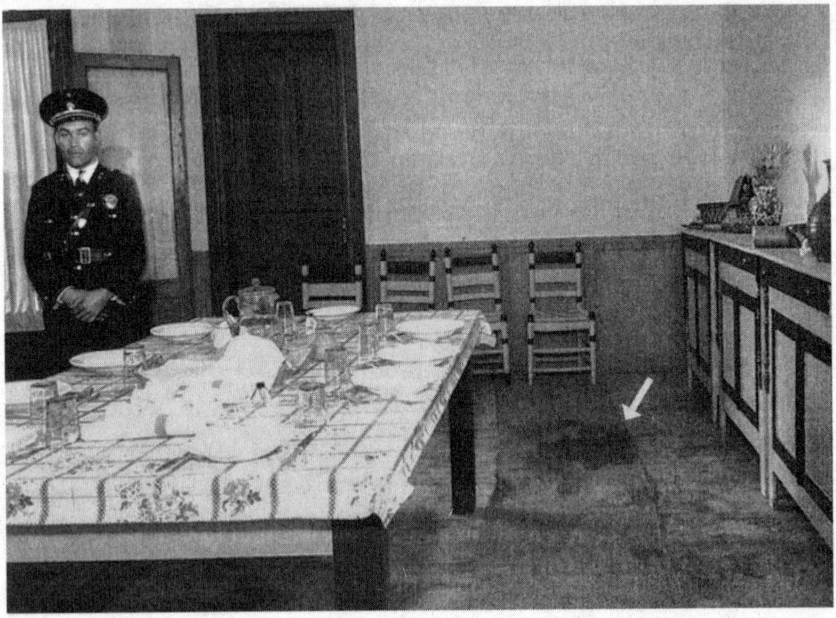

77. The dark bloodstain at the far end of the dining room (see arrow) marks the spot where Trotsky collapsed.

condition spoke for itself. His left arm was paralyzed. His right hand moved in small, uncontrolled motions. The injury was grave.

"He was a political assassin," Trotsky whispered once more. "Most likely the GPU." He did not know that the typed confession—Stalin's calling card—lay folded in Jacson's* pocket.[44]

When the ambulance from Green Cross Hospital finally arrived, medics entered the dining room and found Trotsky motionless on the floor at the far end of the table. For a brief, horrifying moment, they believed he was already dead.

Then he stirred.

Extraction Under Guard

Natalia refused to allow the medics to remove Trotsky. Two years earlier, her son, Lev Sedov, had died mysteriously in a Paris hospital—a suspected GPU poisoning. Now she feared history would repeat itself. The guards agreed. If Trotsky left the villa, they believed, the ambulance might be a GPU ploy to finish what Jacson* had begun. Natalia deferred to Hansen, who insisted the chief of police must first be present.

General José Manuel Núñez, Mexico City police chief, arrived soon, assumed control, and searched Jacson*. In his coat were a typed confession and $890.[45] Jacson*, severely beaten, was sent to Green Cross Hospital under guard.

Only then was Trotsky carried through a double cordon of police, past the assembled crowd of onlookers. The extraction took roughly thirty minutes.

A Fortress Breached

Hansen and Natalia rode in the ambulance beside Trotsky as motorcycle police cleared the way through Mexico City. His voice was a whisper. His breathing shallow. His right hand traced small circles.

Outside Green Cross Hospital, news of the attack traveled quickly, and a crowd had gathered. Natalia warned Hansen quietly that enemies might be among them.

As the gates of the villa closed behind the ambulance, a heavy silence fell. The fortress they had built—steel doors, shutters, wire nets, sirens, guards—might have withstood bullets and bombs.

It could not withstand a calm voice, a familiar face, and a rehearsed story delivered on orders from Moscow.

Trotsky's final campaign did not end in triumph. It was undone by treachery . . . and an axe.

Yet for the moment, the Old Man still clung stubbornly to life.

CHAPTER XXVI

LONELY VIGIL

The Hospital

"He was bleeding terribly . . . I ran alongside the stretcher, and I knew he was dying. But he looked at me—just once—and it was the same Trotsky. The same fire in his eyes."

—Joseph Hansen, recalling Trotsky's final moments at the villa

"There may be enemies among them, as there always are in such cases."

—Natalia Sedova, fearful of a GPU plot at the hospital

"A single blow ended a life—but not the revolution it helped ignite."

—Anonymous historian

Hospital of Shadows

News of the attack reached Green Cross Hospital before the ambulance arrived. Staff were already preparing for emergency surgery when Trotsky was wheeled in, his stretcher flanked by a double phalanx of officers and shielded by police.

Colonel Salazar's detectives soon arrived to oversee Trotsky's protection. Anticipating further violence, they couldn't be sure whether the next attack would target Trotsky—or Jacson*, who might talk. Because Jacson* had been beaten by Trotsky's guards during the scuffle, he

78. Mercader was severely pistol-whipped by the guards before the police arrived.

too was sent to Green Cross Hospital under heavy police escort. By a grim irony, the attacker and his victim were in examining rooms only fifteen feet apart.[1] Mercader, bruised and battered, was placed under guard just two doors down from the examination room where Trotsky clung to life. To isolate the prisoner, authorities installed a grated partition between the two areas, preventing outside contact and shielding him from possible assassins from the jail.

Final Words, Final Hours

In the exam room, nurses began cutting Trotsky's hair to access the wound. With Natalia beside him and only one arm responsive, he feebly gestured for Joseph Hansen to approach. His voice strained and halting, Trotsky dictated his final message to Joseph Hansen:

> I am close to death from the blow of a political assassin. I was struck out in my room. I struggled with him. We had entered . . . Talked

> about French statistics. He struck me. Please say to our friends . . . I am sure of history . . . of the Fourth International. Go forward![2]

As the nurses prepared him for surgery, Natalia pressed ice against the wound and stood vigil at his head. When the attendants moved to undress him, Trotsky stopped them. "I don't want them to undress me . . . I want you to do it,"[3] he said softly—his last words to Natalia before falling into a coma.

A surgical team of five had been assembled—the best that could be gathered on short notice despite the infancy of neurosurgery in Mexico. Leading them was Dr. Joaquín Mass Patiño, a pioneer in the field. President Cárdenas, who viewed Trotsky's safety as a national obligation, condemned the attack and ordered his personal representative, Dr. Gustavo Baz Prada, to join the operation.[4]

As the doctors assessed the wound, they immediately understood its severity and that Trotsky's chances of survival were slim. Although the axe had missed its intended target—the back of his skull—it still penetrated deeply, inflicting irreparable damage to soft tissue.

After reviewing X-rays, doctors began surgery at 9:00 p.m.—about three hours after the attack. They shaved Trotsky's head and performed a 25-cm^2 craniectomy (removing a portion of the skull to relieve pressure) to expose the injury. A broken bone at the crown of the skull revealed fragments embedded inside. The wound measured ¾ of an inch wide and 2¾ inches deep.[5] The brain's protective membrane was torn, and both blood and tissue were visible. Dr. Mass Patiño carefully extracted the bone fragments and thoroughly cleaned the site. By 10:00 p.m., Trotsky was transferred to a nearby recovery room. Given the state of neurosurgery in Mexico at the time, the doctors believed they could do little more than wait.

After the surgery, Dr. Baz briefed reporters, stating the prognosis was extremely grave, with a ninety percent chance of death due to the severity of the injury.[6]

Outside the hospital, large crowds of onlookers and press quickly gathered. Journalists and photographers demanded access to Trotsky but were denied entry, and the lack of updates from hospital and police sources only heightened tensions. One enterprising reporter even

79. General Manuel Núñez displayed the ice axe to the press hours after the attack. It would be sixty-five years before the weapon was shown publicly again.

bribed an ambulance stretcher bearer for his uniform and badge, becoming the only outsider to enter the room.

Colonel Salazar began his investigation at Trotsky's bedside and remained at the hospital for the duration of the Old Man's life. Natalia stayed by his side, holding his hand, clinging to hope that his legendary strength might still save him. Joseph Hansen, with guards Harold Robins and Charles Cornell, stood watch at the door, carefully vetting everyone who entered.

General Núñez held an unscheduled press conference at the hospital hours after the attack and displayed the assassin's weapon for the world to see. The images from his press event would become iconic as it was the first, and last, time the public would see the ice axe for the next sixty-five years.

Word of the attack reached Trotsky's New York colleagues shortly after he arrived at the hospital and again after General Núñez's press conference. Given the severity of the injury, transporting him to a US hospital was impossible. Instead, they proposed flying a leading American surgeon to Mexico City—Dr. Walter Dandy, founder of the

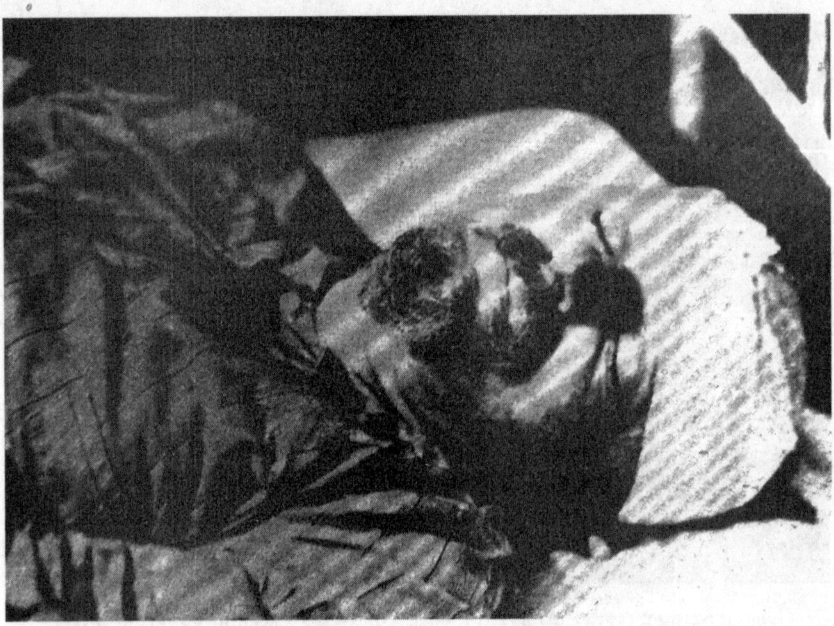

80. Trotsky's doctors believed there was little they could do beyond cleaning the wound.

renowned "Brain Team" at Johns Hopkins and widely considered the world's foremost neurosurgeon.[7]

Contacted at home in the middle of the night, Dr. Dandy quickly agreed to depart the next day. The flight plan routed him through Brownsville, Texas, before continuing to Mexico City—a trip of at least sixteen hours. But Trotsky's condition declined too rapidly, and the plan was abandoned.

The operation had done nothing to improve the Old Man's condition. Natalia remained at his bedside through the night, watching as his eyes stayed shut. His breathing occasionally eased, offering brief glimmers of hope.

That night, Trotsky's secretariat prepared a press release sent out the next day, August 21. It began,

> Leon Trotsky is fighting against death, with few chances. He was hit by an agent of Stalin's GPU. This second assault was foreseen and predicted by Leon Trotsky immediately after the preceding

assault of 24 May 1940. The manner in which this would happen was unknown. The facts of yesterday's attack are summarily as we describe: Mr. Trotsky personally knew the assassin, Frank Jacson*, for six months. Jacson* enjoyed Trotsky's confidence for his connections with the Trotskyist movement in France and the United States. He was known as a financially generous sympathizer. Jacson* often visited the house. At no time did we have any slightest suspicion that he was a GPU agent.

Through the morning of August 21, Trotsky's condition remained unchanged—unconscious, with only fluttering eyelids and shallow breaths as signs of life. Despite receiving oxygen and serum, there was no improvement. By midday, Dr. Mass Patiño noted heavy bleeding from the wound and signs of blood pooling in the brain's ventricles.

The Last Breath

In the afternoon, Trotsky's breathing grew rapid and erratic. The medical team informed Natalia that her husband's life was slipping away. As the final breath escaped his body, Trotsky's clenched hand—once so fierce in argument and resolve—slowly unfurled, as if surrendering at last to history.

At 6:00 p.m., Dr. Mass Patiño issued the final medical report, outlining Trotsky's critical state: a temperature of 38.1°C, pulse at 140, respiratory rate of 41, and blood pressure at 78 × 68 in the right arm and 78 × 64 in the left. The diagnosis was "flooding of the cerebral ventricles." These interconnected cavities produce cerebrospinal fluid, which cushions the brain and spine. When fluid accumulates abnormally, it creates pressure that can severely damage brain tissue and lead to death. The doctors surrounding the Old Man knew the end was near.[8]

At 7:25 p.m. on August 21, 1940, Colonel Salazar addressed the assembled crowds and journalists in front of the Green Cross Hospital saying, "Gentlemen! Trotsky is dead!"[9] Outside, the press jostled for headlines and the world held its breath, but inside Green Cross Hospital, history quietly shifted. The rush to reach one of the hospital's six telephones was so frantic that two were destroyed, and press photographers demanded access to the mortuary for final images.

The long, defiant struggle of Leon Trotsky had come to an end. After fighting to stay alive for more than twenty-five hours after the ice axe struck his head, his breathing slowed, then ceased, as Natalia held his hand in the dim hospital room surrounded by loyal guards and exhausted doctors. The man who had outrun the tsar's prisons, civil war, exile, and Stalin's assassins for more than a decade finally succumbed—not on the battlefield of revolution, but beneath fluorescent lights in a foreign land. The voice that had once stirred millions into action fell silent forever.

But even in death, Trotsky's ordeal was not over—the struggle would now shift to the postmortem that would raise as many questions as it answered.

CHAPTER XXVII

AFTER THE AXE

Autopsy and Aftermath

"The ice-axe entered from the front—not the back—it was not a blow in the dark. It was an execution."

—Dr. José Rojo de la Vega, surgeon, Alcázar Funeral Home

"The line of mourners stretched for blocks. He died hunted and in exile, but here, in Mexico, he was laid to rest as a revolutionary hero."

—Joseph Hansen

"In more experienced hands or in a US hospital the Old Man might have survived the attack, even if it was with some diminished capacity."

—Dr. Robert Lacin, a distinguished US neurosurgeon

The Body as Evidence

Trotsky's ordeal did not end with his final breath. For the next several days, his body became the final terrain on which truth, error, medicine, and politics converged. Surgeons debated what might have been done. Pathologists searched for certainty inside a shattered skull. Journalists rushed to impose narratives before facts could harden. And governments—Mexican, American, and Soviet—moved quickly to manage the consequences.

The autopsy that followed was not a bureaucratic ritual. It was a forensic reckoning that corrected early false reports, fixed the direction of the blow, and established that Trotsky was not struck from behind in darkness but executed face-to-face. It also exposed the limits of emergency neurosurgery in 1940 Mexico—and the narrow margin by which survival might once have been possible.

Beyond the walls of the operating room, a public drama of rare scale unfolded. A hunted exile became a revolutionary martyr. Hundreds of thousands lined the streets of Mexico City. Diplomats debated where his remains could be buried—and where they could not—while the political meaning of his death rippled outward across borders.

What followed moved from the autopsy table to the funeral cortege, from medical findings to political decisions, and finally to the quiet garden in Coyoacán where Leon Trotsky was laid to rest—while those who ordered his death remained unnamed and untouched.

The Funeral Procession

On the morning of August 22, 1940, a solemn procession formed outside Green Cross Hospital. Natalia Sedova [Trotsky], dressed in black—grief-stricken yet composed—walked beside the coffin of her murdered husband. The casket, draped in a red revolutionary banner and covered with flowers, marked the end of a life pursued across continents and extinguished in exile. At her side were Joseph Hansen and Otto Schüssler, along with Charles Cornell and Harold Robins, the members of Trotsky's security detail and household staff who had stood watch over him in his final months.

Under police escort, the cortege moved slowly through the streets of Mexico City toward the Alcázar Funeral Home. Crowds lined the route in extraordinary numbers—tens of thousands by conservative estimates, with some accounts placing the figure near two hundred thousand. They had come not simply to witness a burial, but to honor a revolutionary who had refused silence, even when struck down by Stalin's axe.

81. More than two hundred thousand people lined the funeral procession route to the Alcázar Funeral Home, making it one of the largest in Mexican history.

The Autopsy Begins

At 2:00 p.m. that day, Trotsky's body arrived at the funeral home, still clad in the Green Cross Hospital gown. Blood had begun to seep through the bandages over the wound. Present were Dr. Joaquín Mass Patiño, the funeral home's embalmers, renowned trauma surgeon Dr. José Rojo de la Vega—noted for operating on bullfighters—and Mexico City police chief General José Manuel Núñez.

Following a court order, Dr. de la Vega began the autopsy. He incised the scalp, sawed through the skull, and removed the brain. Inside his skull, Dr. de la Vega discovered a subdural hematoma—a collection of blood under pressure beneath the dura mater, the brain's outer membrane, caused by the penetrating trauma of the axe severing one of the brain's largest veins. A hematoma of this kind can compress the brain and increase intracranial pressure, leading to downward transtentorial herniation. As blood poured out of this large vein, the accumulation led to the compression of Trotsky's brain within the rigid skull and likely ultimately caused his neurological decline, including the paralysis of his left side.

What the Autopsy Revealed

The autopsy reported,

> Trotsky's chest measured 37½ inches and the abdomen 36 inches; the scalp was divided into sections and the skull sawn through. The brain, of extraordinary dimensions, was extracted and placed on a white enamel table. The examination showed hemorrhage on the inner aspect of the lesion, that the orifice of the lesion was ¾ inch wide, 2¾ inches deep, and traversed the whole of the brain substance, with some loss of it. The wound penetrated the second parietal convolution, above the ridges of Rolando at 1.5 inches from the longitudinal sinus and at 4 inches from the right frontal pole. The direction followed by the weapon was from top to bottom, from front to back, and from right to left.[1]

The trajectory confirmed the assassin struck from the front, not from behind as early newspaper reports claimed. The sharp pick of the ice axe penetrated the parietal lobe, passing through the gray matter and driving deep into the center of the brain into the right lateral ventricle (a deep chamber in the brain that contains cerebrospinal fluid). This injury caused massive bleeding within the brain, and, in combination with the subdural hematoma, led to downward transtentorial herniation, a fatal condition where blood flow to the brain is disrupted and the brainstem, which controls breathing, is compressed.

A Missed Opportunity in Surgery

Despite the grave wound, Trotsky survived more than twenty-five hours. A modern neurosurgeon reviewing the case noted that "in more expe-

82. During the autopsy, doctors carefully examine the area of Trotsky's brain where the axe struck.

rienced hands" or in a major US hospital, Trotsky might have survived with disabilities. The surgical team at Green Cross performed only a 25-cm^2 craniectomy (removal of a portion of the skull). This was insufficient to examine internal structures or stop deep arterial bleeding. It is widely accepted that a craniectomy for trauma and decompression should be approximately 12 × 15 cm.

In the early twentieth century, physicians widely believed that bleeding into the brain's ventricles was almost always fatal. Trotsky's doctors might have considered the mention of intraventricular hemorrhage sufficient to explain his death. This likely explains why Dr. Mass Patiño noted "the ventricles were filling up with blood" in his final report—but it raises the troubling question of why no effort was made to stop the bleeding.

In fact, Dr. Mass Patiño believed that brain surgery was ineffective and potentially harmful—a view outdated even in 1940. Dr. Harvey

Cushing, one of the founders of modern neurosurgery, had championed decompressive craniectomy and other methods to relieve increased intracranial pressure decades earlier. He also developed electrocauterization, which uses a high-frequency electrical current to cut tissue and coagulate blood vessels. He introduced it into neurosurgical operative practice. Ligating blood vessels within the brain at that time was extremely challenging and risky. By 1940, electrocautery was commonly used in neurosurgery and became standard practice. It had been widely used in Europe and in the Spanish Civil War as well. It is difficult to explain why such techniques were not employed at Mexico's premier hospital by 1940.

In addition, placement of a ventricular drain to remove accumulated blood or cerebrospinal fluid was already an accepted neurosurgical technique in the 1930s. No mention of this type of intervention is mentioned in the operative report, despite the emphasis on "the ventricles filling with blood."

Trotsky's symptoms and the pooling of blood indicated his brain was swelling dangerously. Electrocauterization, hemostatic clips, an external ventricular drain, and more extensive surgical access might have saved him. Dr. Mass Patiño even noted blood and brain tissue oozing from the wound during the initial exam—a warning sign of internal bleeding and pressure buildup.

Despite all signs pointing to it, the autopsy curiously omitted any reference to transtentorial herniation, a life-threatening medical condition in which part of the brain is pushed from one compartment of the skull to another due to increased intracranial pressure.

Transtentorial herniation occurs when pressure from bleeding, swelling, or a mass (like a hematoma) forces the temporal lobe to herniate downward through the tentorial notch—an opening in a semirigid membrane (the tentorium cerebelli) that separates the upper brain from the cerebellum below.

When pressure builds up—such as from a brain bleed like the ones Trotsky suffered—it can force brain tissue downward, compressing vital structures like the brainstem, which controls breathing and heart rate. In the 1930s, physicians understood that intraventricular bleeding (bleeding into the brain's central fluid chambers) was almost always fatal. Dr. Mass Patiño and his team likely considered the presence of hemorrhaging a sufficient explanation for Trotsky's condition—even though they failed to intervene surgically with a large enough craniectomy to allow the pooling of blood to drain outward rather than continue bleeding internally, thereby relieving the pressure instilled on the brain.

A properly sized cranial opening would have allowed Trotsky's brain to swell upward into the space created rather than downward, which ultimately caused sufficient brainstem compression to lead to his death. Even given the state of neurosurgery in Mexico in 1940, there was more that the surgeons could have done to save his life.

What Might Have Been?

Had Trotsky survived the attack—and the grueling emergency surgery that followed—it is fair to ask what life might have looked like in the aftermath. Though survival was unlikely, it was not impossible. And had he lived, he would almost certainly have been physically diminished.

As a right-handed individual, Trotsky's language and writing abilities were housed in the left hemisphere of his brain—the dominant side in over 85 percent of right-handed people. That hemisphere governs language production, comprehension, reading, writing, and symbolic reasoning. These functions are not replicated in the nondominant hemisphere. Thus, a traumatic injury to the right side of the brain—while serious—typically spares core language functions.

Had the damage remained confined to the right hemisphere, Trotsky likely would have retained his ability to speak, read, and write. However, he almost certainly would have lost mobility on the left side of his body, a result of right hemisphere motor cortex damage. He would have required a wheelchair and constant care, but his intellect and voice—his greatest weapons—might still have endured.

In such a scenario, it is possible to imagine him continuing to write, to dictate, and to lead the Fourth International. Though diminished physically, he might have remained, for a time, the unrelenting revolutionary voice he had always been—scarred but unbroken.

Mapping the Wound

H. Keith Melton, the author and current owner of the ice axe used in the assassination, measured the weapon 2.75 inches from the tip of the pointed pick. At that point, the shaft measured 0.75 by 0.375 inches—dimensions that exactly correspond to the entrance wound described in Trotsky's autopsy.[2]

According to the autopsy, the blow came from above and slightly in front—delivered from right to left, front to back, and top to bottom.[3] The weapon—a shortened mountaineer's piolet—had a forged iron head with a narrow pick on one side and a flat adze on the other.

A closer reading of the autopsy confirms that the pick, not the adze, was used. The entry wound was far too narrow to have been caused by the adze's 2.5-inch-wide blade. Ironically, had that broad edge struck Trotsky's skull, it would almost certainly have shattered the cranium and produced immediate unconsciousness—precisely the outcome the assassin was attempting to achieve, and the one he narrowly failed to secure.

Nevertheless, misconceptions have persisted. Even the chief investigator of the case, Colonel Leandro A. Sánchez Salazar, writing years later in *Murder in Mexico*—and presumably with access to the original case files—asserted that Trotsky had been struck with the adze end of the ice axe.[4] That error was subsequently repeated by otherwise careful historians, including Mahoney,[5] Mosley,[6] Payne,[7] and others. The forensic record, however, leaves no ambiguity: the wound was inflicted by the pick, not the broad adze.

Trotsky's last-minute rotation of his body and look upward to the assassin weakened the blow just enough to prevent his instant death. This action made the mission personal—a frontal execution, not a silent ambush.

Mourning and a Political Decision

Trotsky's body lay in state at Alcázar Funeral Home, opposite Alameda Park. His casket was guarded day and night by comrades and American supporters. Over three hundred thousand mourners are estimated to have filed past[8]—a striking number considering that worldwide Trotskyists numbered fewer than five thousand in 1940.

The funeral announcement read,

> The last of the Great Leaders of the Universal Proletariat has been murdered by Joseph Stalin, who sought—through a traitor's hand—to extinguish the October Revolution and make world socialism impossible.[9]

Trotsky's American attorney, Albert Goldman, flew to Mexico and requested US permission to repatriate the remains. Some believed Trotsky should be buried in a land of free speech and asylum. But on August 26, the Roosevelt administration declined. Two reasons likely guided the decision. First, the US hoped to maintain its fragile wartime relationship with the Soviet Union. Second, there was concern that burying Trotsky in American soil might make him a martyr and trigger unrest.[10]

Final Rest

On August 27, 1940, in a garden behind the now-silent villa in Coyoacán, Natalia watched as Trotsky's ashes were laid to rest beneath a simple stone marker. The ceremony was brief, the mourners few—his widow, his grandson, his guards, and a handful of loyal friends. Yet the act itself defied Stalin's intent. The man whom no nation would claim was claimed instead by history. His assassins silenced his voice but not his last command:

> I am sure of history . . . of the Fourth International. Go forward![11]

These final words did not perish with his body. They endured as a challenge, a prophecy, and a banner raised against tyranny. Still near the rabbit pens he once tended, Leon Trotsky—revolutionary, exile, survivor—left behind not just a garden but a silent witness to one of

83. Trotsky's memorial in his garden in Coyoacán holds the ashes of both Leon and Natalia.

the twentieth century's great betrayals—a scar on history that could never be entirely erased.

Even as his ashes were placed within the monument, those who had plotted his murder were already vanishing into the shadows. Their flight—deliberate and disguised—marked the beginning of a frantic exodus through city streets, safe houses, and international borders as Stalin's executioners struggled to escape the justice that had begun to close in.

CHAPTER XXVIII

FLIGHT OF THE EXECUTIONERS

"The hardest part of an assassination is
not the kill. It's the getaway."
—Pavel Sudoplatov

"Assassination ends a life, but escape protects the lie."
—GPU field manual

"A good assassin is never seen arriving or leaving."
—GPU training maxim

The Trap Is Sprung

As investigators moved to secure the bloodstained villa in Coyoacán, the two GPU officers responsible for the attack were already in motion. Caridad Mercader, the mother of the assassin and operational leader of Operation MAT, and Nahum Eitingon, the architect of Operation UTKA, fled as soon as the sirens sounded. They understood immediately that Ramón had failed to escape. Whether Trotsky was already dead was unknown, but the operation had crossed its point of no return.

Now their own survival depended on disappearance. In GPU doctrine, assassination was only the opening act. The mission was not complete until its architects had escaped and vanished beyond reconstruction. What followed was not flight alone but erasure—an operation layered in false identities, misdirection, and overlapping contingency plans whose purpose was not merely to evade pursuit but to defeat history itself.

The Watchers

Later reconstructions suggest that Caridad Mercader and Nahum Eitingon positioned themselves close enough to Avenida Viena to intervene if Ramón escaped, yet far enough away to avoid immediate detection. Their role was limited and conditional. They were there to extract—or to vanish.

At 5:20 p.m., they saw Jacson* enter the villa. At 5:50 p.m., the contingency collapsed. Sirens cut through the street, signaling the imminent arrival of additional police and the failure of a clean escape. Ramón did not emerge. That confirmation was unnecessary. The alarm itself marked the abort signal.

Caridad and Eitingon withdrew immediately. Continued presence near the villa now carried only danger. They abandoned the area at once, blending into the city and activating prearranged escape plans. Whatever had happened inside the house was now irrelevant. The assassination phase was over. Survival—and disappearance—had become the only objectives.

A Vanishing Act by Design

From that moment forward, the escape of Caridad Mercader and Nahum Eitingon passed from event into record—and into contradiction. No single, authoritative narrative of their flight ever emerged. Instead, the historical record preserves a series of sharply conflicting accounts that diverge in geography, chronology, and intent. These contradictions reflect not confusion but design. They arise from the nature of the operation itself and from the limitations of the sources that later attempted to reconstruct it: investigators working with partial information, postwar journalists assembling retrospective narratives, Soviet memoirists writing with institutional motives, and historians forced to navigate fragments.

What survives is not clarity, but pattern.

Early Reconstructions and Postwar Syntheses

Colonel Leandro Sánchez Salazar noted that false passports and contingency escape plans were already in place before the assassination. Writing nearly two decades later, Isaac Don Levine produced one of the earliest synthetic accounts, reporting that Caridad Mercader escaped Mexico using a new passport under an assumed name in a neighboring country, while Eitingon—assisted by a GPU chauffeur—was believed to be traveling toward Acapulco, where a Soviet freighter awaited extraction.[1] Levine's account was not contemporaneous. It represented a postwar reconstruction drawn from interviews, investigative recollections, and secondary police material. Its value lies less in precision than in its attempt to impose narrative order on an event deliberately engineered to resist it.

Compressed and Divergent Accounts

Other historians offered markedly different versions. E. P. Sharapov asserted that both Eitingon and Caridad fled directly to Cuba, where they lived under illegal status.[2] His account is notably compressed, preserving outcome while discarding operational detail.

A more complex narrative appears in the writings of Eduard Puigventós, drawing on testimony attributed to Garmabella. In this version, Eitingon flew to New York on the night of August 20, 1940, while Caridad briefly remained in Mexico City to secure legal counsel for her son. She contacted Lombardo Toledano, who directed her to Octavio Medellín Ostos—Ramón Mercader's first lawyer—before departing via Tampico aboard a freighter bound for Japan. Japanese authorities supposedly detained her for two months before GPU intervention enabled her return to Moscow.[3]

Additional variations persist. Luis Mercader later claimed his mother fled via California and Vladivostok before reaching Moscow on the Trans-Siberian Railway, while Julián Gorkin believed she traveled through the United States. Each account bears the haze of disinformation—intentional or not—that followed the operation.

Weighing the Evidence

These accounts are best understood not as competing truths but as sources of unequal evidentiary weight. Levine's narrative reflects organized memory rather than direct observation. Sharapov preserves outcome but little else. Puigventós offers the most textured account of Caridad's immediate actions, though full verification remains elusive. Sudoplatov's memoir is indispensable for understanding Soviet intent and internal procedure yet marked by retrospective expansion and institutional self-justification. No version stands alone. Each must be read against the others—and against the logic of GPU tradecraft itself.

The Sudoplatov Version: Authority and Self-Justification

Pavel Sudoplatov, who supervised the operation from Moscow, provided the most expansive account. He wrote that Caridad Mercader and Nahum Eitingon flew to Cuba immediately after the assassination aboard a small aircraft held in readiness. They remained underground for six months before sailing to New York. With forged documents and the assistance of long-embedded GPU operatives, they crossed the United States by rail, reestablishing contact with Soviet assets in California planted years earlier. In February 1941, they sailed to China and returned to Moscow via the Trans-Siberian Railway. Sudoplatov claimed to have met them at Kazan Station. There was no written report. Eitingon briefed Beria and Merkulov orally; Sudoplatov submitted a short summary to the Central Committee titled "On the Liquidation of Trotsky."[4]

"We had accomplished our mission," Sudoplatov later said. "Trotsky was no longer a threat. Stalin was pleased."[5]

Rewards followed swiftly. Eitingon was promoted. Sudoplatov received the Order of the Red Banner. Grigulevich was decorated.[6] One man, however, remained absent from these calculations.

Synthesis: Confusion as Evidence

What ultimately matters is not which route Caridad Mercader and Nahum Eitingon took out of Mexico but that no single, stable account of their escape exists. Later reconstructions attempted to impose order on events deliberately structured to resist clarity.[7] Soviet memoirs expanded the geography and chronology, revealing as much about institutional motives as historical fact.[8] Other accounts emphasize Caridad's brief return to Mexico City before her disappearance.[9]

These versions negate one another. That incompatibility is not a flaw in the record. It is evidence of professional tradecraft. What survives is not a route but an outcome: the planners escaped and were reintegrated. The record remains deliberately unresolved.

The Assassin Left Behind

For Caridad Mercader and Nahum Eitingon, escape marked the successful conclusion of the operation. For Ramón Mercader, it marked the beginning of captivity. While his superiors vanished behind false names and international borders, the man who carried out the assassination remained in a Mexican prison—isolated, beaten during later incarceration, and ultimately expendable.

Sudoplatov later related advice that he had given the Operation MAT team during their training in Paris: "If you're caught, try a hunger strike in jail but do it in such a way that you do not arouse the suspicions of your jailers. At first just eat less and less, preparing yourself for the hunger strike. Eventually, they will feed you artificially, and the whole investigation will be delayed." Mercader responded in 1969 that he employed the tactic for two or three months and then kept to the story that he was a disgruntled supporter of Trotsky.[10]

Stalin framed the calculus with characteristic coldness: "As for the comrade who carried out the sentence, the highest tribute will be awarded to him after he gets out of custody. Let's see what kind of professional revolutionary he is—how he behaves when times get tough." Loyalty would be measured not by the act itself, but by what followed—discipline, endurance, silence.

Mercader upheld his cover without deviation. He did not wait for rescue or even recognition. In Soviet doctrine, success was not survival or applause but containment: kill cleanly, leave no trail, speak nothing. His real name disappeared from cables. His handlers receded. Moscow offered no acknowledgment. By remaining silent, he fulfilled the final requirement of the mission. He had succeeded—though the reward for that success was a prison cell.

As investigators failed to trace the fleeing conspirators, they turned to the only figure still within reach: Sylvia Ageloff. Innocent witness? Naive accomplice? Or something more deliberate? The answers, it soon became clear, were as obscured as the operation itself.

CHAPTER XXIX

THE DUPE

Love as a Weapon

"I have only been used . . ."
—Sylvia Ageloff at the crime scene

"Some betrayals come from malice. Others from love."
—Postwar intelligence aphorism

"She was never part of the conspiracy, only the means to its end. When the blade fell, it cut her loose as well."
—Western intelligence officer, memoir (unpublished)

The Moment of Collapse

At 7:45 p.m. on August 20, 1940, Sylvia Ageloff stepped into the Swastika restaurant—named for a long-standing good luck symbol that predated its Nazi appropriation—unaware that the life she thought she had was already collapsing. She had come to dinner expecting to find her husband waiting at their usual table. Instead there was only absence, and the first tremors of a betrayal so complete it would strip meaning from everything she believed: two years of intimacy, plans, and love. Within hours, the truth would crash down around her. The man she adored had attacked Leon Trotsky, and what she had lived inside was not a romance but a constructed deception—patiently built, directed, and protected. Her unraveling would be as public as it was devastating.

Dinner and Deception

Sylvia arrived fifteen minutes late for their 7:30 p.m. dinner with Otto Schüssler and his fiancée, but Frank* was nowhere to be seen. Earlier that afternoon, Ramón Mercader—using the alias Frank Jacson*—had also failed to meet her in their room at the Hotel Montejo before their planned late afternoon visit to Coyoacán to say goodbye to the Trotskys. Concern rising, she phoned the room. No one answered. Otto suggested calling Trotsky's villa directly. Sylvia resisted, insisting, "It is impossible for Jacson* to be there. He never goes without me."[1] Still clinging to routine, she offered another explanation: he had said he might stop at the Banco Nacional de Crédito Ejidal on business for a client named Alfredo Viñas.[2]

Sylvia and Otto walked to the bank on Calle Venustiano Carranza. The staff had never heard of Jacson* or Viñas. Otto insisted again: call the villa. Sylvia's voice wavered as she yielded: "If anything has happened, it must be serious."[3] At 9:30 p.m., Otto reached the guards. The reply was immediate and shattering: "Come at once. Jacson* has just tried to kill the Old Man!"[4]

As the taxi raced toward Coyoacán, Sylvia's panic broke into open hysteria. "She became very nervous and began to cry," Schüssler later recalled.[5] In minutes, the life she believed in—two years of intimacy, plans, a future—was annihilated. Mercader had not merely lied to her; he had used her. "I wish it were Jacques* who had died instead of the Old Man," she whispered, trembling, fearing Trotsky was already dead.

The Scene at the Villa

The villa was chaos. Reporters shouted from behind barricades. Mounted police circled the perimeter. Inside, the dining room floor was still wet where Trotsky had lain while awaiting the ambulance. As Sylvia moved through the house, the meaning of what had happened sharpened into horror. In the study, chairs were overturned, books were scattered, and a large stain of blood congealing behind the desk marked the place where the assassin had struck.

84. Trotsky's position at the moment of the attack is indicated by the pool of blood beneath the desk.

Witnesses watched her unravel. Journalist Gregorio Luri described her small frame, sailor-style blouse, and worn brown leather coat. "She was like a child lost in the disorder of her own life," he wrote. Room to room she wandered, dazed, sobbing uncontrollably. Over and over, she screamed, "I have only been used!"[6]

Accusations came quickly. As Trotsky's supporters poured into the villa, grief gave way to fury—and it fell squarely on Sylvia. She had vouched for Jacson*. She had lived with him. She had helped normalize his presence. How, they demanded, could she have been so close to him for two years and seen nothing? The possibility that she had been deceived—not simply by a lover but by a disciplined intelligence machine designed to weaponize intimacy—was almost too staggering to accept.

The police at the villa strongly suspected Sylvia's complicity. Levine wrote that she was arrested as soon as she arrived.[7] A more detailed sequence appears in later accounts: when Sylvia arrived, "The Mexicans were not buying her play-acting," and after the ambulance took

Trotsky to the hospital, Commander Galindo, the lead investigator, told her, "You are detained."[8]

At the villa, Octavio Fernández—a senior Trotskyist and longtime friend of Sylvia's—asked to accompany her to the police station. Galindo allowed it. "The car held the driver, Sylvia, and me," Fernández later recalled. "Behind us sat Galindo and two agents. I'd known Sylvia since 1934. She was hysterical, sobbing, and kept repeating, 'Why did they let Jacson* enter [the villa]?' I asked, 'But Jacson* is your husband, no?' 'Yes,' she repeated, again and again. 'But why did they let him enter?'"[9] Her question landed like an inadvertent confession—not that she knew of the plot, but that she had harbored misgivings about her husband that she had never shared with the guards.

During the ride, Sylvia offered a halting explanation. Jacson*, she said, had once mentioned a man named Bills—a name she had only heard him say in passing. According to Sylvia, Bills was involved with Jacson* in vague "suspicious things" and operated out of the Edificio Ermita.[10] The detail immediately raised red flags. Trotsky's circle knew the Edificio Ermita had housed the office of David Alfaro Siqueiros, the muralist and GPU asset who had led the failed May 24 assault on the villa.

Fernández pressed her: If she knew that—and knew Siqueiros had operated out of Edificio Ermita after the May attack—why had she never warned them? Sylvia gave no answer. "I never spoke to her again," Fernández said.[11]

The Arrest and the Spiral

At the Green Cross Hospital, police took care to keep Sylvia separated from Jacson*, who was being treated for his wounds. The aim was simple: prevent their accounts from aligning. Over the next four months, she remained in custody while detectives tried to determine her role—if any—in the operation.

Her appearance and behavior left authorities unsettled. Sylvia seemed fragile, dazed, emotionally unmoored—pale and disheveled, hollow-cheeked, thick glasses perched over wide nearsighted eyes, her gaze

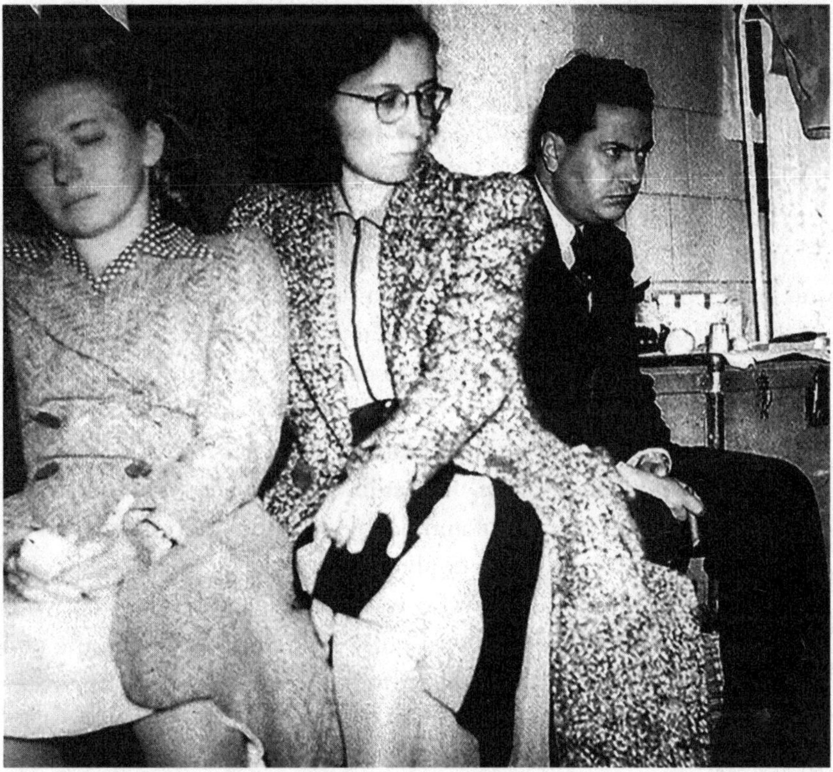

85. Sylvia Ageloff (left) with her sister Hilda and brother, Monte, at the Sixth Delegation police station.

unfocused as if she could no longer attach meaning to what she saw. Again and again, she screamed, "Kill him! Kill him!"—a hoarse, broken cry that echoed through corridors and rooms.[12] Detectives had witnessed staged hysteria before, but this struck them differently. It did not read as performance—no control, no rhythm—only anguish spilling out in jagged fragments.

Suspicion remained all around her. How could she have missed it? How could she have failed to recognize that Jacson* was not who he claimed to be? To many, her claim of ignorance seemed impossible. But Sylvia offered one explanation and clung to it: the man she knew as Jacques Mornard* had never truly existed. The man she loved had been a fabrication—an operative trained to manipulate her idealism, her loneliness, her heart. And it had worked.

A Locked Room and a Reckoning

For Sylvia Ageloff, the real reckoning came not amid the bloodstained chaos of the villa but under the cold fluorescence of a locked room in the hospital—where illusions could not survive routine, silence, and repetition. There, stripped of comfort and certainty, she began to see what she had refused to imagine: the man she had loved, defended, and built a future around was a GPU assassin.

Their life together—shared glances, tenderness, promises—had been the scaffolding of a lie, engineered to carry a killer through the front gate. Now alone and disgraced, Sylvia faced the question that would define what remained of her life: Had she been a willing accomplice, a willfully blind facilitator, or the last human casualty of an operation that treated intimacy as a tool and people as disposable assets?

While Sylvia wrestled with doubt and disgrace, a more urgent question consumed investigators: Who was Frank Jacson*? The man who had driven the axe into Trotsky's skull offered only a false name and a cover story, but the truth behind him would prove more complex—and more dangerous—than anyone yet understood.

CHAPTER XXX

THE PRISONER WITHOUT A NAME

"The success of an operation depends not only on the plan, but on the silence of the man behind the mask."
—Pavel Sudoplatov

"You are not going to get anything out of me."
—Ramón Mercader

"Beneath the mask of the prisoner in Mexico lurks the Kremlin's happy robot of the future."
—Isaac Don Levine, *The Mind of an Assassin*

The First Lies

In the hours after the attack on Trotsky, the man calling himself Jacson* gave police two names—Frank Jacson* and Jacques Mornard Vandendreschd*.[1] Calm and composed, he claimed to be a thirty-six-year-old Belgian journalist. It was a performance rehearsed for years, one designed to delay identification long enough for confusion, legal maneuvering, and outside pressure to take hold.

But the story he told—carefully memorized and artfully delivered—was about to be dismantled one lie at a time.

Crafting a Cover: GPU Tradecraft

The fledgling Bolshevik intelligence service began dispatching operatives abroad as early as 1921. Lacking diplomatic recognition in most countries, Soviet agents could not rely on embassies for immunity or protection. Instead, they operated under false identities supported by carefully constructed cover stories and legends.

In GPU training, a cover referred to the visible identity—name, profession, nationality—while the legend provided the detailed personal history used to sustain it under questioning. Selecting the right combination was a tailored process, matched to an operative's language skills, education, appearance, and behavior, as well as the expected level of scrutiny, local security competence, and the resources of GPU forgery teams.

Such legends were designed to withstand routine inspection. They were far less resilient under sustained, hostile interrogation by determined investigators—especially when time, isolation, and contradiction began to erode rehearsed answers.

The Passport of a Dead Man

Ramón Mercader's primary cover identity—Frank Jacson*—was constructed in 1939 for travel to the United States and Mexico. It rested on a genuine Canadian passport originally issued to Tony Babich, a Yugoslav-Canadian born in 1905 in Lovinac, Yugoslavia, and naturalized in 1929. Babich obtained the passport to visit family in Europe but instead joined the Mackenzie-Papineau Battalion in Spain, where he was killed early in the Spanish Civil War.[2]

The GPU routinely confiscated passports from International Brigades volunteers upon their arrival in Spain, claiming they would be returned after service. In reality, the documents were retained for future covert use. Passports belonging to the dead were especially valuable—no one would report them stolen. GPU technicians substituted photographs, forged signatures, and, when necessary, modified names.[3]

For an operation as sensitive as Trotsky's assassination, the GPU's Operative Technical (OT) unit—led by their specialist in "document work," Austrian émigré George Miller—was tasked with forging Mercader's papers. The work was skilled but imperfect. Intending to use the common Canadian surname Jackson, the forgers dropped a letter, producing the misspelled Jacson*.[4] The error would later draw attention rather than deflect it, marking the assassin's trail instead of concealing it.

Selling the Alias to Sylvia

To explain his false identity to Sylvia Ageloff and her family, Mercader claimed he had purchased the passport for $3,500 on the Paris black market. The unusual spelling, he said, was the result of a careless forger.[5] The story was plausible. By 1939, with war looming, thousands of draft-aged men in France sought forged papers to avoid conscription.

Despite its flaw, the passport was convincing enough to allow Mercader—under the name Jacson*—to enter the United States twice without a visa, passing through New Orleans and Laredo without challenge.

For Sylvia and her family, the use of an alias raised little suspicion. Within the Socialist Workers Party, pseudonyms were common—political masks rather than full identity replacements. The SWP assigned false names to many members in a symbolic attempt to mimic underground security, but it lacked true counterintelligence discipline and conducted no vetting of new recruits. These gestures toward secrecy were no match for the professional apparatus of GPU intelligence and left the movement vulnerable to precisely the kind of infiltration that had claimed Trotsky's life.

Exposing the Legend

Early in the investigation, Mexican police confirmed that the Canadian passport was genuine but altered after Canadian authorities reported that Tony Babich had died in Spain in 1937. On May 12, 1939, the Spanish government issued Babich's death certificate.[6]

The Mornard* identity—the name by which Sylvia first knew him—proved more complex. Unlike the Babich passport, which could be externally verified, the Mornard* legend relied entirely on invented biographical claims that investigators had to dismantle line by line.

Mercader had presented himself as Jacques Mornard Vandendreschd*, a Belgian aristocrat, the son of a diplomat, educated at elite French institutions. He spoke flawless French, was well-mannered and cosmopolitan, drove a luxury car, and traveled with ease—details that lent surface credibility to the role.

Colonel Salazar's investigators contacted the Belgian consulate. The response was immediate: no such person existed. Mornard* was not Belgian. His alleged father had never served in Persia or in any diplomatic post. The military academy he claimed to attend did not exist. The address he gave for his mother turned out to be a department store in central Brussels. The legend collapsed under even modest verification.

While Jacson* answered general questions smoothly, sustained scrutiny exposed widening inconsistencies. The more investigators pressed, the more the mask began to crack.

Cracks in the Armor

During Jacson's* detention at the Sixth Delegation police station, Salazar shifted tactics. One day, he casually brought Jacson* a few books and remarked that a Russian acquaintance wished to greet him.[7] "I have no Russian friends," Jacson* replied flatly.

Moments later, a Russian man entered the room and greeted him in Russian: "Hello, friend Torkof!" He explained that Jacson*—using the name Salvador Torkof—had worked for him in Spain during the Civil War. When the exchange shifted into Spanish, the attending physician, Dr. Alfonso Quiroz Cuarón, listened closely. The speech was not merely fluent; it was native. Quiroz was convinced the man before him had served the GPU.[8]

Quiroz Cuarón, one of Mexico's most distinguished criminologists and forensic psychologists, would later spend a cumulative 972 hours interviewing and observing the assassin. His analysis laid critical groundwork for later identifying Jacson* as Ramón Mercader—Stalin's trained killer.[9]

The Mask Begins to Slip

Mexican authorities now held a confessed assassin who refused to confirm his name, nationality, or past. Isaac Don Levine later observed that Jacson* had "successfully played Dr. Jekyll and Mr. Hyde—Jacques Mornard* and Frank Jacson*—in his intimate relationships with Sylvia Ageloff and the Trotsky household." Since his arrest, Levine noted, Mercader wore "without change the mask of a man of mystery," disclosing nothing of his origins, military service, family ties, or birthplace.[10]

The dismantling of Jacson's* identity exposed one of the most elaborate legends in Soviet intelligence history—built on a dead man's passport, forged papers, and a manufactured aristocratic past. While the aliases withstood brief inspection, methodical investigation by Mexican authorities—supported by foreign consulates—gradually stripped them away.

Despite his silence, Mercader's language mastery, his Spanish Civil War connections, and the accumulating contradictions pointed investigators toward Spain—and the GPU. Though his true name remained unknown, the illusion crafted in Moscow was already failing. Nearly a decade would pass before the world learned that Frank Jacson* was Ramón Mercader.

Colonel Salazar, however, required no final name to proceed. He had seen enough masks to recognize concealment. What mattered were not aliases but patterns—hesitation, contradiction, silence. Now, facing the prisoner who still called himself Jacques Mornard*, Salazar prepared to breach the final barrier: not with force, but with questions.

CHAPTER XXXI

THE COLONEL AND THE ASSASSIN

"Even if you cut the skin off me centimeter
by centimeter, I'll stick to my story."
—Ramón Mercader

"Interrogation is the art of patience—
watching lies unravel themselves."
—Old police proverb

"One man sought the truth. The other was trained to survive it."
—Mexican proverb on interrogation

No Protection for the Guilty

President Lázaro Cárdenas, a revolutionary socialist whose administration included influential pro-Soviet figures, was informed of the attack on Trotsky on the evening of August 20, 1940. He immediately condemned it as "the dirtiest crime committed in Mexico for a long time."[1] Visiting the villa the following day with his wife, Cárdenas assured Natalia Sedova [Trotsky] that the investigation would not spare any guilty party—"Regardless of their position."[2]

Yet behind these public assurances lay a less reassuring reality. Cárdenas's administration was nearing its end, and Stalinist sympathizers occupied sensitive posts within Mexico's security apparatus. For those officials, uncovering the assassin's true identity—and any Soviet connection—posed not merely a diplomatic embarrassment but a political reckoning. Avoiding that outcome became an unspoken concern within certain quarters of the state.

Three Agencies, One Crime

The magnitude of the crime immediately triggered a jurisdictional struggle. Three agencies competed for control of both the investigation and its narrative:

1. Departamento de Policía de la Ciudad de México (Mexico City Police Department), led by General José Manuel Núñez.
2. Servicio Confidencial (Confidential Service), a Ministry of Interior bureau widely penetrated by Communist agents.
3. Policía Secreta Mexicana (Mexican Secret Service), Mexico's elite secret police under Colonel Leandro Sánchez Salazar, assigned by Cárdenas in 1937 to safeguard Trotsky.

The stakes were high. Had the Servicio Confidencial prevailed, the investigation risked suppression, misdirection, or quiet burial—outcomes that would have shielded Moscow at the expense of Mexican sovereignty. Recognizing this danger, the Servicio Confidencial was quickly sidelined.

Shrewd and politically astute, Colonel Salazar publicly deferred to General Núñez as the investigation's senior officer and official spokesman. In return, Núñez quietly ceded operational control to Salazar, who managed the case on behalf of the federal government. The arrangement worked to mutual advantage: Núñez received the publicity; Salazar did the police work.[3] That night, the Policía Secreta launched what would become the largest murder investigation in Mexican history, initially focused on two suspects—Frank Jacson* and Sylvia Ageloff.

86. Colonel Sánchez Salazar, chief of the Mexican Secret Service, led the investigation into both attacks against Trotsky.

The Interrogation Begins

Initial questioning began almost immediately and continued intermittently over five days and nights, with formal interrogations extending into early 1941. When questioning commenced, Jacson's* head and eye were heavily bandaged. In the chaotic seconds after the attack, Trotsky's guards—Harold Robins, Charles Cornell, and Joseph Hansen—had beaten him and shattered his eyeglasses.

The injuries produced an unexpected complication. Unable to read documents placed before him, Jacson* stalled until a local optician, Dr. Gaona, produced a replacement pair. Only then did sustained interrogation proceed in earnest.

Murder, Memory, and the Ice Axe

Once Jacson* could see clearly, Salazar began dismantling the assassin's story methodically. His opening question was direct: How had the murder been carried out?

Jacson*, reverting to the alias Jacques Mornard Vandendreschd*, answered,

> I had the idea of killing him seven or eight days beforehand . . . I brought the ice axe from France . . . I used to detach great blocks

> of ice with it when climbing snow-covered mountains. I intended to kill him and then kill myself afterwards, with the revolver and dagger I carried. That's why I took the dagger.[4]

Mercader's legend as Jacques Mornard* was far more robust than his Jacson* cover and required substantially greater investigative effort to penetrate.[5]

He claimed his hatred of Trotsky stemmed from personal betrayal: "He forced his followers to harm themselves for his own profit . . . That's why I decided to kill him and not just commit suicide."

Describing the attack itself, Mornard* stated,

> He asked if I had brought him an article. He invited me into his study and began reading it. I placed my raincoat behind him. I removed the piolet and brought it down on his head. He shrieked and bit my hand. Then the guards burst in and began to beat me. I made no effort to escape.[6]

The account explained the blow—but not the preparation, the access, or the discipline with which it had been carried out.

When questioned about the Star semiautomatic pistol found in his possession, Jacson* offered an implausible explanation involving a man named Bartolo, allegedly met at the Bar Kit-Kat:

> I asked him for a revolver of any kind. On Tuesday [August 20], I gave him money and a typewriter as a gift. I wanted the weapons to kill myself after the act.[7]

The Letter That Lied

In Mornard's* pocket, investigators found a multipage confession typed in French. It immediately aroused suspicion. Salazar noted that it had been produced on a different typewriter than the article Jacson* had submitted to Trotsky.[8] More damaging still, Jacson* struggled to recall its contents. The letter appeared prepared in advance—designed not to explain the crime, but to contain it.

It opened,

> In writing this letter I have no other object . . . than to explain the motives that have forced me to commit the act of justice I propose to carry out.

The author claimed to belong to an "old Belgian family," accused Trotsky of moral cruelty, and alleged that Trotsky had attempted to recruit him to assassinate Stalin—an assertion no investigator had raised. He wrote of insults to the Mexican people and of historical destiny.

The letter concluded,

> I am sure history will vindicate me . . . I demand the publication of this letter.
>
> JAC 20.8.1940[9]

The document rang hollow. It answered questions no one had asked, echoed familiar Soviet propaganda themes, and contradicted known facts. To Salazar, it was less a confession than a script.

Unraveling a False Identity

Salazar pressed forward. Within hours of the investigation, Jacson* abandoned one fabrication only to retreat into another, claiming to be Jacques Mornard Vandendreschd*, born in Tehran in 1904, the son of a Belgian ambassador. He described an elite education in Brussels, in Dixmude, and at the Sorbonne, supposedly financed by a substantial family fortune.

Investigators dismantled the legend almost immediately. No Belgian ambassador had been posted to Persia in 1904, and the schools he cited proved fictitious. When the Belgian chargé d'affaires addressed him directly in prison, it became clear that he spoke no Flemish, prompting the official conclusion: "He is not a Belgian and has no knowledge of Belgium."[10] The deception unraveled further when the real Jacques Mornard—a journalist with *La Nation Belge*—confirmed that his identity had been appropriated.[11]

Under scrutiny, the cover story collapsed. It was a patchwork identity assembled by GPU specialists who understood that such legends were designed to delay investigators, not withstand professional examination.

The Woman Who Knew

Three days after the attack, Salazar turned to a different instrument—a surprise meeting between Jacques* and Sylvia on August 23, 1940. The encounter was deliberate—designed not as cruelty but as confrontation. Jacson* was told he would see an optician for his injured eye. Instead, he was led into a room where Sylvia lay on a cot, sobbing.

"Colonel, what have you done? Take me out of here!" Jacson* cried, struggling against the guards.

Sylvia screamed: "Take the murderer away! Kill him! Kill him!"[12]

Salazar urged her to speak with her husband.

"A thousand times no! He is a hypocrite and an assassin!"

Jacson* tried again. "Colonel, why am I here?"

When Salazar asked whether her husband had been disillusioned with Trotsky, Sylvia exploded: "Nonsense! Don't lie, traitor! Tell the truth!"

Questioned about money, Sylvia admitted receiving $3,000 but now insisted it must have come from the GPU. Jacson* had claimed it came from his mother.

"Lies! Lies! He's a liar and a scoundrel."[13]

Truth, Torture, and Silence

Toward the end of his investigation, and unhappy with the information being provided, Salazar warned Jacques* that Mexican police possessed other "methods."

"We've treated you with respect. It will be unfortunate if we have to change our methods."

Jacson* replied calmly, "Even if you cut the skin off me centimeter by centimeter, I'll stick to my story."

The letter with his confession, he insisted, contained the whole truth. Salazar knew it did not.[14]

Return to the Scene

Ten days after the attack, the court ordered a walk-through of the crime at the villa. Jacques*, still suffering from his injuries, complied. The atmosphere was volatile. Trotsky's guards were disarmed and separated to prevent retaliation. The man they had watched for months had murdered their mentor—and now recited ideology in place of remorse.[15]

In Salazar's report, the facts required no confession. The lie had already been exposed.

Ramón Mercader—still cloaked in the alias Jacques Mornard*—had been trained for this moment. He did not respond like a man surprised by capture but like a disciplined operative executing a mission. For Salazar, it became a contest of patience rather than force. The interrogation did not break the prisoner—but it left fractures. Small, invisible, and accumulating.

The Duel Ended Without Surrender

What followed lay beyond the police cell. By court order, two psychiatrists entered the case—tasked not with extracting a confession, but with probing the architecture of Mercader's silence. Where Salazar had tested the lie against evidence, they would test the mind against itself.

The struggle would continue—this time in identity, memory, and endurance.

CHAPTER XXXII

TRAINED TO KILL, TRAINED TO LIE

"Trotsky was so blind to his immediate human surroundings that, although living behind the high walls of a fortified villa in constant fear of assassination, he failed to recognize in his own entourage the man assigned to kill him."

—Isaac Don Levine

"To understand the mind of a killer is not to excuse it—but to fear its logic."

—Anonymous psychiatrist

"The perfect operative is not the one who kills without hesitation, but the one who lies without memory."

—GPU manual, 1938

The Case Opens

On September 3, 1940, examining magistrate Raúl Carrancá Trujillo formally opened the legal case against Jacques Mornard* and Sylvia Ageloff. Determined to pierce Jacson's* false identity, Trujillo and prosecutor Francisco Cabeza de Vaca launched international inquiries and compiled documentation from all three Mexican police agencies involved. Fourteen days after the assassination, Trujillo ordered a psychiatric evaluation of the prisoner by two court-appointed criminologists: Dr. José Gómez Robleda, head of social medicine at the National Autonomous University of Mexico (UNAM), and Dr. Alfonso Quiroz Cuarón, professor of criminology at UNAM. Though

87. Dr. Quiroz Cuarón began his court-ordered examination of the assassin in September of 1940.

Robleda outranked him administratively, it was Quiroz Cuarón who pursued the inquiry with singular intensity—continuing the investigation well into the 1950s.[1]

Resisting public pressure for a rapid trial, Trujillo insisted that psychological evaluation precede judgment. For six months, the doctors examined Jacson* six hours a day—972 hours in total—producing a monumental study titled *Organic-Functional and Social Study of the Assassin of Leon Trotsky*. At 1,359 pages, the report comprised more than half the final court record and represented the first comprehensive psychological profile ever conducted on a living political assassin.[2]

The report depicted a disturbing paradox. Beneath Jacson's* calm, cooperative exterior lay a narcissistic and emotionally detached personality fortified by ideological absolutism and a fractured inner identity. He was intelligent, methodical, and capable of sustaining an elaborate double life without remorse. Though not legally insane, he was described as fanatical—fully competent to stand trial yet incapable of moral reflection. For him, murder was not a crime but a duty.

Under Mexican law, such examinations formed part of the judicial process but were independent of police investigation. Their purpose was to assist the judge—who alone determined guilt, sentencing, and confinement. The psychologists were not therapists; no privileged relationship existed, and the scope of inquiry was broad and unrestricted.[3]

Mornard's* Reluctant Consent

Mornard* greeted the psychologists' request with guarded amusement. They assured him their role was strictly technical, not political—that they were impartial court experts, not interrogators. Having already endured questioning by multiple police agencies, he viewed the process with wary curiosity.[4]

Nearly twenty years later, Isaac Don Levine—who collaborated with Quiroz Cuarón on *The Mind of an Assassin*—observed that Mornard* might never have cooperated had his defense counsel fully explained the court's mandate. Mexican law required the court to consider the offender's background, upbringing, education, motives, and social milieu—an inquiry that necessarily threatened to expose his GPU ties and lifelong ideological conditioning. The most dangerous line of inquiry, however, was the simplest: his true identity.

Levine identified five reasons why Mornard* agreed to participate.

First, although Mexico abolished the death penalty in 1929 for ordinary crimes, an obscure statute still permitted it under "exceptionally atrocious conditions." Mornard* might have believed cooperation would yield a favorable report and reduce that risk—though the doctors anticipated his calculated compliance, noting that prisoners routinely attempted to emphasize positive traits while concealing violent ones.

Second, Mornard* worried about Sylvia Ageloff. However instrumental his manipulation of her may have been, he repeatedly expressed guilt over her arrest. He insisted—to police and in written statements—that she was innocent and uninvolved, a claim met with skepticism. Cooperation may have seemed a way to mitigate her situation.

Third, the examination delayed his transfer to the Palacio de Lecumberri, the feared "Black Palace," where conditions were harsher and the risk of a GPU-placed assassin among guards or inmates was real.

Fourth, Mornard* was gregarious and articulate. He enjoyed conversation, storytelling, and psychological sparring. The interviews gave him an audience, and for six months he held it—deploying crafted narratives and layered evasions.

Finally, vanity. Even in captivity, Mornard* relished intellectual combat and the chance to assert superiority. He agreed to cooperate—but only after issuing a warning: "You will not get anything out of me."[5] When the study concluded, he might have been correct.

The Assassin's Persona

The examination began with a full medical and physical assessment, followed by tests of intelligence, memory, coordination, dexterity, and reasoning.

Levine, quoting directly from the court record, described the prisoner:

> Jacques* was 5'10" tall, slender and light-boned, with broad, slightly stooped shoulders and long proportional arms. His hands and feet were thin and elongated. He had abundant curly hair, large green myopic eyes, and wore glasses. His nose was narrow and straight; his teeth strong and regular; his brows heavy; his forehead broad and deeply furrowed.[6]

Quiroz Cuarón noted Mercader's evenly toned light olive skin and wiry physical conditioning, unremarkable in strength but efficient and controlled.[7] The doctors also discovered an unusual hypersensitivity to pain.[8] During interviews, Mornard* complained indignantly about the bite inflicted by Trotsky during the struggle—recounting the incident as if it were an injustice, seemingly oblivious to the fact that Trotsky had been fighting for his life after receiving a skull fracture.[9]

Even in custody, Mornard* remained meticulously groomed. He shaved daily, kept himself impeccably clean, and dressed with care. When police removed a small fabric sample from his bloodstained jacket for analysis, he later filed a complaint accusing them of destroying his clothing.[10]

Dress was not incidental to him. He had arrived in Mexico with multiple trunks of tailored garments and, shortly before leaving for New York in June 1940, shipped a large wardrobe ahead—clear evidence that he expected to survive the operation and reclaim his belongings. Even in prison, once his clothing was returned, he appeared for interviews in suit, vest, and hat—what the doctors termed a "studied, careless elegance."

Asked to define *elegance*, he replied: "Elegance is that quality which makes it possible for those who know how to dress well, but it is very difficult to be elegant."[11]

The doctors associated this fastidiousness with a Don Juan personality—sexually confident, emotionally shallow, and accustomed to easy relationships. Questioned about women, Mornard's* responses were superficial. He claimed to prefer slim Nordic types and—maintaining his cover—remarked that Sylvia Ageloff could have been the mother of his future child. There was no indication of unmet sexual needs prior to arrest.[12]

In a written self-evaluation, he described himself as irascible, impulsive, vengeful, excitable, rebellious, and dominating—yet elsewhere insisted on absolute emotional control. The doctors noted the contradiction. He might appear lost in thought, but when startled, reemerged instantly, fully aware and composed.[13]

The Language Test

One of the most consequential examinations targeted Mornard's* claim that he did not understand Russian. He asserted that French was his native language, that he had learned Spanish in Mexico, and that he spoke some English—but no Russian.

To test this, Quiroz Cuarón devised an experiment using an electroencephalographic (EEG) booth fitted with electrodes to record emotional response. Without warning, a handwritten note in Cyrillic was placed before the prisoner:

> You are done for. All your accomplices have already begun to talk. The police have their hands on all the threads and know who sent you to Mexico. Nevertheless, you have not said a word. Your mother will be put to death.

At first, Jacson* showed no reaction. Nearsighted, he leaned forward to read. As comprehension registered, his complexion paled, his jaw tightened, and his eyes shifted. He turned away and said quietly, "I do not understand."

But the EEG trace told a different story. At the precise moment he read the message, the graph registered a sharp neurological response. The conclusion was inescapable: Jacson* understood Russian. The denial was deliberate.

Profile of a Political Killer

Despite months of intensive police investigation, Mornard's* true identity remained elusive, obscured by a succession of calculated falsehoods that only deepened the mystery. Psychological examiners, however, believed they had assembled a coherent operational profile. They described a man fluent in multiple languages, possessing an exceptional memory, and capable of absorbing complex instructions with remarkable speed. He demonstrated athletic reflexes, unusually strong night vision, and the ability to navigate in complete darkness with ease. He could disassemble and reassemble a Mauser rifle blindfolded in under four minutes, had received formal military instruction, and was trained in alpine climbing.

The examiners also noted his extraordinary emotional control. He was able to convincingly feign deafness despite perfect hearing and appeared to take a calculated pleasure in psychological games of deception and misdirection—traits consistent with advanced intelligence training rather than ideological fanaticism.

When asked his date of birth, he claimed February 17, 1904, placing himself at thirty-six years of age. Only years later would Alfonso Quiroz Cuarón uncover the truth: Mornard* had been born on February 7, 1913. He was just twenty-seven when he killed Trotsky.

In his personal reflections, he expressed open contempt for his father but spoke of his mother with reverence, describing her as fearless, resilient, and heroic. She served as his ideological anchor and emotional compass.

Final Judgments

Despite meticulous interviews and carefully constructed psychological traps, the examination produced little of direct judicial value. The final report resembled a clinical autopsy: traits cataloged, behaviors dissected, motives inferred—yet no confession, no GPU names, no verifiable personal history. The court had tasked science with penetrating a mind trained not merely to conceal secrets, but to erase them.

Mornard* remained confined beneath a sheet, subsisting largely on warm milk and bread, clinging to the fiction that he was Jacques Mornard*. The doctors knew the name was false. But the man behind it offered no past and volunteered none.

Though the escape from the villa had failed, Mercader had fulfilled his function within the Soviet design. Leonid Eitingon, who recruited and shaped him, had chosen well. Mercader was not merely an assassin; he was a constructed instrument. No confession linking him to the GPU was ever extracted—neither by Salazar's interrogations nor by psychiatric inquiry. His mind was a fortress, built to protect the mission and erase the man.

The psychologists gained little. Investigators, however, increasingly turned their attention elsewhere. With Mercader sealed in disciplined silence, scrutiny shifted toward Sylvia Ageloff. The unresolved question confronting authorities was no longer who the assassin was—but whether Sylvia's role had been as innocent as she claimed, or more deliberate than she admitted.

CHAPTER XXXIII

FORTUNE'S FOOL

Love, Denial, and the Death of Trotsky

"ROMEO: Oh, I am fortune's fool."
—*Romeo and Juliet*, Act 3, Scene 1

"Only a moron could live with a GPU
agent and not become cognizant."
—Whittaker Chambers, former GPU operative

"Ageloff saw no evil, heard no evil, and above all, did no evil."
—Eric London

The Invention of Innocence

Few figures associated with the assassination of Leon Trotsky have been so persistently present in the historical record—and yet so thoroughly insulated from judgment—as Sylvia Ageloff. From the first hours after the attack on August 20, 1940, her name appeared in police reports, press accounts, court filings, and intelligence memoranda. Almost immediately, however, a counternarrative took hold: that of the tragic innocent, a woman undone by love and misjudgment rather than by agency or intent.

Contemporary portrayals framed Ageloff neither as conspirator nor facilitator but as an incidental victim. She was depicted as emotionally vulnerable, politically inexperienced, and psychologically overwhelmed. Blame was confined to the assassin, Ramón Mercader; Sylvia was reduced to the unwitting intermediary through whom he reached his target.

This narrative endured not because it was well supported by evidence, but because it was useful. It spared Trotsky's followers from confronting the possibility that Soviet intelligence penetrated their movement not only through deception, but through accommodation, denial, and silence within their own ranks. It also allowed Ageloff to withdraw quietly into postwar anonymity, shielded by sympathy and ambiguity.

As historian Eric London has observed, sustaining this narrative required accepting a portrait of Ageloff stripped almost entirely of agency. She had to be seen as "fortune's fool"—"A woman without agency, wandering blindly through life, and so monumentally stupid as to be incapable of recognizing the transparent and bizarre contradictions in the mysterious life story and activities of the man with whom she had been sleeping for nearly two years."[1]

Agency Without Conspiracy

Stripped of rhetoric, London's formulation exposes the implausibility at the heart of the innocence narrative. The historical record does not require accepting Ageloff as malevolent—but it does require acknowledging agency. Sylvia possessed the intellectual and experiential capacity to recognize contradictions in Mercader's identity and behavior. She understood the implications of his reliance on secrecy, coded communications, false addresses, and guarded correspondence. And she made conscious choices—whether motivated by love, denial, fear, loyalty, or self-preservation—to ignore, excuse, conceal, or fail to report those contradictions.

In 2021, London reopened this question in a four-part investigative series examining Ageloff's role in the assassination. Drawing on Mexican judicial records, FBI memoranda, contemporary journalism, and earlier scholarship, he argued that the traditional portrayal of Ageloff as an unwitting victim collapses when the full evidentiary record is examined.[2] His work introduced no new archive; rather, it insisted that existing sources be read in full and taken seriously.

This chapter reaches the same conclusion through independent analysis. When examined chronologically and without sentiment, the record reveals a sustained pattern of conduct—before, during, and after the assassination—that consistently advanced the assassin's access and obstructed accountability.

Arrest, Detention, and Legal Posture

Sylvia Ageloff was not treated by Mexican authorities as a traumatized bystander. In the immediate aftermath of the attack, she was detained and formally charged as an accomplice with knowledge of Jacson's* intention to kill Leon Trotsky.[3]

Her confinement at Green Cross Hospital was procedural rather than medical. Colonel Leandro Salazar arranged for her admission under a false diagnosis—a "liver condition"—to register her and place her under controlled observation, hoping that isolation from Jacson* might induce cooperation.[4]

Instead, investigators encountered resistance. Salazar described Ageloff as visibly nervous and prone to histrionics, repeatedly insisting that Jacson* had used her to gain access to Trotsky while loudly calling for his death.[5] She refused to answer substantive questions and disrupted interrogation with emotional outbursts. Gregorio Luri recorded that she spent days in bed wearing the same white sailor's blouse, screaming and turning away whenever anyone entered the room.[6]

Federal investigators were less sympathetic. An FBI memorandum dated August 27, 1940, noted that attempts to interview her were unsuccessful because she was "very adept in pulling hysterical fits at any time."[7]

Performance, Psychology, and Resistance

Medical staff privately questioned the authenticity of these episodes. Although Ageloff appeared panicked, her heart rate reportedly remained normal—an anomaly inconsistent with genuine hysteria. Shortly after

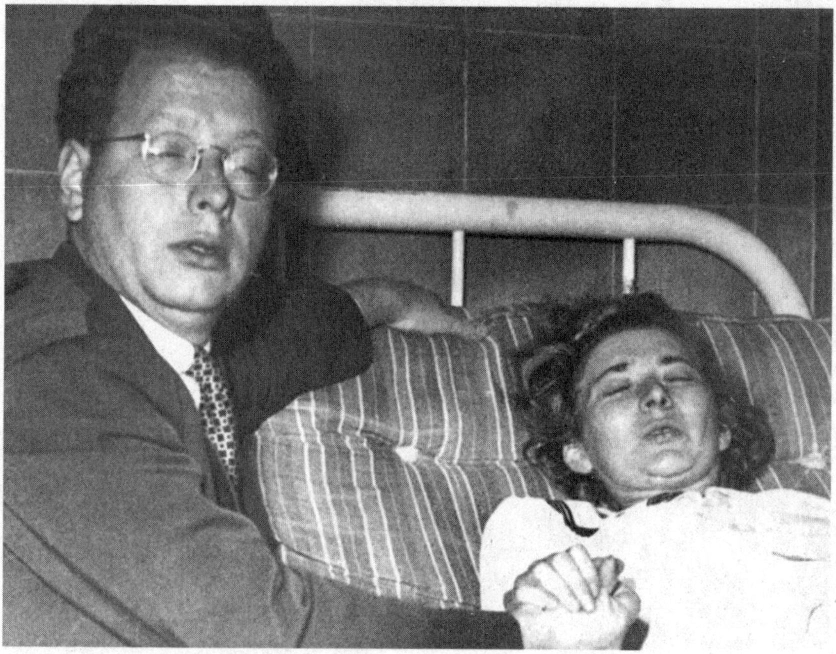

88. Monte Ageloff comforting his sister.

her incarceration, she began refusing food, accepting only bread and milk in what authorities interpreted as an effort to exert pressure on investigators.[8]

Ageloff held graduate-level training in psychology and understood the dynamics of interrogation, including behaviors that could interrupt or suspend questioning. Mexican police increasingly concluded that her emotional displays were not spontaneous expressions of trauma, but performances intended to delay questioning, avoid confrontation with Mercader, limit legal exposure, and buy time as the investigation unfolded.

This interpretation sharply contradicts later caricatures of Ageloff as intellectually incapable or psychologically overwhelmed. As Eric Gurevitch observed in a 2020 interview with historian Eric London, portrayals have oscillated between depicting her as "the duped idiot" and as a collection of crude stereotypes—"But these are just clichés and tropes." He added pointedly, "whatever one thinks happened, Sylvia was not stupid."[9]

89. Sylvia Ageloff never explained the many inconsistencies in her two-year love affair with the assassin.

What She Knew—and Chose Not to Report

Mexican prosecutors did not build their case on a single incriminating act. Their theory rested on accumulation: conscious accommodation of behavior Ageloff recognized as suspicious. They assembled a record that rendered her claim of total ignorance implausible.

Ageloff arranged a despedida dinner on the evening of the assassination involving Otto Schüssler, a Trotsky secretary and guard—an event investigators believed was intended to keep him away from the villa during the attack.[10] She admitted to having relatives in Russia, raising concerns that threats to their safety could have been used as leverage.[11] She observed Mercader working with ciphers and exchanging coded correspondence incompatible with his claimed identity.[12] She acknowledged that he obsessively guarded sealed correspondence and his suitcase during travel from New York to Mexico—yet reported none of this to Trotsky's guards or the Socialist Workers Party.[13]

Mercader's repeated insistence on her innocence further alarmed prosecutors. He challenged Judge Carrancá Trujillo's decision to detain her, a move interpreted as self-serving and strategic.[14] Prosecutor Francisco Cabeza de Vaca dismissed Mercader's claim that the murder stemmed from a romantic dispute as "unbelievable by any reasonable person, or in the brain of a child."[15]

Taken together, these elements formed a pattern that authorities believed could not reasonably be explained by naiveté alone.

A Circle Under Suspicion: Hilda Ageloff

By late August 1940, investigators no longer viewed Sylvia Ageloff's conduct in isolation. Attention widened to the circle around her—who knew what, and when.

Among those examined was her sister Hilda Ageloff. As previously established, Sylvia had asked Hilda to verify Jacson's* supposed import–export office in the Edificio Ermita after telephone calls to the listed room went unanswered. Hilda confirmed that no such room existed and relayed the discrepancy to Sylvia.

The issue did not end there. When confronted, Jacson* revised his account, claiming his office was actually in room 620—a detail that later assumed far greater significance. Following the May 24 assault, it became publicly known that room 620 had been leased by David Alfaro Siqueiros, leader of the attack squad.[16]

For investigators, the matter was not the clerical error itself but the sequence: a false address identified, a correction offered, and an office later tied directly to the first assassination attempt. That Hilda had verified the original false location—and discussed its implications with Sylvia—did not prove complicity. But it complicated assertions of total ignorance.

Contemporary reporting reflected that concern. The *Brooklyn Daily Eagle* noted that Sylvia's father traveled to Mexico City in late August 1940 to appeal directly to President Cárdenas. On September 4, defense attorneys sought an injunction to prevent Hilda's arrest upon her arrival from New York, acknowledging that she was "liable to detention as an accomplice" if questioning revealed prior suspicions. By November, Prosecutor Cabeza de Vaca threatened to arrest Hilda and broaden the inquiry into the Ageloff family, even as US diplomatic pressure intensified.

Money, Mobility, and Means

Ageloff's finances and travel history further unsettled investigators. Despite earning approximately $1,500 annually as a New York welfare investigator, she traveled internationally with unusual frequency.

On August 7, 1940, she abruptly booked passage on the newly inaugurated Eastern–Pan American "Mexican Flyer"—an exclusive overnight route carrying just ten passengers and completing the journey in approximately sixteen hours.[17]

FBI records traced Sylvia's itinerary through Washington, Atlanta, New Orleans, Houston, Brownsville, and Tampico before reaching Mexico City at 12:35 p.m. on August 8.[18] The cost—approximately $35,000 in 2025 dollars—exceeded twenty times her annual income.

Authorities also questioned her vague recollection of receiving $3,000 from Jacson* before he left for Mexico in October of 1939—later revised to $3,500—$85,000 in 2025 dollars. She could not recall the bank involved, later claiming her sister deposited the funds on her behalf. Analysts noted that such transfers mirrored patterns observed in other Soviet intelligence operations.[19] Mercader's explanation—that the money came from an inheritance—convinced no one.

Public Judgment and Professional Fallout

Three days after the murder, *The New York Times* labeled Sylvia Ageloff "The Woman Who Introduced Killer to Trotsky."[20] Her employer placed her position under review, and by September 12 her employment contract was rescinded. While officially attributed to overstaying a vacation, internal records also cited "low moral turpitude."[21]

The response was inconsistent with a presumption of innocence.

Pressure, Threats, and Judicial Retreat

Under Mexican law, guilt or innocence was determined by a judge rather than a jury—a structure vulnerable to political pressure. That pressure arrived swiftly. Threats were delivered to Judge Carrancá Trujillo and to Prosecutor Francisco Cabeza de Vaca warning against forcing Mercader to reveal his affiliations.[22]

Behind the scenes, US diplomatic channels worked quietly to secure Ageloff's release. An FBI memorandum from December 1940 acknowledged confidentially that she would soon be discharged and returned to the United States, where "further questioning . . . might develop more than has been developed in the difficult questioning of her in Mexico."[23]

When Judge Carrancá ordered her release, his justification rested largely on Mercader's insistence that she was uninvolved—despite the original charge of complicity.[24]

Vanishing into the Fog

Ageloff returned to the United States in late December 1940. Met in Newark by her family, she declined further participation in the case. Asked whether Sylvia or her relatives would testify at Jacson's* trial, Hilda replied, "As far as we are concerned, the case is closed."[25]

Rather than assist investigators, Ageloff issued a press statement through her father's office portraying herself as "the victim of a chain of circumstances."[26] The statement attempted to recast her role after the fact. Mexican authorities, by contrast, had charged her as an accomplice.

She emphasized that she had never formally introduced Jacson* to Trotsky—a claim technically correct but materially misleading. Her two-year relationship and repeated vouching made his access possible. She brought him into the villa on March 26 to assist with luggage, and on May 28 he met Trotsky after being introduced as her husband—a fiction that conferred legitimacy and disarmed suspicion.[27]

The FBI Years, HUAC, and Postwar Silence

Ageloff did not vanish from official attention. Under her mother's maiden name, Maslow, she remained under FBI surveillance. Agents regarded both her and Mercader as accomplices and believed she possessed undisclosed knowledge.[28]

In a May 11, 1942, interview, Sylvia acknowledged that Jacson* might have acted under coercion and that the murder was planned earlier in 1940—yet simultaneously denied any indication of GPU ties.[29]

In 1950, she testified before HUAC for approximately seventy-five minutes but did not disclose that she had been jailed in Mexico or charged as an accomplice. The omission allowed her to present herself as peripheral rather than central, and she was not challenged on inconsistencies. She thereafter withdrew completely from public life.

Whittaker Chambers's Warning

In the late 1940s, Socialist Workers Party leaders sought the opinion of Whittaker Chambers, a former GPU agent. Chambers rejected the Ageloff sisters' claims of innocence outright. He argued that no one could live with a GPU agent without becoming aware of it, and that Sylvia's conduct after the assassination only reinforced his judgment. He urged systematic investigation of the entire Ageloff family and warned that Mercader might conveniently die in custody, leaving behind only a scripted confession.[30]

Final Accounting: Dupe or Enabler?

To much of the world, Sylvia Ageloff remains the tragic dupe—seduced, used, and discarded. Yet for that account to hold, she must be accepted as fortune's fool, incapable of recognizing the contradictions in the life of the man beside her.

Her story is not merely personal tragedy but a cautionary tale of how ideology, love, and denial can converge with devastating consequence. Whether naive, manipulated, or willfully blind, Ageloff exercised choice—and those choices helped open the gates to one of the most consequential political assassinations of the twentieth century. History does not require proof of conspiracy to assign responsibility; it requires only a clear accounting of knowledge, choice, and consequence.

She attempted to disappear into history's shadows. History did not oblige. In the final accounting, Sylvia Ageloff was not simply fortune's fool. She was the indispensable enabler of Leon Trotsky's assassin.

And when justice finally moved, it did so incompletely. Only two men ever stood trial for Trotsky's murder—and one vanished before judgment could be rendered.

CHAPTER XXXIV

JUSTICE SUBVERTED

The Amparo Escape

"The May 24 attack was not intended to kill Trotsky but only to steal some of the archives."
—David Alfaro Siqueiros at trial

"A country without justice is a jungle."
—Carlos Fuentes

"In Mexico, justice does not die—it simply changes sides."
—Anonymous remark during the Siqueiros amparo hearings, 1941

A Crime Too Large for Its Court

The trial of David Alfaro Siqueiros opened under the weight of an unfinished crime. This was not a riot, not a spontaneous political clash, and not an act of individual fanaticism. It was a coordinated paramilitary operation—planned in advance, equipped with military hardware, and executed with tactical precision—directed at the home of a single man. Much of what follows was observed directly in the courtroom by contemporaries present throughout the proceedings, later corroborated by documentary records and subsequent findings.[1]

In the early hours of May 24, 1940, more than twenty armed attackers descended on Leon Trotsky's fortified residence in Coyoacán. They arrived with ladders to scale walls, automatic weapons and machine guns, electric saws, incendiary bombs, and destructive explosives. Disguised in police and army uniforms, they carried complete plans of the house and possessed detailed knowledge of where its occupants slept. For several minutes, they poured sustained automatic fire into bedrooms known to be occupied. One assailant entered the bedroom afterward, ostensibly to deliver a final *coup de grâce*. Incendiary devices were thrown in an attempt to burn Trotsky's archives.

By chance—nothing more—Trotsky and his wife survived. Robert Sheldon Harte, a twenty-four-year-old American guard, did not. He was taken alive by the attackers as they withdrew. Weeks later, his bullet-riddled body was found in a shallow grave, covered with lime.

This was the crime the Mexican courts were asked to judge.

David Alfaro Siqueiros: Artist, Operative, Defendant

David Alfaro Siqueiros was no ordinary accused. Internationally celebrated as a muralist, revered in Communist circles as a revolutionary artist, and hardened by experience as a GPU operative during the Spanish Civil War, he stood at the intersection of culture and clandestine violence. His reputation did not merely precede him into the courtroom—it accompanied him, hovered over the proceedings, and quietly shaped them.

In the months preceding the attack, Siqueiros had overseen surveillance of Trotsky's residence through intermediaries, including women tasked with cultivating relationships with guards in order to observe routines, security habits, and daily rhythms inside the compound. These visits were not casual. They were deliberate, recurrent, and timed. On the day of the assault itself, the same intermediaries reportedly returned to the house to confirm that nothing unusual had disrupted the routine.

From the outset, political insulation surrounded Siqueiros. In the immediate aftermath of the assault, Stalinist organizations advanced the claim that the attack had been staged by Trotsky himself as a provocation against Mexico. When that fiction collapsed under scrutiny, it was replaced by a second line of defense. The assault was not criminal but political—a revolutionary act against a reactionary enemy.

Siqueiros adopted this framing as both shield and sword. While still in hiding, he wrote letters to the chief of police and published articles promising that, at the proper moment, he would clarify the "very justified assault" on Trotsky's house and explain the "grave political responsibilities" that had made it necessary. From the beginning, he insisted that the case be treated as political in character, not criminal—a distinction that would soon become decisive.

A Court Without Urgency

When proceedings finally began, the atmosphere inside the courtroom was curiously unhurried. Sessions were postponed. Testimony unfolded slowly. Procedural digressions consumed hours. There was no sense of urgency commensurate with the scale of the crime. Time itself appeared to favor the defendant.

Journalists whispered among themselves. Guards lounged. Judges listened with practiced detachment. The tone suggested not a reckoning, but a negotiation—an unspoken understanding that the purpose of the trial was not to establish the full truth, but to contain it.

Siqueiros refused to make any statement until he had been permitted to read the complete testimony of all other defendants. This extraordinary privilege was granted without protest. Only after absorbing the evidentiary landscape did he take the stand, careful to avoid contradiction and alert to every opening created by earlier testimony.

The courtroom was not hostile to him. If anything, it was accommodating.

The Performance of Responsibility

Siqueiros's testimony followed a precise script. He admitted organizing surveillance of the Trotsky residence. He acknowledged coordinating with known collaborators, including his brother and several Communist Party operatives. He conceded involvement in the preparatory stages of the operation. None of this was denied.

What he denied—firmly, repeatedly, and with emphasis—was responsibility for what happened inside the house.

His role, he insisted, had been limited to "external operations." The machine-gun fire, the attempted destruction of documents, the abduction of Robert Sheldon Harte—these, he claimed, lay beyond his authority. To reinforce this distinction, Siqueiros asserted that he had issued explicit orders not to shoot to kill. Several codefendants echoed the claim as though rehearsed.

The assertion stood in grotesque contrast to the physical evidence: bedrooms riddled with bullets, beds shredded by automatic fire, walls perforated at close range. Yet the court made no effort to reconcile the contradiction. No judge asked how hundreds of rounds fired into sleeping quarters could plausibly be reconciled with an order to avoid lethal force. The performance was not challenged. It was absorbed.

Turning Gunfire into Psychology

The judges eventually transformed this contradiction into doctrine. More than three hundred shots had been fired inside the house, they acknowledged—but not with homicidal intent. The purpose, they ruled, was "psychological." The assault was meant to terrorize, not to kill. Under this interpretation, there could be no attempted homicide.

The logic bordered on the surreal. Testimony revealed that when Siqueiros learned Trotsky had survived, he reportedly exclaimed that all the work had been "in vain." Such a reaction made sense only if death had been the objective. Nevertheless, the court treated the inconsistency as irrelevant. Intent, it ruled, could be inferred away.

In this way, a failed assassination was judicially transformed into an act of intimidation. Automatic gunfire became symbolism. Bullets became rhetoric.

With attempted homicide dismissed, the most serious charge evaporated.

Robert Sheldon Harte: The Case the Court Would Not Hold

The murder of Robert Sheldon Harte remained the trial's suppressed center. Harte had been abducted during the assault and later found dead near a property Siqueiros himself had visited. Furniture purchased by Siqueiros's wife was discovered there. The man guarding the property testified that he had been paid to act under Siqueiros's orders and that he had been "guarding a gringo" for him.

On one occasion, drunk, the guard told his companion exactly whom he was guarding—and for whom.

This evidence demanded explanation. The court's solution was displacement. Responsibility for Harte's murder was assigned to two men—relatives of Siqueiros's wife—who had conveniently disappeared. Their absence made contradiction impossible. With blame transferred to missing figures, the court concluded that Siqueiros bore no responsibility for Harte's death.

The murder was not disproven. It was simply orphaned.

Harte's name appeared less frequently as proceedings continued. His death became a procedural inconvenience rather than a moral anchor. The court acknowledged that a man had died—but seemed determined that no one of consequence would answer for it.

Press Whiplash and the Manufacture of Forgetting

Outside the courtroom, a parallel trial unfolded in the newspapers. In the days immediately following the May 24 assault, the Stalinist press spoke with a voice of indignation. Party-aligned papers denounced the attack as a provocation and called for punishment of those responsible. The tone suggested alarm—an attempt to distance Communist organizations from a crime too violent, too naked, to be defended openly.

This posture did not survive contact with evidence.

As the investigation tightened around Siqueiros and senior Communist Party figures, the editorial line shifted with remarkable speed. Condemnation gave way to ambiguity. Ambiguity softened into silence. Silence was eventually replaced by defense. Within months, newspapers that had demanded justice now framed the prosecution itself as suspect. The question was no longer who had organized the attack but whether the Mexican state had the right to prosecute a "revolutionary artist."

The assault itself faded from view. Machine guns, incendiary bombs, abducted guards—these details receded, replaced by long reflections on Siqueiros's murals, his service to the working class, and his importance to national culture. The violence was not denied so much as submerged beneath rhetoric. Memory was not challenged; it was redirected.

By the time the trial reached its decisive phase, the press no longer functioned as a record of events. It had become an instrument of erasure.

Artists, Unions, and the Moral Laundering of Violence

Pressure on the courts did not come from the press alone. Labor federations and cultural organizations mobilized in Siqueiros's defense, transforming a criminal case into a referendum on revolutionary legitimacy. Resolutions were passed demanding his release. Committees of artists and "independent intellectuals" petitioned the president, urging that Siqueiros be treated with special consideration.

These appeals were carefully constructed. They avoided the language of the indictment entirely. There was no mention of machine guns fired into bedrooms, no reference to the abduction and murder of Robert Sheldon Harte. Instead, they spoke of murals, cultural heritage, and the indispensable role of artists and scientists as "bulwarks of progress."

That many of the same organizations had condemned the assault only months earlier went unmentioned. Political memory proved elastic. What had first been denounced as criminal violence was recast as political misunderstanding; what had been a liability became a cause for defense. In this way, the act itself was laundered through culture—its brutality muted, its consequences softened—and returned to public discourse in sanitized form.

By the time these petitions circulated, the trial's outcome was no longer in doubt.

Bought Justice, Performed Justice

The dismantling of the prosecution proceeded with a choreography that appeared almost rehearsed. One by one, the charges that carried real consequence were reduced, reinterpreted, or dismissed outright. The court did not deny the facts; it neutralized them.

The doctrine of criminal association—ordinarily central to cases involving coordinated violence—was redefined out of usefulness. A criminal association, the judges ruled, must possess permanence, stability, and a generalized intent to disrupt public order. A band assembled for a single operation, directed at a single household, did not qualify.

By this reasoning, a professional assassination squad fell short of being a criminal organization.

Other charges met similar fates. The impersonation of police and army officers was dismissed on the grounds that while the attackers had worn uniforms, they had not attempted to exercise official authority. They had disguised themselves but not impersonated anyone. The distinction was absurd, but it was decisive.

The law was not broken. It was bent—precisely, deliberately, and with the appearance of technical rigor. Justice was performed, not delivered.

The Defense Without Shame

The tone of impunity was set most clearly by Siqueiros's lawyer, Federico Sodi. On the day of his client's release, Sodi offered a set of explanations for Robert Sheldon Harte's murder that bordered on parody.

There were, he said, three possibilities. Harte might have been killed for robbery. He might have been an accomplice murdered to silence him. Or—most extravagantly—Trotsky himself, "author of many deaths during his period of power in Russia," might have organized a Fifth Column to track Harte down and kill him in vengeance.

Such claims were not rebuked. They were not even seriously examined. They were allowed to stand not as credible explanations but as rhetorical fog—sufficient to obscure responsibility and exhaust inquiry.

In that courtroom, absurdity carried no penalty.

Amparo and the Mechanics of Magical Escape

With the most serious charges dismantled, what remained were minor offenses: trespass, property damage, theft of vehicles used to block pursuit. These were insufficient to deny bail.

Siqueiros secured two amparos—protective judicial writs—one from a higher court and another from a trial judge. Both overturned earlier decisions by Judge Raúl Carrancá Trujillo, who had originally pressed the case forward. Trujillo's removal from effective control of the proceedings marked the final collapse of prosecutorial momentum.

In Mexican law, an amparo is not an appeal in the conventional sense, nor is it a ruling on guilt or innocence. It is a constitutional remedy designed to protect individuals from acts of authority deemed to violate fundamental rights. Rooted in nineteenth-century Mexican constitutionalism, the amparo functions as a judicial shield: it can suspend enforcement of laws, halt prosecutions, or nullify specific judicial actions while leaving the underlying case technically intact. In practice, an amparo allows a defendant to step outside the ordinary criminal process and seek protection directly from a judge on constitutional grounds.

There is no close analogue in the United States. Unlike habeas corpus, which challenges unlawful detention after conviction or confinement, the amparo can be invoked preemptively and repeatedly, even while a case is ongoing. Nor is it equivalent to an interlocutory appeal. In politically sensitive cases, the amparo has historically provided a powerful means of delay, fragmentation, and procedural exhaustion. When granted in succession—as in Siqueiros's case—it can effectively paralyze a prosecution, neutralize adverse rulings by lower courts, and create a legal pathway to release without resolving the substance of the charges themselves.

Released on bail, Siqueiros was legally prohibited from leaving the federal district. The restriction proved meaningless. Within weeks, he obtained travel documents and departed the country without interference. Officials professed ignorance. Bureaucratic confusion served as camouflage.

Through diplomatic assistance, Siqueiros reached Chile, where he resumed work on murals commissioned for public institutions. When Chilean police briefly detained him—having learned that he was legally a fugitive—the Mexican embassy intervened to secure his immediate release.

The escape required no drama. It required only indifference.

The Trial That Never Closed

After Siqueiros's departure, the case entered a peculiar legal limbo. Officially it remained open. A later district attorney would state plainly that Siqueiros had withdrawn from the action of justice and that the proceedings should continue until his reapprehension.

In the end, the matter stalled. No serious effort was made to pursue extradition. No renewed investigation examined the source of funds used to finance the assault. Siqueiros's claim that he had paid for the operation by selling paintings was accepted without scrutiny. Connections between Siqueiros and other Stalinist operatives—some of whom would later surface in Trotsky's assassination—were ignored entirely. The machinery of justice remained intact. It simply stopped moving.

What the Trial Refused to See

What the trial ultimately refused to confront was not complexity but consequence. A man had been abducted and murdered. A household had been subjected to sustained automatic fire. An assassination attempt had been organized with military precision. These facts were not disputed.

What was disputed—successfully—was responsibility.

By dispersing blame, redefining intent, and elevating political and cultural considerations above criminal accountability, the court ensured that no figure of consequence would answer for the crime. The result was not acquittal in the ordinary sense but something more corrosive: the normalization of impunity.

Robert Sheldon Harte disappeared from the record not because his death was insignificant, but because it was inconvenient.

The Verdict That Endured

The trial of David Alfaro Siqueiros did not fail because guilt could not be established. It failed because enforcing guilt conflicted with political necessity. The courts spoke, but their words were drained of force.

Siqueiros walked free, protected by culture, politics, and law carefully emptied of meaning. Harte lay dead, his murder acknowledged but unassigned. That asymmetry was the trial's true verdict. And it was precisely the verdict that made the final act—Trotsky's assassination three months later—not only possible, but predictable.

Closing: From Impunity to Instruction

The trial of David Alfaro Siqueiros accomplished nothing in the way justice is ordinarily understood. No organizer of the May 24 assault was held meaningfully accountable. No chain of command was established. No institutional reckoning followed the murder of Robert Sheldon Harte. Yet in another sense, the proceedings were not a failure at all. They delivered a lesson—one that was closely observed.

The message was unmistakable. A politically protected organizer could assemble an armed assault, deploy machine guns and explosives, abduct a guard, and still evade punishment through procedural fragmentation, cultural prestige, and judicial restraint. Responsibility could be diluted, intent redefined, and evidence rendered inert. The law, it became clear, would not pursue such crimes to their source.

Three months later, a different kind of operation would be carried out—simpler, quieter, and far more disciplined. It would rely not on mass violence but on intimacy; not on firepower but on access; not on escape but on silence. Where Siqueiros's assault had been loud and deniable, the next attack would be precise and final.

The trial that failed did more than absolve a man. It revealed the limits of prosecution and the dangers of exposure. For those planning Trotsky's murder, it was not a warning. It was instruction.

The courtroom had spoken. The assassin was listening—and learning.

CHAPTER XXXV

MERCADER CONVICTED

Stalin Acquitted

"But Siqueiros, assailant, assassin, incendiary, and agent in the GPU services, is free. Why not Jacson*?"
—Natalia Sedova [Trotsky]

"He killed Trotsky, yes—but he did not choose the target, acquire the weapon, or write the script."
—From *The Case That Ended in Silence*

"The court convicted the hand that held the axe but left untouched the mind that directed it."
—*Reflections of a Mexican Prosecutor*, unpublished memoir

Natalia's Warning

The release of all participants in the May 24 raid—most notably David Alfaro Siqueiros—laid bare the political nature of the Mexican legal system. Despite being arrested with a signed confession in hand, Ramón Mercader nevertheless hoped that the same legal sleight-of-hand and amparo appeal that had freed Siqueiros might eventually work in his favor.

This hope was not limited to the assassin himself. Even Trotsky's closest associates doubted that justice would be done. In 1942, Natalia Sedova [Trotsky] bitterly remarked that if judges could accept the fiction that Siqueiros had merely attempted to steal archives, or that the gunmen were "cothinkers" firing for psychological effect, then they might just as well free Jacson* too. "Siqueiros, assailant, assassin, incendiary, and agent in the GPU services, is free," she wrote. "Why not Jacson*?"[1]

Her skepticism was well-founded. Charging Siqueiros—a celebrated muralist and Communist icon—with murder would have embarrassed new President Manuel Ávila Camacho and implicated senior Communist figures. Under conspiracy law, every participant bore equal responsibility for the murder of Sheldon Harte. The stakes were enormous. Mexico's Communist Party and its allies moved swiftly to shield their own, and in the end—defying logic, evidence, and law—Siqueiros walked free.

With the assassin, however, the roles were reversed. Jacson* was a nobody who refused even to disclose his true name. His victim, by contrast, was a world-renowned revolutionary whose murder instantly became a historic event. The crime was not merely personal but political: a direct affront to former President Lázaro Cárdenas, who had granted Trotsky asylum in 1936 and regarded himself as responsible for his protection. It was also an affront to the Mexican nation itself—that a foreigner, traveling under forged papers, had violated Mexico's sovereignty by staining the principle of political asylum with an act of murder.[2]

A Trial in Two Phases

Meanwhile, the geopolitical landscape was shifting. As the Soviet Red Army began to gain ground against Nazi Germany, Stalin's international prestige rose—particularly within Mexico's left. The disappearance of Sheldon Harte, an obscure American Trotskyist, faded from public concern. Trotsky's murder, however, remained an international scandal. Cárdenas regarded the assassination not only as a national insult but as a personal betrayal.[3]

Mexican trials had no juries. Judges both investigated and ruled, typically within a year. Trotsky's assassination unfolded in two judicial phases—first from August 1940 to January 1941, and then from 1942 until the final ruling in April 1943.

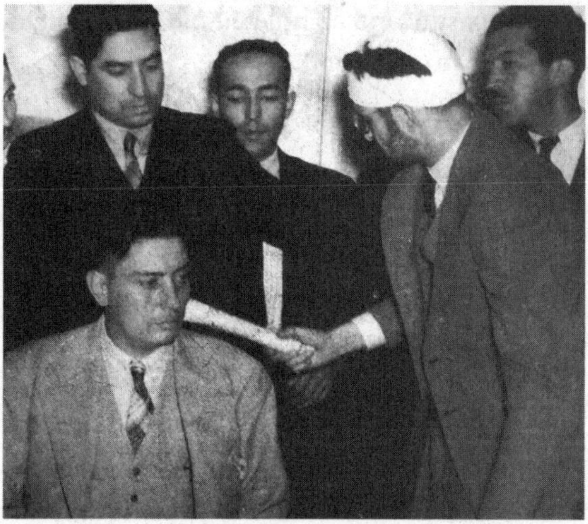

90. Ten days after the attack, the assassin reenacted how he struck Trotsky.

Phase One: The Psychologists and the Prisoner

During the first phase, the GPU remained silent. Mercader, operating under the alias Jacson*, claimed to be a disillusioned Trotskyist acting on behalf of the Fourth International. He adhered closely to the narrative laid out in his "confession letter," prepared by his handlers in New York, though he occasionally forgot key details.

The exhaustive psychological profile prepared by Drs. Alfonso Quiroz Cuarón and José Gómez Robleda would later haunt Mercader. Though they found him legally sane, the doctors described a fanatical personality, pronounced criminal tendencies, and clear indications that he understood Russian—despite his denials. They also pointed to the probable involvement of accomplices. These conclusions would later play a decisive role in denying him parole. In response, the defense retained its own expert, Dr. Millán, whose rebuttal amounted to a predictable effort to blunt the impact of the diagnosis.

On August 30, 1940—only ten days after the assassination—Jacson*, still bandaged and bruised from his beating by the guards, was brought back into Trotsky's study. Ordered to reenact the killing using a rolled-up newspaper, he visibly trembled as he stepped into a congealed pool of Trotsky's blood and had to be physically supported by officers. The guards and Salazar's detectives were unmoved, and

Jacson* soon recovered his composure and completed the reenactment, depicting the fatal blow coming from behind.

In early 1941, Judge Raúl Carrancá Trujillo was promoted, and the case was reassigned to Judge Manuel Rivera Vázquez. On January 8, 1941, the GPU formally retained Octavio Medellín Ostos—a politically astute and unscrupulous attorney—to represent Mercader.[4]

New Defense and New Distractions

Only after Ostos formally entered the case did Mercader's legal posture harden into systematic obstruction. Under Ostos's counsel, Jacson* abruptly ceased cooperating with the court. He never again submitted to questioning and demanded the right to compose a new confession letter. The defense now pursued delay and disruption rather than explanation. It faced daunting obstacles: a confession letter found in his coat pocket, destroyed evidence, a forged passport, and Jacson's* own admission that he had deceived Trotsky to gain access to his study. Together, these acts met the legal threshold for premeditation and fraud—offenses punishable by the maximum sentence allowed.

By late 1940—three months into proceedings—the trial had already become a public spectacle, even before Ostos assumed Mercader's defense. After Ostos's entry in January 1941, the strategy escalated. Jacson* announced that his key statements had been made while he was under the influence of some mysterious "liquid" with which he had been injected.[5] The defense now claimed that his confessions were therefore invalid.

Ostos also challenged the admissibility of the August 30 reenactment, arguing that Jacson* lacked legal representation at the time. He further asserted that Trotsky had not been struck from behind, contradicting the prosecution's allegations. The judge rejected both claims and upheld the confession's validity. A later reexamination of the autopsy, however, lends unexpected support to Ostos's assertion that Trotsky was indeed facing his assailant—looking up—when the axe fell.[6]

In the final months of the first phase, Ostos pursued an unusual line of questioning, probing Trotsky's age, strength, and temperament—and repeatedly emphasizing the loaded pistol kept on his desk—hinting at a possible shift toward a claim of self-defense.

A Fabricated Self-Defense

As the verdict approached, Ostos accused Judge Rivera Vázquez of bias, filing a formal complaint intended to delay proceedings. The accusation rested on a misquotation published in *Estampa* magazine, which falsely attributed hostile remarks about Jacson* to the judge. Ostos submitted the article to a higher court, alleging that the judge "professed a manifest hate for the accused."

At the same time, Ostos formally retracted the original confession and introduced a new version of the events of August 20, 1940. He claimed that Jacson* had been mentally unstable, depressed, and beaten by police, and therefore incapable of understanding the documents he signed. Colonel Salazar directly contradicted this assertion, testifying that he had personally ordered the prisoner be treated "with utmost propriety."[7]

In his revised statement, Jacson* alleged that Trotsky insulted him as a "military blunderer." He further wrote,

> I want to note that Leon Trotsky began to fight and shout before the blow in order to free himself from the pressure of my left hand on his coat, no doubt so as to draw his revolver, but I was faster than he [and struck first].[8]

The claim collapsed under scrutiny. Trotsky was unarmed, while Jacson* had arrived carrying a concealed pistol, a dagger, and a shortened ice axe. The court found the account implausible and directly contradicted by the confession letter Jacson* had carried in his coat pocket on the day of the murder. The judge dismissed the self-defense claim as a calculated fabrication.[9]

Phase Two: Changing Allegiances, Shifting Lies

By 1942, international politics had shifted once more. With the Soviet Union now allied with the United States against Nazi Germany, the political winds demanded a new narrative. Washington—formerly hostile to Stalin's purges and secret police—now required public support for a wartime alliance. Propaganda adjusted accordingly. The American press began portraying the USSR as a heroic bulwark against fascism, while Hollywood and the Office of War Information promoted sympathetic depictions of Soviet virtue.

Mercader and his attorney adapted in turn. To explain the contradictions between his new story and the hundreds of pages of court testimony already on record, the defense now claimed:

> He [Jacson*] was in no condition to make statements after the crime; the bandages prevented his being able to read the documents he signed; he was maltreated by the police; he suffered from a moral depression after his crime that caused him to lose all interest in what he was saying and signing, etc.[10]

He abandoned earlier claims linking Trotsky to Wall Street financiers and the Dies Committee—accusations tailored to a prewar world in which the USSR remained a pariah. Now he embraced the opposite line: that Trotsky had betrayed the workers' cause and was secretly a Nazi agent. As Isaac Don Levine observed, Jacson* "managed to say all of this without laughing," calling it a "diplomatic somersault."

The court found no credibility in these revised confessions. Judges concluded that Mercader had traveled to Mexico under false pretenses with a single objective: to assassinate Trotsky. He had never been a member of the Fourth International.[11]

Unexplained Funds

One issue remained conspicuously unresolved: Jacson's source of funding. Throughout his imprisonment, he enjoyed privileges far beyond those normally afforded a murder defendant. Press reports described gatherings held in his cell, attended by prison officials themselves. Journalists returned with remarkably consistent accounts—a private library, special meals, and conditions of confinement bearing little resemblance to ordinary incarceration.[12]

Beyond these comforts lay the far greater expense of his legal representation in the case itself, now three years old and likely to continue. Jacson* claimed all costs were covered by a bank account funded with five thousand dollars ($110,000 in 2025) provided by his wealthy "mother." The explanation strained credulity. That sum would long since have been exhausted, and Jacson's* attorney—who alone could clarify who was paying the mounting legal and personal expenses—offered no explanation. The silence spoke volumes.[13]

Final Judgment

Mexico neither permitted capital punishment nor imposed life imprisonment. Prosecutors sought the maximum sentence allowed by law, twenty-three years: twenty years for premeditated murder, two years for armed assault, and one year for illegal weapons possession. Sentencing was delayed when Ostos filed yet another appeal.

On April 17, 1943, the court finally rendered its decision. *Time* magazine reported nine days later that Jacques Mornard* had been convicted of the August 20, 1940, assassination of Leon Trotsky and sentenced to twenty years in prison. The court declined to rule on whether Mornard* had acted as a Soviet agent.[14]

Shortly after the sentencing hearing of Mornard* adjourned, Cabeza de Vaca, the court prosecutor, walked out onto the street in central Coyoacán and was murdered. The assassin was never identified, but it bore the hallmarks of the GPU seeking revenge for de Vaca's efforts to link Trotsky's assassination to the GPU and Stalin in court. His widow fled with her six children to the city of Leon, Guanajuato, for their safety.

91. Natalia Sedova was dismayed that the trial failed to hold Soviet leader Joseph Stalin—figuratively holding the bloody ice axe—accountable for her husband's murder.

After the Verdict

Mercader filed an appeal. On May 19, 1944, the court of appeals rejected it and upheld the sentence.

For Natalia Sedova, the verdict offered no closure. She knew with certainty that the assassin was a Soviet agent, trained by the GPU and dispatched by Stalin. What enraged her was the court's refusal to identify—or pursue—those in Moscow who had orchestrated the crime. The trial exposed only the man who held the ice axe; the conspiracy behind him remained untouched. To Natalia, Mexican justice had failed—not from ignorance, but from cowardice, corruption, or both.

Unlike Siqueiros, Mercader had no hope of escape or pardon. When his final appeal failed, he remained behind bars as Jacques Mornard*—the false name he refused to surrender. The trial ended, but the role endured. For years at Lecumberri, he demanded to be addressed by the name that had once concealed the crime.

CHAPTER XXXVI

GUEST OF THE BLACK PALACE

Twenty Years of Silence

"He never confessed. He never apologized.
He simply outlasted the truth."
—Mexican reporter, 1960

"There are no secrets in prison, only debts and disguises."
—Anonymous cellmate

"A cell cannot contain a cause, nor iron
bars a revolution betrayed."
—Former Trotskyist prisoner

From Custody to Confinement

Mornard* possessed the determination of a survivor. As his biographer Eduard Puigventós observed, "In early 1941, he had already been in prison for almost seven months—long enough to digest what had happened and to understand what he was going to have to live." The relative comfort and privileges afforded to him in his cell at the Sixth Delegation police station, however, had done little to prepare him for what lay ahead.

Colonel Salazar's investigation uncovered a dense web of aliases—Frank Jacson* of Canada, Jacques Mornard* of Belgium, and even Salvador Torkof* of Russia, a name Ramón had used earlier under unclear circumstances.[1] Mercader displayed no fear, only a steely determination to maintain his current assumed identity, Jacques Mornard

Vandendreschd*.[2] Salazar would later describe Mornard* as "a totalitarian soldier, a blind agent of an absolute power—his task to lie and to deceive."[3] Mercader remained faithful to the core GPU tradecraft directive: "Never, never, never, break cover."

In GPU tradecraft, the directive "Never, never, never, break cover" was a foundational rule, not a slogan. An operative's cover was meant to be lived as a complete identity, sustained under interrogation, imprisonment, and even after conviction. Breaking cover endangered handlers, safe houses, and intelligence networks, not merely the agent himself. Silence retained operational value long after arrest by preserving deniability and shielding others; endurance itself became proof of loyalty, reinforced by the GPU's hard-earned experience that agents who held to their legend survived longer and compromised less.

Mexican law permits prisoners to be confined in a penitentiary even while awaiting trial. With Colonel Salazar's examination completed in early 1941, Mornard* was loaded into a prison van on March 4 and, under siren-blaring escort, transferred to Lecumberri Prison—the infamous "Black Palace."[4] Long used to hold political enemies and foreign nationals, Lecumberri had inspired fear for decades.

For prisoners without money, influence, or protection, incarceration at Lecumberri was not merely confinement but a daily ordeal shaped by extortion, overcrowding, and institutional violence. Survivors consistently described Lecumberri as a system governed by corruption at every level. Confessions were extracted through beatings, forced immersion in sewage, and other forms of physical coercion. One of the most feared punishments—known as el chocho—required prisoners to grind a heavy stone or brick against the floor for days or even weeks unless bribes of thousands of pesos were paid to halt the ordeal. It was into this environment—designed to break bodies and enforce submission—that Jacques Mornard* was delivered.

Welcome to the Black Palace

Opened in 1900 as Mexico City's central penitentiary, Lecumberri was a steel-framed structure clad in stone that darkened over time, likely

92. The Palacio de Lecumberri, or the Black Palace, was Mexico's most notorious prison. It now houses Mexico's national archives.

from nearby drainage runoff. Its architecture followed the panopticon model: seven radiating corridors, all visible from a central thirty-five-foot watchtower. The design imposed constant psychological pressure. Inmates, never certain when they were being observed, were compelled toward self-discipline through the illusion of perpetual surveillance.

Inside Lecumberri, daily life operated on a brutal hierarchy defined by wealth and deprivation. The prison was stratified by wealth: inmates with money or influence secured private cells, ordered meals from outside restaurants, and obtained personal services, while those without resources were confined to filthy, overcrowded barracks and subjected to routine abuse. Access to nearly everything—from sleeping space to sanitation—was governed by bribery. Punishment was often arbitrary, enforced through beatings, isolation, and physical degradation. The administration tolerated unusual freedoms for the affluent even as poorer prisoners endured squalor and neglect.[5]

Prison is not designed to be pleasant, but the Black Palace was so dangerous, dirty, and degraded that *LIFE* magazine described it as "an animal cage for great and petty criminals who . . . murdered each other in knife brawls and lived in depravity in overcrowded cells."[6]

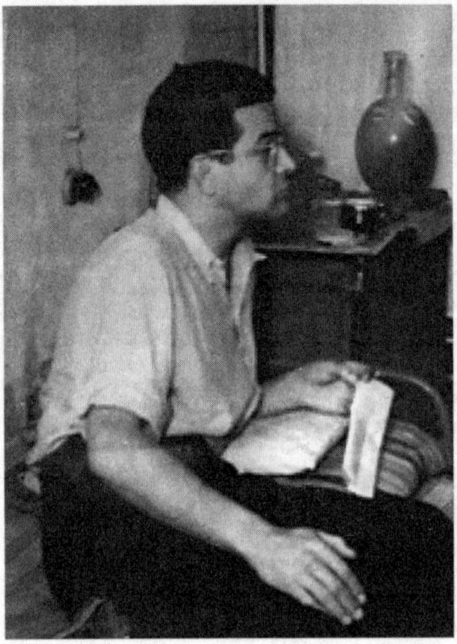

93. Jacques Mornard* shortly after arriving at Lecumberri prison.

Jacques Mornard*, however, was never among the wretched. The GPU understood the value of his silence and ensured his protection. His prison account began receiving deposits almost immediately—some direct, but mostly routed through his local lawyer, likely originating from Soviet rezidentura in Mexico City or New York. These payments continued for years and were widely known within the prison, even if their source remained concealed.

Mornard*, consistent with his legend, claimed the money came from a wealthy Belgian family, asserting that his mother and sister had become millionaires after his father's death. He offered no verifiable details. Years later, a former cellmate told reporters that Mornard* received three thousand pesos (approximately $350) per month. His lawyer confirmed only that the funds came from an account opened before his arrest.

Survival, Protection, and Paranoia

Even as the press labeled him "the world's most notorious assassin," Mercader adapted quickly to prison life.[7] According to his biographer Eduard Puigventós, by early 1941 he had mentally accepted the life that awaited him. His demeanor was not desperate but composed—focused on maintaining control over his new environment. One of his first acts was to purchase bleach and hire another inmate to clean and repaint his cell.

Mornard* imposed a strict personal regimen: cold showers, daily shaving, light morning exercise, and punctuality. For twenty years, he was always the first to answer roll call. During his first year he avoided the prison yard, keeping to himself while other inmates viewed him with suspicion. Over time, his rigid routine became a symbol of stoic defiance.

Though Lecumberri was notorious for brutality, Mercader escaped the worst. While he later claimed he was beaten daily and confined in a windowless cell, Puigventós regarded this as exaggeration. His steady flow of bribes and the pro-Communist orientation of Lecumberri's administration between 1941 and 1947 likely shielded him. Still, his life was not without danger.

On one occasion, he received a box of chocolates from an unknown admirer. When he asked the prison laboratory to examine them, they were found to contain enough poison to be lethal.[8] The sender was never identified—possibly a Trotskyist avenger, possibly a GPU agent—and Mornard* was forced to remain vigilant.

According to Puigventós, guards made several offers to Natalia Sedova [Trotsky] to have Mercader killed: one by a fellow inmate, another by a guard for fifty thousand pesos, and even one from the family of a counterfeiter who had befriended him. Natalia refused them all.[9]

The Man in Cell 27

Mercader's trial dragged on until 1943, when he was sentenced to nineteen and a half years for Trotsky's assassination, plus six months for carrying a concealed weapon. Throughout his imprisonment, he remained a national figure. One newspaper described his living conditions:

> He lives in the maximum-security section, cell 27 in block one. His quarters include a sleeping room, a living room, and an open patio. The bars over his patio are only two inches apart—tight enough to stop a grenade. Most other cells have wider bars, or none at all. Mornard* moves freely through the prison, often accompanied by two prisoners who appear to be bodyguards.[10]

In mid-1944, as his lawyers pursued a final appeal of his sentence, a new threat emerged. Authorities considered transferring him to the

Federal Penal Colony at Islas Marías, roughly seventy miles offshore in the Pacific—a six-to-eight-hour journey by boat through often rough seas. Originally conceived as a modern, escape-proof prison, Islas Marías had by the early 1940s become a dumping ground for inmates considered unsuitable for Lecumberri, notorious for disease, violence, and forced labor.

Mornard* alerted the press and successfully campaigned to remain at Lecumberri, arguing that transfer to a more remote—and, paradoxically, less secure—facility was a pretext to have him killed. He was successful and ultimately served nearly his entire sentence at Lecumberri.[11]

In 1945, President Ávila Camacho expanded Mexico's national literacy campaign into the prison system, promising amnesty to inmates who taught others to read and write. Mornard*, well-educated, joined the program alongside fellow inmate Isidro Cortés, a convicted family murderer. Their informal rivalry began in September 1945 and lasted until May 1947. Mornard* taught 347 inmates; Cortés taught 463.

Prison Director Ricardo Núñez Sáenz praised their efforts and in 1946 petitioned the president for pardons, noting that together they had educated more than a thousand prisoners. Despite the appeal—and Camacho's earlier promise—no sentence reductions were granted.[12]

Love, Privilege, and Poison

Conjugal visits were permitted under Mexico's permissive penal codes—not only for spouses and mistresses but, for a fee, for prostitutes as well. Visits could last until 2:00 p.m. on weekdays and 6:00 p.m. on Sundays, and nighttime excursions to local brothels could even be arranged. The system benefited prisoners and guards alike, who profited from its lax enforcement.

In June 1945, with discreet assistance from his mother, Caridad—then in Mexico attempting to arrange his escape—Mercader met Roquelia Mendoza Buenabad, a nightclub singer with aspirations of becoming an actress.[13] She enrolled in Ramón's prison class teaching English and was drawn not only to his charm but to the quiet authority he exercised within Lecumberri. Their relationship deepened quickly. Roquelia soon began smuggling messages on his behalf and, for the next two years, brought him all his meals from outside as a precaution.

Mornard* feared assassination—not only by a vengeful Trotskyite but, paradoxically, by the GPU itself, which might have preferred him dead to ensure his silence. He therefore rarely trusted prison food. His suspicions were not unfounded; a later attempt on his life would arrive concealed as a gift.

Roquelia later became his common-law wife and remained with him for life. In a later interview, she admitted, "I never really knew who he was. But he looked at me like I was the only real thing in his world—and I wanted to believe that was true. If I had doubts, I buried them." She maintained until her death that whatever else he had been, he had loved her honestly.

Until 1947, Mercader lived in relative comfort: silk pajamas, imported meals, liqueurs, cigars, books, and a radio. Under a sympathetic warden and a pro-Communist prison administration, he wielded near-authority, issuing instructions like a deputy warden. When leadership changed, his privileges diminished, but his spotless conduct ensured continued favor.

In December 1952, Mornard* was appointed head of the prison's radio and television repair shop, a coveted post that involved training apprentices in woodworking and teaching a popular electrical engineering course. The arrangement proved lucrative. He earned a salary for instruction and shared in the shop's profits, which expanded as it began servicing clients outside the prison. Eventually, he was entrusted with maintenance of Lecumberri's entire electrical system, including lighting, motors, and refrigeration.[14]

In August 1953, he became eligible for parole upon completing two-thirds of his sentence. At the same time, the warden decided to publicly announce that police had finally identified the assassin's true identity. Despite this revelation, Mornard* refused to acknowledge any name other than Jacques Mornard*. The warden stated that although he was eligible, it was doubtful he would apply. The following year,

Mornard* retained attorney Eduardo Ceniceros, a prominent political figure, and launched a vigorous legal campaign for parole.

Although Mexican law treated parole after two-thirds of a sentence as a right rather than a privilege, Mornard's* petitions were denied. His refusal to acknowledge his true identity weighed heavily against him, as did an unfavorable report by Dr. Alfonso Quiroz, who concluded that Mornard* felt no remorse and believed Trotsky's death had benefited the working class. He was denied parole.[15]

For twenty years, the man who murdered Leon Trotsky did not live in regret. He lived like a soldier still following orders. His prison cell was not a place of penance but a shelter for the lie he had become. Backed by Soviet gold, loyal to GPU doctrine, and watched by both admirers and enemies, Mercader remained silent. He was not a broken man, only one who survived inside his own false identity.

He had silenced the voice of the revolution and buried its truth, but no one—not Natalia, not the press, not the Mexican state—could compel him to speak.

And while Mercader kept his silence inside the Black Palace, half a world away, Moscow had already begun preparing his rescue—and carefully orchestrated plans that would never come to pass.

CHAPTER XXXVII

THE ESCAPE THAT NEVER WAS

"An agent's silence is his final disguise."
—GPU training manual

"In the end, silence is also a form of obedience."
—Soviet internal security doctrine

"A man who has killed for a cause cannot be left to rot—unless the cause is finished with him."
—Victor Serge

The Silence from Moscow

From the moment of Mercader's arrest, the Soviet government categorically denied any connection to Trotsky's assassination. As World War II escalated, the case gradually faded from public view, subsumed by larger events and diplomatic necessities. Behind the scenes, however, Caridad Mercader (MOTHER)—the leader of Operation MAT—pressed relentlessly to secure her son's release. With GPU backing, she pursued discreet, tightly compartmentalized efforts through CPUSA channels and trusted intermediaries in Mexico to support Ramón and explore the possibility of escape.

Even before Ramón had gone on trial, the Soviet underground operating from New York began cautiously organizing an attempt to rescue him. During the war years—especially as Hitler's armies drove deep into Soviet territory and the Kremlin became increasingly dependent on American aid—Stalin was careful not to provoke the United

States through overt acts of abduction or terror on its soil or within its sphere of influence. Political restraint, however, did not mean inactivity.

In 1942 and 1943, numerous suspicious communications passing between New York City and Mexico City were intercepted at the US border by postal censorship officials in Texas. Laboratory examination revealed that these letters were written in invisible ink and disclosed a conspiracy to "spring" Trotsky's assassin from prison. A network of "letter-drops" had been established in both the United States and Mexico to handle clandestine communications. These interceptions did more than delay the plan—they effectively doomed it.[1]

Cipher Plots and Compromised Couriers

Jacob Epstein, a veteran of the Communist-controlled American Lincoln Brigade—part of the International Brigades in Spain—received encrypted correspondence concerning the proposed rescue from comrades in Spain and Mexico until November 1943. Shortly thereafter, Pavel Klarin, a Soviet vice consul based in New York and, in reality, an aide to General Vasili Zubilin, the former GPU rezident in the United States, was posted to Mexico. Epstein followed him there and would later be accused of having communicated with Klarin on at least eight occasions.[2]

The correspondence implicated Simon Travis, alias Maxine Levi, a former *Daily Worker* journalist, who transferred $3,700 to a man identified as Enrique de los Ríos in Mexico City—apparently in response to an urgent appeal for funds from conspirators in Mexico. Another participant was Anna Vogel Colloms, a New York City schoolteacher alleged to have served as both a letter drop and courier.[3]

What the conspirators did not yet realize was that their communications channel had already been penetrated. As later revealed through a border interception, clandestine correspondence linking New York and Mexico had fallen into the hands of US authorities. The breach did not immediately expose the full scope of the rescue attempt, but it compromised the network at its core.

When interrogated by the House Committee on Un-American

Activities in 1950, Epstein, Travis, Colloms, and several other alleged accomplices were asked whether they were Communists and whether the charges against them were true. All refused to answer, invoking the Fifth Amendment. Their silence mirrored, in miniature, the discipline that had sealed Ramón Mercader's fate years earlier.[4]

The first known effort to rescue Ramón did not merely fail—it collapsed under the weight of compromised tradecraft. Once exposed, the network could not be rebuilt without unacceptable political risk. The escape that never was had already become impossible.[5]

Exiled in the Soviet Motherland

In Moscow, Caridad Mercader received assurances from her lover Nahum Eitingon (TOM) and from his GPU superiors that once the most critical phase of the war had passed, an operation to rescue her son would be launched. Alongside the legendary La Pasionaria—Spain's fiery Communist leader—Caridad ranked among the most privileged members of the enclave of elite Spanish exiles who had taken refuge in the Soviet Union.

According to El Campesino, the celebrated guerrilla commander who later escaped the USSR, this privileged circle lived in relative comfort while others endured far harsher conditions.[6] Caridad now observed life in the so-called "Workers' Fatherland" at close range. With few exceptions, Spanish refugees were assigned tasks for which they were ill-suited and untrained. They received starvation rations; many died of malnutrition. Spanish women resorted to prostitution for scraps of bread. Abandoned children formed roaming bands of homeless youths, surviving through begging, theft, and violence. Some were executed—not as petty criminals but as Spanish Fascists, a political designation that sealed their fate.[7]

Unlike La Pasionaria, who maneuvered within the Comintern's upper reaches, Caridad was a fighter. She did not avert her eyes from what she saw. Yet she was acutely aware that discretion was essential—not only for her own survival but to preserve any hope of securing Soviet assistance for her son.

The Watchdog

Caridad shared an elegant Moscow apartment with her former radio operator, Carmen Brufau—one of the schoolteachers Caridad herself had recruited into the apparat. Carmen, blue-eyed and in her early thirties, was both companion and constraint. Her first husband, now a Mexican citizen, was the Juan who had accompanied Caridad on the initial mission to Mexico in 1936.[8]

Carmen had known Ramón well. During psychological interviews, Ramón once inadvertently let slip her Christian name, quickly covering himself by describing her as a "champion swimmer" he had known in Paris. On another occasion, he referred to his mother's companion as "a very mannish sportswoman." These evasions reflected the enduring necessity of silence.[9]

Officially, Caridad was under strict instructions never to discuss Trotsky's murder or her son's role in it. Carmen Brufau—devoutly loyal to Moscow—served as both confidante and GPU watchdog. Her devotion would later be underscored by her expulsion from Switzerland in the 1950s as a suspected Soviet spy.[10]

War Turns, Plans Resume

As the war turned in the Soviet Union's favor and Red Army forces advanced into Poland, Caridad renewed her pressure on the Kremlin to redeem its promises. Stalin's hesitation reflected not indifference but calculation: he was unwilling to jeopardize relations with the United States while negotiating the postwar order.

Caridad escalated her demands, writing directly to Lavrentiy Beria and insisting on authorization to return to Mexico. She threatened to seek protection from the Cuban ambassador, citing her Cuban citizenship, if permission were denied. The pressure worked. Stalin approved the plan, and Beria provided Caridad with jewels valued at $55,000 to $60,000 to finance the operation.

According to contemporaneous accounts, a scheme was devised involving a Mexican physician, identified as Dr. Carlos D., who would inject

Ramón with the virus of a contagious but treatable disease. His condition would require transfer from Lecumberri to a hospital for infectious patients outside the prison, where escape could be arranged. Whether this plan advanced beyond preparation remains uncertain, but its conception illustrates the lengths to which Caridad and her handlers were prepared to go.[11]

Back in Mexico

On March 9, 1945, Caridad arrived in Mexico City and rented a flat in the Azteca Apartments on Hamburgo Street. Carmen Brufau soon joined her from Odessa, and the two resumed their shared life.

Caridad quickly discovered that other rescue schemes were already underway, directed by Carlos Contreras and elements of the local Communist underground. She soon grew alarmed. These plans bore the unmistakable hallmarks of Stalin's earlier "rescues"—operations that frequently ended in convenient "accidents," with the intended prisoner emerging not freed but dead. In one proposal, Contreras offered $100,000 to a prominent Spanish refugee to bribe a prison guard who would escort Ramón out of Lecumberri at night under the pretense of visiting a brothel. The scheme was rejected.[12]

Caridad now feared not failure, but success achieved at the cost of her son's life.

She appealed to a trusted Spanish friend in Mexico whom she had aided during his desperate years in Moscow. She urged him to organize the escape independently, promising unlimited funds provided he alone controlled the operation and relied only on trustworthy participants. Though deeply indebted to her, the man refused. Grateful to the Mexican government for granting him refuge, he would not repay that hospitality with a crime against the state.

Final Retreat

During her final months in Mexico, Caridad lived in constant fear. GPU protocol forbade her from visiting Ramón in Lecumberri Prison in order to protect his false identity, and she was convinced that Soviet agents monitored her movements closely. She managed once to slip into the prison, desperate for a glimpse of her son, but failed. Not long afterward, an automobile nearly struck her as she crossed an unlit street at night—a moment she interpreted as a warning.[13]

From then on, fear governed her life. She suspected the GPU might silence her as she had once helped silence others. The realization was bitter and inescapable: she had become what she once hunted. Her anxiety was well-founded. Stalin's secret services forgot nothing, and in the unstable postwar climate, even loyal revolutionaries could disappear for knowing too much. In that system, a single act of disloyalty could outweigh a lifetime of faithful obedience.

In mounting desperation, Caridad sought refuge at the French embassy and requested permission to settle in France, where her daughter Montserrat and her son Jorge were living. In her application, she stated that she had no occupation but received an income of $950 a month from Cuban properties. With her visa secured, she fled first to Cuba and then to Paris, where she would remain for years—safe, but marked—an exile haunted by what she knew.[14]

None of the escape schemes advanced beyond cautious discussions and aborted overtures. What had once been celebrated within Soviet circles as a decisive act against a mortal enemy had, by the final years of the war, become a political liability. In the new alliance with the United States, Trotsky's assassination was an embarrassment the Kremlin preferred to bury. Within that enforced silence, Caridad—mother of the assassin and veteran of the plot—had become a dangerous reminder of a crime Moscow wished erased.

Years earlier, Trotsky had remarked that life inside the fortified villa was a form of imprisonment—protective yet confining. The walls shielded him, but they also limited him. In the end, Ramón Mercader found himself in the same paradox. Lecumberri confined him, but it also protected him. The same prison that held him now shielded him from the GPU itself. So long as he remained silent and contained, he was safer behind bars than free in the hands of those who had sent him to kill.

Ramón Mercader remained in prison—his cover intact, his silence unbroken, and Soviet responsibility for Trotsky's assassination still officially denied. He was never rescued, not because the GPU lacked resources but because silence had become more valuable than survival. His usefulness had shifted—from protected asset to enduring liability. Behind the scenes, however, another intelligence struggle was unfolding. Only decades later would the decryption of a Soviet cipher system—VENONA—confirm what this abandonment already implied: that rescue efforts had not merely failed but had been deliberately abandoned once exposure threatened greater secrets. The encryption that shielded Soviet intelligence during the war would become a fabulous source for Anglo-American counterintelligence agencies.

CHAPTER XXXVIII

OPERATION GNOME

The Plot to Free the Assassin

"The perfect agent is one who never speaks—even when abandoned."
—Pavel Sudoplatov

"Every code conceals a lie, and every lie serves the state."
—Soviet cryptographer's proverb, 1943

"The Party never forgets its heroes—only its promises to them."
—Eastern Bloc (Soviet) proverb

A Prisoner Too Dangerous to Abandon

From the moment Ramón Mercader buried the ice axe into Leon Trotsky's skull, the Kremlin faced a new and dangerous problem: a captured assassin who knew too much. Publicly, Moscow denounced the murder and denied any involvement. Privately, Soviet intelligence moved to contain the damage—to sever all visible connections with Operation MAT, suppress exposure, and, if possible, recover the man who had carried out the deed.

What followed was not a single rescue attempt but a prolonged covert effort conducted through layers of intermediaries, coded correspondence, and ideological volunteers. Spanning Mexico, New York, Chile, and Moscow, the operation—later known by one of Mercader's early cover names, GNOME—became one of the earliest sustained intelligence struggles of the emerging Cold War, though neither side yet recognized it as such.

Intercept on the Border

The first decisive break in the rescue effort came not through sophisticated counterintelligence but by chance.

In August 1941, US Customs officers inspecting luggage at the border encountered a traveler carrying a box of personal stationery. The blank pages aroused suspicion. Laboratory testing revealed invisible writing—secret ink used to conceal clandestine correspondence on the final five sheets.

The stationery belonged to Anna Vogel Colloms, a New York–born schoolteacher with graduate degrees from Cornell and Columbia. Unaware of the discovery, she was allowed to proceed to Mexico without the box, which authorities retained. Government agents photographed and analyzed the hidden messages, then quietly replaced the original sheets with blank paper. Weeks later, Colloms retrieved the box and continued her travel, unaware that the communications channel had been compromised.

What US authorities had stumbled upon—without fully grasping its full significance—was a covert Soviet link between the New York rezidentura and operatives in Mexico. The messages tied intermediaries in the United States to financial transfers and planning efforts connected to Ramón Mercader's potential extraction from Lecumberri.

At the time, investigators could not yet see the full network. But the thread had been pulled. The illusion of secure communication had already collapsed, even as those involved continued to operate as though the channel remained intact.

A Network Revealed

Over the next two years, the US Bureau of Censorship identified twenty-four encrypted messages concealed in similar fashion. Together, they implicated a web of couriers, cutouts, and sympathizers—many linked to the Communist Party USA—operating across state and national borders.

Among those identified were Jacob Epstein, a veteran of the Abraham Lincoln Brigade; his wife Ruth; courier Anna Colloms; journalist Simon Travis (alias Maxine Levi); and others who facilitated communications, money transfers, and safe addresses. The system was deliberately indirect. Soviet officials rarely appeared on paper. Instead correspondence passed through ideologically reliable intermediaries whose political loyalty doubled as operational camouflage.

At this stage, American investigators still lacked the decisive key. They could see the outlines of a conspiracy but not its full intent.

VENONA: What Was Learned Later

During World War II, the US Army Signal Intelligence Service initiated a highly secret project—eventually code-named VENONA—that succeeded in partially decrypting ciphered cable traffic sent between Soviet intelligence services and their foreign stations. By exploiting repeated-use errors in Soviet one-time pads, American (and later British) cryptanalysts were able to reconstruct portions of thousands of GPU and GRU (Soviet military intelligence) messages from the 1940s, revealing Soviet espionage networks, tradecraft, and decision-making at senior levels.

The decrypts were fragmentary and often ambiguous, but they provided unprecedented insight into Soviet intelligence operations. To protect sources and methods, the existence of VENONA was kept strictly classified and was not publicly acknowledged until 1995. Only then would the full significance of the intercepted communications from the early 1940s become clear. Taken together, the decrypts revealed plans and priorities that had gone undetected at the time—including references to a single prisoner identified by the code name GNOME.

Operation GNOME Takes Shape

The VENONA traffic from 1943 and 1944 revealed that GNOME was Ramón Mercader and that his recovery had become a matter of sustained attention to the GPU. Messages identified a coordinating group centered on Jacob Epstein and his associates, with Anna Colloms acting as a courier between Mexico and New York.

The cables did not describe a single escape plan but an evolving effort: surveillance of Mercader, assessment of prison conditions, identification of sympathetic officials, and—most critically—the establishment of a medical conduit inside Lecumberri Prison.

What appeared in code was stark in implication. Mercader was, at that time, still considered rescuable. And the effort had reached high levels.

Codes, Cutouts, and Book Ciphers

To shield GPU agents from exposure, communications relied on a layered system of cutouts and coded references. When earlier channels were compromised, correspondence was rerouted through Santiago, Chile, and possibly Buenos Aires. One message instructed that future communications use a book code based on a specific edition of a 1942 paperback *Defense Will Not Win the War.* When the FBI acquired the same edition, they were able to follow the cipher.

The GPU sometimes employed book codes as a simple but effective method of clandestine communication in which sender and recipient used the same published book as a shared key. Words, letters, or phrases were encoded by referencing page numbers, line numbers, and word positions within the agreed-upon text. Because the message appeared meaningless without knowledge of the specific book and edition, book codes allowed indoctrinated intelligence personnel to pass instructions discreetly through ostensibly ordinary correspondence, minimizing suspicion while preserving secrecy.

These measures reflected both the sophistication and the fragility of the operation. Each new layer reduced risk—but also increased complexity and delay.

The Prison Doctor

The most consequential VENONA messages, dated June 1944, referred to a figure code-named LATA, identified by analysts as Dr. Esther Chapa, a physician at Lecumberri. According to the traffic, she had provided Mercader with medical treatment and was viewed as a potential liaison.

Other code names pointed to senior Mexican political figures, including SNOW LEOPARD, identified as Dr. Javier Rojo Gómez, then governor of Hidalgo and later mayor of Mexico City.

Whether these individuals knowingly participated or were merely assessed as exploitable remains uncertain. But the volume and urgency of the messages made one point clear: the rescue of GNOME had become a high priority in Moscow. Between December 1943 and November 1944 alone, more than eighty encrypted cables were sent from Mexico City to Moscow concerning the operation—some addressed directly to GPU chief Lavrentiy Beria.

Why the Plot Failed

Yet for all its reach, Operation GNOME stalled. Serial numbers in the VENONA traffic suggest a sharp decline in communications after the war's end. By 1945, the flow of messages slowed dramatically. The political landscape had changed. Trotsky's murder, once celebrated in secret, had become a diplomatic liability. Mercader, once an asset, now represented risk.

The operation did not collapse from lack of effort. It failed because silence had become more valuable than rescue.

Exposure Without Rescue

In 1950, many of the same individuals identified through earlier investigations were summoned before the House Committee on Un-American Activities. Most refused to testify. But the questions alone revealed how much American counterintelligence had learned—knowledge that had been quietly accumulating for years.

The irony was profound. Mercader remained imprisoned, his identity hidden. But the machinery built to free him had exposed itself.

VENONA would remain classified until 1995. By then, the escape no longer mattered. The codebreakers had captured something far more important than a man: the structure of Soviet clandestine power in motion.

Operation GNOME failed to free the assassin. But in tracing it, American intelligence mapped an invisible war already underway—one that would define the Cold War to come.

And even as Moscow chose silence, the pressure on Mercader's false identity continued to build. The alias of Jacques Mornard* would not survive forever. The unmasking had begun.

CHAPTER XXXIX

UNMASKING THE ASSASSIN

"Silence is not protection. It is strategy."
—Former GPU officer

"Mercader was not a fanatic. He was an obedient instrument, trained to kill and trained to keep silent."
—Julián Gorkin, *Murder in Mexico* (1950)

"History leaves footprints, even on the most carefully cleaned floor."
—Forensic proverb

The Silence Begins

As Leon Trotsky lay mortally wounded on August 20, 1940, he issued one final instruction to his guards: "Let him live. He must talk." The assassin, calling himself Frank Jacson*, did neither. He offered only a string of carefully rehearsed falsehoods—about his origins, his motives, and his past. Trotsky himself had known the assailant only under that alias. When pressed by Mexican authorities, the prisoner retreated into a second identity, Jacques Mornard*, and then into silence once again. For the next two decades, he buried his true identity as deeply as the ice axe had struck—becoming one of the most famous and enigmatic political prisoners of the twentieth century.

This silence was not instinctive. It was learned. GPU tradecraft demanded that an operative's cover be lived as a complete identity, sustained not only under interrogation but through trial, imprisonment, and even exposure. To reveal his true name was to endanger handlers, networks, and safe houses. To remain silent preserved deniability long after arrest. Mercader's refusal to acknowledge his true identity—even when disclosure might have improved his legal position—or bought his freedom—was not obstinacy, but the final execution of his assignment.

Inside Mexico City's Lecumberri Prison—the notorious "Black Palace"—reporters, guards, and fellow inmates who attempted to engage him throughout the years encountered icy detachment or open hostility. The assassin of Leon Trotsky withdrew into a rigid routine: reading, studying languages, repairing electrical equipment, and serving out his twenty-year sentence with mechanical discipline. He spoke little, revealed nothing, and never deviated from the role he had been trained to inhabit.

Silence was not merely a defensive posture. It was the last remaining form of control.

Clues, Leaks, and Betrayal

The prisoner's silence only intensified curiosity among journalists and Western intelligence services seeking to uncover his real identity. According to Pavel Sudoplatov, the Soviet intelligence officer in overall charge of Operation UTKA, the first major breach in Mercader's anonymity occurred in 1946, when a distant Spanish relative defected to the West and disclosed his true identity. Sudoplatov asserted that the leak could ultimately be traced back to Mercader's mother, Caridad Mercader. During the early years of World War II, Caridad had been evacuated to Tashkent, Uzbekistan, as German forces approached Moscow. There, Sudoplatov claimed, she confided in a minor Spanish Communist refugee—unaware that he would later defect and reveal the information to Western authorities in an attempt to secure his own freedom.[1]

By the time Caridad returned to Moscow, Sudoplatov wrote, the damage had already been done. Yet despite his proximity to events, no corroborating documentation has surfaced in Western intelligence archives to independently substantiate his claim. Most telling is that the FBI shows no record of such a revelation—an omission that would be difficult to explain if the account were accurate. The assertion remains plausible but unverified and must therefore be treated as retrospective testimony rather than established fact.

At the end of the war, Caridad was granted permission by Lavrentiy Beria to travel covertly to Mexico City in March 1945 and given $55,000 to $60,000 in jewels to finance her son's escape operation. There she worked quietly to improve her son's prison conditions and explored possible avenues for escape. Although she was ordered to never meet with her son face-to-face, Caridad remained in contact with him through intermediaries and played a role in arranging his introduction to Roquelia Mendoza, the woman who became his mistress and later his wife.[2]

Despite efforts to remain inconspicuous, Caridad was well-known among Spanish Republican exiles in Mexico, many of whom remembered her from her 1936 and 1937 fundraising tour during the Spanish Civil War. Her presence alone risked exposing Ramón's identity long before official confirmation.

The Mask Begins to Slip

Within days of the attack, photographs of the would-be assassin circulated in Mexican newspapers and quickly spread abroad. Isaac Don Levine later noted that veterans of the Spanish Civil War living in Mexico recognized Mornard* almost immediately yet chose silence out of fear of Soviet retaliation.[3] Among these Spanish exiles—many of them former Stalinists—the recognition was unmistakable. One acquaintance, Rossend Cabré, reportedly identified him without hesitation, saying, "That is Ramón Mercader," but like the others, he remained silent.[4]

Mercader's recognition did not produce disclosure. It produced dread. Many Spanish Republicans in Mexico had already seen comrades disappear, reputations destroyed, and families ruined through association with Soviet intelligence. To speak was not merely to accuse an assassin—it was to invite retribution. Fear enforced what loyalty could not.

In a 2001 article, journalist Stephen Schwartz credited Spanish Republican veteran and crime reporter Víctor Alba as the first to identify Ramón Mercader as Trotsky's assassin, claiming that Alba reached this conclusion as early as 1946 and that it was later confirmed by the VENONA decrypts. Yet no authoritative primary source establishes the year Alba first made this identification. In addition, the VENONA materials were not declassified until 1995, rendering claims of contemporaneous corroboration implausible absent proof that Alba had access to those highly classified files decades earlier. While NSA records do confirm that the individual referenced in the decrypts was ultimately identified as Mercader, they do not specify the year that determination was first reached.[5]

Recognition Without a Name

A more substantiated identification emerged in 1950, when Spanish exile Julián Gorkin collaborated with Colonel Salazar on *Murder in Mexico*, the first published work to publicly link the assassin to the Mercader family. Gorkin reported that Catalan refugees—veterans of the Spanish Civil War—recognized Mercader "without a shadow of a doubt." He claimed access to police archives and described personally verifying a scar on the prisoner's forearm, allegedly sustained during the fighting in Spain.[6]

In the book's appendix, Gorkin went further, identifying the assassin as one of Caridad Mercader's sons. He accurately described her as a "fanatical Catalonian," fluent in French, with years spent in France and Belgium, and alleged that she had worked for the GPU in Paris undercover within the French Socialist Party since 1928. During the Spanish Civil War, he wrote, she had been an active member of the United Socialist Party of Catalonia (PSUC), aligned with the Comintern.[7]

According to Gorkin, Soviet intelligence had drawn on Caridad's children for covert operations, and following the failed Siqueiros raid of May 1940, "one of her sons" was activated for the final assassination. He characterized the killer as a "docile instrument" of Soviet espionage. While Gorkin correctly linked the assassin to Caridad, he lacked the final confirmation—his given name, Ramón.[8]

Telltale Speech

Mercader's own behavior also unwittingly undermined his carefully constructed legend. He told Mexican police that French was his native language and claimed to have learned Spanish only after arriving in Mexico. Yet local workers noted that he spoke Spanish flawlessly, while FBI linguists observed that his French carried a distinct Spanish accent.[9]

Two Catalans hired by Mexican police detected unmistakable Catalan pronunciation during interrogations. On one occasion, Mercader inadvertently hummed a Spanish Loyalist song. When Dr. Alfonso Quiroz Cuarón asked him to write out the lyrics, he did so in perfect Spanish.[10] To Cuarón, this moment further confirmed that Mercader's roots lay not in Belgium but in Catalonia.

Skeptics and Secrets

As late as early 1950, the House Committee on Un-American Activities still listed the assassin as unidentified. Public uncertainty persisted, but behind the scenes, the FBI was moving closer to a determination of his identity. In April 1950, a memorandum from the New York Field Office to Director J. Edgar Hoover, using information from Gorkin, stated,

> JACSON* is in reality the son of CARIDAD MERCADER, a Catalan who was active in the Spanish Civil War and who, with her sons, was drawn into the ranks of the GPU.[11]

Although the Bureau still lacked Mercader's full legal name, the mask was beginning to fracture.

94. The Mexican police later prepared juxtaposed photos of the assassin and his mother, with each showing half a face of the other.

The Final Confirmation

Definitive identification came later in 1950 through forensic persistence rather than confession. Dr. Alfonso Quiroz Cuarón, attending the World Congress of Criminology in Paris as a representative of the National University of Mexico, brought several sets of Mercader's fingerprints with him. Taking advantage of the trip, he made an unofficial journey to Spain—despite Mexico's lack of diplomatic relations with Franco's regime.

Cuarón wrote:

> In the Spanish capital, I interviewed Florentino Santamaría, director of the Identification Archive of the General Directorate of Security. I had with me Jacson's* fingerprints and gave them to Pablo Valcárcel, his primary assistant. Thus, in a matter of minutes, I had in my possession a file with the name, photograph, and fingerprints of Jaime Ramón Mercader del Río, born in Barcelona on February 7, 1913. The fingerprints perfectly matched, without a doubt, the man arrested in Barcelona in 1935 and who was imprisoned in Mexico under the name Jacques Mornard* for murdering León

Police Photographs of the Assassin - Ramon Mercader

1935 passsport photo from Spain | 1939 forged passsport photo | 1940 police mugshot

95.

> Trotsky was the same person. Days later . . . I obtained the file of the mother of the murderer, that is, María Eustasia de la Caridad del Río Hernández, born in Santiago de Cuba in 1892 . . .[12]

Despite nearly a decade of calculated silence and a lifetime of GPU training, Mercader could not evade identification indefinitely. His cover was broken not by a confession or a slip of the tongue but by fingerprints and the methodical determination and perseverance of a criminologist.

Living Your Cover

Following Cuarón's discovery in the fall of 1950, news of Jacques Mornard's* identification spread through the Mexican justice system but wasn't made public. Mercader's response was predictable. When he was confronted with his true name, he refused to acknowledge it. He lived by a single commandment learned in GPU tradecraft training: never break cover. The identity of Jacques Mornard* had ceased to be a disguise; it had become a second skin he would never shed.

For the remainder of his incarceration, he still answered only to Jacques Mornard*, or Monsieur Mornard*, as he was respectfully called by guards and inmates who admired his composure and envied his steady income—believed to derive from family wealth, but it came from Soviet channels through his lawyer. He cultivated a reputation as an educated gentleman, reading European literature and maintaining an air of calm superiority even as journalists published his birth records and Soviet affiliations.

To break cover would have meant psychological collapse as much as political betrayal. Jacques Mornard* was no longer an alias—it was the architecture of survival.

Radio Shop and the Birdcage

By 1952, Mercader was transferred to Circular Cell Block No. 1, known as "The Birdcage," reserved for dangerous inmates or those at risk of assassination. The move placed him under constant surveillance, but it also conferred a measure of protection. Within the brutal ecosystem of Lecumberri, isolation could serve as sanctuary.

That December, having served half his sentence, he was placed in charge of Lecumberri's radio and television repair shop. A trained engineer, he launched a training program for inmates and was eventually placed in charge of the prison's entire electrical infrastructure. By 1953, he was servicing equipment for both prisoners and external clients.[13] One prisoner later recalled that Mornard* began each class by quoting Cervantes: "To learn to read is to learn to think." He rarely spoke of politics but insisted his students write in clear, elegant script, "as if the words might be inspected by history." At the radio shop, he was equally exacting—reprimanding inmates for careless soldering and praising them when the static cleared from a transmission. "He acted," one former inmate remarked, "as if he were training us for something far beyond these walls."

According to Isaac Don Levine, prison rumors held that Mornard* had grown wealthy from the radio shop—so much so that he was said to be "wallowing in luxury."[14] The workshop repaired radios and refinished wooden cabinets for both the penitentiary and the surrounding community, and as its manager, Mornard* received the largest share of the profits. This arrangement produced a sharp irony. A professed Communist who denounced profit as inherently dishonest—and who had previously refused to participate in prison "businesses" he claimed existed to exploit fellow inmates—now benefited directly from a small capitalist enterprise.[15] The shop brought him income, protection, and status: guards indulged him, inmates deferred, and whispers circulated that Mercader lived in relative comfort while others endured deprivation.[16]

Unrepentant and Unparoled

On August 20, 1953, Mercader became eligible for parole. During a press conference, the warden publicly revealed his true identity for the first time. According to *The New York Times*, Mercader appeared shocked but remained composed when the information was made public.[17] His distress reflected the depth of his indoctrination. For thirteen years, Jacques Mornard* had been more than an alias—it was a constructed self, sustained with absolute discipline.

The court denied parole, and in 1954 Mercader retained attorney Eduardo Ceniceros and submitted a new petition for parole. Dr. Quiroz Cuarón's psychological evaluation again proved decisive: Mercader continued to justify Trotsky's murder, refused to acknowledge his true identity, and expressed no remorse.[18]

A Hero's Exit to Cuba

After eighteen years in Lecumberri, Mercader was transferred to a modern correctional facility outside Mexico City at Puebla in 1958 to allow him to transition back into society. On May 6, 1960, he was released fourteen weeks short of his full sentence. Natalia Sedova reportedly remarked wisely, "Mornard* is now going to his reward—or his elimination."[19]

96. Mercader (right) was escorted by his attorney, Eduardo Ceniceros (second from right), and two Czech diplomats on the flight to Cuba.

Mercader was handed to Czech diplomats and flown to Cuba under a diplomatic passport. In Havana, he was greeted by Che Guevara.[20]

Moscow had not abandoned him. It had simply waited.

Silence, System, and the Fatal Gap

Mercader left Mexico as he had lived inside Lecumberri: silent, disciplined, and intact. He had never confessed, never explained, never apologized. The GPU had asked only one thing of him—that he protect the system that sent him. In that task, he succeeded. His loyalty was not expressed in words but in refusal. Silence was his final service.

Yet Mercader's success revealed something larger than his own training. His ability to penetrate Trotsky's inner circle, to live undetected for months inside a guarded world, and to strike at the center of it exposed a structural weakness far beyond one man. The assassin had not forced his way in. He had been invited in as a friend.

The failure was not one of walls, gates, or guards. It was a failure of recognition—of understanding that modern political struggle had become an intelligence war, and that devotion, ideology, and personal trust were no defense against a professional clandestine service. The GPU did not defeat Trotsky through brute force. It defeated him through patience, infiltration, and silence.

Mercader never spoke publicly. He did not need to. The conditions that made his act possible had already been created. The fatal breach occurred long before August 20, 1940—not in the study at Avenida Viena, but in the blind spots of a movement that underestimated its enemy and overestimated its own immunity.

The narrative moves from the assassin to his victim—and to the structural vulnerabilities within the Fourth International that enabled Stalin's war to achieve its final objective.

CHAPTER XL

THE REVOLUTIONARY WHO FORGOT TO FIGHT BACK

"All they [the GPU] know about my movements is what they learn from the newspapers."
—Leon Trotsky, 1932

"Trotsky died not just from a blow to the skull, but from a failure to believe in betrayal."
—Rita Kronenbitter, CIA memorandum, 1972

"He built a fortress for the people—but left the gates open to the enemy."
—Victor Serge, reflecting on Trotsky's exile

The Fatal Underestimation

Leon Trotsky—once celebrated for his strategic genius and mastery of revolutionary warfare—fatally underestimated the one adversary he should have understood best: the Soviet secret police. Despite a lifetime immersed in political struggle, clandestine organization, and intelligence operations, he failed to grasp how thoroughly the GPU could infiltrate, subvert, and ultimately dismantle both the Fourth International and the physical defenses of "Fortress Trotsky."

His approach to security combined vigilance without structure and suspicion without system. Physical defenses were reinforced, guards were armed, walls were thickened—but the internal mechanisms necessary to detect deception, screen loyalty, and disrupt infiltration were never institutionalized. Stalin's assassins tested those defenses once and failed. The second time, they succeeded. What followed was not only Trotsky's death but the quiet collapse of the last organized revolutionary resistance to Stalin from the left.

None of this implies that Trotsky's survival could have been guaranteed. No counterintelligence system—particularly one operating in exile and with limited resources, against a state intelligence service with global reach—can ensure absolute protection. What it can do is alter probabilities: delay penetration, expose hostile actors, and disrupt long-term operational planning. Trotsky's failure lay not in believing himself invulnerable but in refusing to adapt his movement to the kind of war being waged against it.

In the decades that followed, intelligence agencies sought to understand how one of the twentieth century's most experienced revolutionaries could be so thoroughly undone. Among the most penetrating assessments was a classified 1972 analysis by CIA counterintelligence officer Rita T. Kronenbitter (a CIA pseudonym for a male counterintelligence analyst), later declassified and released in the mid-1990s under the title *Leon Trotsky: Dupe of the NKVD*."[1] Drawing on intelligence reporting, postwar interrogations, and archival synthesis, Kronenbitter identified a recurring pattern of misjudgment, organizational openness, and resistance to counterintelligence discipline that, in her view, made Trotsky uniquely vulnerable to Soviet penetration.

Kronenbitter's memorandum is best read not as a source-driven monograph but as an intelligence community analytical synthesis—valuable for identifying operational patterns rather than establishing every factual detail. Scholars such as Susan Weissman have challenged aspects of Kronenbitter's conclusions, particularly where evidentiary support is thin or inferential. Even so, the memorandum remains useful precisely because it highlights how intelligence services evaluate failure: not as moral weakness but as a convergence of structural blind spots and repeated decision-making errors.

A Movement Without Defenses

The Fourth International, established in Paris in September of 1938, quickly became the GPU's most important foreign target. Modeled in form on Lenin's revolutionary structures—with congresses, internal bulletins, and a central secretariat—it projected discipline and cohesion. What it lacked was a permanent counterintelligence function.

There was no formal vetting of recruits, no mechanism to evaluate suspicious behavior or dispel rumors, and no internal security service empowered to investigate infiltration. As a result, the movement proved highly susceptible to penetration. While Lev Sedov oversaw the Paris-based *Bulletin of the Opposition*, he remained unaware that his most trusted confidant and perhaps others in his immediate circle were reporting directly to Moscow. Trotsky's organization functioned on trust, ideological commitment, and personal familiarity—qualities that revolutionary movements prize, but intelligence services deliberately exploit.

This vulnerability did not stem from ignorance. It stemmed from a belief that counterintelligence was a defensive reflex incompatible with revolutionary openness—a belief that left the movement exposed to an adversary that viewed deception as its most dependable instrument.

Stalin's Global War on Trotskyism

Throughout the 1930s, Soviet intelligence—first the GPU, then the Unified State Political Administration (OGPU)—waged a global campaign to eliminate Trotsky, his family, his associates, and the international network aligned with the Fourth International. Within the Soviet Union, "Trotskyism" became a political weapon, a catchall label used to justify purges, show trials, and executions. Abroad, the campaign took a different form: infiltration, disinformation, provocation, and targeted violence.

Trotsky's denunciation of Stalinism energized disillusioned Communists across Europe and the Americas, giving rise to a transnational movement that soon became a priority target for Soviet intelligence.

What began as political sabotage escalated into organized elimination. GPU mobile units of assassins eradicated key Trotskyist figures in Europe, narrowing the circle until the campaign culminated in the final attack on Trotsky himself on August 20, 1940.

Paris Headquarters, Global Reach

From exile in Mexico, Trotsky directed his movement largely through Sedov and the Paris headquarters. The *Bulletin of the Opposition* circulated his writings across France, Germany, Britain, and the Low Countries, sustaining an international network of supporters.

The GPU exploited this openness. From Moscow, operations were directed with methodical precision—sowing distrust, fragmenting leadership, and placing agents inside administrative and personal roles. Trotsky, operating without an intelligence apparatus of his own, failed to recognize the cumulative pattern. He had once mastered the mechanics of clandestine organization and understood the logic of Soviet tradecraft. Yet he never applied those lessons systematically to his own cause. Awareness of danger existed; institutional response did not.

Admiration Turned Blindness

During the Russian Civil War, Trotsky openly praised Felix Dzerzhinsky and the Cheka (the GPU's forerunner) for their effectiveness. That respect, forged in revolution, lingered long after exile. Even as the GPU turned its full machinery against him, Trotsky retained a residual belief in the intelligence service as an instrument that could, in theory, be separated from Stalin's abuses.

This blind spot was evident when GPU agent Yakov Blumkin visited Trotsky in Turkey soon after he had gone into exile. Rather than sever ties, Trotsky urged him to remain within Soviet intelligence, still imagining a distinction between the institution and the regime that controlled it. It was a misjudgment rooted not in naiveté but in an inability to accept that the apparatus he once helped legitimize had become irrevocably hostile.

The Blind Spot

Though fully aware that Stalin intended to destroy him, Trotsky never created a counterintelligence service within the Fourth International. He resisted proposals to do so, convinced that ideological commitment and revolutionary purpose would protect the movement from corruption. Security measures—aliases, double-envelopes, coded correspondence—were used, but inconsistently and without institutional enforcement.

Trotsky remained, at heart, a theorist and polemicist. He fought with ideas and persuasion, not with the sustained operational rigor demanded by clandestine warfare. The GPU, by contrast, understood that deception was not episodic but structural—and that successful infiltration required patience, redundancy, and control.

The Enemy Within

The consequences were catastrophic. The GPU filled the vacuum Trotsky left behind, embedding agents at every level of his organization—from the offices of his American supporters in New York, to his European offices in Paris, and to his household in Coyoacán. Individuals posing as secretaries, couriers, translators, and intimate companions relayed information directly to Moscow. Internal factionalism, already present within the Fourth International, further complicated detection.

Trotsky's trust decisions were shaped by familiarity and shared revolutionary experience. Long-standing personal relationships were assumed to imply continuity of loyalty. Warnings from comrades were weighed against fears of paranoia and organizational fracture. The result was hesitation at precisely the moment when decisive internal action was required.

Warnings Ignored

By the late 1930s, Trotsky's writings reflect growing awareness of the danger surrounding him. Assassinations of allies and defections to Stalinism underscored the scope of GPU penetration. Yet repeated warnings—from Natalia, from trusted aides, and later from members of the Socialist Workers Party—failed to prompt decisive internal reform.

After the May 24, 1940, raid on the villa, concerns about Jacson's* finances, movements, and inconsistencies intensified. Trotsky's response was caution rather than exclusion. Notes from the period show that he resisted expelling Jacson*, preferring instead to draw him further into the organization. After the assassination, Joseph Hansen acknowledged that Jacson* had not been investigated with sufficient rigor.

Physical security was strengthened. Internal security was not. Both assassination attempts in 1940 bypassed walls, towers, and guards—not through force but through access.

Legacy and Lessons

The Mexican government maintained armed protection around Trotsky's residences, from the Blue House to Avenida Viena. What could not be imposed from outside was discipline within. Trotsky's resistance to advice, his confidence in political judgment over operational caution, and his reluctance to institutionalize suspicion left him exposed.

The justification offered by Jacson* in his confession letter after the murder echoed Soviet propaganda, branding Trotsky a traitor and enemy of the people. Victor Serge recognized the unmistakable imprint of Soviet intelligence in the construction of that narrative. The GPU had not only killed its target but shaped the story of his death.

Trotsky's assassination reveals both the efficiency of Stalin's intelligence apparatus and the structural weaknesses of a revolutionary culture unprepared for sustained clandestine warfare. The contrast is stark: persuasion versus coercion, openness versus paranoia, ideological conviction versus operational control. Trotsky understood power, but he underestimated the necessity of defending against it in modern form.

His death was not merely Stalin's victory. It was the result of a failure to adapt—to recognize that the tools of revolution had been transformed into weapons of annihilation. Counterintelligence would not have ensured survival, but its absence ensured vulnerability. He saw the threat, warned others about it, and yet refused to meet it on its own terms. The movement he created to preserve the ideals of 1917 became the most thoroughly penetrated revolutionary organization of its time.

Trotsky's failure to guard against betrayal sealed his fate. But to fully understand the crime, we must turn to the instrument that made it possible. The ice axe—utilitarian, exotic, and chilling in its precision—was no random choice. It had its own history: how it was selected, how it passed from Soviet hands to the assassin's grip, and how, decades later, its trail would lead to its recovery by author H. Keith Melton after a forty-year search.

AFTERWORD

Tracking the Axe That Killed the Revolution

"A single blow in the right place can
silence an entire revolution."
—KGB Colonel Oleg Tsarev

"The weapon may rust, but the wound it
leaves remains fresh in history."
—Julián Gorkin

"The past leaves fingerprints. Some are made in blood."
—Forensic motto

The Vanishing Weapon

It was small. Silent. And it vanished. The ice axe that tore into Leon Trotsky's skull in 1940 disappeared almost as soon as it struck—swallowed by panic, politics, and deliberate concealment. It wasn't a gun or a knife, but something stranger: a mountaineer's tool, compact enough to hide and lethal enough to change history.

General Manuel Núñez, Chief of the Mexico City police, remained at Trotsky's villa to oversee the ambulance departure for Green Cross Hospital. He then took custody of the badly beaten Frank Jacson*, followed the police car to the hospital, and hours later convened an impromptu press conference, producing the ice axe—still in his possession—for assembled reporters. Photographs from August 20,

1940, show General Núñez holding the weapon, clearly revealing the distinctive rust pattern on the pick that would later prove central to its authentication. It was the first—and for the next sixty-five years, the only—public appearance of the weapon.

For decades, historians reconstructed the assassination in microscopic detail but offered little new information about the murder weapon or its whereabouts. Theories proliferated: destroyed, sent to Moscow, locked in a vault, used as a presidential paperweight, stolen by spies, sold online, displayed in dubious museums. Many stories. No proof. The trail went cold.

A Tool Turned Murder Weapon

Contemporary accounts variously described the weapon as a "pick-axe," an "alpenstock," an "Eispickel," or simply an "icepick." In fact, it was a shortened piolet—an ice-climbing axe. In form, it resembles the small hand-held ice axes still used in some ice houses to move large blocks of ice, a usage reflected in the terminology adopted in this book.

During interrogation, Jacson* explained his choice of weapon: "I used the alpine stock [alpenstock] because I had made excursions in the Switzerland mountains on various occasions . . . Because of its use when cutting footholds into the ice-covered mountains, I thought that one blow would be enough to kill Trotsky."[1]

The terminology was wrong. An alpenstock is a five-foot walking stick fitted with a spiked ferrule; the murder weapon was a piolet, equipped with a serrated pick and an adze, its shaft shortened from roughly thirty-two inches to about twelve—short enough to conceal beneath the assassin's Clifton gabardine overcoat. Forged of steel, the piolet's head was designed to anchor with its serrated pick and cut footholds with its broad adze. Criminologist Alfonso Quiroz Cuarón later recalled Mercader boasting that he could split a block of ice in two blows—an assertion that aligned with the weapon's design and lethality.[2]

Forged in the Alps

Stamped with the maker's mark "GARANTIE, WERKGEN FULPMES," the piolet was forged in the Austrian village of Fulpmes by the Werkgenossenschaft, a guild of blacksmith workshops in the Tyrolean Alps renowned in the 1920s and early 1930s for crafting coveted piolets distinguished by elegant steelwork and polished wood handles.

Disputed Accounts—and the Credible One

Mercader's Account: He told police: "I bought the pick-axe, or alpine stock, in Switzerland and sent it with a collection of arms to New York."[3] The account is possible, but other explanations appear more probable.

Sylvia's Account: Sylvia Ageloff told the FBI she had seen an "alpine axe" in the apartment she shared with Jacson* as early as January or February 1940.[4] Historian Martín Gabriel Barrón Cruz argued that this conflicted with accounts placing the weapon's acquisition only days before the murder. However, while Mornard* may have kept ordinary climbing gear at his hotel or apartment in early 1940, he had little reason to retain a modified murder weapon for months—or even hours—particularly in the presence of the already suspicious Sylvia. Most piolets are visually similar, and the object she recalled seeing was almost certainly not the weapon used in the attack.

Neither Mexican police nor the FBI recovered Jacson's* other climbing gear. It was not among the trunk of clothing he shipped to New York in June 1940, and Caridad Mercader likely destroyed it before leaving Mexico on August 20, 1940.

The Garmabella Story: Barrón Cruz recounts an alternative origin he attributes to José Ramón Garmabella. In this version, Jacson* allegedly acquired the axe "by chance" after James Shirley, owner of Shirley Courts, invited Caridad Mercader, Nahum Eitingon, and Jacson* to a child's birthday celebration on August 16, 1940. One of the gifts presented was said to be an ice axe. Jacson*, the story continues, then regaled the child with invented tales of mountaineering prowess, persuading the parents to allow the child to accompany him on a hike to Popocatépetl on Sunday, August 18. Barely half an hour into the excursion, Jacson* supposedly feigned illness, returned to the hotel, waited for the child to exit the car, and then drove off—retaining the ice axe.[5]

The story collapses under scrutiny. Its timeline strains plausibility and contradicts established facts: GPU tradecraft would never have permitted Caridad, Eitingon, and Mercader to appear together in public; Mercader was reportedly ill on August 16 and remained at the hotel with Sylvia; and the notion that a rare Austrian-made ice axe would be given as a child's birthday gift in 1940s Mexico is implausible. The account also assumes the assassination's primary weapon was acquired only at the last moment. At every level, it is improbable and unsupported.

Jim Shirley's Story: While early theories abounded, Colonel Salazar's account—backed by FBI investigation and later verification—remains the most convincing. In *Murder in Mexico* (1950), Salazar described how the future assassin stole the weapon from Jim Shirley Jr., an American mountaineer and son of James Shirley Sr., proprietor of the Shirley Courts motor court in Mexico City.[6] The Austrian-made piolet matched one Shirley Jr. purchased in 1936 and stored with his climbing gear in a back room behind the motel office.[7]

From mid-April to mid-June 1940, while Sylvia Ageloff was in Brooklyn, Jacson* rented a cabin at Shirley Courts. The location served as both his residence and a safe house for clandestine meetings. During this period, he struck up a casual friendship with Shirley Jr., joined him on climbs, and stored his gear alongside Shirley's in the shared storage room—access he retained even when Shirley was away. Salazar concluded the axe was likely stolen, and discreetly shortened, only a day or two before the attack on August 20.

The theft allegedly went unnoticed until the morning after the assassination, when James Shirley Sr., reading of the attack over breakfast, asked his son about the ice axe. Discovering it missing, they immediately reported the loss to Salazar, providing the first solid lead on the weapon's origin.

The FBI, already monitoring the case, assigned Special Agent Ken Crosby—who, by coincidence, had once served as an usher at Shirley's wedding. Traveling to Mexico City, Crosby interviewed Shirley and determined the connection to the assassin was incidental: the men had climbed together briefly, but their acquaintance was limited. Shirley's prompt report of the theft, combined with the match to the Austrian piolet purchased in 1936, confirmed it as the weapon Mercader used.[8]

Salazar's account of the ice axe's origin—corroborated by documentary evidence and subsequent investigation—remains the most credible explanation.

The Axe Comes Home

Across four decades, H. Keith Melton—a historian of intelligence and the clandestine world, accustomed to working where access is limited and evidence is deliberately obscured—pursued Trotsky's ice axe, the small, silent weapon that helped end a revolution. The search pulled him into the margins where Cold War loyalties, unfinished histories, and the habits of secrecy still endure. What began as a historian's question became a sustained inquiry conducted in places where memory is guarded, archives open selectively, and suspicion remains a form of self-preservation.

That inquiry would ultimately converge on a single object—long hidden, fiercely contested, and burdened with the unresolved legacy of Stalin's war on Trotsky.

A simple question followed the search for years: Why pursue a rusted implement so fiercely guarded by rumor, fear, and disinformation? The answer lay not in relic-hunting but in accountability. The axe was the only surviving physical link between Stalin's covert apparatus and the mortal blow in Coyoacán. To recover it was to confront the machinery that had tried to erase its own trace. Finding it meant excavating not myth, but proof.

A Marketplace of Secrets

The international market for espionage artifacts is not a world for the naive. It is crowded with former intelligence officers, smugglers, ideologues, con men, organized crime figures, syndicates, opportunists—

and, occasionally, an honest collector. Many regarded Melton with suspicion. They were rarely sure whether he was a collector, a journalist, or something more dangerous.

His background did little to quiet such doubts. He had written books about the CIA and helped cut the ribbon at the agency's fiftieth anniversary alongside President Clinton and CIA Director George Tenet. To some, those credentials did not clarify who he was. They complicated it.

Surveillance and Warnings

During repeated trips to Russia and the former Eastern Bloc in the 1990s, Melton was followed, questioned, and sometimes detained at airports and border crossings. On two occasions he was ordered to leave the country on the first flight the next morning. At times the harassment turned physical. In one incident in Tbilisi, Georgia, the message became unmistakable when a bullet narrowly missed him as he was atop a telephone pole at midnight.

There were people who preferred that Stalin, Trotsky, and the weapon used in Coyoacán remain untouched subjects.

The suspicion was not wholly misplaced. The search for the axe intersected with Melton's larger effort to build what would become the world's most extensive private collection of authentic espionage artifacts—an endeavor viewed with equal parts fascination and distrust by those who guarded their own secrets.

The Object—and the Truth—Worth Pursuing

For Melton, the purpose never shifted. The axe was not a trophy; it was missing historical evidence. Its reappearance could illuminate a sweeping intelligence operation executed with precision, protected by layers of Soviet denial, and blurred by decades of incomplete or distorted accounts. To document its provenance was to recover a fragment of history deliberately scattered.

As the search pushed deeper into that opaque world, access widened. He sat across from retired spies, Cold War spymasters, arms traffickers, black market dealers, organized crime figures, mercenaries, and, at times, respected historians. He met the man whose real-world job helped inspire Ian Fleming's fictional Q—an inventive mind behind genuine espionage technology—with whom he would later coauthor a half-dozen books. These were people trained to guard what they knew, yet for reasons he never fully understood, they allowed him into their circles. Perhaps they sensed he was not there to expose them but to pursue a truth long hidden.

Methods Outside the Archive

The search demanded persistence—and methods far beyond conventional scholarship: border crossings under scrutiny; encrypted, untraceable communications; discreet financial channels; unconventional shipping routes for artifacts moving out of the Eastern Bloc; assumed identities and press credentials; secure storage for sensitive material; meetings arranged in places where questions were neither expected nor wise; and a ready supply of cash. When the objective was locating the most infamous assassination weapon of the twentieth century, Melton did not choose his company. He moved carefully, hoping each encounter tightened the circle around the axe—and that he returned home unscathed.

The Call

And then, after years of dry holes and wild-goose chases, on the morning of July 11, 2005, it all changed. H. Keith Melton was eating breakfast at a hotel in Los Angeles when his phone rang. The call came from a friend at the FBI, his voice urgent: "It's breaking on the wire—Trotsky's ice axe has been found!"

Not by a spy. Not by an arms dealer. But by a journalist—Mark Stevenson of the Associated Press.

97. A blood rust pattern of a fingerprint is visible on the right side of the ice axe (see arrow).

And where had it surfaced? Not in a sealed vault, nor in a Kremlin archive, nor through a Cold War exchange. It lay instead in a simple pasteboard box beneath a young girl's bed in Mexico City—an extraordinary detail later confirmed in a 2005 interview with that girl, Ana Alicia Salas.

Melton bolted to his hotel room, located Stevenson's email address, and made contact within minutes. After establishing his bona fides—and with Stevenson's cooperation—he arranged to meet the woman who had inherited the axe forty-eight hours later in Mexico City. He had no intention of missing the opportunity.

First Contact

Ana Alicia arrived for the first meeting at Melton's hotel carrying photographs, accompanied by her son and—out of caution—an armed guard. She declined to bring the axe itself. Melton, however, came prepared with three specific criteria for authentication. The first was the Austrian maker's stamp, known from the original police report and familiar to only a small circle of specialists. The second was the weapon's shortened overall length—approximately twelve inches—consistent with Mercader's documented modification.[9] The third was the distinctive rust "fingerprint" pattern visible in the photograph

98. Seeing the axe for the first time in 2005. The remnants of the fingerprint (see arrow) proved crucial in establishing the axe's provenance.

taken on August 20, 1940, showing General Manuel Núñez holding the weapon during his first press conference.

Ana Alicia's photographs satisfied every requirement. The forensic confirmation would follow.

Proof—and Preservation

At a second meeting at her home the following day, Ana Alicia produced the axe. She did not allow Melton to handle it, but he photographed it extensively. Back in the United States, retired FBI supervisory special agent and photographic forensic specialist Jerry Richards joined him in a detailed comparison of the weapon's distinctive rust pattern with that visible in the 1940 archival photograph. The pattern functioned as a physical signature, linking the object in Ana Alicia's possession to the axe shown in General Núñez's hands. Richards's analysis was conclusive: every contour aligned. It was the same weapon.

The physical match was reinforced by documentary evidence, including a 1946 receipt from the Mexico City police evidence room and a 1960s transfer letter awarding the axe to police captain Alfredo Salas as a retirement gift. Taken together, the chain of custody was complete.

The Negotiation

Negotiating with Ana Alicia Salas proved nearly as demanding as the years-long search for the weapon itself. She was not interested in spectacle or profit. What mattered to her was that her father's story—and the story of the axe—be told with care, accuracy, and dignity. That insistence on historical integrity aligned with the mission of the International Spy Museum in Washington, DC—the world's largest public museum devoted to espionage. The connection was more than institutional. The majority of the artifacts on display in the museum came from Melton's own collection, assembled over decades of research into intelligence history. If the axe were to emerge from obscurity, it would do so in a setting dedicated not to myth, but to documented clandestine history.

Yet the axe was also a private legacy, bound to Ana Alicia's family memory and national trauma. Parting with it was never going to be simple.

For more than three years, discussions advanced and stalled, shaped by uncertainty, hesitation, and the influence of her "kitchen cabinet"—her son, her sister, and her hairdresser—whose counsel repeatedly shifted the direction of the talks. And when an agreement seemed final, that inner circle could veto it, sending negotiations back to the beginning. They did so more than once. Both sides stepped away at times. Eventually, through her son's intervention, an agreement emerged that satisfied the family and preserved her father's legacy. It appeared the hardest part was over—and that the axe would soon be in Melton's hands.

Banking Regulations—and a Failed Bridge Exchange

Paying for the axe and getting it out of Mexico proved nearly as difficult as finding it. Melton ran into legal red tape, shifting regulations, and banking delays—complications sharpened by post–9/11 safeguards designed to block illicit cross-border transfers. Those same safeguards now obstructed the lawful purchase of a single murder weapon turned artifact.

Melton's American banker explained that while a wire transfer could be guaranteed to leave the United States, there was no guarantee it would arrive in Mexico. In 2008, he warned, the banking system between the US and Mexico behaved like a black hole: funds went in, then disappeared. He also could not reliably determine which Mexico City banks were credible and which might be compromised by criminal enterprises.

As frustration mounted and Ana Alicia pressed for payment, Melton proposed a solution drawn from Cold War logic: a cash-for-artifact exchange at midday on the international bridge linking Ciudad Juárez, Mexico, and El Paso, Texas. He would bring a suitcase of money from the US side; she would bring a suitcase containing the axe from the Mexican side. At the midpoint, the international border, they would swap cases and walk back to their respective countries.

Melton enlisted a retired friend from SEAL Team Six—now running a private security firm in Texas—to shadow the operation from an El Paso bank to the bridge, then back to a waiting car, and an armed driver for the nineteen-hundred-mile return to Florida. Convincing an El Paso bank to release a large cash withdrawal legally also proved difficult. The amount triggered multiple Treasury Department safeguards designed to detect trafficking and money laundering. Explaining that the cash was intended for a historically significant murder weapon did not simplify the conversation. Melton ultimately mailed the branch manager a copy of one of his books, professional references, and the contact information of an FBI agent willing to vouch for him.

Everything was set, but at the last minute, Ana Alicia withdrew. Melton understood why. He had security and options; she had neither. Seeking protection from Juárez police, she believed, would have been suicidal. She feared any request for help would quickly reach the cartels, and she would not make it home alive with the money. Bound to proceed lawfully, Melton was forced back to the slow path of legitimate transfer.

Unorthodox Channels

After the setback, Melton searched anew for a reliable financial institution in Mexico City. Because he had attended high school in Utah and maintained ties to friends now prominent in the Mormon Church, he briefly considered whether the vetted church banking network might provide a discreet and lawful bridge. The plan was simple: open an account at Zions Bank in Salt Lake City, deposit the funds, then withdraw them through a vetted partner in Mexico. He even promised a significant donation to the church's charitable fund as thanks.

The idea went nowhere. Friends stopped returning calls. The church, it appeared, had no interest in facilitating a Cold War relic transaction—however historically justified.

Ultimately, Melton used a little-known method employed by both the current Russian intelligence service—the SVR—and the Israeli Mossad to move payments discreetly and legally across borders. The transfer was primed for completion within the law in both countries.

Transportation: The Last Hurdle

One major obstacle remained: how to transport a murder weapon safely from Mexico to the United States. Melton and a small circle of confidants in Washington weighed multiple options. One California media magnate and close friend, Craig, offered to fly it out by private jet. Others proposed hiding it in checked luggage on a nonstop flight from Mexico City to Miami. But Melton remembered the blunt advice of an American Airlines baggage specialist who, after the airline lost his suitcase twice on consecutive flights, told him, "Why would anyone place something valuable in their luggage and trust it to us?" The airlines were ruled out.

Ideally, payment and transfer would occur simultaneously. But without a secure and lawful method of removal, there could be no deal. As

99. Melton's wife, Karen, just before delivering the ice axe to its new home at the International Spy Museum in 2019.

complications mounted, Melton began considering the use of diplomatic pouches from sympathetic embassies—which was sounding promising. Instead, an inventive friend from the intelligence community—"Bill"—devised a legal solution, legitimate in both countries, that delivered the axe safely to Florida.

The cost? Less than $100 and a dozen red roses. The details remain confidential to protect those involved. When the axe finally reached Florida, the pursuit had come to an end. The weapon that killed Leon Trotsky was finally in Melton's hands.

Today, Trotsky's ice axe resides at the new International Spy Museum in Washington, DC, displayed prominently alongside Ramón Mercader's shattered eyeglasses from his beatings by Trotsky's guards, and the gold watch awarded to him—under his alias Agent López*—by the Soviet Politburo in 1965 for the assassination. After nearly eighty years, the three most important artifacts of the assassination are together at last, and on public display, where they belong.

100. The assassin's eyeglasses were broken when he was pistol-whipped by Trotsky's guards.

Trotsky's Axe—and the Imitators

Even after the weapon was recovered and authenticated, imitation axes continued to appear. The object carried too much symbolic weight—too closely bound to a murder that reshaped the twentieth century—to recede quietly into a museum case. Its notoriety guaranteed the persistence of replicas, misidentified artifacts, and deliberate fabrications.

One early false offering surfaced online. A seller offered an ice axe of similar appearance alongside a high-quality forensic model of Trotsky's skull. The listing claimed both items had been present at Mercader's trial and later exhibited at Knott's Berry Farm in Southern California. The story collapsed under scrutiny. The axe was the wrong size, bore incorrect markings, and lacked the features consistent with the 1940 weapon. The skull model also displayed a wound at the rear—contradicting the documented forensic record of Trotsky's injury.[12] When challenged, the seller withdrew the listing.

Misidentified examples also appeared in several European museums. Some institutions, presented with photographic comparisons and forensic documentation, acknowledged the error and quietly removed the displays. Others did not.

The Prague KGB Museum

A small privately run KGB Museum in Prague is among the institutions unwilling to reconsider its claim. Located on a narrow street not far from the US Embassy, the museum markets an interactive experience: tourists can don KGB uniforms, pose for photographs, and handle Cold War–era submachine guns. The museum also displays a purported "Trotsky murder weapon" in a spotlighted case, accompanied by dramatic interpretive text and surrounded by Soviet-era memorabilia.

Melton visited in 2013, years after the real axe had been authenticated and featured in the updated edition of his best-selling book, *Ultimate Spy*. Asked how the museum had verified its axe, the curator offered an elaborate narrative involving unnamed contacts, a shadowy acquisition in Moscow, and vague associations with the GPU, the KGB, Stalin, and even "Eitingon's mother." The story invoked intrigue and large sums of money but offered no verifiable details. There was no paperwork, no chain of custody, and no plausible explanation—historical or logistical—for why Mexican authorities, still under international scrutiny in the 1940s, would have returned the murder weapon to the regime that ordered the killing and spent decades denying involvement.

Visual comparison was decisive. The Prague axe was the wrong make, wrong profile, and wrong dimensions and lacked the distinctive rust "fingerprint" pattern visible on the authentic weapon in the August 1940 press photographs.

Melton informed the curator, calmly and respectfully, that he owned the genuine axe and offered documentation demonstrating its authenticity. He brought along a copy of his *Ultimate Spy* containing high-resolution photographs and provenance documentation and gave the museum the opportunity to remove the mistaken exhibit quietly, without fanfare or embarrassment. The curator listened, said nothing, and just walked away.

In the gallery at the rear of the museum, Melton noticed a wall of enlarged images of espionage devices copied directly from *Ultimate Spy*, reproduced without acknowledgment or permission. The only notable omission was, of course, the authentic ice axe—the one object whose documentation would have forced the museum to abandon its claim.

The episode underscored a broader truth: in the marketplace of dark historical memory, a compelling fiction can be more profitable than a documented fact. Myths circulate easily; evidence must fight its way in. And when proof arrives—photographs, measurements, forensic comparison—some simply turn their backs and walk away. In such places, truth is not merely inconvenient. It threatens their business model.

As of the summer of 2025, the KGB Museum in Prague remains open and continues to promote its display as "the weapon used to kill Trotsky."

Closing Reflection

The passage of the ice axe—from a tool forged in the Alps, to a weapon wielded in a study in Coyoacán, to an artifact hidden beneath a child's bed, and finally to authenticated display in a major museum—traces more than the path of an object. It charts the collision of ideology, violence, secrecy, and memory that shaped the twentieth century. The weapon vanished because powerful forces wanted it forgotten. It survived because history, however obscured, leaves traces for those willing to follow them.

In recovering the axe, the record regained a missing piece of evidence. In restoring it to public view, the story regained a measure of its truth.

EPILOGUE

Sylvia Ageloff (Maslow) (1909–1995): After Sylvia's father, Samuel Ageloff, used his political connections in Washington, DC, to pressure the Mexican government to release Sylvia from her Mexican jail cell in late December 1940, Sylvia flew back to New York City and retreated to her family residence in Brooklyn. For privacy, she adopted the use of Maslow, her mother's maiden name. With the exception of her required communications with the Mexican and American authorities, Sylvia never publicly discussed the issue and refused all interviews with comrades, academics, or reporters on the subject. The FBI report of her final interview in 1942 stated that "She believed she was merely a 'catspaw' and dupe for Jacson*."[1] At some point she married and became Sylvia Mohr. Sylvia lived a comfortable life in New York City and died in 1995 at the age of eighty-six, having outlived the events in Coyoacán by more than a half century.

Louis Budenz (1891–1972): The labor activist and senior member of the Communist Party USA who helped initiate the selection of Sylvia Ageloff as the intended seductee of Jacques Mornard* later renounced Communism and, like Elizabeth Bentley and Whittaker Chambers, became a paid informant for the FBI. He estimated that he spent three thousand hours explaining the Communist Party's inner workings to the FBI and received some $70,000 for his expert testimony at trials of Communists and before many of the Senate and House committees that were formed to investigate Communists. He voluntarily confessed that he had participated in espionage and other efforts on behalf of the Soviet Union, including discussion of the assassination of Leon Trotsky with CPUSA chairman Earl Browder. He wrote several books and became a popular lecturer exposing the espionage activities of the Communist Party USA and the penetration of America by Soviet agents. He died at age eighty.

Francisco Cabeza de Vaca (?–1943): The Mexican court official assigned to prosecute Jacques Mornard* and Sylvia Ageloff was injected with poison on a street in central Coyoacán on April 23, 1943—the same day Mornard's* sentence was announced. With no known antidote available, he died soon afterward. The assassin was never identified, but the family's belief is that the GPU was behind it. His grandson, Daniel Cabeza de Vaca, served as the Mexican Attorney General from 2005 to 2006.

Nahum Eitingon (1899–1981): The GPU field commander of the assassination attacks against Trotsky (Operation UTKA) in Mexico City continued his loyal service to Stalinism and the GPU as the deputy to Sudoplatov in the Fourth Directorate (sabotage and infiltration operations). He was awarded the Order of Lenin on June 17, 1941, for his role in the assassination. Eitingon later ran afoul of Moscow politics and was arrested in 1951 for his alleged role in the so-called Doctors' Plot but was released after the death of Stalin in 1953. He was soon arrested again for his well-known association with Lavrentiy Beria and sentenced to twelve years in prison following Beria's death. Eitingon was released in 1964 and had a private reunion with Ramón in Moscow in the late 1960s. His ashes are in Moscow's Donskoi Monastery Cemetery, near those of Grigulevich. Each year on the May 24 anniversary of Operation KON, the children and families of the raid's participants gather at Eitingon's gravesite for a private ceremony.

Lilia Estrin (Dallin) (1898–1981): Estrin moved to New York City in early 1941 and married David Dallin, a Menshevik and anti-Communist historian. The Dallins inexplicably facilitated Mark Zborowski (TULIP)'s move to the United States and his arrival in Philadelphia on December 29, 1941. In 1955, defector Alexander Orlov confirmed that Mark Zborowski was a GPU agent and that he suspected Lilia of being one as well, a claim he reiterated during his CIA debriefings. In March 1956, Lilia appeared before a Senate subcommittee to publicly denounce Zborowski and describe her role in the Trotskyist faction. In 1972, a classified CIA counterintelligence report (*Leon Trotsky: Dupe of the NKVD [GPU]*) named Lilia as a GPU agent, cover name LYDIA. Declassified in 1994, it offered no evidence beyond what was known two decades prior. Was Lilia Estrin a knowing agent, a manipulated conduit, or simply a comrade caught in forces she scarcely understood? The record is silent. The consequences are not. Each reassurance to Sedov and each message to Trotsky tightened the circle of trust and bought the GPU time. Whatever her intent, her actions aligned with Mark Zborowski's designs and the GPU's interests—shaping events far beyond what she may have imagined.

Sylvia Callen (1914–1994): The secretary and assistant to SWP president James Cannon was exposed in 1947 following the publication of Louis Budenz's autobiography, *This Is My Story.* Although Budenz—the very man who had recruited her to spy on Cannon—identified her as a Stalinist infiltrator, members of the Socialist Workers Party initially dismissed the accusation. In 1954, Callen was summoned before a federal grand jury but invoked the Fifth Amendment. Four years later, however, she testified before a secret grand jury, admitting that she had regularly met with GPU officer Gregory Rabinowitz and his GPU successor, Jack Soble, and had passed confidential Trotskyist materials to them through an intermediary, Lucy Booker, at a rented apartment. Sylvia's role as a GPU agent and her 1958 testimony remained unknown to the public until the mid-1970s. In 1995, the declassification of the VENONA Project decrypts revealed her cover name—SATYR—and definitively confirmed her treachery.

Iosif Grigulevich (1913–1988): The GPU illegal officer using the cover name FELIPE was brought to Mexico City to design the attack plan for Operation KON, the unsuccessful raid on Trotsky's villa on May 24, 1940. Grigulevich later received the Order of the Red Star in June 1941 for his role in Trotsky's assassination. Under the cover name ARTUR, Iosif Grigulevich was sent to Argentina to run Soviet sabotage against the Nazis. There he married another agent, Laura Araujo Aguilar—cover name LUIZA. In 1948 Moscow seized her as a hostage, testing his loyalty by ordering him to handle a New York dead drop for KGB spy Rudolf Abel. By 1952 Grigulevich had become Teodoro B. Castro and served as Costa Rica's ambassador to Italy and Yugoslavia. His real mission was to kill Yugoslav leader Josip Broz Tito. Only Stalin's death spared the target. Grigulevich returned to Moscow, turned historian, and wrote fifty-eight books, including a biography of Cuban revolutionary Che Guevara. Grigulevich's role in the Trotsky assassination plans was only revealed in the 1990s with the release of *The Mitrokhin Archive* and Sudoplatov's 1994 autobiography, *Special Tasks*. His ashes are in Moscow's Donskoi Monastery Cemetery, near those of Eitingon.

Joseph Hansen (1910–1979): Trotsky's most trusted secretary and guard returned to the United States after Trotsky's death, started working as a merchant seaman, and later became editor of the SWP's newspaper, *The Militant*. Hansen was in contact with the GPU in 1938, though he claimed that it was with Trotsky's blessing, and with the FBI in 1940. Volkogonov points out that by protecting GPU agent Sylvia Callen, Hansen might have also been a double agent for the GPU all along.

África de las Heras (1909–1988): One of the GPU's legendary illegal officers, she later served during World War II in a partisan unit on the Eastern Front as a radio communicator. As the Cold War heated up, she served in various undercover roles in Europe before being assigned to manage a network of informants under the cover of an antique store in Montevideo, Uruguay, in 1947. In 1967 she returned to Moscow where she taught spycraft to the next generation of Soviet intelligence officers. Colonel África de las Heras is buried in Moscow's Khovanskoye Cemetery.

Frida Kahlo (1907–1954): Despite her role in arranging for Trotsky's asylum in Mexico in 1936, Frida Kahlo sought to be readmitted to the Communist Party after 1945. She recalled meeting the future assassin seven years earlier in Paris: "In 1938 I had met Mornard*, the one who killed him [Trotsky], and he went around insinuating to me that I should take him to Trotsky's house. 'Not me, because I am quarreling with the old Trotsky,' I told him. 'I only ask you, please, to find me a house near there.' 'Well look for it yourself, because I am too sick to look for houses for anyone, and I cannot give you lodging in my house, nor can I introduce you to Trotsky, I never will introduce him to you.'" In later life, as Kahlo was gaining recognition in Mexico for her paintings, her health was declining rapidly. In her last days, Kahlo was mostly bedridden, but made a public appearance on July 2, 1954, participating with Rivera in a demonstration against the CIA invasion of Guatemala. Frida died a committed Communist on July 13, 1954 . . . likely of a self-induced overdose of painkillers.

Caridad Mercader (1892–1975): Caridad received the Order of Lenin in Moscow on June 17, 1941, for directing Operation MAT in the Trotsky assassination. Following the failure of Operation GNOME to rescue her son from prison in Mexico City, she resettled in Paris, where she lived the rest of her life. Following Ramón's release from prison in 1960, she was twice able to visit her sons Ramón and Luis and children who were then living in Moscow. Though Caridad remained a committed Stalinist, she was disillusioned by the version of Communism that she experienced in Moscow and anxious to return to France. Her final employment from 1960 to 1967 was as the director of public relations for the Cuban embassy in Paris, where "she organized receptions, protocols, and received dignitaries from France and other countries." However, the secret official history of the KGB references Caridad's operational activities controlling a small cell in Paris during the 1960s without providing further details, but likely involving reporting on activities within the Cuban Embassy. As a result of Operation UTKA and her wartime service, she received a lifetime pension from the Soviet government that should have enabled her to live comfortably and peacefully. However, friends remembered her being forever haunted by her failure to secure Ramón's release from his twenty-year imprisonment in Mexico City. At the end of her life, she was cared for by her son Jorge and daughter-in-law Germaine before passing away in Paris at age eighty-two in 1975. One writer describing Caridad's final days observed that "she was in a luxurious setting, surrounded by her collection of jewels, perfumes, and extravagant clothing, remaining an unapologetic Stalinist who reputedly consumed 40 cups of coffee and smoked 80 cigarettes daily."

Ramón Mercader (1913–1978): After spending nineteen years and eight months in a Mexican prison without divulging a single word, Ramón was finally released on May 6, 1960, at the age of forty-seven. Hours after his release, he and his wife Roquelia flew with two Czech diplomats and his personal attorney to Cuba, where they were officially welcomed by former guerrilla leader Che Guevara, then serving as the President of the National Bank of Cuba. Following a year of exile in Cuba, Ramón returned to the USSR using the alias of Ramón Ivanovich López*.

On June 8, 1961, Ramón was awarded the title of Hero of the Soviet Union, the Order of Lenin, and the Gold Star medal for displaying bravery and heroism in carrying out a "special task"—Trotsky's assassination. The award was originally conferred by Stalin himself and was personally presented by Alexander Shelepin, the head of the KGB. Ramón became one of only forty-one foreigners to receive this prestigious accolade. Mercader and Roquelia adopted two children in Moscow but never adjusted to the harsh Moscow climate. He yearned to return to his native Catalonia, Spain, but was denied permission because of politics. Writer Leonardo Padura clarified Ramón's reasons for returning to his mother's birth country of Cuba: "He and his wife had become accustomed to Mexico and could not live in Moscow, the cold, the atmosphere, not for himself, but for her. They looked for a better option. Cuba was the choice because it was closer to Spain where he wanted to live and that he could not return because Franco was still alive." In 1974, Ramón, still using the alias Ramón López*, received permission to emigrate to Cuba as a "Spanish Republican refugee with his family." Officially he was an esteemed guest of the Cuban government and served his final years as an adviser to the Ministry of the Interior. However, his health declined as a result of lung cancer, and when he was terminally ill, he was attended to in a nursing habanera reserved for the exclusive use of the Cuban Communist Party elite.

Ramón Mercader died of cancer on October 19, 1978, with Roquelia at his side. His last words to Roquelia related to the murder he committed thirty-eight years earlier: "I hear it always. I hear [Trotsky's] scream. I know [Trotsky's] waiting for me on the other side." His body was removed to Moscow, where he is interned at the Kuntsevo Cemetery as Ramón Ivanovich Lopez*. His modest gravesite is located only a few yards away from that of the GPU's prize recruit in the 1930s, Kim Philby.

Alexander Orlov (1895–1973): A high-ranking defector from the GPU in 1938, Orlov changed his name and lived clandestinely in New York for many years under the name Alexander L. Berg. He published a number of accounts of his life and work after the death of Stalin in 1953 that embarrassed both the CIA and FBI. Orlov died in 1973 in Cleveland, Ohio.

Gaik Ovakimian (1898–1967): The high-ranking GPU officer who ran Soviet espionage operations in the US since 1934 was arrested in May 1941 on a charge of not registering as a foreign agent. As an illegal officer, he did not have diplomatic immunity and was swapped back to the Soviet Union in July 1941 for the release of several Americans that were imprisoned. In Moscow, Ovakimian became the head of the GPU's American desk, and later was the deputy director of the GPU's foreign intelligence service.

Diego Rivera (1886–1957): Post–World War II, Diego attempted to be readmitted to the Communist Party and proudly claimed that he had secured Trotsky's asylum only for the purpose of having him assassinated. While some have argued that Diego and Frida had their hands in the plot to kill Trotsky, no proof exists of their involvement. Diego's boast is better explained as an example of his "clownish political opportunism."

Henry Schnautz (1911–2010): An American guard in Coyoacán in July and August 1940, he was the last of Trotsky's guards to die, in 2010. His papers were saved by historian Terry Priest.

David Alfaro Siqueiros (1896–1973): After the unsuccessful attack on Trotsky's compound on May 24, 1940, Siqueiros fled to Guadalajara and then to the mountainous region of Jalisco in central-western Mexico, where he was arrested. Siqueiros later served just a year in prison and three years in exile in Chile before returning to Mexico in 1944. Throughout his life, Siqueiros maintained strong ties with the USSR and insisted on being addressed as El Coronelazo—the big colonel—in remembrance of his service in the Spanish Civil War. In a touch of irony, the Soviet Union awarded him the International Lenin Prize "for strengthening peace among peoples" in 1966.

Jack Soble (1903–1967): In 1941 he became the top GPU spy in the US under the name Vasili Zubilin. He was exposed by Boris Morros as a Soviet spy in 1947 and again by Alexander Orlov. Soble was finally arrested on January 25, 1957, was convicted of espionage, and received a reduced prison term of seven and a half years for "valuable assistance" in other espionage cases, including testifying against his brother in 1961. Soble attempted suicide twice in prison and was released on parole in 1962.

Pavel Sudoplatov (1907–1996): During World War II, his unit organized guerrilla operations behind enemy lines as the head of the GPU's Department of Special Tasks. According to Sudoplatov's autobiography, he played a key role in stealing important atomic secrets from the Americans. This claim has subsequently been questioned by the FBI and others. After Stalin's death and, like Eitingon, due to his close association with Beria, he was imprisoned and feigned madness to avoid being executed. Sudoplatov was later convicted and served fifteen years in prison. His autobiography, *Special Tasks*, was authored with the help of his son Anatoliy and two American writers in 1994. He died in 1996 at age eighty-nine.

Lev Davidovich Trotsky (1879–1940): Trotsky's remains were cremated and interred in the garden of his home in Coyoacán. For the protection of the Old Man's ashes, the Mexican painter and architect Juan O'Gorman designed the still-standing monolithic funeral column that bears the name of the old revolutionary, crowned by the red flag and the symbol of the Communist struggle: the sickle and the hammer.

Natalia Sedova [Trotsky] (1882–1962): Trotsky's wife died twenty-two years after her husband in Paris in 1962 at age seventy-nine. Her ashes were returned to Mexico and are preserved, together with those of Leon Trotsky, inside the monument in the courtyard of their last home in Coyoacán. She survived her husband and both sons. Lev Sedov died in a Paris hospital, and Sergei Sedov was executed in 1937 in his homeland.

Esteban "Sieva" Volkov (1926–2023): Trotsky's grandson, likely the last living witness to the attack on May 24, 1940, and his grandfather's final moments three months later, died on June 16, 2023, in Tepoztlán, Mexico, at age ninety-seven. Volkov was instrumental in opening the Leon Trotsky House Museum in 1990 and dedicated his final years as the "keeper of the flame" upholding Trotsky's legacy. Unfortunately, he refused to be interviewed for this book.

Ruby (Lewis) Weil (1904–1953): The American woman from Indiana who engineered the introduction of Sylvia Ageloff to the future assassin had publicly renounced the Communist Party in 1938 to gain Ageloff's trust within Trotskyist circles. After Trotsky's murder in 1940, she tried to rejoin the CPUSA but was refused. In 1950, both Ruby and Sylvia Ageloff were summoned to testify before the House Committee on Un-American Activities. At the time she testified, Ruby said that she was the women's editor for *Wide World Photos*. Afterward she faded into obscurity. According to Irving Howe, Ruby suffered from tuberculosis and remained gravely ill for several years before her death in 1953.

Mark Zborowski (1908–1990): With the Nazi invasion of France in 1940, TULIP fled to the south of France but ended up in a Vichy concentration camp. With the help of Lilia Estrin, now married to anti-Communist historian David Dallin, his passage was arranged to the US, and he arrived in Philadelphia on December 29, 1941. Zborowski moved to New York and, without any visible means of support, lived in the same upscale apartment building as the Dallins. Zborowski reported directly to GPU officer Jack Soble while continuing his surveillance of the remaining Trotskyist circles in the United States and assisting in the search for Soviet defector Victor Kravchenko. Despite the suspicions and partial exposure of his role as a GPU agent during his lifetime, Zborowski evaded full accountability for his actions for many years. He took up an academic career in 1945 and was granted US citizenship in 1947, as at that time there was no information confirming his role with the GPU. Mark was finally unmasked by GPU defector Alexander Orlov in 1955 and appeared before a Senate hearing in 1956, where he admitted to having been a GPU agent. Zborowski was eventually convicted of perjury in 1962 and served four years in prison. Because TULIP's espionage activities for the GPU in Paris occurred before the United States entered World War II—and the statute of limitations had long since expired—he could not be prosecuted under the Espionage Act, nor could his US citizenship be revoked. In his later years—despite his central role in the murders of at least four Trotskyists during the 1930s—Zborowski reinvented himself as a respected anthropologist, gaining full acceptance within the academic community and publishing several well-regarded books. He resided in an upscale area of San Francisco and died peacefully on April 30, 1990, at age eighty-two.

PHOTO CREDITS

1. Public Domain, Wikipedia Creative Commons
2. Public Domain, Wikipedia, http://levoradikal.ru/archives/1923/bezyimyannyiy
3. José Ramón Garmabella, *El grito de Trotsky*, Random House, 2006
4. Public Domain, Wikipedia Creative Commons
5. Leonardo Daniel Pérez Bautista, "Fachada Museo Frida Kahlo," CC BY-SA 4.0, via Wikimedia Commons
6. Public Domain, Wikipedia Creative Commons
7. Public Domain, Wikipedia Creative Commons
8. Anton Mironov, KGB Archives
9. Anton Mironov, KGB Archives
10. Henry R. Schlesinger
11. Anton Mironov, KGB Archives
12. Henry R. Schlesinger
13. José Ramón Garmabella, *Operación Trotsky*, Editorial Diana, 1972
14. Public Domain, Wikipedia Creative Commons
15. Pavel Sudoplatov, *Special Tasks: The Memoirs of An Unwanted Witness*, Little, Brown, 1994
16. Public domain, forged passport photo from a nonexistent nation
17. Casasola Archive, Wikipedia Creative Commons Attribution-Share Alike 4.0 International license
18. *Brooklyn Daily Eagle*, 1923
19. Anton Mironov, KGB Archives
20. Henry R. Schlesinger
21. Photo from an NKVD file circa 1933
22. Public domain, forged passport photo from a nonexistent nation
23. Anton Mironov, KGB Archives
24. General Archive of the Nation, Mexico; Díaz, Delgado and García Fund, box 77/10 "Trotsky Jury"
25. Anton Mironov, KGB Archives
26. The collection of H. Keith Melton
27. Jerrold and Leona Schecter, *Sacred Secrets: How Soviet Intelligence Operations Changed American History*, Brassey's, 2002
28. Barton Whaley, "Guerrillas in the Spanish Civil War" (master's thesis, Massachusetts Institute of Technology, 1969)
29. The photograph is from David Mink; the excerpt of text is from the *Socialist Appeal*, Vol. 2, No. 16, April 16, 1938
30. José Ramón Garmabella, *Operación Trotsky*, Editorial Diana, 1972
31. The collection of H. Keith Melton

32. The collection of H. Keith Melton
33. The collection of H. Keith Melton
34. José Ramón Garmabella Collection
35. General Archive of the Nation, Mexico; Díaz, Delgado and García Fund, box 61/21 "Trotsky"
36. The collection of H. Keith Melton
37. Enrique Díaz Delgado y García, Chronological/box EDDG/77/10, subject: Leon Trotsky, assassination
38. General Archive of the Nation, Mexico; Díaz, Delgado and García Fund, box 61/21 "Trotsky"
39. Tom Sharpe and the *Sante Fe New Mexican*
40. Anton Mironov, KGB Archives
41. Casasola Archive, unknown author, Wikipedia, http://mediateca.inah.gob.mx/repositorio/islandora/object/fotografia%3A207882
42. Leon Trotsky, *Los Gangsters de Stalin*, Editorial América, 1940
43. Anton Mironov, KGB Archives
44. The collection of H. Keith Melton
45. Leon Trotsky, *Los Gangsters de Stalin*, Editorial América, 1940
46. Anton Mironov, KGB Archives
47. General Archive of the Nation, Mexico; Díaz, Delgado and García Fund, box 61/21 "Trotsky"
48. General Archive of the Nation, Mexico; Díaz, Delgado and García Fund, box 77/10 "Trotsky Jury"
49. The collection of H. Keith Melton
50. General Archive of the Nation, Mexico; Díaz, Delgado and García Fund, Box 75/8 "Trotsky Affair"
51. The collection of H. Keith Melton
52. FBI archive; CPUSA logo from *Workers Age*, Vol. 2, No. 1, October 15, 1932
53. The collection of H. Keith Melton
54. Anton Mironov
55. Anton Mironov
56. FBI Trotsky file
57. Hank Schnautz photographer, Terry Priest collection
58. The collection of H. Keith Melton
59. This photograph, believed to have been created circa 1940 in Mexico City, is of unknown authorship and has not been previously published to our knowledge. Despite diligent research, no copyright holder or estate could be identified. This photograph is in the public domain in Mexico because anonymous works are considered in the public domain until the author or the owner of the rights is identified
60. The collection of H. Keith Melton
61. The collection of H. Keith Melton
62. Anton Mironov
63. Oleg Yunakov, Wikimedia Creative Commons
64. Hank Schnautz photographer, Terry Priest collection
65. Sanchez Salazar, *Murder in Mexico: The Assassination of Leon Trotsky*, Secker and Warburg, 1950
66. Hank Schnautz photographer, Terry Priest collection
67. The collection of H. Keith Melton
68. Thayne Tuason, Wikipedia Creative Commons
69. The collection of H. Keith Melton
70. Anton Mironov
71. Anton Mironov

72. Samuel Johnson Wolf; CCO: Creative Commons Zero
73. José Ramón Garmabella Collection
74. This photograph, believed to have been created circa 1940 in Mexico City, is of unknown authorship and has not been previously published to our knowledge. Despite diligent research, no copyright holder or estate could be identified. This photo is in the public domain in Mexico because anonymous works are considered in the public domain until the author or the owner of the rights is identified
75. Anton Mironov
76. The collection of H. Keith Melton
77. General Archive of the Nation, Mexico; Díaz, Delgado and García Fund, box 75/8 "Trotsky Affair"
78. Historical Archive of the Federal District Carlos de Sigüenza y Góngora, México, box 5, exp. 39
79. Enrique Díaz Delgado y García, Chronological/box EDDG/77/10, subject: Leon Trotsky, assassination
80. José Ramón Garmabella, *El grito de Trotsky: Ramón Mercader, el Asesino de un Mito*, Random House, 2006
81. General Archive of the Nation, Mexico; Díaz, Delgado and García Fund, box 77/10 "Trotsky Jury"
82. General Archive of the Nation, Mexico; Díaz, Delgado and García Fund, box 77/10 "Trotsky Jury"
83. FEDARO–Wikipedia Commons
84. General Archive of the Nation, Mexico; Díaz, Delgado and García Fund, box 77/10 "Trotsky Jury"
85. José Ramón Garmabella, *El grito de Trotsky: Ramón Mercader, el Asesino de un Mito*, Random House, 2006
86. Sanchez Salazar, *Murder in Mexico: The Assassination of Leon Trotsky*, Secker and Warburg, 1950
87. Anton Mironov, KGB Archives
88. General Archive of the Nation, Mexico; Díaz, Delgado and García Fund, box 77/10 "Trotsky Jury"
89. Anton Mironov, KGB Archives
90. José Ramón Garmabella, *Operación Trotsky*, Editorial Diana, 1972
91. *The Militant*, March 8, 1947
92. Wikipedia Creative Commons
93. General Archive of the Nation, Mexico; Díaz, Delgado and García Fund, box 75/8 "Trotsky Affair"
94. José Ramón Garmabella, *Operación Trotsky*, Editorial Diana, 1972
95. José Ramón Garmabella, *Operación Trotsky*, Editorial Diana, 1972
96. José Ramón Garmabella, *Operación Trotsky*, Editorial Diana, 1972
97. Dan Treado for the International Spy Museum
98. Dan Treado for the International Spy Museum
99. The collection of H. Keith Melton
100. The collection of H. Keith Melton

ENDNOTES

INTRODUCTION

1. Pavel Sudoplatov and Anatoli Sudoplatov, *Special Tasks: The Memoirs of an Unwanted Witness—A Soviet Spymaster* [Boston: Little, Brown, 1994], 3
2. Robert Service, *Trotsky: A Biography* [London: Pan Books, 2010], 371–372
3. Ibid., 386–387
4. Ibid., 431
5. "Soviets Exonerate a Son of Trotsky," *The New York Times*, Reuters, November 23, 1988
6. International Committee of the Fourth International, "How the GPU Murdered Trotsky: Sedov Is Killed in the Clinic" [London: New Park Publications, 1981]
7. Leon Trotsky, "Exile and Assassination," Encyclopedia Britannica
8. Service, 420–425
9. Service, 425–427; *Singapore Morning Tribune*, August 31, 1936
10. Mahoney, 227
11. Ibid., 228
12. Ibid., 228–229
13. Ibid., 229
14. Ibid., 231–232
15. Isaac Don Levine, *The Mind of an Assassin*, 36
16. Levine, 126–127

CHAPTER I: THE BLUE HOUSE: SANCTUARY, SUBVERSION, AND SEDUCTION

1. Dmitri Volkogonov, *Trotsky: The Eternal Revolutionary* [New York: Free Press, 1996], 410
2. Bertrand M. Patenaude, *Stalin's Nemesis: The Exile and Murder of Leon Trotsky* [London: Faber & Faber, 2009], 12–13
3. Ibid., 11–12
4. Hayden Herrera, *Frida: A Biography of Frida Kahlo* [New York: Perennial Library, 1983], 205
5. Ibid.
6. Patenaude, Kindle Loc 15
7. Ibid.
8. Ibid.
9. Herrera, *Frida*, 205–206
10. Jean van Heijenoort, *With Trotsky in Exile: From Prinkipo to Coyoacán* (Cambridge: Harvard University Press, 1978), 104
11. Ibid., 118
12. Bertrand Patenaude, *Stalin's Nemesis* [London: Faber & Faber, 2009], 52
13. Herrera, *Frida*, 207
14. Ibid.

15. John Dewey et al., *The Case of Leon Trotsky* [New York: Harper & Brothers, 1937], 514
16. Patenaude, *Stalin's Nemesis*, 49
17. Herrera, *Frida*, 209
18. Ibid., 257–258
19. Ibid., 113
20. Ibid., 209
21. Ibid., 210
22. Herrera, *Frida*, 210
23. Ibid.
24. Ibid., 201
25. Patenaude, *Stalin's Nemesis*, 82–83
26. Ibid., 207
27. Kronenbitter, *Leon Trotsky: Dupe of the NKD*
28. Pierre Broué, *Trotsky: A Biography* [Chicago: Haymarket Books, 2005], n.p.
29. Herrera, *Frida*, 212
30. Ella Wolfe, interview with Victor Serge, 1946, Serge Papers, Yale University Library
31. Herrera, *Frida*, 212
32. Jean van Heijenoort, *With Trotsky in Exile*, 112
33. Patenaude, *Stalin's Nemesis*, 152
34. Ibid., 151–154
35. Jean van Heijenoort, *With Trotsky in Exile*, 138
36. Ibid., 139

CHAPTER 2: THE ASSASSINATION OF LEV SEDOV

1. *Security and the Fourth International: How the GPU Murdered Trotsky* [London: Labor Publications, 1976], Kindle Loc 135
2. Bertrand M. Patenaude, *Stalin's Nemesis: The Exile and Murder of Leon Trotsky* [London: Faber & Faber, 2009], Kindle Loc 98
3. *Los Angeles Times*, November 23, 1988
4. Trotsky, Leon, "Leon Sedov, Son, Friend, Fighter," obituary of Lev Sedov
5. Pierre Broué, *Léon Sedov: Fils de Trotsky, Victime de Staline* [Paris: Éditions Ouvrières, 1993], n.p.
6. Lev Sedov, *The Red Book on the Moscow Trial* [New York: Pioneer Publishers, 1936]
7. *How the GPU Murdered Trotsky*, Kindle Loc 152
8. Mahoney, 176
9. Poretsky, 237–238
10. Mahoney, 176
11. Ibid., 175–176
12. Ibid.
13. Ibid.
14. Mahoney, 182
15. Mahoney, 182; Rayfield, *Stalin and His Hangmen*, 352–353
16. Mahoney, 183; Kronenbitter, however, writes that the building was opposite Sedov's building and not adjacent
17. Mahoney, 182; *A Near Miss: Renata Steiner in Juan-les-Pins*
18. Swiss Federal Archives, the Assassination of Ignace Reiss; the floor plan of the Blue House was likely compiled by África de las Heras before she was withdrawn in late 1938
19. Mahoney, 182
20. Rita T. Kronenbitter, "Leon Trotsky, Dupe of the NKVD," *Studies in Intelligence* 40, No. 1 (1996), CIA Center for the Study of Intelligence, 28
21. Mahoney, 182; eavesdropping on Lilia's phone adds weight to the argument that she was not a GPU agent

22. Kronenbitter, 41
23. Tom Peters, "How the GPU Murdered Leon Sedov and other Trotskyists," World Socialist Website
24. Mahoney, 184
25. Catriona Kelly, "Coded Confessions," *Times Literary Supplement*, November 21, 2004, posted online at Powells.com
26. Mahoney, 184
27. Ibid.
28. Patenaude, Kindle Loc 97; Mahoney, 184; *How the GPU Murdered Trotsky*, Kindle Loc 129
29. Weissman, 605, endnote 95
30. Mahoney, 185
31. Patenaude, Kindle Loc 98
32. Ibid.
33. Ibid.
34. Mahoney, 187
35. Weissman, 603
36. Weissman, 605
37. Weissman, 605, citing *Cahiers Leon Trotsky*, no. 13, March 1983, p. 46
38. Ibid.
39. Weissman, 605–606
40. Weissman, 606
41. Ibid., 187
42. *How the GPU Murdered Trotsky*, Kindle Loc 130
43. Weissman, 603
44. Ibid.
45. Ibid.
46. Ibid.
47. Mahoney, 184
48. Weissman, 603
49. Weissman, 604, note 89
50. Testimony of Mark Zborowski, US Congressional hearings, 1955
51. Weissman, 603
52. Weissman, 605, endnote 96
53. French judicial archives, 1938
54. Mahoney, 184
55. Fourth International, *How the GPU Murdered Leon Trotsky*, Kindle Loc 131
56. Ibid.
57. Ed Gazur, *Alexander Orlov*, n.p.
58. Alexander Orlov testimony, 1955 US Senate Internal Security Subcommittee
59. Ibid.
60. Walter Krivitsky, FBI debriefing notes, 1939–1940
61. Jack Soble, US Congressional testimony, 1958
62. Weissman, 603
63. Weissman, 605
64. Sudoplatov, 82; Volkogonov, 338
65. Sudoplatov, 82
66. Ibid., 83
67. Summary of irregularities compiled from Patenaude, Broué, Orlov, and French judicial records
68. International Committee of the Fourth International, Security and the Fourth International, *How the GPU Murdered Trotsky*, Kindle Loc 133
69. Service, 435

CHAPTER 3: THE US PLOT TO KILL TROTSKY: STALIN'S AMERICAN NETWORK

1. Sudoplatov, 69
2. Mahoney, 259–260
3. FBI Memorandum, "Subject: Gaik Ovakimian," New York Field Office, 1941
4. Whitewood, "The Purge of the Red Army . . . ," *Slavonic & East European Review*, 2015, 286–314
5. HUAC Testimony, 1950, "The Role of Earl Browder in Soviet Intelligence"
6. Mahoney, 261
7. Ibid., 257
8. Budenz, *This Is My Story*, 184
9. Haynes, *Cover Name, Cryptonym, Pseudonym, and Real Name Index*
10. HUAC Testimony, "Gregory Rabinowitz and Soviet Red Cross Operations," *Congressional Record*, 1953
11. Budenz, *This Is My Story*, 244
12. London, *Agents*, Kindle Loc 66
13. Fourth International, "Trotsky's Assassin at Large," 15
14. Thomas L. Black, FBI Deposition, New York, 1954
15. London, *Agents*, Kindle Loc 85

CHAPTER 4: SATYR: STALIN'S MOLE IN THE SWP

1. London, *Agents*, Kindle Loc 5
2. Ibid.
3. London, *How the GPU Murdered Trotsky*, Kindle Loc 25
4. Sylvia Callen Franklin, 1954 US Grand Jury testimony
5. London, *How the GPU Murdered Trotsky*, Kindle Loc 73
6. London, *Agents*, Kindle Loc 85
7. Herbert Romerstein and Eric Breindel, *The Venona Secrets* [Washington, DC: Regnery, 2000], 360
8. London, *Agents*, Kindle Loc 86
9. Ibid.
10. Louis Budenz, *Men Without Faces* [New York: Harper & Brothers, 1950], 124
11. Romerstein and Breindel, *The Venona Secrets*, 361
12. Budenz, *Men Without Faces*, 221
13. Ibid., 223
14. Moscow interview with KGB historian Colonel Oleg Tsarev, 1996

CHAPTER 5: THE HANDS BEHIND THE AXE: STALIN'S KILLERS

1. Patenaude, Faber & Faber, 320
2. Levine, 14
3. Luri, *El Cielo Prometido*, 27–30
4. Javier Juárez, *Patria: Una Española en el KGB* (in Spanish) [Barcelona: Random House Mondadori, 2008], 103
5. Luis Mercader and Germán Sánchez, *Ramón Mercader, Mi Hermano. Cincuenta Años Después* [Madrid: Espasa-Calpe, 1990], 179
6. Ibid., 15
7. Mercader and Sánchez, 30
8. Juárez 2008, 103
9. Mahoney, 220
10. Service, 249–251
11. Mahoney, 223
12. Levine, 61–62
13. Ibid.

14. Lev Voroviev (1998), "L'assassinat de Trotsky décrit par ses assassins," *Critique Communiste* (in French), Translated by Jean-Michel Krivine, 449–450
15. Mercader and Sánchez 1990, 56
16. Rodrigo Fernández, "Dos españoles quisieron acabar con Trotski antes que Mercader," *El País*, November 16, 1997
17. Levine, 18
18. Mahoney, 219
19. Mahoney, 220–221
20. Ibid., 221
21. Ibid., 222
22. Ibid.
23. Levine, 21
24. Patenaude, Kindle Loc 146
25. Voroviev, 1998
26. Wilmers, 275
27. Voroviev, 1998
28. Wilmers, 275; citing Federal Security Service (FSB) of Russia archives that place Ramón's training in France—likely instruction in maintaining his Jacques Mornard* alias
29. E. P. Sharapov, *Stalin's Avenging Sword* [St. Petersburg: "Neva" Publishing House, 2003], 9
30. Ibid., 10–13
31. Levine, 33
32. Sharapov, 21–24
33. Sudoplatov, 69
34. Sudoplatov, 67
35. Ibid., 69
36. Ibid., 7
37. Pavel Sudoplatov, *Special Tasks: The Memoirs of an Unwanted Witness, a Soviet Spymaster* [Boston: Little, Brown]
38. Ibid., 45–49
39. Ibid., 22–23
40. Ibid., 65–69
41. Ibid., 67
42. Andrei Znamenski, "Joseph Grigulevich: A Tale of Identity, Soviet Espionage, and Storytelling," *The Soviet and Post-Soviet Review*, 44 (3): 314–341 (September 7, 2017)
43. Patenaude, Kindle Loc 249
44. Ibid.
45. Patenaude, Kindle Loc 248–250
46. Sudoplatov, 74
47. Mahoney, 235
48. Philip Stein, *Siqueiros: His Life and Works* [New York: International Publishers, 1994], 14
49. Mahoney, 237
50. Ibid., 14–28
51. Ibid., 237
52. Ibid.; the KGB surfaced the same idea in 1971: see John Barron, *KGB* [New York: Readers Digest Press, 1974], 312
53. Levine, 69; Mahoney, 237
54. Stein, 102
55. Mahoney, 237; Stein, 103
56. Herbert L. Matthews, *Half of Spain Died* [New York: Charles Scribner, 1973]
57. Mahoney, 237
58. Ibid.
59. Ibid., 238

60. Ibid., 237–238
61. Levine, 69, he was a brevet lieutenant colonel from his service in the Republican Army in the Spanish Civil War
62. Levine, 190

CHAPTER 6: THE SEDUCTION AND BETRAYAL OF SYLVIA AGELOFF

1. Budenz, *This Is My Story*, 244
2. Ibid., 245
3. Mahoney, 258
4. Levine, 45
5. Levine, 46
6. van Heijenoort, 146
7. Levine, 46
8. Ibid.
9. Ibid.
10. Levine, 47
11. Ibid., 46
12. Ibid., 47
13. House Committee on Un-American Activities, "Testimony of Sylvia Ageloff," Eighty-First Congress (December 4, 1950), Washington, DC
14. Mahoney, 324
15. Ibid.
16. Sudoplatov, 70
17. Mahoney, 325
18. Mahoney, 324
19. Ibid., 325
20. Ibid., 326
21. Ibid.
22. House Committee on Un-American Activities, "Testimony of Sylvia Ageloff," Eighty-First Congress, (December 4, 1950), Washington, DC
23. FBI Memorandum #100–7751 of May 11, 1942, by R. S. Garner; in her FBI interview in May 1942, Sylvia states her initial introduction to the assassin took place in Paris on July 1, 1938
24. Ibid.
25. Mahoney, 327
26. Levine, 139
27. Francis Wyndham, *Trotsky*, 176
28. Isaac Deutscher, *The Prophet Outcast: Trotsky 1929–1940* [New York: Oxford University Press, 1963], 483
29. Wyndham, 176
30. Levine, 50
31. Mahoney, 327
32. Ibid.
33. House Committee on Un-American Activities, "Testimony of Sylvia Ageloff," Eighty-First Congress, (December 4, 1950), Washington, DC
34. Levine, 51
35. Mahoney, 307
36. Mahoney, 327
37. Mahoney, 327
38. Levine, 51
39. Mahoney, 328
40. Levine, 52

41. Mahoney, 219
42. Deutscher, *The Prophet Outcast; Trotsky 1929–1940*, 330
43. Levine, 54
44. Interview with KGB Colonel Oleg Tsarev in Moscow in 1997
45. Leon Trotsky, "The Murder of Rudolf Klement," *The New International* [New York: Socialist Workers Party], Vol. 4, No. 9 [September 1938], 257–259
46. Interview with KGB Colonel Oleg Tsarev in Moscow in 1997
47. Levine, 55
48. Ibid.
49. Ibid.
50. Mahoney, 319
51. David Dallin, "Mark Zborowski, Soviet Agent," *The New Leader*, New York (March 19, 1952)
52. Gani Jakupi, *Les Amants de Sylvia* [Paris: Futuropolis, 2010], n.p.
53. Some have written that Ramón met the Rosmers in Paris in 1938. However, Jacson's* own words contradict that. See: Goldman, *The Assassination of Leon Trotsky*, 11, and Deutscher, *The Prophet Outcast*, 365
54. Robert J. Alexander, *International Trotskyism, 1929–1985: A Documented Analysis of the Movement* [Duke University Press, 1991], 270
55. Mahoney, 331
56. Ibid.
57. Ibid.
58. Eric London, "Sylvia Ageloff and the Assassination of Leon Trotsky: Part Two," *Security and the Fourth International*; Gani Jakupi, *Les Amants de Sylvia* [Paris: Futuropolis, 2010], n.p.
59. *A Study of "PRESTIGE" and "OBJECTIVE" Factors in Suggestibility and a Comparison of Racial and Sex Differences*, Columbia University, May 1934
60. Levine, 57
61. Mahoney, 332
62. Ibid.; the truth was that Caridad Mercader had just arrived in Paris after the fall of the Spanish Republic, accompanied by a wave of GPU operatives bound for Mexico
63. Conquest, *The Great Terror*, 247–252
64. Sudoplatov, 64
65. Ibid., 69
66. Ibid., 333
67. Sayers, *The Great Compromise*, 319, points out additional aliases that Ramón used but have not been previously reported, Leon Jacome* and Leon Hiakys*
68. Ibid., 334
69. Sudoplatov, 73
70. Ibid., 334–335
71. Ibid., 334

CHAPTER 7: THE SIAMESE TWINS: STALIN'S SPIES INSIDE THE FOURTH INTERNATIONAL

1. Dallin, *Soviet Espionage*, 285
2. NKVD file, Bundle (Papka) 28, June 3, 1933 to November 12, 1952, F 31660, d. 9067, p. 22; FBI interviews December 6, 1954, file 65–58681, Section No. 6, Serials 56x, 62
3. Weissman, *Portrait of Deception*, 586
4. Zborowski's GPU file
5. Zborowski testimony, US Senate Committee (February 29, 1956), 89
6. Kronenbitter, note 39, p. 37
7. Weissman, 588
8. Kronenbitter, *Trotsky: Dupe of the NKVD*, 1972, note 43, p. 42

9. Kronenbitter, 39
10. Mahoney, 180
11. Kronenbitter, 39
12. Ibid.
13. Robert Service, *Trotsky, a Biography* [London: Pan Books, 2009], 415–416
14. Weissman, 588; Patenaude, Kindle Loc 112
15. Letter 4, February 23, 1935, NKVD file
16. Kronenbitter, 37
17. Mahoney, 179
18. L. Yakovlev [L. Estrin], "Leon Sedov," 1–2
19. Central Archive of the Federal Security Service of the Russian Federation, f. 17548, d. 0292, t. 2, 159–165
20. Kronenbitter, 37; Mahoney, 177
21. Patenaude, Kindle Loc 112–113; Zborowski testimony, US Senate Hearings, February 29, 1956, Part 4, 88–89
22. Kronenbitter, 37
23. Ibid.
24. Mahoney, 178
25. Christopher Andres and Vasili Mitrokhin, *The Sword and the Shield: The Mitrokhin Archive and the Secret History of the KGB* [New York: Basic Books, 1999], 71; Mahoney, 178
26. US Senate Subcommittee, Testimony of Mark Zborowski, 1956
27. Weissman, 595
28. Weissman, 590
29. Mahoney, 183
30. Deutscher, 315
31. Gary Kern, *A Death in Washington: Walter G. Krivitsky and the Stalin Terror* [New York: Enigma Books, 2004], n.p.
32. Mahoney, 184
33. Ibid.
34. Ibid., 187
35. Ibid., 175
36. Weissman, 605, claims Zborowski made the statement to Elsa Poretsky, the widow of Ignace Reiss
37. Patenaude, Kindle Loc 117
38. Interview with KGB spokesperson Colonel Oleg Tsarev, Moscow, May 1991
39. Mahoney, 187
40. Interview with KGB historian Colonel Oleg Tsarev, Moscow, 1996
41. Volkogonov, 351
42. Ibid., 361
43. Kronenbitter, 40
44. Ibid., 40–41
45. Ibid., 41
46. Ibid., 42
47. Ibid., 52
48. Ibid.
49. Ibid., 53
50. Ibid., 51–53
51. Orlov admitted that he was the author of the anonymous letter before a hearing held by the US Senate Committee on the Judiciary, February 14–15, part 51
52. Ibid.
53. Ibid., 54

54. Ibid., 54
55. Ibid., 55
56. Weissman, 606
57. Jean van Heijenoort, letter to George L. Weissman, November 2, 1981. G.L. Weissman Collection, Box 1, Folder 58, Walter Reuther Library, Wayne State University
58. Weissman, 607, incorrectly states that "it was at this meeting that Sylvia Ageloff met Ramón Mercader, alias Jacson*"
59. Executive Confidential Testimony, US Senate Subcommittee, Scope of Soviet Activity in the US, February 29, 1956, p. 268

CHAPTER 8: STALIN'S MISTAKE: THE ONE WHO GOT AWAY

1. Leon Trotsky, *The Comintern and the GPU,* Fourth International, Vol. 1, No. 6, November 1940, 148–163
2. David M. Cole, *Josef Stalin: Man of Steel* [London/New York: Rich & Cowan, 1942], 68
3. Robert Service, *Trotsky: A Biography* [Cambridge, MA: Harvard University Press, 2009], 318
4. Volkogonov, 1996, 439
5. Volkogonov, 1996, 439
6. Slava Katamidze, *Loyal Comrades, Ruthless Killers, The Secret Service of the USSR 1917–1991* [Miami: Lewis International, 2003], 36
7. Coşar, *Troçki İstanbul'da,* 45–46
8. *Socialism Today*, No. 49 (2000), summarizing Trotsky's 1932 writings
9. Volkogonov, 441
10. *Leon Trotsky: An Open Letter to the French Workers*, Marxists.org, June 10, 1935
11. Geoffrey Swain, *Trotsky* (London: Routledge, 2014), 199–202
12. Oddvar Høidal, *Trotsky in Norway: Exile, 1935–1937*, n.p.
13. *Leon Trotsky in Norway (1936)*, Marxists.org, January 1937
14. Oddvar Høidal, *Trotsky in Norway: Exile, 1935–1937*, n.p.
15. *Leon Trotsky in Norway (1936)*, Marxists.org, January 1937
16. *En Sensasjonell Rettssak*; Oddvar Høidal, *Trotsky in Norway: Exile, 1935–1937*, n.p.
17. Ibid.
18. *The Moscow "Confessions"*, Marxists.org, n.p.
19. Oddvar Høidal, *Trotsky in Norway: Exile, 1935–1937*, n.p.
20. Volkogonov, 441
21. Sudoplatov, 69–70
22. Sudoplatov, 69–70
23. Sudoplatov, 74
24. Volkogonov, 443
25. Nikita Petrov and Marc Jansen, *Stalin's Loyal Executioner: People's Commissar Nikolai Ezhov, 1895–1940* [Stanford: Hoover Institution Press, 2002], 182
26. F. I. Firsov, Harvey Klehr, John Earl Haynes, *Secret Cables of the Comintern, 1933–1943* [New Haven: Yale University Press, 2014], 21–23
27. "Stalin's Hand in Rotterdam: The Murder of the Ukrainian Nationalist Yevhen Konovalets in May 1938," *Intelligence and National Security*, 9 (4), 1994
28. Elisabeth K. Poretsky, *Our Own People: A Memoir of "Ignace Reiss" and His Friends* [London: Oxford University Press, 1969], 208–226
29. Sudoplatov, 38, 91
30. Pierre Broué, (1979), n.p.
31. Sudoplatov, 48, claims that Agabekov was actually killed in Paris by the assassin and a young illegal officer, Aleksander Korotkov; they lured him to a safe house, knifed him, stuffed his body into a suitcase, and tossed it into the sea
32. Volkogonov, 443

33. Sudoplatov, 67
34. Volkogonov, 443
35. Volkogonov, 444

CHAPTER 9: AVENIDA VIENA: TROTSKY'S FINAL REFUGE

1. van Heijenoort, 138–139
2. Ibid.
3. Lubitz' TrotskyanaNet, "Leon Trotsky–The Trotsky Museum," accessed May 16, 2025, https://trotskyana.net/Leon_Trotsky/The_Trotsky_Museum/trotsky_museum_feature_engl.html
4. van Heijenoort, 138–139
5. Ibid.
6. Patenaude, *Downfall of a Revolutionary*, Kindle Loc 237
7. Bertrand Patenaude, "Trotsky in Exile," *Hoover Digest*, April 21, 2010
8. Ibid.
9. Charles Cornell, "With Trotsky in Mexico," *Fourth International* 5, No. 8 (August 1944), 246
10. Patenaude, *Downfall of a Revolutionary*, Kindle Loc 3
11. van Heijenoort, 145
12. Bertrand Patenaude, "Trotsky in Exile," *Hoover Digest*, April 21, 2010
13. John Earl Haynes, *Cover Name, Cryptonym, Pseudonym, and Real Name Index*, updated 2009, http://www.john earlhaynes.org/page66.html

CHAPTER 10: OPERATION UTKA: STALIN'S SECRET WAR ON TROTSKY

1. John Earl Haynes, *Cover Name, Cryptonym, Pseudonym, and Real Name Index*, http://www.john earlhaynes.org/index.html
2. Sudoplatov, 66
3. Ibid., 67
4. Kotkin, *Stalin: Waiting for Hitler*, 709–710; Roberts, *Stalin's Wars*, 20–22
5. Conquest, *The Great Terror*, 123–126; Khlevniuk, *Stalin: New Biography*, 207–209
6. Volkogonov, *Trotsky*, 369–371; Deutscher, *Prophet Outcast*, 421–423
7. Kotkin, *Stalin: Waiting for Hitler*, 741–744; Conquest, *The Great Terror*, 275–278
8. Ibid.
9. Ibid., 68
10. Volkogonov, 443
11. Sudoplatov, 69
12. Mahoney, 8
13. Sudoplatov, 70
14. Ibid.
15. Sudoplatov, 72
16. Ibid., 72–73
17. Ibid.
18. Ibid.
19. Salazar, 179–180
20. Sudoplatov, 74; Deutscher, 391, described him as "handsome and well-groomed"; Mahoney, 327, described him as being "tolerably handsome" and "impeccably dressed"
21. Sudoplatov, 74
22. Ibid., 74; Sudoplatov was incorrect when writing that the KON raiders relied upon the floor plan provided by Maria de la Sierra (PATRIA)
23. van Heijenoort, 138–139
24. John Earl Haynes, *Cover Name, Cryptonym, Pseudonym, and Real Name Index*, http://www.john earlhaynes.org/index.html

25. Salazar, 49
26. Sudoplatov, 74
27. Ibid.
28. Sudoplatov, 73
29. Patenaude, Kindle Loc 249 of 371
30. Jerold and Leona Schecter, *Shared Secrets*, 55
31. Sharapov, *Stalin's Avenging Sword*, [St. Petersburg: Neva Publishing House, 2003], 56
32. Ibid.

CHAPTER 11: THUGS, ENFORCERS, AND ASSASSINS

1. Julius Ruiz, *The "Red Terror" and the Spanish Civil War* [Cambridge University Press, 2014], 18–21
2. Ruiz, 19
3. Burnett Bolloten, *The Spanish Civil War: Revolution and Counterrevolution* [University of North Carolina Press, 1991], 341–359; Paul Preston, *The Spanish Civil War* [New York: HarperCollins, 2006], 217–220
4. Ronald Radosh, Mary Habeck, and Grigory Sevostianov, *Spain Betrayed: The Soviet Union in the Spanish Civil War* [New Haven, CT: Yale University Press, 2001], 52–58
5. Helen Graham, *The Spanish Republic at War, 1936–1939* [Cambridge: Cambridge University Press, 2002], 284–289
6. Bolloten, 341–359; Preston, 217–220
7. Paul Preston, *The Spanish Holocaust* [New York: HarperCollins, 2012], 442–445; Bolloten, 355–359; Radosh et al., 176–183
8. Radosh et al., 47–49, 77–84; Bolloten, 350–352; Stanley Payne, *The Spanish Civil War, the Soviet Union, and Communism* [New Haven, CT: Yale University Press, 2004], 219–223
9. Radosh et al., 301–305; Hugh Thomas, *The Spanish Civil War*, 4th ed. [New York: HarperCollins, 2004], 890–898
10. Ángel Viñas, *El Escudo de la República* [Barcelona: Crítica, 2003], 312–319
11. Radosh et al., 225–230
12. Barry Carr, *Marxism and Communism in Twentieth-Century Mexico* [Lincoln: University of Nebraska Press, 1992], 92–103; Radosh et al., 310–314; Leon Trotsky, *Writings 1938–39*, [New York: Pathfinder Press, 1974], 176–180
13. Preston, *The Spanish Holocaust*, 412–416
14. Carr, "Crisis in Mexican Communism," 49–56
15. Bolloten, *Spanish Civil War*, 353–359; Radosh et al., *Spain Betrayed*, 176–183
16. Viñas, *El Escudo de la República*, 264–267
17. Patenaude, *Downfall of a Revolutionary*, 232–233; Preston, 412–414
18. Beevor, *The Battle for Spain*, 229–234
19. Carr, 50–56
20. Carr, 52–54
21. Trotsky, *Writings 1939–40*, 219–221
22. US House Special Committee on Communist Activities, Investigation of Communist Propaganda, 1939, 441–445
23. Ibid., 443
24. Preston, *Spanish Holocaust*, 416–418
25. Trotsky, *Writings 1938–39*, 298–299
26. FBI file 65–58335, interview, 1942
27. Carr, 54–55; *Excélsior*, May 2, 1940

CHAPTER 12: COMRADES AND LOVERS: MEXICO (JANUARY TO MARCH 1940)

1. Mahoney, 335
2. Mahoney, 334–335

3. FBI Report of Special Agent R.S. Garner, dated March 2, 1942
4. Levine, 71–75
5. Ibid.
6. Mahoney, 336
7. Levine, 64
8. Patenaude, Kindle Loc 245
9. Mahoney, 336
10. Ibid.
11. "Sylvia Ageloff and the Assassination of Leon Trotsky: Part Two," *Security and the Fourth International*; 55 Calle Dinamarka address is called out as at the "GPU operational headquarters in the city"
12. Levine, 75
13. Goldman, 11; Ramón states that it was in Mexico when "I met the Rosmer couple," and not in Paris, which many authors have written
14. Patenaude, Kindle Loc 244
15. Puigventós, Kindle Loc 146
16. *How the GPU Murdered Trotsky* [London: New Park Publications, 1981], 103
17. Luri, 238
18. Mahoney, 336
19. Ibid., 239
20. Mahoney, 337
21. Ibid.
22. Ibid., 243
23. Ibid.
24. Levine, 76–77
25. Mahoney, 239
26. Levine, 77
27. *How the GPU Murdered Trotsky* [London: New Park Publications, 1981], 239
28. Albert Goldman, *The Assassination of Leon Trotsky: The Proofs of Stalin's Guilt* [New York: Pioneer Publishers, 1940], 16
29. Levine, 77
30. Olivia Gall, *Trotsky en Mexico y la Vida Política en Tiempos de Lázaro Cárdenas (1937–1940)* (Mexico DF: UNAM, 2012), 354–355
31. Ibid.
32. Mahoney, 339; Sylvia told the Mexican police investigator of Ramón's promise to her during questioning after the fatal attack; she explained that her request was motivated by a desire to avoid drawing negative attention to Trotsky should Frank's* false passport be discovered by the Mexican police or the press

CHAPTER 13: THE INVISIBLE SIEGE: STALIN'S SPIES ENCIRCLE TROTSKY (APRIL TO MAY 1940)

1. José Garmabella, *El Asesinato de Trotsky* [Mexico City: Siglo XXI, 1972], 134; Melton's 2009 visit to the Museo Trotsky included a guided tour from guide Beatrice Mestre, who explained the rumors of the "automatic firing devices"; in hindsight, had such devices existed, they would have been far more dangerous to Natalia and Leon than to the GPU
2. Colonel Oleg Tsarev interview, Moscow, 1997
3. Mahoney, 422
4. Sharapov, 52
5. Colonel Oleg Tsarev interview, Moscow, 1997
6. Mahoney, 322
7. Ibid.
8. Ibid., 323

9. Ibid., 406
10. Patenaude, Kindle Loc 35
11. Ibid., Kindle Loc 36
12. Mahoney, 406
13. Ibid., 407
14. Sharapov, 56; Puigventós wrote in Chapter 9 that the safe house was at 55 Calle Dinamarka; it is possibly the same address as Marta Meller's apartment
15. Mahoney, 409
16. Ibid.
17. Ibid., 408

CHAPTER 14: ASSASSINS AT THE GATES: OPERATION KON BEGINS

1. Patenaude, Kindle Loc 6; Levine, 84
2. Mahoney, 376
3. Ibid., 417–418
4. Mahoney, 373
5. Ibid., 374
6. Ibid., 375
7. Barrón Cruz, "The Assault on Trotsky's Villa: A Ballistic Analysis," *Mexican Historical Quarterly* 12, No. 3 (1987): 45–48
8. Patenaude, Kindle Loc 254
9. Levine, 87; the Mexican police investigation determined that the improvised bombs had a technical defect
10. Archivo General de la Nación (AGN), Mexico City, Policía Secreta Files, May 1940, Raid Report on Avenida Viena; it was never explained by Sudoplatov or Eitingon why they did not simply plant explosives in the garden at the base of the southern wall of the Old Man's bedroom; with Trotsky sleeping less than ten feet away on the other side of the brick wall, his death would have been a certainty
11. Salazar, 3
12. Patenaude, Kindle Loc 6; Levine, 87
13. Salazar, 10
14. Levine, 87
15. Patenaude, Kindle Loc 254
16. Ibid., 6
17. Archivo General de la Nación (AGN), Mexico City, Policía Secreta Files, May 1940, Raid Report on Avenida Viena
18. Patenaude, Kindle Loc 255
19. Levine, 87

CHAPTER 15: ON THE RUN: STALIN'S ASSASSINS VANISH

1. Patenaude, Kindle Loc 259
2. Levine, 82
3. Pavel Sudoplatov, *Special Tasks*, 1994, 192–193
4. E. B. Held, *A Spies Guide to Santa Fe*, 7–10
5. Ibid., 5
6. Schecter, 55
7. Marjorie Ross, *El Discreto Encanto de la KGB: Las Cinco Vidas de Iósif Griguliévich* [San José, Costa Rica: Farben/Norma, 2004]
8. Held, 8
9. Held, 8
10. Held, 8
11. Interview with E. B. Held, November 2025

12. Sudoplatov, 193
13. Andrei Znamenski, "Joseph Grigulevich: A Tale of Identity, Soviet Espionage, and Storytelling," *The Soviet and Post-Soviet Review*, 44 (3): 314–341 (September 7, 2017)
14. Leon Trotsky, *Stalin's Gangsters*, XIII
15. Levine, 95
16. Stein, 119
17. Salazar, *Así Asesinaron a Trotski*, 65
18. Stein, 121–122
19. Stein, 122
20. Stein, 123
21. Daniela Spenser, *"Unidad a Toda Costa": La Tercera Internacional en México Durante la Presidencia de Lázaro Cárdenas* [Mexico City: CIESAS, 2007], 426 No. 19
22. Spenser, 431–432
23. Julio Scherer García, *Siqueiros: La Piel y la Entraña* [Mexico City: Fondo de Cultura Económica, 2003], 41–43
24. Herner, 211
25. Salazar, *Así Asesinaron a Trotski*, 214
26. Scherer, 46–47

CHAPTER 16: INSIDE JOB: THE MOLE HUNT

1. Leandro A. Sánchez Salazar, *Así Asesinaron a Trotski*, 5
2. Salazar, 5
3. Salazar, 10
4. Salazar, 10
5. Salazar, 10
6. Nicholas Mosley, *The Assassination of Trotsky*, 42
7. Levine, 89; Salazar, 7
8. Salazar, 41; Patenaude, *Trotsky*, Kindle Loc 252
9. Salazar, 8–9
10. Salazar, 48–49
11. Salazar, 14
12. Patenaude, Kindle Loc 249–250
13. Patenaude, Kindle Loc 249–250
14. Patenaude, 248–250; having lost Maria de la Sierra (PATRIA), the GPU's only source inside the Trotsky's entourage in late 1938, it appears unlikely that Grigulevich had sufficient intelligence on the new Avenida Viena residence to prepare a detailed attack plan in the summer of 1939
15. Ibid.
16. Ibid.; Patenaude's account omits Grigulevich's trip to Santa Fe in January 1940
17. Salazar, 45
18. Ibid.
19. "Trotsky Home Attacked by Gunmen," *New York Times*, May 25, 1940
20. Mahoney, 373
21. David North, "A Tribute to Harold Robins: Captain of Trotsky's Guard 1908–1987," World Socialist Web Site, November 27, 1987
22. Ibid.
23. North, "A Tribute to Harold Robins"
24. Salazar, 18
25. Salazar, 18
26. Salazar, 20
27. Salazar, 24
28. Mahoney, 385

29. Mahoney, 385; Salazar, 13
30. Patenaude, Kindle Loc 6
31. Patenaude, Kindle Loc 6
32. Patrick Marnham, *Dreaming with His Eyes Open: A Life of Diego Rivera* [New York: Knopf, 1998], n.p.
33. Patenaude, 248–250; Levine, 95
34. Levine, 95

CHAPTER 17: OPERATION CASA CHICAS: SEX, LIES, AND THE ROAD TO COYOACÁN

1. Salazar, 35
2. Ibid., 40
3. Mahoney, 513–514
4. Salazar, 44
5. Ibid., 44–47
6. Ibid., 48
7. Ibid., 49
8. Ibid., 18
9. Ibid., 43
10. Salazar, 67
11. Ibid., 64
12. Ibid., 65
13. Ibid., 65–66
14. Levine, 95–96
15. Salazar, 69
16. Ibid., 65–67
17. Ibid., 45
18. Ibid., 46
19. Ibid.
20. Ibid., 48

CHAPTER 18: PAWN OF STALIN: THE TRAGEDY OF SHELDON HARTE

1. Salazar, 16–17
2. Salazar, 30–33
3. Julia Harte, *Rebel Without a Cause*
4. Sudoplatov, 74
5. Ibid.
6. Ibid.
7. Joseph Hansen, "The Attempted Assassination of Leon Trotsky," *Fourth International*, Vol. 1, No. 4 (August 1940), 85–91
8. Salazar, 92
9. Salazar, 46
10. Ibid., 49
11. Mahoney, 388; *New York Times*, May 26, 1940
12. Ibid.
13. Telegram from Trotsky to American press, May 26, 1940
14. Julia Harte, *Rebel Without a Cause*
15. Salazar, 35
16. Ibid., 75
17. Ibid., 70
18. Ibid., 82
19. Ibid., 74
20. Ibid., 77

21. Patenaude, Kindle Loc 260
22. Today, the chain-link gate opens into a cramped anteroom that functions largely as storage for the museum's refuse bins. The steel gates that once marked the villa's sole entrance and exit have been reduced to a service passage—largely forgotten, opened now only to roll the bins in and out
23. Service, 488
24. Fourth International, *Trotsky's Assassin at Large* [New York: Labor Publications, 1979], 3
25. Mahoney, 422
26. Sudoplatov, 74
27. Sharapov, *Stalin's Avenging Sword*, 57–58
28. Ibid., 57
29. Ibid., 58

CHAPTER 19: THE SPY WHO LOVED AND LIED

1. Volkogonov, 454
2. Ibid., 459
3. Sharapov, 59
4. Sharapov, 57–58
5. Sharapov, 59
6. Ibid.
7. Ibid.
8. Mahoney, 396
9. Levine, 77–78
10. Mahoney, 396
11. Goldman, 46
12. Levine, 78
13. Goldman, 46
14. Levine, 80–81
15. Levine, 80
16. Melton, *The Secret History of KGB Spy Cameras*, 23
17. FBI Trotsky Files, Vol. 2, 146–148
18. Ibid.
19. His Leica camera was not found among Jacson's* personal effects at the Hotel Montejo after the assassination

CHAPTER 20: OPERATION MAT: LICENSE TO KILL

1. Mahoney, 396
2. Hansen, *The Assassination of Leon Trotsky*, 44–47
3. Salazar, 14; while both of their vehicles were stolen by the raiders and later found by the police, they were still being processed and had not been returned to the family
4. Mahoney, 396
5. Levine, 93–94
6. Levine, 94
7. Mahoney, 397
8. Hansen, *The Assassination of Leon Trotsky*, 44–47
9. Levine, 102
10. Ibid.
11. Levine, 102
12. Ibid., 101
13. Archive General de la Nación (México). Tribunal Superior de Justicia del D.F. Año 1940. Caja 3265 Folio 602993, 30–31
14. H. Keith Melton and Robert Wallace, *Spy Sites of New York City*, 118–119; Mahoney, 410,

makes a mistake and identifies that Frank* and Sylvia stayed in the Hotel Lexington; his source for the data was a mistake in the FBI files; the FBI corrected the mistake in a later memorandum on August 27, 1940, which is shown as document No. 45–57 of "trotsk2.pdf"

15. Harry Mahoney, 410; Levine, 102; however, Puigventós writes in Chapter 9 that Ovakimian and others from the US were not present at the June meetings to reduce the number of people involved
16. Sudoplatov, 77
17. The New York rezidentura had access to much better radio equipment at the consulate for faster communications with Moscow
18. The meeting is often mistakenly attributed to happening on May 28, 1940, but Ramón was driving Natalia and the Rosmers to Veracruz all that day
19. Sudoplatov, 78
20. Levine, 100–101
21. Sudoplatov, 24–27
22. Ibid.
23. Sudoplatov, 77
24. Ibid.
25. Levine, 111–112
26. Andrew-Gordievsky, 170; the body was subsequently wrapped in a rug and disposed of
27. Levine, 72–73
28. Moscow interview in 1997 with KGB historian Lieutenant Colonel Oleg Tsarev
29. Sudoplatov, 77
30. H. Keith Melton, *Ultimate Spy*, 25–27; the Cheka produced suppressed Nagant revolvers during the Russian Civil War, and suppressed Tokarev pistols were introduced in the 1930s
31. Whittaker Chambers, statement to the Fourth International directing committee, quoted in *The Gelfand Case*, Vol. 1 [Detroit: Labor Publications, 1985], 15
32. Salazar, 219
33. Eric London, "Sylvia Ageloff and the Assassination of Leon Trotsky: Part Three," *Security and the Fourth International*
34. Salazar, 119–120
35. Ibid.
36. Ibid., 220
37. Mahoney, 103
38. FBI report on September 13, 1940

CHAPTER 21: FORTRESS TROTSKY: THE HOUSE UNDER SIEGE

1. Bertrand M. Patenaude, *Trotsky: Downfall of a Revolutionary* [New York: HarperCollins, 2009], Kindle Loc edition, 266
2. Joseph Hansen, "With Trotsky to the End," *Fourth International* 1, No. 5 (October 1940)
3. Isaac Don Levine, *The Mind of an Assassin*, 85
4. Bertrand M. Patenaude, *Trotsky*, 278
5. Harry Thayer Mahoney and Marjorie Locke Mahoney, *The Saga of Leon Trotsky*, 385
6. Henry Schnautz letters
7. Patenaude, Kindle Loc edition, 264
8. Patenaude, Kindle Loc 278
9. Patenaude, Kindle Loc 264
10. Albert Goldman, *The Assassination of Leon Trotsky* [New York: Pioneer Publishers, 1972]
11. Patenaude, Kindle Loc 251
12. Schnautz letter
13. Joseph Hansen to Ferrell Dobbs, July 31, 1940, SWP Archive
14. Patenaude, Kindle Loc 264
15. Patenaude, Kindle Loc 255

CHAPTER 22: FINAL REHEARSAL: HAT, RAINCOAT, AND AXE

1. Eduard Puigventós Lopez, *Ramón Mercader: El Hombre del Piolet*, Kindle Loc 4526
2. Eric London, "Sylvia Ageloff and the Assassination of Leon Trotsky: Part Three," World Socialist Web Site, February 7, 2021
3. *Trotsky: The Eternal Revolutionary*, 459
4. Eric London, Part 3
5. Interview with José Ramón Garmabella, Mexico City, 2009
6. Mahoney, 411
7. Ibid.
8. Mahoney, 412
9. Ibid.
10. Isaac Deutscher, *The Prophet Outcast*, 496
11. Mosley, 142
12. Ibid.
13. Leon Trotsky, letter to Jean van Heijenoort, August 2, 1940, in *Writings of Leon Trotsky (1939–40)*, ed. George Breitman [New York: Pathfinder Press, 1977], 419
14. Interview with José Ramón Garmabella, Mexico City, 2009
15. Mosley, 144
16. Natalia Sedova, "How It Happened"
17. Mahoney, 433
18. Ibid.
19. Mosley, 145
20. Mahoney, 433
21. Leon Trotsky, quoted in Isaac Deutscher, *The Prophet Outcast: Trotsky, 1929–1940* [New York: Oxford University Press, 1963], 503

CHAPTER 23: AUGUST 20, 1940: TROTSKY'S FINAL DAY

1. Mahoney, 426
2. Natalia Sedova, "How It Happened," *Fourth International*, Vol. II, No. 4 (May 1941), 100–103
3. Ibid.
4. Natalia Sedova, "How It Happened"
5. Ibid.
6. Letter from Albert Goldman to Leon Trotsky, August 1940; Deutscher, *The Prophet Outcast*, 499
7. Leon Trotsky, *Writings of Leon Trotsky (1939–1940)*, ed. George Breitman [New York: Pathfinder Press, 1977]
8. Natalia Sedova, "How It Happened"

CHAPTER 24: THE ASSASSIN'S LAST DAY

1. Mahoney, 431
2. Hotel Montejo brochure, ca. 1940
3. FBI Memorandum file No. 62–20, by R. N. Hosteny, 9–25–40
4. FBI Memorandum re: Jacques Mornard Vandendreschd*, by M. R. Griffin, December 9, 1940, p. 12
5. Goldman, 17
6. Mahoney, 413
7. Puigventós, Kindle Loc 4546
8. Mahoney, 431
9. Señorita Noriega statement, August 1940 in José Ramón Garmabella collection
10. Mahoney, 431
11. José Ramón Garmabella, *El Asesino Entró Sin Llamar*, 1975
12. Mahoney, 432

13. Ibid.
14. London, "Sylvia Ageloff and the Assassination of Leon Trotsky: Part Three," citing Barrón Cruz, 47
15. Mahoney, 433
16. Barrón Cruz, 166
17. Eric London, "Sylvia Ageloff and the Assassination of Leon Trotsky: Part Three"
18. Mahoney, 434
19. Isaac Don Levine, *The Mind of an Assassin*, 1950
20. Interview in 2025 with neurosurgeon Dr. Robert Lacin

CHAPTER 25: THE AXE FALLS: TROTSKY'S FINAL BATTLE

1. Joseph Hansen, "With Trotsky to the End," *Fourth International*, Vol. I, No. 5 (October 1940), 115–123
2. Ibid.
3. Mahoney, 438
4. Natalia Sedova, "How It Happened," *Fourth International*, Vol. II, No. 4 (May 1941), 100–103
5. Ibid.
6. Mahoney, 440
7. Sedova, "How It Happened"
8. Ibid.
9. Ibid.
10. Ibid.
11. Ibid.
12. Ibid.
13. Ibid.
14. Ibid.
15. Levine, 124
16. Mahoney, 443
17. Ibid.
18. Deutscher, 408
19. Salazar, 135
20. Sudoplatov, 78; the meeting took place at the Union of Writers Club in Moscow
21. Sedova, "How It Happened"
22. Ibid.
23. Patenaude, Kindle Loc 265
24. Mercader, 444
25. Hansen, "With Trotsky to the End"
26. Ibid.
27. Mahoney, 445
28. Sedova, "How It Happened"
29. Ibid.
30. Hansen, "With Trotsky to the End"
31. Ibid.
32. Puigventós, Ch. 10, n.p.; Sudoplatov, 77; his statement undercuts his prior boasts about killing a sentry with a knife during the Spanish Civil War
33. Ibid.
34. Deutscher, *The Prophet Outcast*, Vol. 3, 408
35. Salazar, 102
36. Hansen, "With Trotsky to the End"
37. Ibid.
38. Ibid.
39. Ibid.

40. Deutscher, 409
41. Ibid.
42. Ibid.
43. Ibid.
44. Ibid.
45. Ibid.

CHAPTER 26: LONELY VIGIL: THE HOSPITAL

1. Melton visited the Green Cross Hospital in 2009, which is still colocated with the police department, and was shown the original examining rooms; they are no longer in use but remain as they were in 1940
2. Hansen, "With Trotsky to the End"
3. Natalia Sedova, "How It Happened," *Fourth International*, Vol. II, No. 4 (May 1941), 100–103
4. Salazar, 103
5. Ibid., 109
6. Enrique Soto-Pérez-de-Celis, MD, *Neurosurgery*, Vol. 67, Issue 2 (August 2010), 417–423
7. Patenaude, Kindle Loc 290
8. Enrique Soto-Pérez-de-Celis, MD, *Neurosurgery*, Vol. 67, Issue 2 (August 2010), 417–423
9. Salazar, 108

CHAPTER 27: AFTER THE AXE: AUTOPSY AND AFTERMATH

1. Salazar, 109
2. H. Keith Melton, technical analysis of the assassination weapon, 2019; private research files
3. Salazar, 109
4. Salazar, 104
5. Mahoney, 444
6. Mosley, 160
7. Payne, 455
8. Isaac Deutscher, *The Prophet Outcast: Trotsky, 1929–1940* [New York: Oxford University Press, 1963], 412
9. Alcázar Funeral Proclamation, author's collection
10. US Department of State, Foreign Relations of the United States (FRUS), 1940, Vol. II: "Mexico and Latin American Affairs," Document 1337
11. Hansen, "With Trotsky to the End"

CHAPTER 28: FLIGHT OF THE EXECUTIONERS

1. Levine, 131
2. Sharapov, 63
3. Puigventós, trans., 90
4. Sudoplatov, 64
5. Interview with Anatoli Sudoplatov, Boca Raton, Florida, 2010
6. It is still unclear why Grigulevich was decorated; Operation KON should have succeeded if he had only confirmed the Old Man's death before withdrawing; perhaps Grigulevich's other contributions—still unreported—merited the award
7. Levine, 131; Sharapov, 63
8. Sudoplatov, 64
9. Puigventós, trans., 90
10. Sudoplatov, 79

CHAPTER 29: THE DUPE: LOVE AS A WEAPON

1. Levine, 129
2. Barrón Cruz, 47–48

3. Salazar, 144
4. Levine, 130
5. Barrón Cruz, 48
6. Eric London, citing Luri, 250–251
7. Levine, 130
8. Eric London, citing Gall, 354–355
9. Ibid.
10. Ibid.
11. Ibid.
12. Levine, 131

CHAPTER 30: THE PRISONER WITHOUT A NAME

1. Salazar, 125
2. Mahoney, 333
3. Ibid., 333–334
4. Ibid.
5. Ibid.
6. Hansen, "With Trotsky to the End"
7. Salazar, 182–183
8. Ibid.
9. Levine, 150
10. Ibid., 207

CHAPTER 31: THE COLONEL AND THE ASSASSIN

1. Levine, 133
2. Ibid., 134
3. *New York Times*, August 21, 1940
4. Levine, 138–140; *New York Times*, August 22, 1940
5. Levine, 139
6. Goldman, 13
7. Murphy, 434–435
8. Ibid.
9. Goldman, 5–8
10. Levine, 142
11. Ibid.
12. Ibid., 146
13. Ibid., 146–147
14. Ibid., 147
15. Salazar, 161

CHAPTER 32: TRAINED TO KILL, TRAINED TO LIE

1. Levine, 149
2. Ibid., 150
3. Ibid., 149–150
4. Ibid., 151
5. Ibid., 151
6. Ibid., 161
7. Ibid.
8. Ibid., 161–162
9. Ibid., 169
10. Ibid.
11. Ibid., 170

12. Ibid.
13. Ibid., 170–171

CHAPTER 33: FORTUNE'S FOOL: LOVE, DENIAL, AND THE DEATH OF TROTSKY

1. Eric London, "Sylvia Ageloff and the Assassination of Leon Trotsky," World Socialist Web Site, *Security and the Fourth International* series, February 5–8, 2021
2. Ibid.
3. *New York Times*, August 31, 1940
4. Interview with José Ramón Garmabella, Mexico City, 2009
5. Salazar, 107
6. Gregorio Luri, *Los días de Trotsky* [Mexico City: UNAM, 1982], 242
7. FBI memorandum, August 27, 1940, RG 65, NARA
8. Associated Press, August 24, 1940
9. London interview with Eric M. Gurevitch, August 17, 2020
10. Martín Gabriel Barrón Cruz, 47
11. Ibid., 39
12. Ibid., 59
13. Ibid., 47
14. Barrón Cruz, 39
15. Albert Goldman, *The Assassination of Leon Trotsky*, 152
16. Ibid.
17. FBI memorandum by R. N. Hostney, September 25, 1940, RG 65, NARA
18. Ibid.
19. FBI memorandum, RG 65, NARA
20. August 23, 1940
21. *New York Times*, September 12, 1940
22. AGN; Victor Serge recollections
23. FBI memorandum, December 1940, RG 65, NARA
24. Barrón Cruz, 39
25. *Washington Post*, December 28, 1940
26. Eric Gurevitch, *Hypocrite Reader*, August 2015
27. Nicholas Mosley, *The Assassination of Trotsky*, 115
28. FBI file 100–7751
29. FBI memorandum by R. S. Garner, May 11, 1942
30. *The Gelfand Case*, Vol. 1, 15

CHAPTER 34: JUSTICE SUBVERTED

1. Walter Rourke, "The Murder of Robert Sheldon Harte: The Aftermath of the Machine-Gun Attack on Trotsky," *Fourth International*, Vol. III No. 5 (May 1942), 139–142

CHAPTER 35: MERCADER CONVICTED, STALIN ACQUITTED

1. Walter O'Rourke, "The Verdict on the Assassin of Trotsky," *Fourth International*, Vol. 4, No. 8 (August 1943)
2. Levine, 191
3. Ibid., 150
4. O'Rourke, "The Verdict on the Assassin of Trotsky"
5. Ibid.
6. Salazar, 109
7. Levine, 192
8. Ibid.
9. Ibid.

10. O'Rourke, "The Verdict on the Assassin of Trotsky"
11. Ibid.
12. Ibid.
13. Ibid.
14. Levine, 194

CHAPTER 36: GUEST OF THE BLACK PALACE: TWENTY YEARS OF SILENCE

1. Salazar, 182–183
2. Levine, 200–203
3. Salazar, 218
4. Puigventós, Kindle Loc 423
5. Ibid.
6. Ibid.
7. Levine, 200
8. Levine, 201–202
9. *The Militant*, Vol. V, No. 50 (December 13, 1941), 6
10. *Excélsior,* "Jacson* en su Celda," November 22, 1943
11. Levine, 202
12. Levine, 203
13. Interview with José Ramón Garmabella, Mexico City, 2009
14. Levine, 204–205
15. Levine, 205–206

CHAPTER 37: THE ESCAPE THAT NEVER WAS

1. US Office of Censorship, Interception and Censorship Reports, RG 216, National Archives and Records; US Congress, Investigation of Un-American Propaganda Activities in the United States, Hearings before a Special Committee, 81st Cong., 2nd Sess., 1950, Vol. 3, 4017–4019
2. US Congress, Investigation of Un-American Propaganda Activities, Vol. 3, 4017–4019
3. CIA, Soviet Intelligence Communications, declassified report, CIA FOIA Reading Room
4. House Committee on Un-American Activities, Hearings Regarding Communist Espionage and Propaganda, 1950, Vol. 3, 4021–4025
5. Levine, 195
6. Ibid., 196
7. Ibid., 196–197
8. Ibid.
9. Ibid.
10. Ibid., 197
11. Ibid., 197–198
12. Ibid., 198
13. Levine, 222
14. Ibid., 199

CHAPTER 39: UNMASKING THE ASSASSIN

1. Sudoplatov, 79–80
2. Sudoplatov, 80
3. Levine, 209
4. Olivia Gall, *Trotsky en México y la Vida Política en Tiempos de Lázaro Cárdenas* (1937–1940), UNAM, 2012, 255
5. Stephen Schwartz, Morton Sobell, and John Lowenthal, "The Gentlemen of Venona," *The Nation*, March 15, 2001
6. Salazar, 231

7. Ibid., 232
8. Ibid., 233
9. Levine, 208
10. Ibid.
11. Federal Bureau of Investigation, "Office Memorandum to Director, FBI," April 14, 1950, FBI Trotsky Files, file TROTSK8
12. Barrón Cruz, trans., Loc 29
13. Levine, 204
14. Levine, 204–205
15. Ibid.
16. Ibid.
17. Ibid.
18. Levine, 206
19. *TIME*, May 16, 1960
20. Warth, *The Spanish Civil War and the Cuban Revolution*, 185

CHAPTER 40: THE REVOLUTIONARY WHO FORGOT TO FIGHT BACK

1. Kronenbitter, 1–53

AFTERWORD: TRACKING THE AXE THAT KILLED THE REVOLUTION

1. Goldman, 2
2. Alfonso Quiroz Cuarón, *Criminología*, Vol. 2 [Mexico City: Universidad Nacional Autónoma de México, 1942], 117
3. Goldman, 13
4. Salazar, 148
5. Barrón Cruz, trans., 66
6. Salazar, 179
7. The piolet is rare, with only a handful known to exist in 2025
8. Ken Crosby, *Crosby's Luck*, unpublished manuscript
9. Mahoney, 433
10. Salazar, 109

EPILOGUE

1. Leon Trotsky FBI file, April 15, 1942, interview by FBI Special Agent R. S. Garner with Sylvia Ageloff at her apartment in Brooklyn

SELECT BIBLIOGRAPHY

1. Andrew, Christopher, and Oleg Gordievsky. *KGB: The Inside Story*. New York: HarperCollins, 1990.
2. Andrew, Christopher, and Vasili Mitrokhin. *The Sword and the Shield: The Mitrokhin Archive and the Secret History of the KGB*. New York: Basic Books, 2001.
3. Andrew, Christopher M, and Vasili Mitrokhin. *The Mitrokhin Archive II: The KGB in the World*. London: Penguin, 2018.
4. Barmine, Alexander. *One Who Survived*. New York: G. P. Putnam's Sons, 1945.
5. Barron, John. *KGB: The Secret Work of Soviet Agents*. New York: Reader's Digest Press, 1974.
6. Barrón Cruz, Martín Gabriel. *Actuaciones Ministeriales En El Homicidio de León Trotsky*. Mexico D.F.: Instituto Nacional de Sciencias Penales, 2018.
7. Boriszkyj, Boris. *The Uses of Terror*. New York: Coward, McGann, & Geoghegan, Inc., 1972.
8. Brossat, Alain. "The Tragedy of the Bronstein Family," posted online at Marxists Internet Archive, accessed December 27, 2024, https://www.marxists.org/history/etol/revhist/supplem/bronstei.htm.
9. Broué, Pierre. *Leon Sedov: Trotsky's Son, Stalin's Victim*. Les Éditions Ouvrières, 1993. French to English translation at: https://katelinterpret.com/2023/01/31/leon-sedov-trotskys-son-stalins-victim-by-pierre-broue-french-to-english-translation/.
10. Budenz, Louis. *Men Without Faces*. New York: Harper Bros, 1950.
11. —. *This Is My Story*. New York: Harper Bros, 1947.
12. Carranca y Rivas, Raúl. *El Caso Trotsky: Presentación de Un Proceso*. Mexico City, 1994.
13. Conquest, Robert. *The Great Terror: A Reassessment*. London: The Bodley Head, 2018.
14. Cookridge, E. H. *The Soviet Spy Net*. London: Frederick Muller, 1956.
15. Costello, John, and Oleg Tsarev. *Deadly Illusions*. New York: Crown Publishing, 1993.
16. Cover, Julian J. *Mass Meeting Called by the American Committee for the Defense of Leon Trotsky, to Answer His Accusers*. New York: Stenographers Minutes at the Hippodrome, 1947.
17. Deutscher, Isaac, and David King. *The Great Purges*. Oxford: Blackwell, 1984.
18. Deutscher, Isaac. *The Prophet Armed: Trotsky, 1879–1921*. London: Verso, 2003.
19. —. *The Prophet: The Life of Leon Trotsky*. London: Verso, 2015.
20. Dewar, Hugo. *Assassins at Large*. Boston: The Beacon Press, 1951.
21. Duff, William E. *A Time for Spies*. Nashville: Vanderbilt University Press, 1999.
22. Dziak, John J. *Chekisty: A History of the KGB*. Lexington: Lexington Press, 1988.
23. Fourth International. *In Defence of Trotskyism [by] the International Committee of the Fourth International*. New York: Labor Publications, 1977.
24. Frank, Pierre. *Those Who Died so that the International Might Live: The Fourth International*. Paris: Intercontinental Press, 1972.
25. Gall, Olivia. *Trotsky En Mexico Y La Vida Política En Tiempos de Lázaro Cárdenas (1937–1940)*. Mexico City: UNAM research institute (CEIICH-UNAM) and Editorial Ítaca, 2012.

26. Garmabella, José Ramón. *El Grito de Trotsky*. Mexico City: Random House, 2006.
27. Gazur, Edward P. *Alexander Orlov: The FBI's KGB General*. New York: Carroll & Graf, 2002.
28. Goldman, Albert. *The Assassination of Leon Trotsky*. New York: Pioneer Publishers, 2013.
29. Hansen, Joseph. *Attempted Assassination of Leon Trotsky (August 1940)*. www.marxists.org, https://www.marxists.org/archive/hansen/1940/08/assas.htm.
30. —. "With Trotsky to the End." *Fourth International* 1, No. 5 (October 1940): 115–23.
31. —. *Leon Trotsky, the Man and His Work. Reminiscences and Appraisals*. New York: Merit Publishers, 1969.
32. Hansen et al. *Leon Trotsky: The Man and His Work. Reminiscences and Appraisals*. New York: Merit Publishers, 1969.
33. Haynes, John, and Harvey Klehr. *Venona: Decoding Soviet Espionage*. New Haven: Yale University Press, 2009.
34. Haynes, John Earl. *Cover Name, Cryptonym, Pseudonym, and Real Name Index*. Accessed April 23, 2025. http://www.johnearlhaynes.org/index.html.
35. Heaps, Willard A. *Assassination: A Special Kind of Murder*. New York: Hawthorn Books, 1969.
36. Heijenoort, Jean Van. *With Trotsky in Exile*. Cambridge: University Press, 1977.
37. Held, E. B. *A Spy's Guide to Santa Fe and Albuquerque*. Albuquerque: University of New Mexico Press, 2011.
38. Herrera, Hayden. *Frida: A Biography of Frida Kahlo*. New York: Harper & Row, 1983.
39. International Committee of the Fourth International. *How the GPU Murdered Trotsky*. London: New Park Publications, 1981.
40. Kamatidze, Slava. *Loyal Comrades, Ruthless Killers*. Miami: Lewis International Inc., 2003.
41. King, David. *Trotsky: A Photographic Biography*. New York: Basil Blackwell Inc., 1986.
42. Kirk, Betty. *Covering the Mexican Front*. Norman: University of Oklahoma Press, 1942.
43. Klein, Christopher. "The Trotsky Assassination." *HISTORY*, August 29, 2018. https://www.history.com/news/the-trotsky-assassination-75-years-ago.
44. Kronenbitter, Rita T. "Leon Trotsky: Dupe of the NKVD." *Studies in Intelligence*, CIA, 1972. Accessed May 1, 2025, https://www.cia.gov/resources/csi/static/Leon-Trotsky-of-NKVD.pdf.
45. Lamphere, Robert J., and Tom Shachtman. *The FBI-KGB War: A Special Agent's Story*. Macon, GA: Mercer University Press, 1995.
46. Leonard, Raymond W. *Secret Soldiers of the Revolution: Soviet Military Intelligence, 1918–1933*. Westport, CT: Greenwood Press, 2000.
47. Levine, Isaac Don. *The Mind of an Assassin*. Westport, CT: Greenwood Press, 1979.
48. London, Eric. *Agents: The FBI and GPU Infiltration of the Trotskyite Movement*. Detroit: Mehring Books, 2021.
49. —. *Sylvia Ageloff and the Assassination of Leon Trotsky*, Parts I-IV, World Socialist Web Site, February 5–8, 2021, accessed March 13, 2025, https://www.wsws.org/en/articles/2021/02/09/sylv-f09.html.
50. Luri Medrano, Gregorio. *El Cielo Prometido: Una Mujer al Servicio de Stalin*. Barcelona: Ariel - Editorial Planeta, S.A., 2016.
51. Mahoney, Harry Thayer, and Marjorie Locke Mahoney. *The Saga of Leon Trotsky*. San Francisco: Austin & Winfield, 1998.
52. Mandel, Ernest. *Trotsky*. London: New Left Books, 1979.
53. Matthews, Herbert Lionel. *Half of Spain Died: A Reappraisal of the Spanish Civil War*. New York: Scribner, 1973.
54. Melton, H. Keith, Lieutenant Vladimir Alekseenko, and Detlev Vreiseleben. *The Secret History of KGB Spy Cameras*. Atglen, PA: Schiffer Military, 2018.
55. Melton, H. Keith, *Ultimate Spy*. 3rd ed. New York: DK Publishing, 2009.
56. Mercader, Luis, and Germán Sánchez. *Ramón Mercader*. Madrid: Espasa - Calpe, 1990.
57. Mosley, Nicholas. *The Assassination of Trotsky*. London: Michael Joseph, 1972.

58. North, David. "A Tribute to Harold Robins: Captain of Trotsky's Guard 1908–1987." World Socialist Web Site. International Committee of the Fourth International. November 27, 1987. https://www.wsws.org/en/special/library/fi-15-1/13.html.
59. Olmsted, Kathryn S. *Red Spy Queen*. Chapel Hill: University of North Carolina Press, 2003.
60. O'Rourke, Walter. "The Murder of Robert Sheldon Harte (May 1942)." www.marxists.org. Accessed August 1, 2024. https://www.marxists.org/history/etol/newspape/fi/vol03/no05/rourke.htm.
61. —. "The Trial of the Assassin of Trotsky (August 1942)." www.marxists.org, 1942. https://www.marxists.org/history/etol/newspape/fi/vol03/no08/rourke.htm.
62. —. "Walter O'Rourke: The Verdict on the Assassin of Trotsky (August 1943)." www.marxists.org, August 1942. https://www.marxists.org/history/etol/newspape/fi/vol04/no08/orourke.htm.
63. Oswald, J. Gregory, and Anthony J. Strover, *The Soviet Union and Latin America*. New York: Praeger Publishers, 1970.
64. Payne, Robert. *The Life and Death of Trotsky*. New York: McGraw-Hill, 1977.
65. Payne, Stanley G. *The Spanish Civil War, the Soviet Union, and Communism*. London: Yale University Press, 2008.
66. Petrov, Vladimir, and Evdokia Petrov. *Empire of Fear*. London: Andre Deutsch, 1956.
67. Phelps, Christopher. *Young Sidney Hook: Marxist and Pragmatist*. Ann Arbor: University of Michigan Press, 2005.
68. Poretsky, Elisabeth K. *Our Own People*. Ann Arbor: University of Michigan Press, 1970.
69. Puigventós i López, Eduard. *Ramón Mercader, El Hombre Del Piolet*. Barcelona: Ara Libres, 2015.
70. Rexroth, Kenneth, and Linda Hamalian. *An Autobiographical Novel*. New York: New Direction, 1991.
71. Romerstein, Herbert, and Eric Breindel. *The Venona Secrets*. New York: Simon & Schuster, 2001.
72. Salazar, General L. A. S. *Murder in Mexico: The Assassination of Leon Trotsky*. London: Secker & Warburg, 1950.
73. Schecter, Jerrold L., and Leona Schecter. *Sacred Secrets: How Soviet Sánchez Intelligence Operations Changed American History*. New York: Potomac Books, 2002.
74. Schnautz, Henry. "Henry Schnautz Letter 1940 Aug 6." www.frfly.com. Accessed August 1, 2024. http://www.frfly.com/esp/trotsky/w_1940_8_6.html.
75. —. "Letter Sylvia Caldwell 1939 Jan 26 to Henry Schnautz." www.frfly.com. Accessed August 4, 2024. http://www.frfly.com/esp/trotsky/j_1940_8_4.html.
76. —. "Night Shift Guard 1940 Aug 5." www.frfly.com. Accessed August 1, 2024. http://www.frfly.com/esp/trotsky/j_1940_8_5.html.
77. Schwartz, Stephen, Morton Sobell, and John Lowenthal. *The Nation*. April 2, 2001. https://www.thenation.com/issue/april-2-2001/.
78. Segal, Ronald. *Leon Trotsky*. New York: Pantheon, 1979.
79. Serge, Victor, and Natalia Sedova Trotsky. *The Life and Death of Leon Trotsky*. New York: Basic Books, 1975.
80. Service, Robert. *Trotsky: A Biography*. Cambridge, MA: Harvard University Press, 2009.
81. Sharapov, E. P. *Nahum Eytingon - Stalin's Avenging Sword*. St. Petersburg: Neva Publishing House, 2003.
82. Solis, Manuel Camacho. *Museo Casa de Leon Trotsky: Memoria de Su Restauración*. Ciudad de México: Departamento del Distrito Federal, 1990.
83. Soto-Pérez-de-Celis, Enrique. "The Death of Leon Trotsky." *Neurosurgery* 67, No. 2 (August 1, 2010): 417–23. https://doi.org/10.1227/01.NEU.0000371968.27560.6C.
84. Stein, Philip. *His Life and Works*. New York: International Publishers, 1994.
85. Sudoplatov, Pavel, and Anatoli Sudoplatov. *Special Tasks: The Memoirs of an Unwanted Witness—A Soviet Spymaster*. Boston: Little, Brown, 1994.

86. *The Gelfand Case; Volume 1.* Detroit: Labour Publications, Inc., 1985.
87. *The Sylvia Franklin Dossier.* New York: Labor Publications Inc., 1977.
88. Trotsky, Leon, and Lev Davidovič Trockij. *Trotsky's Diary in Exile.* London: Faber & Faber, 1958.
89. Trotsky, Leon. "Leon Trotsky: Stalin Seeks My Death (1940)." Marxists.org, May 24, 1940. https://www.marxists.org/archive/trotsky/1940/05/stalin.htm.
90. —. *Stalin's Gangsters.* London: New Park Publications, 1977.
91. Trotsky, Natalia Sedova. "How It Happened." *Fourth International* II, No. 4 (May 1941).
92. —. "Natalia Sedova Trotsky: How It Happened (November 1940)." www.marxists.org. November 1940. https://www.marxists.org/archive/sedova-natalia/1940/08/20.htm.
93. "Trotsky Guard 1940 Aug 6 Journal Entry." www.frfly.com. http://www.frfly.com/esp/trotsky/j_1940_8_6.html.
94. Valtin, Jan. *Out of the Night.* New York: Alliance Book Corporation, 1941.
95. Volkogonov, Dmitrij, and Harold Shukman. *Stalin: The Eternal Revolutionary.* London: Free Press, 1996.
96. Volkogonov, Dmitri. *Trotsky: Eternal Revolutionary.* New York: Free Press, 2007.
97. Warth, Robert D. *Leon Trotsky.* New York: Macmillan Reference USA, 1977.
98. Weinstein, Allen, and Alexander Vassiliev. *Haunted Wood.* New York: Random House, 1999.
99. West, Nigel. *Soviet Penetration of the Manhattan Project.* New York: Enigma Publishing, 2005.
100. —. *Venona.* London: HarperCollins, 2000.
101. Wilmers, Mary-Kay. *The Eitingons: A Twentieth-Century Story.* London: Verso, 2012.
102. Wright, Peter. *Spycatcher.* New York: Viking, 1987.

INDEX